Subject Pronoun Expression in Spanish

GEORGETOWN STUDIES IN SPANISH LINGUISTICS
JOHN M. LIPSKI, SERIES EDITOR

Spanish as a Heritage Language in the United States: The State of the Field
Sara M. Beaudrie and Marta Fairclough, eds.

Subject Pronoun Expression in Spanish: A Cross-Dialectal Perspective
Ana M. Carvalho, Rafael Orozco, and Naomi L. Shin, eds.

Spanish Phonology: A Syllabic Perspective
Sonia Colina

Fundamentos y modelos del estudio pragmático y sociopragmático del español
Susana de los Heros and Mercedes Niño-Murcia, eds.

Sonido y sentido: Teoría y práctica de la pronunciación del español con audio CD
Jorge M. Guitart

El español en contacto con otras lenguas
Carol A. Klee and Andrew Lynch

Varieties of Spanish in the United States
John M. Lipski

Sociolingüistica y pragmática del español
Carmen Silva-Corvalán

Subject Pronoun Expression in Spanish

A Cross-Dialectal Perspective

ANA M. CARVALHO
RAFAEL OROZCO AND
NAOMI LAPIDUS SHIN
EDITORS

Georgetown University Press
Washington, D.C.

Library of Congress Cataloging-in-Publication Data

Subject pronoun expression in Spanish: a cross-dialectal perspective / Ana M. Carvalho, Rafael Orozco, and Naomi Lapidus Shin, Editors.
pages cm. — (Georgetown studies in Spanish linguistics)
Includes bibliographical references and index.
ISBN 978-1-62616-170-2 (pbk. : alk. paper) — ISBN 978-1-62616-171-9 (ebook)
1. Spanish language—Pronouns. 2. Spanish language—Terms and phrases. 3. Spanish language—Dialects. 4. Spanish language—Parts of speech. 5. Spanish language—Grammar. I. Carvalho, Ana Maria, editor. II. Orozco, Rafael, editor. III. Shin, Naomi Lapidus, editor.
PC4261.S83 2015
465'.55—dc23

2014014998

♾ This book is printed on acid-free paper meeting the requirements of the American National Standard for Permanence in Paper for Printed Library Materials.

17 16 15 9 8 7 6 5 4 3 2
First printing

Printed in the United States of America

Cover by M Madrid Design Studio.

We would like to thank David G. Nicholls from Georgetown University Press for his valuable assistance throughout the preparation of this manuscript. We also wish to express our immense gratitude to the series editor, John Lipski, as well as to the copy editors. We are especially thankful to the anonymous reviewers whose insightful comments helped us improve the overall quality of this compilation. In addition, we are indebted to the authors for contributing with their unique research and for serving as peer reviewers. Our gratitude also goes to our students who assisted us in the preparation of the manuscript: Ryan M. Bessett, Ryan McGowan, and Joshua Rodríguez. Most of all, we are infinitely grateful to the countless speakers from around the Hispanic world who made it all possible by providing the data for the studies in this volume.

Contents

Preface

Ricardo Otheguy

A half century has now passed since William Labov grew impatient with the dismissal in phonology of what was then called free variation. His impatience led to the quantitative analysis of centralized diphthongs in the English of Martha's Vineyard, Massachusetts, and to the realization by linguists that statistical procedures could illuminate the nature of sound systems. A few years later, this realization had been made extensive to morphosyntax, as Henrietta Cedergren and David Sankoff relied on the use of *que* in French in Canada to stress to linguists the importance of the crucial difference between statistics and probability. Their nuanced contention that linguistic competence was not statistic but probabilistic still stands, as does their inclusion of morphosyntactic phenomena within the purview of what has come to be known as variationist sociolinguistics. With these two things (i.e., morphosyntactic features and probabilistic competence) in place, the stage was set for the study of the topic that occupies the authors of the present volume, the variable absence and presence of subject personal pronouns in Spanish (e.g., *canta* alternating with *ella canta* to mean 'she sings').

The topic is a mature one, with a very large literature. Most of it has been inspired by the developments in variationist theory just described, but qualitative studies have not been lacking. Authors of academic grammars like Emilio Alarcos Llorach have had something to say about subject pronouns, as have authors like Olga Fernández Soriano who have devoted entire chapters of their grammars to the topic. With the familiar depth to which her readers were accustomed, Erica García too had important things to say about subject pronouns, placing what she proposed as their constant semantic contribution within her general theory of pronoun meaning in Spanish. And even earlier, Dwight Bolinger had insightful ideas about these pronouns as they appeared in Spanish discourse. Universalist generative approaches have paid attention also, as in the valuable contributions by Haegeman, Pérez-Leroux, and Toribio, while from the field of pragmatics the ideas of Sarah Blackwell and Brad Davidson have added positively to this ample literature.

Still, it has been within the quantitative paradigm where the study of Spanish subject personal pronouns has flourished, with contributions coming from scholars in

Europe and the Americas. Early studies by Ana María Barrenechea and Paola Bentivoglio developed statistical approaches to these forms in Latin American settings, and Emilia Enríquez did the same in Spain. And as always, when it comes to Spanish linguistics in the home country of variationism, an important contribution was already available in the United States more than 30 years ago from Carmen Silva-Corvalán, who provided insights into the variable use of pronouns not only by monolingual speakers but also by bilinguals in Los Angeles. Many of the statistical predictors of pronoun use today owe their widespread application to the work of pioneers like Silva-Corvalán. Thanks to them and to the many variationists who followed them, far too many to mention by name here, we have started to develop a detailed understanding of how the choice by the speaker to insert or leave out a subject pronoun is made; this choice is conditioned not only by external factors (who the speaker is, what socio-demographic groups provide primary identifications) but also by what have come to be called internal factors (what is the person-number and the tense of the associated verb, what is the nature of the discourse referent, what is the lexical content of the verb). The works in the present volume, led by three members of a new generation of Spanish *pronombristas*, deepen that understanding, studying the pronouns in several settings where Spanish is a majoritarian language of official status that is relatively free of crosslinguistic influences, but also in places where Spanish is a (usually thriving) minority language or one that operates under the rich pressures of contact.

The road that has brought us here has not been a conceptually smooth one, and the theoretical boulders that have been removed to make it passable still insist on rolling back, requiring attention if forward movement is to be sustained. Two scholars are deserving of gratitude for pointing out rocks lying in the way. Back in the 1970s, Beatriz Lavandera raised the problem, still with us, of whether probability grammars could deal with features where the choice of one form or another involved two different meanings. And more recently, Frederick Newmeyer raised the question of whether these grammars were grammars at all. Many, including Labov and Sankoff, endeavored to answer Lavandera's challenge. Newmeyer too did not lack responses, notably from Gregory Guy. But the questions, to some extent, still remain.

To Lavandera, one could still say, with Labov, that the "same meaning" requirement for doing variationist work was never an absolute one. And adding to Labov, we could point out that even in phonology the requirement is, fortunately, violated. With a definition of meaning that is not confined to truth-value (a confinement from which linguistics has already suffered enough), every choice, even the choice to articulate a coda consonant more or less forcefully, or to elide it altogether, is meaningful. The problem, if it indeed it were one, would thus not be by any means unique to the study of variability in morphosyntax. It never deterred anyone from studying variable phonological phenomena, and it should not be a deterrent in variationist morphosyntax either. To be sure, subject personal pronouns in Spanish, like *que* in French, are meaningful elements, as Erica García reminded us. But what we need to see, even if she didn't, is that variationist sociolinguistics is the study of semantic-contextual factors that, along with purely social-external considerations, creates probabilistic favorings in the exercise of meaningful choice. These favorings in one direction or the other give us clear insight into the nature of grammars that, as they must, constitute one of the elements that provide guidance to the usage of speakers and writers, grammars that are therefore necessarily probabilistic and meaningful.

To Newmeyer, one should still say that speech and writing (and signing for the deaf) are, every bit as much as introspective judgments, and perhaps much more, the natural object of linguistic analysis, of what gets explained by the postulation of grammars. Usage, then, is not just usage, but is the object of study, the *explanandum* of grammar. And large parcels of the grammars that would account for usage have to be, necessarily, probabilistic, reflecting the user's knowledge of under what conditions a linguistic choice (say, the use of a Spanish subject pronoun) is a better one to make and when it is better inhibited.

As these problematic boulders get pushed out of the road and fall back onto it, yet another waits ahead—the one associated with the need to better understand the notions of the null pronoun and the internal predictor. Internal predictor variables are, in most cases, internal in the sense that they're meaningful, and thus part of the internal semantic apparatus that constitutes the grammar of the language. (To be sure, some internal predictors are purely morphological, but we can set them aside for now.) It is the meaning of, say, one tense as opposed to a different tense that drives the Spanish speaker's choice of whether to use or omit a pronoun. And it is the meaning of one mental verb as opposed to the meaning of an action verb that motivates the deployment or omission of the pronoun and that makes these decisions by the user understandable. When not meaningful, these so-called internal variables are usually not internal at all. The queen of variables in the study of subject personal pronouns in Spanish, continuity of reference (a.k.a. switch reference), has little of the internal about it. Continuity of reference is not internal to the language. It constitutes an external, communicative motivation, a thing you want to say and which pushes you to tend to make pronominal choices in the direction of insertion or omission. Plainly, the continuity variable has to do with the speaker's or the writer's intent to stay with the same referent or direct the attention of the hearer or reader to a new one, and there's nothing internal about that.

Seen in this light, there are not overt and null pronouns in Spanish since explanation requires that we see why the pronoun is absent, whereas a null pronoun is always present, just in null form. What the student of pronouns is confronted with is speakers choosing to display or to omit these forms. This choice is conditioned in almost every case by the meanings of the surrounding contextual items, the user's communicative intent, and the very meaning of the forms on which the choice is centered, that is, the meanings—the constant semantic contributions—of the pronouns themselves. When considered from this perspective, the variationist's grammars are not only probabilistic, but meaningful, and it is in the blending of these two traits of grammar that some of the most important theoretical vistas open up in the study of subject personal pronouns.

As we continue the analysis of Spanish subject personal pronouns, the chapters here will build a most necessary platform on which to erect a full understanding of linguistic choice, one that will grow hand in hand with our grasp of the empirical realities, in both monolingual and bilingual settings, and of the theoretical conceptualizations brought to bear in order to understand them.

Introduction

Ana M. Carvalho,
Rafael Orozco, and
Naomi Lapidus Shin

Research on structured linguistic variation suggests that usage patterns are deeply embedded in speakers' knowledge of grammar: While speakers of the same language may vary widely in how much or how often they use a particular linguistic variant, usage patterns reveal sensitivity to a shared set of conditioning factors or constraints (e.g., Guy 1997; 2011; Otheguy and Zentella 2012; Tagliamonte 2012, 13; Torres Cacoullos and Travis 2011). Yet there remain several outstanding questions regarding structured variation, such as: What is the nature of this variable component of grammar? Is it consistent across speakers of a language? Is variable grammar susceptible to contact-induced change? How does variable grammar develop during language acquisition? In order to begin to answer these questions, we present here a unified volume of studies focusing on the same variable morphosyntactic feature: Spanish subject personal pronoun expression (SPE).

In Spanish, as with other so-called pro-drop languages, subject personal pronouns (SPPs) are often omitted; for example, one may say *yo canto* ('I sing') or *canto* ('[I] sing'), without changing the basic meaning of the utterance. A great deal of sociolinguistic scholarship has been dedicated to discovering the linguistic and extra-linguistic factors that probabilistically condition the expression or omission of Spanish subject pronouns, so much so that this feature has recently been called "a showcase variable of sociolinguistics" (Bayley et al., 2012, 50). Moreover, a careful review of the literature suggests that patterns of use are remarkably similar across geographical settings and communities, lending support to the notion that structured linguistic variation is an intrinsic part of speakers' grammatical knowledge. Table 1 provides a general overview of some of the most commonly studied variables conditioning SPE.

While table 1 shows that there has been abundant research on the same factors impacting SPE, most prior research has been published as individual studies with little or no connection between them. By bringing together SPE studies from a variety of

Table 1 Significant variables conditioning Spanish subject pronoun use in monolingual and bilingual settings

Conditioning variable	General trend of variable	Monolingual settings	Bilingual settings
Grammatical person/ number	Varies which pronoun is expressed most often. Broadest generalization is that singular pronouns (*yo, tú, él, ella, usted, uno*) are expressed at higher rates than plural pronouns (*nosotros, ellos/ellas, ustedes*).	Abreu 2009, 2012; Bentivoglio 1987:36, 60; Claes 2011; Posio 2011; Ortiz López 2011; Prada Pérez 2009	Abreu 2009, 2012; Bayley and Pease-Álvarez 1996, 1997; Carvalho and Child 2011; Erker and Guy 2012; Flores-Ferrán 2002, 2004, 2007, 2009; Otheguy and Zentella 2012; Otheguy, Zentella, and Livert 2007
Switch-reference/co-reference, distance from previous mention of referent	Pronouns are expressed when reference is switched more often than when reference is maintained across two consecutive grammatical subjects. Also, the further back in the discourse the previous mention of the referent is, the greater the likelihood a pronoun will be expressed.	Bentivoglio 1987:60; Cameron 1992, 1993, 1994, 1995; Claes 2011; Enríquez 1984; Orozco and Guy 2008; Ortiz López 2011; Prada Pérez 2009; Travis 2007	Abreu 2009, 2012; Bayley and Pease-Álvarez 1996, 1997; Carvalho and Child 2011; Erker and Guy 2012; Flores-Ferrán 2002, 2004; Hurtado 2005; Ortiz López 2011; Otheguy and Zentella 2007, 2012; Otheguy, Zentella, and Livert 2007, 2010; Shin and Otheguy 2009; Silva-Corvalán 1994; Torres Cacoullos and Travis 2010, 2011; Travis 2007
Priming	Expression of pronoun triggers further expression of pronoun.	Travis 2007	Abreu 2009, 2012; Cameron and Flores-Ferrán 2004; Carvalho and Child 2011; Torres Cacoullos and Travis 2010, 2011; Travis 2007
TMA morphology	Ambiguous verb morphology (e.g., imperfect forms) promotes more pronoun use than unambiguous forms.	Abreu 2009, 2012; Almeida and Castellano 2001; Claes 2011; Bentivolgio 1987:45; Cameron 1994; Prada Pérez 2009; Travis 2007	Bayley and Pease-Álvarez 1996, 1997; Erker and Guy 2012; Flores-Ferrán 2002, 2004, 2009; Hochberg 1986; Hurtado 2005; Otheguy and Zentella 2007, 2012; Otheguy, Zentella, and Livert 2007; Shin 2014; Shin and Montes-Alcalá 2014

Table 1 *(continued)*

Conditioning variable	General trend of variable	Monolingual settings	Bilingual settings
Lexical semantics of verbs	Cognitive-psych verbs promote use of pronouns more than other types.	Abreu 2009, 2012; Bentivoglio 1987:52, 60; Enríquez 1984; Posio 2011; Miyajima 2000; Orozco and Guy 2008; Travis 2007	Carvalho and Child 2011; Erker and Guy 2012; Flores-Ferrán 2002, 2004, 2009; Hurtado 2005; Otheguy and Zentella 2007, 2012; Otheguy, Zentella, and Livert 2007; Silva-Corvalán 1994; Torres Cacoullos and Travis 2010, 2011; Travis 2007
Clause type	Pronouns are most likely to be expressed in main clauses, less likely in dependent clauses, and least likely in coordinate clauses.	Abreu 2009:125; Enríquez 1984:256-258, Orozco and Guy 2008:77	Otheguy and Zentella 2012, Flores-Ferrán 2009, Shin and Montes-Alcalá 2014. Others find no effect for clause type: Carvalho and Child 2011; Prada Pérez 2009:97; Torres Cacoullos and Travis 2011:254, 258
Reflexive	Verbs that occur with a reflexive pronoun are more likely to promote pronoun omission than verbs that occur without a reflexive pronoun.		Abreu 2009, 2012; Bayley and Pease-Álvarez 1996, 1997; Carvalho and Child 2011; Otheguy and Zentella 2012
Conflict	Conflict narratives promote pronoun expression more than non-conflict parts of narratives.		Flores-Ferrán 2010

perspectives, the current volume provides synthesis, connections, and directions in the growing line of inquiry related to Spanish SPE and, more generally, the nature of the variable component of grammar and how it is affected by extra-linguistic factors, such as setting, bilingualism, and age.

This volume comprises twelve chapters and is thematically divided into three parts of four chapters each. The first part addresses SPE in monolingual speech communities in the Dominican Republic, Colombia, Mexico, and Spain, respectively. Determining the distributional patterns and conditioning forces on subject pronoun expression in these four locations allows for cross-dialectal comparisons, and sets the baseline for understanding how adult monolingual Spanish speakers use subject pronouns. The second part comprises studies that assess the impact of bilingualism on SPE based on the analyses of Spanish in contact with English, Catalan, Maya, and Portuguese, respectively. The analyses of four different language pairs contribute to a longstanding debate on whether language contact results in grammatical change (e.g., Müller 1871, 86; Silva-Corvalán 1994; Thomason and Kaufman 1988; Weinreich 1953), while also exploring the role language typology plays in the outcome of contact. The third part examines acquisition among monolingual and bilingual children as well as adult second language learners. This section sheds light on the development of the grammar underlying SPP use in both child and adult populations. Bringing together studies on this variable in monolingual, bilingual, and developmental varieties of Spanish addresses questions that have either emerged as a result of four decades of research on variable SPE in Spanish or that remain open in spite of that extensive research. In doing so, this compilation brings both breadth and depth to the empirical analysis of this variable in Spanish in a single, coherent volume.

PART I: MONOLINGUAL VARIETIES

It is well known that SPE is subject to marked regional differences in Latin American and Peninsular Spanish. Overall frequency of use differs dialectally—with the highest overt pronoun expression rates occurring in the Caribbean (Orozco and Guy 2008; Otheguy and Zentella 2012, among others). At the same time, usage patterns reveal remarkable similarities. For instance, previous research has shown that subject pronouns are expressed more often a) when the referent of the verb is singular than when it is plural, b) when the referent of two consecutive grammatical subjects is different rather than the same, and c) with verbs conjugated in the imperfect than with other tense-mood-aspect (TMA) forms (Bentivoglio 1987; Cameron 1992, 1993, 1994, 1995; Enríquez 1984; Otheguy and Zentella 2012; Torres Cacoullos and Travis 2011; Travis 2007, among others). These same trends emerge in the studies presented in the current volume. In addition to confirming broad generalizations uncovered by previous research, the studies in Part I provide new information about variables that have been less clearly understood, such as textual genre and verbal semantics. Also, by carefully examining social factors, several of these studies reveal that SPE may be undergoing change in some monolingual varieties, a finding that has important ramifications for our analyses of grammatical change in contact situations.

This first section of the volume opens with a study by Alfaraz, who explores SPE in the Spanish of Santo Domingo, Dominican Republic, in order to test the hypothesis that higher pronominal expression rates represent a change in progress towards mandatory overt subjects. The author reports an overall pronominal expression rate of 42 percent, the highest among the monolingual varieties, corroborating previous reports of a high pronominal rate in Dominican Spanish (cf. Martínez-Sanz 2011; Ortiz López 2011; Othegey, Zentella, and Livert 2007; Shin and Otheguy 2013). Alfaraz finds that SPE is significantly conditioned in Dominican Spanish by the same major variables that condition other varieties of Spanish, such as switch reference and number, with singular subject contexts favoring pronoun expression and plurals favoring omission. She also finds some evidence for the weakening of the switch reference constraint, which might support other scholars' (e.g., Toribio 2000) assertion that this variety is experiencing a change in progress involving increasing subject expression and fixed SVO word order. In Alfaraz's study, gender is the only social constraint conditioning SPE, with women exhibiting a higher pronominal rate than men, a tendency also prevalent in Barranquilla, Colombia and—although not significantly—Mexico City (chapters 2 and 3).

Our regional focus remains on the Caribbean, as we turn to Orozco's study of SPE in Colombian Costeño Spanish, where he finds an overall pronominal rate of 34.2 percent. As with other studies throughout this compilation, his results reflect overall congruence with the conditioning effects on SPE prevalent across varieties. His paper's in-depth analysis of the effects of verb semantics constitutes an important contribution to our knowledge of the conditioning forces on SPE. We learn that the classification of verbs into the categories traditionally used by numerous scholars to explore Lexical Content (estimative, mental activity, stative, external activity) is problematic, as Orozco uncovers clear divergences between verbs within each Lexical Content category. For instance, most stative verbs favor overt SPPs, but *tener* 'to have' has a rather neutral effect. Within the category of verbs denoting mental activity, both *creer* 'to believe' and *saber* 'to know' favor SPE, while all other mental activity verbs favor null subjects. These findings tell us that analyses of verbal semantics must take into account the configuration of the corpus at hand, the characteristics of different verbs, and, more importantly, lexical frequency. Orozco's chapter also reveals an interesting trend whereby younger speakers exhibit lower pronominal rates than older speakers do, which appears to be the result of this Caribbean variety's sustained contact with Mainland varieties.

Next, Lastra and Martín Butragueño take us to Mexico City, the world's largest Spanish-speaking city. Chapter 3 constitutes the first large-scale variationist analysis of SPE in that metropolis and thus provides valuable baseline data for further study of Mexican Spanish. Lastra and Martín Butragueño find an overall pronominal rate of 21.7 percent, which is in keeping with the very few other studies conducted on SPE in Mexico (e.g., Michnowicz, this volume), as well as studies of Mexicans living in the United States (e.g., Otheguy and Zentella 2012; Silva-Corvalán 1994). With respect to the factors conditioning SPE, like the previous studies, Lastra and Martín Butragueño find the same effects for switch reference, person and number of the verb, and verb tense. In addition, they uncover the significant effect of textual genre, with argumentation favoring pronoun expression, and narrative favoring omission. They also find that young *defeños* (Mexico City residents) use fewer overt pronominal subjects than their elders, a tendency that is congruent with the trend found in Barranquilla (chapter 2). If we consider the typical evolution in Romance languages to be one that moves from pro-drop to non-pro-drop (as evidenced by diachronic change in French and Brazilian Portuguese), then the increasing pronoun omission found in Orozco's and Lastra and Martín Butragueño's studies might be evidence of what Labov (2001) calls "retrograde movement," that is, a reversal in the direction of change (75).

Peninsular Spanish is examined by Posio, who adopts a usage-based, constructional approach to examine data from *Corpus de referencia del español contemporáneo* (COREC, Marcos-Marín 1992). His analysis focuses on local contexts where subject pronouns acquire formulaic status as part of the construction where they occur. Posio finds that formulaicity, understood as a combination of high token frequency and low type frequency, plays a role in accounting for variable SPE. At the same time, as reported in this part of the volume for Costeño Spanish, not all frequently occurring verbs behave similarly. Posio's study reveals that only lexical verbs used for various discourse-pragmatic functions exhibit recognizable formulaic sequences where the presence and placement of SPPs follows local, construction-specific patterns. While the general factors affecting SPP expression (e.g., tense/mood/aspect, grammatical person or switch reference) show similar effects across Spanish dialects, formulaic sequences constitute a potential site for cross-dialectal differences. Such differences can be observed, for instance, between the frequently occurring items in Colombian Costeño Spanish (Orozco, this volume) and Peninsular Spanish. Thus, in addition to the mere frequency of use of a given verb token, the degree of formulaicity enabling the entrenchment of token-specific usage patterns should be considered in order to account for dialectal divergences in subject pronoun expression (cf. Bybee 2010; Erker and Guy 2012).

In sum, the first section of our volume confirms previous findings on some of the well-known constraints, such as switch reference, and also sheds light on new factors such as textual genre. We also learn that verbal semantic categories are not monolithic, as individual lexical items within those categories show divergent behavior with respect to SPE, and that certain verbs lend themselves to formulaic sequences. Finally, the studies in Part I suggest possible changes in progress. While Alfaraz's study lends some support to the idea that there is some relaxing of discourse constraints on SPE in the Dominican Republic, Orozco's and Lastra and Martín Butragueño's studies suggest retrograde movement towards lower rates of pronoun expression in Barranquilla and Mexico City, respectively.

PART II: BILINGUAL VARIETIES

Having increased our understanding of SPE in monolingual varieties of Spanish, we move on, in the second section of the volume, to the issue of whether language contact triggers any change in SPE. Subject pronoun expression is a productive tool to diagnose cross-linguistic transfer, but it has primarily been examined in studies of Spanish in contact with English, with some scholars arguing for contact-induced change (e.g., Otheguy and Zentella 2012; Shin, forthcoming; Shin and Montes-Alcalá 2014), and others against it (e.g., Flores-Ferrán 2004; Torres Cacoullos and Travis 2010, 2011). Research on other language pairs is sorely needed, then, to better understand the outcomes of language contact. Thus far, a few studies have examined SPE in other languages. For example, Nagy (in press) studied heritage speakers of Russian, Italian and Cantonese in Canada, and found no significant effect of contact with English. In a study of Spanish in contact with a typologically similar language, Veneto (a northern Italian dialect), Barnes (2010) finds an increased rate of pronoun expression among bilinguals, but no significant difference in linguistic constraints. In contrast, Meyerhoff's (2009) study of Bilama creole and its substratum, Tamambo, reveals some partial replication of Tamambo on the distribution of subject pronoun expression in Bilama. Guided by the variationist approach to exploring language contact set forth by Poplack and her associates (2010, 2011) and the premises of comparative sociolinguistics (Tagliamonte 2012), the chapters in this section contribute to this discussion by measuring the effect of contact on SPE through comparisons of pronoun rates, factor group rankings, and constraint rankings between bilingual and monolingual varieties of four language pairs.

This part of the volume opens with a study by Torres Cacoullos and Travis that demonstrates the need to investigate structured variation not only in Spanish, but also in English. Their study shows that, even though Spanish and English differ quantitatively with respect to SPE (English overall rate for first person singular subject expression reaches 95 percent in the corpus analyzed by the authors, while the highest rate in Spanish approximates 50 percent), there are, in fact, some commonalities between the two languages. The authors show that both grammars favor first person singular subject omission in co-referential coordination headed by 'and' (or '*y*' in Spanish), as in "I went and **Ø saw** their house the other night" (cf. Shin & Montes-Alcalá 2014). Also, both 'I' and *yo* are subject to priming effects; expressed 'I' triggers expressed 'I' and expressed *yo* triggers expressed *yo*. However, a close look at the position of 'I' and *yo* in intonation units (IUs) reveals a marked difference between the two languages: In English, unexpressed 'I' in non-coordinated structures is restricted to IU-initial position. This prosodic constraint does not apply to Spanish. In addition, the well-known tendency in Spanish for cognition verbs to favor subject expression is not replicated in English. These newfound conflict sites between English and Spanish can and should be used to better assess crosslinguistic influence in Spanish–English bilingual SPE.

The effect of contact between two pro-drop languages is analyzed in the next three chapters, starting with Michnowicz's study of Maya–Spanish bilinguals in Yucatán, Mexico. The author compares SPE among monolingual speakers of Yucatan Spanish and bilingual speakers of Maya and Spanish. He finds that while monolinguals share similarities with results found for the rest of Mexico, bilinguals use higher overt pronoun rates and different constraint rankings with respect to reference. More specifically, bilinguals show less sensitivity to contexts of continuity, which strongly promote pronoun omission in monolingual Yucatán Spanish. Both the increase in SPE rates and weakening of pragmatic constraints are seen by the author as evidence of simplification rather than crosslinguistic transfer. Following Prada Pérez's distinction between convergence and simplification (2009, this volume), Michnowicz interprets his findings as evidence that bilinguals simplify the discourse rules that govern the use of overt pronouns, a situation also detected among Spanish–English bilinguals in New York (Shin and Otheguy 2009, cf. Shin 2014).

The next two chapters deal with Spanish in contact with other pro-drop Romance languages. First, Prada Pérez investigates the impact of Catalan on the expression of first person singular subject pronouns among bilinguals in Spain. Based on results extracted from a group of Spanish-dominant bilinguals and one of Catalan-dominant bilinguals, and on their comparison with Spanish monolinguals and speakers who know Spanish but speak mostly Catalan (henceforth 'near-monolingual' Catalan speakers), she finds that the overall pronoun rates are very similar in all groups (around 20 percent). In addition, all groups present the same variable rankings, showing similarities regardless of language dominance and proficiency. Most importantly, the two bilingual groups were not significantly different from each other, suggesting a shared variable SPP grammar in Spanish, at least for first person singular. Nevertheless, bilinguals diverged in some ways from the two control groups, the Spanish monolinguals and the Catalan near-monolinguals. For example, while discourse connectedness had the same strong effect in all groups, verb form ambiguity and verb type did not impact first person singular pronoun expression among bilinguals the same way as in the control groups. More specifically, ambiguity was significant in the control groups but not among the bilinguals. On the other hand, verb type was significant in the bilingual groups but not the control groups. The subtle differences that emerge are viewed by Prada Pérez as a case of simplification since the results indicate an overall decrease in variability among the bilinguals. The author proposes the Vulnerability Hypothesis (Prada Pérez, in progress), which establishes a categorical-variable continuum of crosslinguistic permeability. According to this hypothesis, variable phenomena are susceptible to inter-lingual effects while more categorical phenomena are not.

Contact between Spanish and Portuguese is analyzed by Carvalho and Bessett, who test the theory that similar languages will converge in situations of prolonged contact (Muysken 2000). Based on a corpus of both Portuguese and Spanish compiled in a bilingual community in northern Uruguay along the Brazilian border, the authors analyze SPE to determine whether bilinguals utilize parallels between languages to develop a single system of variable grammar. Spanish and Portuguese are suitable for assessing the effect of language contact on SPE because Spanish tends to favor null subjects while Brazilian Portuguese is transitioning toward overt pronominal subjects (e.g., Barbosa, Duarte, and Kato 2005, among others). Although the results do not indicate significantly divergent crosslinguistic behavior, the authors consider previous accounts of monolingual Spanish and Portuguese varieties and show abundant parallel variability in the source dialects, highlighting the challenges of distinguishing language-specific properties from crosslinguistic tendencies in cognate languages. Nevertheless, some differences emerge and attest to the independence of the linguistic codes, such as discrepant overall pronominal rates (25 percent in Spanish and 46 percent in Portuguese within the same bilingual consultants). The results also show dissimilarities in constraint rankings for grammatical person, such as the use of grammaticalized *a gente* as the first person plural pronoun in Portuguese (absent in Spanish) and the importance of first person singular as a major conditioning factor for SPE in Spanish but not in Uruguayan Portuguese. By pinpointing similarities between these border dialects and previous results, the authors detect clear continuities with their monolingual counterparts and lack of substantial crosslinguistic convergence.

These studies on contact varieties show that, on one hand, knowledge of another language may bring about subtle changes in this variable component of the Spanish grammar, while on the other hand, many of the same conditioning factors influence both monolingual and bilingual usage. Furthermore, while Torres Cacoullos and Travis, as well as Carvalho and Bessett, do not find that patterns in bilingual Spanish depart significantly from the monolingual varieties they study, Michnowicz and Prada Pérez detect patterns that seem to derive from contact-induced language change, although both agree that the driving force behind this type of change is not necessarily linguistic convergence whereby one language approximates another (cf. Bullock and Toribio 2004), but instead bilingualism itself (Sorace 2011).

PART III: DEVELOPMENTAL VARIETIES

The third section of our volume focuses on acquisition of Spanish SPE, and reveals developmental sequences that have broad implications for both first and second language development and for our understanding of crosslinguistic influence during acquisition. The two chapters on developmental sequences show similarities between first and second language acquisition: The variables that most strongly constrain subject pronoun expression among adult native speakers of Spanish are the same variables that emerge first during language acquisition. The following two chapters, which focus on bilingual children, find that English exerts influence over Spanish subject pronoun expression, especially among children who are English-dominant bilinguals. Below we provide a brief description of each study in order to demonstrate how they deepen our understanding of crosslinguistic influence and developmental patterns.

In the first chapter in the acquisition section, Shin and Erker explore SPE among 24 monolingual Spanish-speaking children in Oaxaca, Mexico, ages six to eight. Their analysis shows that at this age children use relatively few subject pronouns and this is particularly true for boys. At the same time, a regression analysis measuring the influence of person/number, switch reference, TMA, clause type, semantic class of the verb, and reflexivity shows that the children's patterns of pronoun use are systematic and demonstrate emerging adult-like sensitivity. More specifically, the two most robust predictors of pronoun use among adults, person/number and switch reference, are the same ones that significantly constrain the children's pronoun expression. There is also evidence of emerging sensitivity to TMA among the children. The authors conclude that the developmental sequence of pronoun use follows directly from adult language patterns: the strongest predictors among adults are the first to emerge among children.

Geeslin, Linford, and Fafulas's study focuses on the developmental sequence of SPE during second language acquisition. A written contextualized task was administered to 207 university students (180 L1English/L2 Spanish speakers evenly distributed across six proficiency levels and 27 native speakers of Spanish). After reading short passages, participants chose between two final sentences that varied only in subject pronoun expression. In terms of rates of selection, the authors found evidence of U-shaped development (moving from target-like language to less target-like and then back to target-like): The learners at the two opposite ends of the proficiency scale (lowest and highest proficiency) were most similar to the native speakers, while the middle-level groups had the highest rate of overt pronoun selection. Such U-shaped development has also been found in child language acquisition of Spanish subject pronouns (Shin and Cairns 2012), suggesting a pattern of development in language learning. Geeslin et al.'s analysis of factors conditioning pronoun selection also reveals similarities between first and second language development. Switch reference was the first constraint to emerge among the second language learners, followed by TMA, a sequence that is similar to the development found in Shin and Erker's study of first language acquisition.

Thus the first two studies in the acquisition section have much in common even though they examine different populations and use different tasks. They both suggest a) a phase during early stages of acquisition in which learners tend to omit subject pronouns, with children omitting more than adults do; and b) that linguistic factors influencing SPE emerge in a predictable order: The strongest predictors of pronoun expression among native speaker adults are also the first predictors to emerge during acquisition.

The third and fourth chapters in the acquisition section concentrate on crosslinguistic influence during bilingual language acquisition. Both investigate the potential impact of English on the Spanish spoken by bilingual children in the United States. Silva-Corvalán's study examines the developmental path of two bilingual siblings in their acquisition of subjects in English and Spanish. The children differ in amount of exposure to Spanish, with the older child, Nico, having had more exposure than the younger child, Bren. This differential amount of exposure appears to impact pronoun expression, as the younger child expresses pronouns more frequently in comparison to his older brother, as well as compared to monolingual children. In addition, Bren's pronouns indicate some weakening of discourse-pragmatic constraints, most specifically switch reference, since he expresses pronouns in redundant contexts, that is, where the pronoun co-refers with the previous subject. Silva-Corvalán concludes that her study provides evidence that language dominance plays a strong role in determining the extent to which crosslinguistic influence occurs during bilingual language acquisition.

In the final chapter of this section, Montrul and Sánchez-Walker examine subject expression in narratives produced by a) children who are exposed to Spanish and English from birth (i.e., 'simultaneous bilinguals'), and b) children who are exposed to Spanish first and then learn English as a second language during childhood (i.e., 'sequential bilinguals'). They also compare these two groups of bilingual children to monolingual children in Mexico. Results show that the bilingual children produced more overt subject pronouns than the monolingual children did, with the simultaneous bilingual children producing the highest rates of all three groups. In addition to studying overall SPE, the authors examine two discourse contexts, one in which two consecutive subjects are co-referential ('same reference') and the other in which there is a switch in reference between subjects ('switch reference'). As is clear from the entire volume, SPE rates are significantly higher in switch reference than in same reference contexts. The authors find that the simultaneous bilingual children are the most likely to express overt pronouns in same reference contexts, followed by the sequential bilinguals, and finally the monolinguals. Since subjects are expressed at very high rates in English, the authors suggest that the bilinguals' higher rates of expression, especially in same reference contexts, are indicative of crosslinguistic influence. There is one caveat that will require more investigation: A majority of the sequential bilinguals in this study were from New York City, while most of the simultaneous bilinguals were from Chicago. Montrul and Sánchez-Walker suggest that, in addition to greater exposure to English, New York bilinguals are possibly more heavily influenced by Caribbean varieties, in which there is a tendency to express more subject pronouns. It remains to be seen whether the combination of dialect-leveling and English influence, both found to impact adults in New York (Otheguy and Zentella 2012), also affects bilingual child language development.

In general both chapters—the one by Silva-Corvalán and the one by Montrul and Sánchez-Walker—reveal similar trends. The more English-dominant bilingual children are, the more pronouns they use. Furthermore, both studies suggest that the switch reference constraint is not as strong among bilingual children as among monolingual children, a finding that is consistent with several studies of adult bilinguals (e.g., Michnowicz, this volume; Otheguy and Zentella 2012; Shin and Otheguy 2009).

CONCLUSION

In sum, the broad generalizations that we can extract from the current volume of SPE are the following:

1. Multiple studies of SPE across communities, across settings, and across the lifespan reveal the very consistent nature of structured variation. All studies in our volume demonstrate the same powerful effects of switch reference; person/number of the verb; and tense, mood and aspect. This consistency points to the existence of a systematic, core variable grammar shared by all Spanish speakers. At the same time, the rankings of factors within each factor group reveal a locus of divergence across varieties. For example, the ranking of singular grammatical persons is not uniform across dialects, with *yo* ranked highest in some varieties and *tú* ranked highest in others. Since factor rankings fluctuate more than factor group rankings do, we propose that this is the area of grammar that is more permeable and susceptible to change.
2. In language contact situations, structured morphosyntactic variation is an area of grammar that may be susceptible to subtle changes. In particular, we find that discourse-related constraints are the most likely to be affected by bilingualism, a tendency previously detected by Silva-Corvalán (1994). At the same time, studies in this volume find more similarities than divergences between monolinguals and bilinguals, pointing to strong continuity between varieties and a lack of convergence of variable grammars.
3. Finally, the investigations of language acquisition show that structured morphosyntactic variation develops in a predictable sequence. The strongest predictors of pronoun expression among native speaker adults are also the first predictors to emerge during both first and second language acquisition.

The first in its content and scope, this compilation is unique in that its chapters are both mutually complementary and inclusive and, as a whole, provide a panoramic view of current research trends on SPE. By bringing together multiple studies that analyze the same variable in various speech communities, this volume sheds light on the methodological and theoretical contributions of cross-dialectal, comparative approaches to our understanding of the factors conditioning SPE in Spanish. The findings reported here constitute an important foundation for further SPE research in Spanish as well as in other languages.

REFERENCES

Abreu, Laurel. 2009. "Spanish subject personal pronoun use by monolinguals, bilinguals, and second language learners." PhD diss., University of Florida.

Abreu, Laurel. 2012. "Subject pronoun expression and priming effects among bilingual speakers of Puerto Rican Spanish." In *Selected Proceedings of the 14th Hispanic Linguistics Symposium*, edited by Kimberly Geeslin and Manuel Díaz-Campos, 1–8. Somerville, MA: Cascadilla.

Almeida, Manuel, and Ángela Castellano. 2001. "On the biological basis of gender variation. Verbal ambiguity in Canarian Spanish." *Estudios de sociolingüística* 2:81–100.

Barbosa, Pilar, Maria Eugênia Duarte, and Mary Kato. 2005. "Null Subjects in European and Brazilian Portuguese." *Journal of Portuguese Linguistics* 4:11–52.

Barnes, Hilary. 2010. "Subject pronoun expression in bilinguals of two null subject languages." *Amsterdam Studies in the Theory and History of Linguistic Science Series IV, Current Issues in Linguistic Theory* 313:9–22.

Bayley, Robert, and Lucinda Pease-Álvarez. 1996. "Null and expressed pronoun variation in Mexican-descent children's Spanish." In *Sociolinguistic variation: Data, theory, and analysis*, edited by Jennifer Arnold, Renee Blake, and Brad Davidson, 85–99. Stanford University: Center for the Study of Language and Information.

———. 1997. "Null pronoun variation in Mexican-descent children's narrative discourse." *Language Variation and Change* 9:349–71.

Bayley, Robert, Norma L. Cárdenas, Belinda Treviño Schouten, and Carlos Martín Vélez Salas. 2012. "Spanish dialect contact in San Antonio, Texas: An exploratory study." In *Selected Proceedings of the 14th Hispanic Linguistics Symposium,* edited by Kimberly Geeslin and Manuel Díaz-Campos, 48–60. Somerville: Cascadilla Proceedings Project.

Bentivoglio, Paola. 1987. *Los sujetos pronominales de primera persona en el habla de Caracas*. Caracas: Universidad Central de Venezuela.

Bullock, Barbara E., and A. Jacqueline Toribio. 2004. "Introduction: Convergence as an emergent property in bilingual speech." *Bilingualism: Language and Cognition* 7:91–93.

Bybee, Joan. 2010. *Language, usage and cognition*. Cambridge: Cambridge University Prcss.

Cameron, Richard. 1992. "Pronominal and null subject variation in Spanish: Constraints, dialects, and functional compensation." PhD diss., University of Pennsylvania.

———. 1993. "Ambiguous agreement, functional compensation, and non-specific *tú* in the Spanish of San Juan, Puerto Rico and Madrid, Spain." *Language Variation and Change* 5:305–334.

———. 1994. "Switch reference, verb class and priming in a variable syntax." In Katharine Beals (ed.), *Papers from the 30th Regional Meeting of the Chicago Linguistics Society: Volume 2: The parasession on variation in linguistic theory,* 27-45. Chicago Linguistics Society.

———. 1995. "The scope and limits of switch-reference as a constraint on pronominal subject expression." *Hispanic Linguistics* 6/7:1–27.

Carvalho, Ana M., and Michael Child. 2011. "Subject Pronoun Expression in a Variety of Spanish in Contact with Portuguese." In *Selected Proceedings of the 5th Workshop on Spanish Sociolinguistics*, edited by Jim Michnowicz and Robin Dodsworth, 14–25. Somerville, MA: Cascadilla Proceedings Project.

Claes, Jeroen. 2011. "¿Constituyen las Antillas y el Caribe continental una sola zona dialectal? Datos de la variable expresión del sujeto pronominal en San Juan de Puerto Rico y Barranquilla, Colombia." *Spanish in Context* 8:2, 191–212.

Enríquez, Emilia V. 1984. *El pronombre personal sujeto en la lengua española hablada en Madrid.* Madrid: Consejo Superior de Investigaciones Científicas.

Erker, Daniel, and Gregory R. Guy. 2012. "The role of lexical frequency in syntactic variability: Variable subject personal pronoun expression in Spanish." *Language* 88:3, 526–557.

Flores-Ferrán, Nydia. 2002. *A sociolinguistic perspective on the use of subject personal pronouns in Spanish narratives of Puerto Ricans in New York City.* Munich: Lincom-Europa.

———. 2004. "Spanish subject personal pronoun use in New York City Puerto Ricans: Can we rest the case of English contact?" *Language Variation and Change* 16:49–73.

———. 2007. "A bend in the road: Subject personal pronoun expression in Spanish after 30 years of sociolinguistic research." *Language and Linguistic Compass* 1/6:624–652.

———. 2009. "Are you referring to me? The variable use of *UNO* and *YO* in oral discourse." *Journal of Pragmatics* 41:1810–1824.

———. 2010. "*¡Tú no me hables!* Pronoun expression in conflict narratives." *International Journal of Sociology of Language* 203:61–82.

Guy, Gregory R. 1997. "Violable is variable: Optimality theory and linguistic variation." *Language Variation and Change* 9:333–347.

———. 2011. "Variability." In *The Blackwell companion to phonology Vol. 4*, edited by Marc Van Oostendorp, Colin J. Ewen, Elizabeth Hume, and Keren Rice, 2190–2213.

Hochberg, Judith. 1986. "Functional compensation for /s/ deletion in Puerto Rican Spanish." *Language* 62, 3:609–621.

Hurtado, Luz Marcela. 2005. "Syntactic-semantic conditioning of subject expression in Colombian Spanish." *Hispania* 88:335–348.

Labov, William. 2001. *Principles of linguistic change, vol. 2: Social factors.* Oxford: Blackwell.

Marcos-Marín, Francisco. 1992. *Corpus oral de referencia del español contemporáneo.* Universidad Autónoma de Madrid. Available at http://www.lllf.uam.es/~fmarcos/index.html.

Martínez-Sanz, Cristina. 2011. *Null and overt subjects in a variable system: The case of Dominican Spanish.* PhD diss., University of Ottawa.

Meyerhoff, Miriam. 2009. "Replication, Transfer, and Calquing: Using variation as a tool in the study of language contact." *Language Variation and Change* 21:297–317.

Miyajima, Atsuko. 2000. Spanish subject pronoun expression and verb semantics. *Sophia Linguistica* 46/47, 73–88.

Müller, Max. 1871. *Lectures on the science of language*. New York: Scribner.

Muysken, Pieter. 2000. *Bilingual speech: A typology of code-mixing*. Cambridge: Cambridge University Press.

Nagy, Naomi. In press "A sociolinguistic view of null subjects and VOT in Toronto heritage languages." *Lingua.*

Orozco, Rafael, and Gregory Guy. 2008. "El uso variable de los pronombres sujetos: ¿Qué pasa en la costa Caribe colombiana?" In *Selected Proceedings of the Fourth Workshop on Spanish Sociolinguistics,* edited by Maurice Westmoreland and Juan Antonio Thomas, 70–80. Somerville, MA: Cascadilla Proceedings Project.

Ortiz López, Luis A. 2011. "Spanish in contact with Haitian Creole." In *The handbook of Spanish sociolinguistics*, edited by Manuel Díaz-Campos, 418–445. Wiley-Blackwell.

Otheguy, Ricardo, and Ana Celia Zentella. 2007. "Apuntes preliminares sobre el contacto lingüístico y dialectal en el uso pronominal del español en Nueva York." In *Spanish in contact: Policy, social and linguistic inquiries*, edited by Kim Potowski and Richard Cameron, 275–295. Amsterdam/ Philadelphia: John Benjamins.

———. 2012. *Spanish in New York: Language contact, dialectal leveling, and structural continuity.* Oxford: Oxford University Press.

Otheguy, Ricardo, Ana Celia Zentella, and David Livert. 2007. "Language contact in Spanish in New York toward the formation of a speech community." *Language* 83:4:770–802.

Poplack, Shana, and Stephen Levey. 2010. "Contact induced grammatical change: A cautionary tale." In *Language and space: An international handbook of linguistic variation vol. I*, edited by Peter Auer and Jürgen Erich Schmidt, 391–419. Berlin: Mouton De Gruyter.

Poplack, Shana, Lauren Zentz, and Nathalie Dion. 2011. "Phrase-final prepositions in Quebec French: An empirical study of contact, code-switching, and resistance to convergence." *Bilingualism: Language and Cognition* 15:203–225.

Posio, Pekka. 2011. "Spanish subject pronoun usage and verb semantics revisited: First and second person singular subject pronouns and focusing of attention in spoken Peninsular Spanish." *Journal of Pragmatics* 43:3, 777–798.

Prada Pérez, Ana de. 2009. "Subject expression in Minorcan Spanish: Consequences of contact with Catalan." PhD diss., Penn State University.

Prada Pérez, Ana. In progress. The Vulnerability Hypothesis.

Shin, Naomi Lapidus. 2014. "Grammatical complexification in Spanish in New York: 3sg pronoun expression and ambiguous verb morphology." *Language Variation and Change* 26(3):303–330.

Shin, Naomi Lapidus, and Helen Smith Cairns. 2012. "The development of NP selection in school-age children: Reference and Spanish subject pronouns." *Language Acquisition* 19:3–38.

Shin, Naomi Lapidus, and Cecilia Montes-Alcalá. 2014. "El uso contextual del pronombre sujeto como factor predictivo de la influencia del inglés en el español en Nueva York." *Sociolinguistic Studies* 8(1):85–110.

Shin, Naomi Lapidus, and Ricardo Otheguy. 2009. "Shifting sensitivity to continuity of reference: Subject pronoun use in Spanish in New York City." In *Español en Estados Unidos y en otros contextos: Cuestiones sociolingüísticas, políticas y pedagógicas,* edited by Manel Lacorte and Jennifer Leeman, 111–136. Madrid: Iberoamericana.

———. 2013. "Social class and gender impacting change in bilingual settings: Spanish subject pronoun use in New York." *Language in Society* 42:429–452.

Silva-Corvalán, Carmen. 1994. *Language contact and change: Spanish in Los Angeles.* New York: Oxford University Press.

Sorace, Antonella. 2011. "Pinning down the concept of "interface" in bilingualism." *Linguistic Approaches to Bilingualism* 1:1–33.

Tagliamonte, Sali. 2012. *Variationist sociolinguistics: Change, observation, and interpretation.* Malden, MA/West Sussex: Wiley-Blackwell.

Thomason, Sarah G., and Terrence Kaufman. 1988. *Language contact, creolization, and genetic linguistics.* Berkeley and Los Angeles: University of California Press.

Toribio, Almeida Jacqueline. 2000. "Setting parametric limits on dialectal variation in Spanish." *Lingua* 110:315–341.

Torres Cacoullos, Rena, and Catherine Travis. 2010. "Variable *yo* expression in New Mexico: English influence?" In *Spanish of the U.S. southwest: A language in transition*, edited by Susana Rivera-Mills and Daniel Villa Crésap, 189–210. Madrid: Iberoamericana/Vervuert.

———. 2011. "Testing convergence via code-switching: Priming and the structure of variable subject expression." *International Journal of Bilingualism* 15:3, 241–267.

Travis, Catherine E. 2007. "Genre effects on subject expression in Spanish: Priming in narrative and conversation." *Language Variation and Change* 19:101–135.

Weinreich, Uriel. 1953. *Languages in contact.* The Hague: Mouton.

PART I

Subject Pronoun Expression in Monolingual Varieties of Spanish

1

Variation of Overt and Null Subject Pronouns in the Spanish of Santo Domingo

Gabriela G. Alfaraz

The high frequency of overt subject pronouns in varieties of Caribbean Spanish (Cameron 1992; Hochberg 1986; Morales 1989) has received great attention within variationist sociolinguistic and other quantitative-oriented work. While studies of linguistic and social constraints on subject pronoun expression (SPE) in Caribbean varieties have dominated the discussion (Avila-Jiménez 1995; Cameron 1992; Hochberg 1986; Morales 1989, 1997; Otheguy and Zentella 2012), the increasing frequency of overt subject pronouns as a change in progress (Cameron 1993; Lunn 2002; Morales 1989, 1997; Toribio 2000) is a question that has drawn considerably less attention.

Comparative work has demonstrated the high frequency of overt subject pronouns in Dominican, Puerto Rican, and Cuban Spanish. Most notably, in their comprehensive cross-dialectal comparison of new arrivals from Latin America to New York City, Otheguy et al. (2007) showed that Caribbean speakers, from the Dominican Republic, Cuba, and Puerto Rico, used 12 percent more overt pronouns than Mainland speakers, from Ecuador, Colombia, and Mexico. In the Caribbean group, Dominican newcomers had a higher rate of overt SPE (41 percent) than Puerto Ricans (35 percent) and Cubans (33 percent), respectively, which leads us to ask whether the rate of subject pronouns in Dominican Spanish is indicative of a larger change in progress.[1] Moreover, pragmatic constraints on pronominal variation appear to be neutralizing, according to Bullock and Toribio (2009), who noted, in light of their findings from research on a rural population of 34 adults and 60 children in Dajabón, Dominican Republic, that "personal pronouns abound, without the anticipated pragmatic functions typically attributed to overt Spanish subject pronouns" (56). Rather than being limited to rural nonstandard speakers, this distribution of overt pronouns is a feature of the standard norm, according to Alba

(2004), who found, in an attitudinal study with 138 participants, that attitudes toward overt pronoun use were highly positive, receiving favorable ratings from 83 percent of participants.

How frequent are overt subject pronouns in Dominican Spanish? Two investigations carried out within the Dominican Republic (Martínez-Sanz 2011; Ortiz López 2009, 2011) found higher rates than the 41 percent Otheguy et al. (2007) found for Dominican newcomers in New York City. It should be pointed out, however, that the higher overt pronominal rates obtained in the Dominican Republic are from communities along the Dominican–Haitian border and, thus, may not be comparable to the New York newcomer sample, nor representative of monolingual speakers beyond the contact areas. Martínez-Sanz (2011) found an overall rate of 51.4 percent for a sample of speakers from Santo Domingo and Dajabón, the rural community studied in Bullock and Toribio (2009), located on the Haitian border in the northwestern Cibao region. A second study, reported by Ortiz López (2009, 2011), based on Spanish in contact with Haitian Creole, found 49 percent expression of overt pronouns for five monolingual Spanish speakers.

Although overt pronominal subject frequency provides a descriptive framework for research on regional and social variation, comparisons across studies may not be reliable because of methodological differences, most obviously in the coding and determination of what counts in the envelope of variation, and less obviously in the collection of data, where characteristics of the interaction can influence discourse, style, and overt pronominal expression. Moreover, it was shown in Cameron (1993), with a statistical comparison of San Juan and Madrid, that percentage rate differences are not necessarily indicative of differences in internal constraints across varieties. The cross-dialectal analyses reported in Otheguy et al. (2007) and Otheguy and Zentella (2012), however, demonstrated differences in both frequencies and constraint rankings for varieties in New York City. Thus, a comparison of overall rates is not necessarily futile when examining variation as a change in progress.

In research on SPE variation, questions remain about the role of overt subjects as functional compensation agents motivated by ambiguity, a topic initially investigated in Hochberg (1986), and renewed in Otheguy and Zentella (2012). Hochberg (1986) tested the functional compensation hypothesis as a means of preserving linguistic information with subject pronouns in Puerto Rican Spanish, examining the correlation between overt pronouns and verb ambiguity produced through deletion of morphological /s/ (as in *tú canta*, cf. *tú cantas*). Hochberg found that the overt pronominal rate was significantly higher for the 2nd person singular *tú* than for a) the 1st and 3rd person singular forms *yo* and *él/ella*, and b) the 1st and 3rd person plural forms *nosotros* and *ellos*. Cameron (1993) further explored these findings through a comparison of Madrid, with no /s/ deletion, and San Juan, with deletion, that showed that even though overt pronominal rates were higher for San Juan, the two dialects had similar constraint rankings; thus, there was no significant difference attributable to verb ambiguity in Puerto Rican Spanish. In a later study, Alba (2004) argued that, given the high rate of /s/ deletion in Dominican Spanish, functional constraints played a role in the occurrence of overt and null pronouns in his study, which found a nearly categorical rate of overt *tú* (96 percent), but 31 percent for other pronouns. Otheguy and Zentella (2012) noted that the pronoun *tú* was overt in 80 percent of cases in which /s/ is deleted from the verb but overt in only 37 percent when there was no deletion.

Cameron (1993) highlighted the importance of the discourse-pragmatic factors specificity and co-reference. He found that one exception to the similarities between San Juan and Madrid was the specificity of the 2nd person singular pronoun *tú*: In San Juan, nonspecific *tú* was ranked higher than specific *tú*, but the opposite was true for

Madrid. Other studies on Puerto Rican Spanish found higher rates for nonspecific *tú*, with the exception of Holmquist (2012), which did not find it significant in the community of Castañer. A small effect was reported in Otheguy et al. (2007), who found that specificity was last in the hierarchy of constraints for Caribbean newcomers, but these results included all forms, not only 2nd person singular.

There has been consensus in the finding that co-reference has a strong influence on pronominal subject expression (Ávila-Jimenez 1995, Bayley and Pease-Alvarez 1997; Bentivoglio 1987; Cameron 1992, 1993, 1995; Flores-Ferrán 2002; Holmquist 2012; Morales 1989; Silva-Corvalán 1977, 1994). In Otheguy and Zentella (2012), reference ranked second, after person, in the constraint hierarchies of both Caribbean and Mainland newcomers. Cameron (1993) reported that in switch reference contexts, San Juan had 66 percent overt pronouns and Madrid 38 percent, but in same reference contexts, the rates dropped to 35 and 14 percent, respectively. Regional differences were eliminated in the logistic regression analysis in which switch reference had a weight of .65 for San Juan and .66 for Madrid and same reference had .35 for both varieties. Holmquist (2012) provides interesting findings on the influence of switch reference in the Castañer community, which had more conservative use of overt pronouns (28 percent) than other Puerto Rican communities, for which frequencies between 35 and 46 percent have been reported. Holmquist found a rate of 42 percent (.70 weight) for switch reference, but only 17 percent (.34 weight) for same reference; recall that Cameron had found 66 percent in switch and 35 percent in same reference contexts. Thus, as we examine findings for evidence of a change in progress, it is necessary to examine overt pronoun frequencies in both switch and same reference contexts, but particularly within the latter, where there is no apparent pragmatic need to reintroduce the referent because its antecedent is accessible and/or unambiguous.

It has been suggested that the high frequency of overt subjects in Caribbean varieties reflects a larger change in progress to a fixed word order with overt pre-verbal subjects (SV) (Jiménez Sabater 1975; Morales 1989, 1997; Toribio 2000). Evidence for the change is supported by the evidence of absence of prepositional object marking with human objects (Alfaraz 2011; Bullock and Toribio 2009; Lunn 2002). Research on word order has found some changes over time; for instance, in a study on Cuban Spanish, Alfaraz (2012) found that there was a generational difference in subject position for intransitive verbs. Similarly, Martínez-Sanz (2011) noted that in Dominican Spanish evidence of a change in progress could be seen for subject position (although it was not evident in overt subject rates). The study of pronominal subject expression in the Dominican variety may shed light on the status of a change toward overt pre-verbal subjects and fixed word order.

The study presented here intends to explore the question of high overt subject pronoun rates as part of a larger change in progress. To this end, this chapter discusses variable SPE in Dominican Spanish with the following goals in mind. First, the overall frequencies are described to establish a rate of overt pronoun use. Second, the influence of linguistic factors on the variation is examined, particularly that of factors that have been found to significantly influence it, namely, the discourse-pragmatic factors co-reference and specificity, and of grammatical factors, including person and number. Third, the influence of social factors is examined, even though studies have mostly found that they do not significantly condition SPE in monolingual varieties (Bayley and Pease-Alvarez 1997; Bentivoglio 1987; Cameron 1992, 1993; Flores-Ferrán 2002), including Santo Domingo (Martínez-Sanz 2011). Nonetheless, some studies have reported significant social factors (see Orozco and Lastra and Martín Butragueño, in this volume); for instance, Ávila-Jimenez (1995) found that in Puerto Rican Spanish, speakers younger than 50 favored overt pronouns more than those over 50. Orozco and

Guy (2008) also reported that age was significant, but for the northern coastal Colombian community studied, the trend ran in the opposite direction, with the younger group (less than 50) using fewer overt pronouns (33 percent, .49 weight) than the older group (41 percent, .60 weight). Shin (2013) and Shin and Otheguy (2013) discussed the influence of gender and social status in the variable use of subject pronouns in the bilingual setting in New York City. In general, linguistic constraints tend to condition variation more strongly than social constraints (Preston 1991). Nevertheless, in the case of Spanish subject pronouns, it is possible that we are not examining social factors in a meaningful manner, more so because we replicate for the Latin American context social variables constructed for the Anglo-American one. The research discussed here is expected to contribute to the larger discussion of variation in subject pronouns in varieties of Spanish, in particular to the question of whether high overt pronoun rates in Dominican Spanish are indicative of a change in progress.

METHODOLOGY

Among the Dominican Republic's regional dialects are the northern (Cibao) dialect, the southern regional dialect, and the south central dialect of the capital city of Santo Domingo, officially named *el Distrito Nacional*, which distinguishes it from the larger metropolitan area that grew from the city's expansion to the north, east, and west. The current study is based on fieldwork conducted in the city of Santo Domingo (*Distrito Nacional*) proper, rather than the larger metropolitan area.

The goal of the fieldwork carried out in Santo Domingo was to build a corpus of speakers born and raised in the city, or who had arrived there before the age of seven. The population of the municipality of Santo Domingo (*Distrito Nacional*) was reported in the country's 2010 *IX Censo Nacional de Población y Vivienda* at 965,040. Sampling the local population was difficult, however, because heavy internal migration from the countryside (*los campos*) as well as from smaller cities and towns had contributed significantly to the number of interlopers: The 2010 *Censo Nacional* reported that 317,773 (33 percent) of the population was born outside the municipality (and another 43,968, or 4.6 percent, was born abroad). Indeed, when conducting fieldwork, it seemed that there were no true locals because most of the people encountered were originally from another city, another town, or some *campo* and had come to Santo Domingo as adults, or had been taken there by parents or siblings as older children. Given these issues with interlopers, and the difficulty of finding individuals native to Santo Domingo, the conditions for being local were expanded along the lines of Chambers's (2000, 2002) interpretation of native-ness as gradient (Regionality Index). Thus, we included participants born or raised outside the city who had immigrated between the ages of 8 and 18 or as adults depending on three criteria: (1) distance: less distance from Santo Domingo was preferred; (2) region: limited to the south central region; (3) residence: they had resided in the city for a significant portion of their lives. This new interpretation of local allowed us to identify suitable participants in a city where interlopers account for nearly 40 percent of the population. We obtained the participation of 21 speakers, 10 men and 11 women in the age groups 18–29, 30–49, and 60+, who were of higher or lower status.

Data Collection

The author and a graduate student fieldworker collected the data used in this study. Both are bilingual Cuban–Americans whose first language was Spanish. A face-to-face sociolinguistic interview (Labov 1984) was the method used for data collection. Modules with topics that would stimulate talk had been designed specifically for the population being sampled and included topics such as life in the city/country, food, family, recreation, and dreams, among others, including a danger-of-death module. Each module contained between two and four submodules, which, in turn, contained two to five questions each. Not all modules were covered with all participants, but each module was referenced as we searched for a topic of interest to the participant. Some participants introduced their own topics (recovery from illness, daily routines, being a single parent, personal history), in which case the person was allowed to speak freely on the topic. We obtained sociolinguistic interviews of at least 30 minutes for the majority of participants.

The participants were recruited based on their age, gender, and social status. Their ages varied from 18 for the youngest to over 70 years old for the oldest. We attempted to obtain data from men and women with diverse educational backgrounds and occupations in order to have a socially stratified sample. Education was used as the most reliable indicator of social status; it was combined with occupation to gain insight into social position. For instance, a university education was not necessarily representative of status and had to be considered along with occupation. Graduates from one of the many nontraditional institutions of higher education are not able to gain employment in their fields of study and often work in positions requiring less education. Furthermore, when determining social status, information was also taken into account about the neighborhood where participants resided, their type of housing, principal mode of transportation, and other indicators of social position in the community. Most participants were candid about the economic hardship they experienced and their struggles to meet basic demands of life with low wages, high inflation, and few opportunities for upward mobility. This information was taken into account when establishing social status.

Quantitative Analysis

The statistical analysis was carried out using Goldvarb and a total of 2,507 tokens. Linguistic and social factors were included in the analysis. The linguistic factors included person, number, tense, specificity and co-reference. Person was coded as first, second, or third, and number as singular or plural. Reference was interpreted as same reference if there was no other human or animate referent in the context between the referent encoded in the verb and its antecedent, as in Erker and Guy (2012) and Travis and Torres Cacoullos (2012), in which the referent expressed as the subject of a target and trigger verb were either the same (same reference) or different (switch reference). The context was considered switch reference if there was a human or animate entity between the referent and its antecedent.[2] Reference was combined with turn to take into account the status of referents in the speech of participants and interviewers: A switch reference could occur within a speaker's turn or in the next speaker's turn; similarly, same reference could be within the turn or the same referent could be maintained in a turn exchange. To ensure reliability, reference was coded by the researcher and a research assistant, who discussed and resolved any discrepancies.

RESULTS

The overall SPE frequency was 42.3 percent (1,060) and the rate of null pronouns was 57.7 percent (1,447), which is shown in table 1.1. These results not only confirm variation in subject expression, they also indicate that Dominican Spanish continues to have more null than overt pronouns. The frequency of overt and null pronouns in switch and same reference contexts, shown in table 1.1, revealed the expected pattern of more frequent overt pronouns in switch reference, 59.2 percent overt and 40 percent null, and fewer in same reference contexts, 40.8 percent overt and 60 percent null. This trend for reference held within and between turn exchanges: More overt pronouns were found for switch reference with a turn change (60.6 percent) or within a same turn (51.5 percent) than for same reference either with a turn change (40.8 percent) or within a same turn (32.1 percent). A change in speaker and reference had the most overt pronouns (60.6 percent) and same reference within speaker turn had the fewest (32.1 percent).

Table 1.1 Reference context in the expression of subject pronoun

		Overt		Null	
		%	N	%	N
Overall		42.3	1060	57.7	1447
Reference	Switch	59.2	627	40.0	579
	Same	40.8	433	60.0	868
Reference and turn	Switch +turn	60.6	43	39.4	28
	Switch -turn	51.5	584	48.5	551
	Same +turn	40.8	73	59.2	106
	Same -turn	32.1	360	67.9	762

Statistical Analysis

The multivariate analysis with Goldvarb included number, co-reference, tense, age, gender, socioeconomic status, person, specificity, and reference. An interaction was found between person and specificity, and these factors were merged to resolve it. Additional interactions in the data between the merged factor with person/specificity and reference were resolved by merging person and specificity with reference. Types of reference according to the type of turn were collapsed into two factors—same and switch—to avoid empty cells in the new analysis. The factor group containing person, specificity, and reference was analyzed along with age, gender, and socioeconomic status. The constraint ranking revealed that the merged group with person, specificity, and reference ranked first with a range value of 81, followed by number (38), and, lastly, by gender (10); neither age nor socioeconomic status was significant in the analysis.

Linguistic Factors

The multivariate analysis results presented in table 1.2 show that overt pronouns are favored mostly by 2nd person specific pronouns in a switch reference context (.87). Similarly, and more interestingly, 2nd person nonspecific pronouns in same reference contexts also strongly favor overt pronouns (.82). This suggests that it is highly probable that *tú*, *usted*, and *ustedes*, when nonspecific, will be overt when in same reference contexts, despite a preceding accessible and unambiguous antecedent. 2nd person specific pronouns in same reference contexts also moderately favored overt pronouns (.66). Overt pronouns were favored for 1st person in switch reference contexts (.69), 3rd person in switch contexts (.69), and 2nd person nonspecific in switch contexts (.64). They were slightly disfavored for 3rd person and 1st person specific when the reference was the same. Overt forms were strongly disfavored for 3rd person nonspecific in both same (.16) and switch reference (.06) contexts. A second analysis, discussed in more detail below, and run with reference as a separate factor, confirmed that overt forms were promoted in switch reference contexts (.64, 52 percent, N = 627/1206) but disfavored in same reference contexts (.37, 33 percent, N = 433/1301). In all, these findings confirmed that the accessibility of the referent is a factor constraining the occurrence of overt forms, with a stronger possibility that they will surface when there is a change of referent.

Table 1.2 Results for person, specificity, and reference

	Switch		Same	
	Weight	**% (N)**	**Weight**	**% (N)**
2nd [+spec]	.87	81.8 (117/143)	.82	78.9 (15/19)
1st [+spec]	.69	59.0 (356/603)	.66	56.2 (36/64)
3rd [+spec]	.69	53.5 (138/258)	.45	34.0 (118/347)
2nd [-spec]	.64	56.0 (14/25)	.40	34.4 (260/756)
3rd [-spec]	.06	1.1 (2/177)	.16	3.5 (4/115)
Range	81		66	

Note: Input .36, total chi-square = 59.17, chi-square/cell = 1.74, log likelihood = –1354.01.

A second configuration of the linguistic factors examined the different pronominal forms in a factor group rather than the features person, number, and so on, separately. In this analysis, too, an interaction was found with pronominal form and specificity, and the two factor groups were combined. Reference context, however, did not interact with the other factor groups and remained a separate factor group, with turn-type collapsed into same and switch context. As in the previous analysis, the social categories age, gender, and socioeconomic status were included. For this analysis the ranking of factor groups—determined here according to statistical range values—was essentially the same as the earlier analysis: Pronominal form (and specificity) ranked highest (86), then co-reference (27), and, lastly, speaker gender (10). Age and socioeconomic status were not significant.

The results for pronoun and specificity in table 1.3 show that specific *tú* had a very strong likelihood of being overt (.89). The pronoun *ella* (.78) also had a strong chance of being overt. Also favoring overt forms were nonspecific *tú* and *usted* (.77), which had been combined because they had similar weights and were frequently used interchangeably. Other grammatical persons that favored overt subjects included *ustedes* (.69), *yo* (.67), and *él* (.64). Note that there is a sharp contrast between forms that favor and the ones that disfavor overt subjects pronouns, including specific *ellos* (.31), *ellas* (.28), *nosotros* (.24) and nonspecific *ellos* (.03).

Number was significant in both models described above. The first analysis showed that overt pronouns were moderately favored with singular pronouns (.63, 55 percent, N = 936/1701) and they were strongly disfavored with plural pronouns (.25, 15 percent, N = 122/801). The second analysis confirmed that singular pronouns promoted overt forms but that plural pronouns did not, with the exception of *ustedes*. Thus, it was found that 1st person singular *yo* (.67) favored overt forms but 1st person plural *nosotros* strongly disfavored them (.24). Furthermore, overt forms were moderately favored for

Table 1.3 Pronoun (with specificity)[a]

Pronoun	Weight	%	N
tú [+specific]	.89	85	91/107
ella [+specific]	.78	68.3	99/145
tú/usted [-specific]	.77	65.9	29/44
usted [+specific]	.75	67.2	41/61
ustedes [+specific]	.69	56.8	21/37
yo [+specific]	.67	51.6	573/1110
él [+specific]	.64	44.4	107/241
ellos [+specific]	.31	22	42/191
ellas [+specific]	.28	22.9	8/35
nosotros [+specific]	.24	17.2	43/250
ellos [-specific]	.03	2.1	6/286
Range	86		

Note: Input .36, total chi-square = 93.18, chi-square/cell = 2.22, log likelihood = –1351.24.

a. The pronoun *uno* was not included in the statistical count, but it commonly varies with *yo* in discourse, appearing to be 1st person specific, rather than nonspecific, which has been described in Bullock and Toribio (2009).

3rd person masculine singular *él* (.64) and its feminine counterpart *ella* (.78), but the plural forms of both disfavored them: *ellos* (.31) and *ellas* (.28). Lastly, nonspecific *ellos* was nearly categorical, strongly disfavoring overt forms (.03). As noted earlier, higher rates of overt pronouns with singular verb forms than with plural forms are commonly found.

Social Factors

The analysis indicated that gender was the only significant social factor. These results are shown in table 1.4. Gender patterning showed that females slightly favor overt pronouns (.54) and males favor null pronominal subjects (.44). Although age was not significant, the percentages showed small increases in the use of overt forms in the middle and older group than among the younger speakers. The cross-tabulation of gender and age (figure 1.1) did not reveal consistent patterns; women in the youngest and middle groups had higher overt pronoun rates (18–29 years: 42 percent; 30–49: 49 percent) than men (18–29: 34 percent; 30–49: 32 percent), with a larger contrast in the 30–49 year old group, but in the older group, men outdid women in the use of overt forms (51 percent vs. 45 percent). Further examination with more participants from this age group will help us understand whether age distribution is specific to this sample or representative of the larger community.

Table 1.4 Gender, age, and SES (range for gender .10)

		Weight	%	N
Gender	Female	.54	45.4	712/1567
	Male	.44	37.1	346/935
Age[a]	18–29	*.49*	39.3	287/730
	30–49	*.49*	41.2	426/1034
	60+	*.52*	46.7	347/743
SES[a]	Higher	*.50*	40.2	513/1276
	Lower	*.50*	44.4	547/1231

a. Not significant (weights in italics).

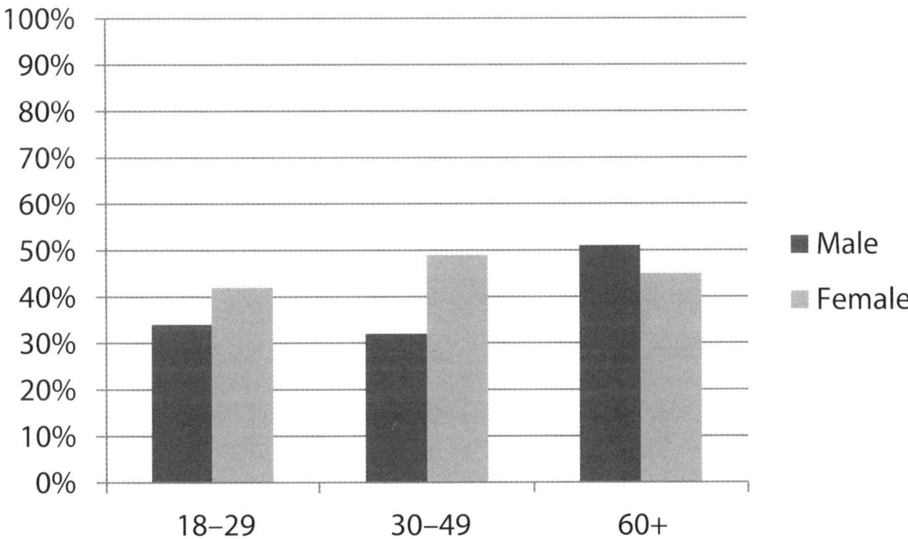

Figure 1.1 Overt subject expression by age and gender.

DISCUSSION

This empirical study of subject pronoun expression in Dominican Spanish was intended to examine variation and a possible change in progress, given the variety's reputation as one with radical use of overt subject pronouns. The distribution of overt and null pronouns may be indicative of this variety being advanced in a change toward becoming a non-pro-drop language (Jiménez Sabater 1975; Morales 1989, 1997; Toribio 2000). To examine whether the occurrence of overt pronouns in Dominican Spanish is extraordinary, the overall rate of overt pronouns is viewed in comparison with other studies. Of particular interest is the overt pronominal rate when the reference is the same and overt forms are not motivated by pragmatic factors, a context in which we may find absence of expected constraints. The behavior of pronouns will be discussed because those that exhibit higher frequencies may be undergoing change. Lastly, the findings for age and other social factors will be discussed because generational differences can provide evidence for a change in progress.

Frequencies

The 42 percent overt pronominal rate reported here is comparable to the 41 percent rate reported in Otheguy and Zentella (2012) for six Dominican newcomers in New York City. Other studies that sampled communities along the Dominican–Haitian border reported higher rates than these: 51 percent was reported in Martínez-Sanz (2011) and 49 percent in Ortiz López (2009, 2011). Taken as representative of the variety, the rate of 42 percent found here or 41 percent in Otheguy and Zentella (2012) does not suggest an extraordinarily high use of overt pronominal subjects. Although these rates are higher than what Otheguy and Zentella found for the Cuban and Puerto Rican varieties (33 percent and 35 percent respectively), and significantly higher than what these authors reported for mainland Latin American varieties (24 percent), this does not necessarily constitute evidence that Dominican Spanish is an outlier. In fact, higher rates have been reported in studies of other dialects; for instance, Cameron (1992) found 45 percent for Puerto Rican Spanish.

Thus, the distribution of overt and null pronouns found in this study does not indicate a sharp divergence from the pan-regional Caribbean norm. Moreover, while overt subject pronouns were found in 42 percent of cases, in 58 percent of tokens, the preferred form was the null one, indicating the strength of null subjects in Dominican Spanish. These rates do not suggest, strictly on the basis of rate comparisons, that this variety is radical or unique in its selection of overt pronouns. Nonetheless, a change may be in progress that is not observable using an apparent-time methodology based on a time depth of thirty to forty years between the oldest and youngest generations sampled.

Reference

Bullock and Toribio (2009) observed that personal pronoun expression in their Dominican corpus from the Haitian border area was not constrained by the pragmatic functions that have been shown to operate on the variation in other varieties. The findings described above indicated that it is a significant constraint for the sample studied here. Our findings showed that there was a moderate preference for overt pronouns with switch reference (.64), compared to same reference (.37), a pattern commonly found across dialects (Bayley and Pease-Alvarez 1997; Bentivoglio 1987; Cameron 1992, 1993; Carvalho and Child 2011; Flores-Ferrán 2002, 2004; Holmquist 2012; Martinez-Sanz 2011; Orozco and Guy 2008; Silva-Corvalán 1994). Furthermore, this analysis showed that reference can interact with other factors, as it did here with person and specificity, depending on the approach taken when representing the dependent variable, whether as the pronoun (with the grammatical features included), or as linguistic and pragmatic features that are separated into different factor groups. Teasing apart the influence of switch reference requires considering various configurations of the variables and then submitting them to statistical modeling to identify the ones that provide relevant and significant material to interpret the variation.

To address the question of a change in progress, the appearance of overt pronouns in same reference contexts, in which they are expected to occur less frequently, is perhaps a site where differences suggesting changes in progress can be examined. The findings for person, specificity, and reference, displayed in table 1.2, showed that in switch reference contexts, every factor favored overt forms, to greater or lesser degrees, with the exception of 3rd person nonspecific. In same reference contexts, on the other hand, only 2nd person specific and nonspecific favored overt forms, but the probability that other factors would disfavor overt forms was not strong (.45 for 3rd person specific and .40 for 1st person specific), and only 3rd person nonspecific strongly disfavored it.

Thus, according to these findings, 3rd person nonspecific is the only context in which it is very likely that overt forms will not appear, but in the others there are varying degrees of likelihood that they will. This distribution could reflect a weakening of constraints on overt pronouns in same reference contexts. Thus, Bullock and Toribio's (2009) observation that overt forms appear without regard to pragmatic function is partially confirmed. Through further study of the connection between reference and subject expression, we can explore changes in the constraints on overt forms in same reference contexts.

Pronouns

The distribution of the variation across the pronominal forms, according to number and person, found here is in line with findings from other variationist SPE research (Bayley and Pease-Alvarez 1997; Carvalho and Child 2011; Otheguy et al. 2007; Otheguy and Zentella 2012). The 2nd person pronoun *tú* (specific) was overt in 85 percent of cases, which although not as high as the 96 percent rate reported for Dominican Spanish in Alba (2004), is, nevertheless, high. The sample from Santo Domingo studied in Martínez-Sanz (2011) also found high rates of specific *tú* (89.1). Both here and in Martínez-Sanz, nonspecific occurrences of *tú* also had high rates (66 percent and 78 percent respectively). In Otheguy et al. (2007), 2nd person singular was the highest ranked factor, followed by 2nd person nonspecific, 3rd person singular, and so forth. Alba (2004) attributed the occurrence of overt *tú* to a compensatory /s/ deletion effect, which was also discussed in Otheguy and Zentella (2012), who noted that an overwhelming number of overt pronouns (80 percent) appeared when /s/ was deleted. The results presented above were not intended to address the issue of functional compensation, but it should be noted, nevertheless, that overt pronouns were favored, with the exception of the plural forms *ellos* (specific and nonspecific), *ellas*, and *nosotros*. In addition to the functional role that overt pronouns may play in a variable system, Erker and Guy (2012) showed that lexical frequency influenced the occurrence of overt pronominal forms according to person and number but the pattern depends on the form: Overt forms decreased in 3rd and 1st person singular forms (37 percent to 35 percent and 39 percent to 37 percent, respectively), but they increased significantly in the 2nd person singular from 40 percent for infrequent verbs to 83 percent for frequent verbs. Moreover, they showed that these effects operate across dialects, similarly influencing, for instance, Dominican and Mexican Spanish. Further study of the role of functional compensation and the effects of lexical frequency may offer insight into the variation observable in Caribbean varieties.

CONCLUSION

This chapter has explored SPE in Dominican Spanish, a variety that has been shown to have high overt pronominal rates. The discussion of the variation of overt and null forms was framed within the question of whether frequent overt subjects are related to other ongoing changes in Spanish, namely, a change to mandatory overt pre-verbal subjects. To find evidence substantiating this claim, statistical analysis was carried out on 2,507 tokens from sociolinguistic interviews with 21 participants from Santo Domingo. The analysis focused on linguistic factor groups that have been shown to influence the variation, including person, number, tense, specificity, and switch reference, as well as on the social factors age, gender, and socioeconomic status, although these have not been consistently found to significantly condition the variation.

Results showed that the overall overt pronoun frequency was in line with that reported in Otheguy et al. (2007) and Otheguy and Zentella (2012) for Dominican newcomers in New York City. The multivariate analysis indicated that person, specificity, and reference interacted to constrain subject pronouns. The majority of contexts favored overt pronouns, whether with switch reference, where overt forms are expected to be more frequent, or with same reference, where they are expected to occur at a significantly lower rate. As in previous studies, this investigation found that the 2nd person pronouns *tú* and *usted* were strongly favored both in switch reference (probability weight .87) and in same reference (.82) contexts. Claims that pragmatic functions do not operate on overt subject expression in this variety (Bullock and Toribio 2009) were not supported because it was found that reference influenced the variation. However, the results suggested a weakening of this constraint, which, it was proposed, may be the location of changes in progress. The effects of social factors did not reveal generational differences to substantiate, in apparent time, a change in progress. There is a likelihood that subject expression may constitute an instance of stable variation, whose gender distribution (a small preference among women) suggests that it may have covert prestige, or even overt, as suggested by Alba (2004).

ACKNOWLEDGMENTS

This research was supported by a HARP Grant from Michigan State University. I would like to express profound gratitude to Dr. Bruno Rosario Candelier, Jacqueline Pimentel, and the staff at the Dominican Academy of Language for their invaluable help.

NOTES

1. Holmquist (2012) noted that overt pronoun rates for Puerto Rican Spanish vary from 28 percent, in Holmquist's own study of Castañer to 46 percent in Morales's (1986) study of San Juan. Shin and Otheguy (2013) showed that in New York City Dominican Spanish is not undergoing change; in fact, the Dominican group shows the least change among the six regional dialect groups in the community.
2. Travis and Torres Cacoullos (2012) showed that the variable expression of the first person singular pronoun *yo* was influenced by the presence of an intervening human subject referent.

REFERENCES

Alfaraz, Gabriela G. 2011. "Accusative object marking: A change in progress in Cuban Spanish?" *Spanish in Context* 8:213–234.

———. 2012. "Word order as a change in progress: Evidence from Cuban Spanish." Presentation at the 6th Workshop on Spanish Sociolinguistics (WSS6), at the University of Arizona, Tucson, Arizona, April 12–14.

Alba, Orlando. 2004. *Cómo Hablamos los Dominicanos: Un Enfoque Sociolingüístico*. Santo Domingo: Grupo León Jiménez.

Avila-Jiménez, Bárbara I. 1995. "A sociolinguistic analysis of a change in progress: Pronominal overtness in Puerto Rican Spanish." *Cornell Working Papers in Linguistics* 13:25–47.

Bayley, Robert, and Lucinda Pease-Alvarez. 1997. "Null pronoun variation in Mexican-descent children's narrative discourse." *Language Variation and Change* 9:349–71.

Bentivoglio, Paola. 1987. *Los Sujetos Pronominales de Primera Persona en el Habla de Caracas*. Caracas: Universidad Central de Venezuela.

Bullock, Barbara E., and A. Jacqueline Toribio. 2009. "Reconsidering Dominican Spanish: Data from the rural Cibao." *RILI* 2:49–73.

Cameron, Richard. 1992. "Pronominal and null subject variation in Spanish: Constraints, dialects and functional compensation." PhD diss., University of Pennsylvania.

Cameron, Richard. 1993. "The scope and limits of switch reference as a constraint on pronominal subject expression." *Hispanic Linguistics* 6/7:1–27.

Cameron, Richard. 1994. "Ambiguous agreement, functional compensation, and nonspecific *tú* in the Spanish of San Juan, Puerto Rico, and Madrid, Spain." *Language Variation and Change* 5:305–334.

Carvalho, Ana M., and Michael Child. 2011. "Subject pronoun expression in a variety of Spanish in contact with Portuguese." In *Selected Proceedings of the 5th Workshop on Spanish Sociolinguistics*, edited by Jim Michnowicz and Robin Dodsworth, 14–25. Somerville, MA: Cascadilla Proceedings Project.

Chambers, J. K. 2000. "Region and language variation." *English World-Wide* 21:1–31.

———. 2002. "Dynamics of dialect convergence." *Journal of Sociolinguistics* 6:117–130.

Erker, Daniel, and Gregory R. Guy. 2012. "The role of lexical frequency in syntactic variability: Variable subject personal pronoun expression in Spanish." *Language* 88:526–557.

Flores-Ferrán, Nydia. 2002. *Subject Personal Pronouns in Spanish Narratives of Puerto Ricans in New York City: A sociolinguistic perspective*. München: Lincolm Europa.

———. 2004. "Spanish subject personal pronoun use in New York City Puerto Ricans: Can we rest the case of English contact?" *Language Variation and Change* 16:49–73.

Hochberg, Judith G. 1986. "Functional compensation for /s/ deletion in Puerto Rican Spanish." *Language* 62:609–621.

Holmquist, Jonathan. 2012. "Frequency rates and constraints on subject persona pronoun expression: Findings from the Puerto Rican highlands." *Language Variation and Change* 24:203–220.

Jiménez Sabater, Maximiliano. 1975. *Más Datos sobre el Español en la República Dominicana*. Santo Domingo: Ediciones Intec.

Labov, William. 1984. "Field methods of the Project on Linguistic Change and Variation." In *Language in use,* edited by John Baugh and Joel Sherzer, 28–54. Englewood Cliffs: Prentice Hall.

Lunn, Patt. 2002. "Tout se tient in Dominican Spanish." In *Structure, meaning, and acquisition in Spanish*, edited by James F. Lee, Kimberly L. Geeslin, and J. Clancy Clements, 65–72. Somerville, MA: Cascadilla Press.

Martínez-Sanz, Cristina. 2011. "Null and overt subjects in a variable system: The case of Dominican Spanish." PhD diss., University of Ottawa.

Morales, Amparo. 1989. "Hacia un universal sintáctico del español del caribe. El orden SVO." *Anuario de Lingüística Hispánica.* 5:139–152.

———. 1997. "La hipótesis funcional y la aparición de sujeto no nominal: el español de Puerto Rico." *Hispania* 80:153–165.

Oficina Nacional de Estadísticas (ONE). Retrieved from http://www.one.gob.do.

Orozco, Rafael, and Gregory Guy. 2008. "El uso variable de los pronombres sujetos: ¿qué pasa en la costa Caribe colombiana?" In *Selected Proceedings of the Fourth Workshop on Spanish Sociolinguistics*, edited by Maurice Westmoreland and Juan Antonio Thomas, 70–80. Somerville, MA: Cascadilla.

Ortiz López, Luis A. 2009. "Pronombres de sujeto en el español (L2 vs. L1) del caribe." *LENSO* 21:85–110.

———. 2011. "Spanish in contact with Haitian Creole." In *Handbook of Hispanic sociolinguistics*, edited by Manuel Díaz-Campos, 418–445. Malden, MA: Blackwell.

Otheguy, Ricardo, and Ana Celia Zentella. 2012. *Spanish in New York: Language contact, dialect leveling, and structural continuity.* Oxford: Oxford University Press.

Otheguy, Ricardo, Ana Celia Zentella, and David Livert. 2007. "Language and dialect contact in Spanish in New York: Toward the formation of a speech community." *Language* 83:770–802.

Preston, Dennis R. 1991. "Sorting out the variables in sociolinguistic theory." *American Speech* 66:33–56.

Shin, Naomi Lapidus. 2013. "Women as leaders of language change: A qualification from the bilingual perspective." In *Selected Proceedings of the 6th Workshop on Spanish Sociolinguistics*, edited by Ana M. Carvalho and Sara Beaudrie, 135–147. Somerville, MA: Cascadilla Proceedings Project.

Shin, Naomi Lapidus, and Ricardo Otheguy. 2013. "Social class and gender impacting change in bilingual settings: Spanish subject pronoun use in New York." *Language in Society* 42:429–452.

Silva-Corvalán, Carmen. 1977. "A Discourse study of word order in the Spanish spoken by Mexican–Americans in West Los Angeles." MA thesis, University of California, Los Angeles.

———. 1994. *Language contact and change: Spanish in Los Angeles.* Oxford: Claredon Press.

Toribio, A. Jacqueline. 2000. "Setting parametric limits on dialectal variation in Spanish." *Lingua* 110:315–341.

Travis, Catherine E., and Rena Torres Cacoullos. 2012. "What do subject pronouns do in discourse? Cognitive, mechanical and constructional factors in variation." *Cognitive Linguistics* 23:711–748.

2

Pronominal Variation in Colombian Costeño Spanish

Rafael Orozco

Variable pronominal usage is a morphosyntactic feature that Spanish inherited from Latin. Consequently, as with all other pro-drop languages, pronominal subjects are variably present in Spanish. That is, speakers consistently alternate between overt and null pronominal subject expression, as illustrated in (1), taken from the data for the present study.

(1) ***Yo sí tengo*** *el interéh, pero es que* ***{Ø} no tengo*** *tiempo.* [BM07016][1]

'**I do have** the interest, but it's that **[I] don't have** time.'

As shown throughout this volume and in numerous prior studies, pronominal rates differ dialectally—with higher overt pronoun rates in the Caribbean than in the rest of the Hispanic World (cf. Barrenechea and Alonso 1977; Bayley and Pease-Alvarez 1997; Bentivoglio 1987; Cameron 1992, 1993, 1995, 1996; Cameron and Flores-Ferrán 2004; Enríquez 1984; Erker and Guy 2012; Flores-Ferrán 2002, 2004; Hochberg 1986; Hurtado 2001; Morales 1980; Orozco and Guy 2008; Ortiz López 2009; Otheguy and Zentella 2007, 2012; Otheguy, Zentella, and Livert 2007; Posio 2011; Prada Pérez 2009; Shin and Otheguy 2013; Silva-Corvalán 1982, 1994; Travis 2005a; inter alios). Dialectal differences also exist in the constraints on pronoun expression. For instance, Cameron (1993) finds differences between Spain and Puerto Rico in the effect of indefinite versus definite reference on second person singular forms.

The empirical study of variable subject personal pronoun (SPP) usage was pioneered by Barrenechea and Alonso (1977), Morales (1980), and Silva-Corvalán (1982) who explored the Spanish spoken in, respectively, Buenos Aires, Puerto Rico, and among Mexican–Americans in East Los Angeles. Those trailblazing studies inspired many others, which include work on Latin American Spanish (Bentivoglio 1987; Cameron 1992,

1993, 1995, 1996; Hurtado 2005a, 2005b; Orozco and Guy 2008; Ortiz López 2009; Travis 2005a, 2005b), Peninsular Spanish (Cameron 1993, 1995, 1996; Enríquez 1984; Posio 2011; Prada Pérez 2009), and Spanish in the United States (Bayley and Pease-Alvarez 1997; Cameron and Flores-Ferrán 2004; Flores-Ferrán 2002, 2004, 2007; Hochberg 1986; Hurtado 2001, 2005a; Otheguy and Zentella 2007, 2012; Othegey, Zentella, and Livert 2007; Shin and Otheguy 2013; Silva-Corvalán 1982, 1994, 1997; inter alios). In addition to numerous syntactic, morphological, and semantic constraints found to condition SPP usage, significant functional effects have been claimed (Erker 2005, Hochberg 1986) and contradicted (Cameron 1993). Despite being extensively explored throughout the Hispanic world, subject personal pronoun expression remains understudied in Colombian Spanish, particularly so in Costeño Spanish. Previous research has explored SPE in Bogotá and among Colombians in Florida (Hurtado 2001, 2005a, 2005b), in the city of Cali (Travis 2005b, 2007), and among Mainlander Colombians in NYC (Otheguy and Zentella 2007, 2012; Otheguy, Zentella, and Livert 2007). The present study expands on Orozco and Guy's (2008) preliminary analysis of SPE in Costeño Spanish. It also seeks to provide a stronger data baseline and answer some lingering questions.

METHODOLOGY

This section describes the speech community constituted by the city of Barranquilla and the data used in this analysis. It also details the main research criteria employed in the present study.

The Speech Community and the Data Set

Barranquilla, known as Colombia's Golden Gate, was first settled in 1629. With a current population of 1,146,359 inhabitants, it constitutes the largest Colombian seaport. The migration pattern of people moving from rural to urban areas found throughout Latin America also affects Barranquilla. Since this city attracts people from all over northern Colombia, its language has become representative of *Costeño*, the Caribbean variety of Colombian Spanish (Orozco 2007b, 104). According to Spanish dialectal classifications (Henríquez Ureña 1921; Lipski 1994, 6; Zamora and Guitart 1982, 182 ff.; inter alios), *Costeño*, is part of the Carib/Arawak macrodialect, which includes varieties spoken in the Antilles and the coastal regions of Colombia, Ecuador, and Venezuela.

The dataset examined here was extracted from *Corpus del Castellano Barranquillero* (CorCaBa) gathered between 1997 and 1999. This corpus consists of 39 hours of sociolinguistic conversations with twenty-two socially stratified consultants: eleven women and eleven men whose ages range from 15 to 85 years old. At the time of data collection, all consultants resided in middle and working class communities in the Barranquilla metropolitan area, having spent most of their lives within a hundred miles of their birthplace. The orthographic transcription of this corpus consists of 186,309 words, or 440 pages.

Research Questions and Hypotheses

As with the other studies in this part of the book, this investigation fills a particular gap by contributing to the formation of a data baseline on contemporary SPE in monolingual Spanish-speaking communities. In exploring pronominal expression in Costeño Spanish, I seek to answer the following research questions.

1. *How are overt SPPs and null subjects distributed in Costeño Spanish? How does Costeño compare with other varieties of Spanish in SPP expression? Is it more like the Caribbean or Mainland dialects?*
2. *Is the internal conditioning on SPP usage in Costeño Spanish similar to that throughout the Hispanic World? Do all verbs within a semantic category have similar effects on SPP usage?*
3. *What is the social distribution of SPP usage? How does the external conditioning in Barranquilla compare to what occurs elsewhere?*

Concurrently, I seek to test the following main hypothesis: *The constraints and individual factor tendencies conditioning overt SPP usage largely reflect uniformity across different varieties of Spanish despite differences in overt pronominal rates with SPP usage being more strongly conditioned by subject-related constraints.* Moreover, I test hypotheses directly addressing each one of the constraints explored here. My research questions and hypotheses have been informed by a multitude of previous studies (Barrenechea and Alonso 1977; Bayley and Pease-Alvarez 1997; Bentivoglio 1987; Cameron 1992, 1993, 1995, 1998; Enríquez 1984; Flores-Ferrán 2002, 2004, 2007; Hurtado 2001, 2005b; Morales 1980; Orozco and Guy 2008, Otheguy and Zentella 2007, 2012; Otheguy, Zentella, and Livert 2007; Silva-Corvalán 1982, 1994, 1997; Travis 2005b; inter alia).

Constraints Examined

To answer the above research questions and test my hypotheses, I explored the effects of 17 constraints (12 internal, 5 external). The internal constraints operate at different morphosyntactic and discourse levels. For this analysis, I divided them into three groups: (a) those pertaining to the whole clause, (b) constraints pertaining to the verb, and (c) constraints pertaining to the subject or SPP, as follows.

a. Clause-related constraints
   —Two constraints fall within this category: *discourse style* and *clause type.*
b. Verb-related constraints
   —This category comprises five constraints: *lexical content of verb, verb regularity, verb class, TMA form of the verb,* and *preceding TMA.*
c. Subject-related constraints
   —Although some of the five constraints in this category deal with factors that are actually located outside the clauses being studied, I grouped them together considering how they condition SPPs. These constraints include *SPP person and number, switch reference, prior subject's person and number, priming,* and *distance from previous co-referential subject.*

I based my choice of internal constraints on prior SPE findings (cf. Enríquez 1984; Flores-Ferrán 2002, 2004, 2007; Otheguy, Zentella, and Livert 2007; Torres Cacoullos and Travis 2011; Travis 2005b, 2007; Travis and Torres Cacoullos 2012). Thus, these internal constraints include eight of those nine explored in Orozco and Guy (2008). Verb reflexivity, not found significant in that study, constitutes the only constraint excluded from this investigation. To further probe verb semantics and priming, I added four constraints to this analysis: *verb class, prior subject's person and number, realization of preceding subject*, and *distance from previous co-referential subject.* Seeking to further probe their finding that younger speakers tend to favor null SPPs, I also explored the five external constraints analyzed by Orozco and Guy (2008): *sex, age, education, socioeconomic status*, and *conversation conditions*.

The Envelope of Variation and the Analysis

The envelope of variation used here adheres to the Principle of Accountability (Labov 1972, 72) by including only uncontestable instances of variable SPE usage. It also follows the parameters advanced by Silva-Corvalán (1982), which have become standard for SPP studies. I included in the dataset only those clauses with ascertainable animate pronominal subjects containing a conjugated verb where the null/overt subject alternation is clearly possible. Thus, all tokens constitute one of at least two possible different ways of saying the same thing. This dataset comprises 3,009 tokens, that is, roughly 135 per speaker. I coded all tokens in terms of the constraints discussed above. Aiming to avoid problematic factor overlaps or interactions while preserving the orthogonality of constraints, I conducted parallel multivariate Goldvarb analyses using two different dataset configurations (cf. Tagliamonte 2006, 233) both including social factors. Thus, I tested *lexical content of verb* and *switch reference* in one data configuration separating them from *verb class* and *prior subject's person* and number, included in the alternate configuration. Among other things, this helped avoid the possible interactions caused by the fact that all motion verbs denote external activity and all perception verbs denote mental activity.

In the subsequent sections, I walk the reader through my results starting with the distribution of overt and null SPPs. My discussion of the internal conditioning on pronominal usage precedes that of external constraints.

DISTRIBUTION OF OVERT AND NULL SPPS

The distribution of overt and null subjects, presented in table 2.1, reflects the dominance of null subjects throughout each grammatical person. The overall 34.2 percent pronominal rate places Barranquilla squarely within the Caribbean dialect region (cf. Henríquez Ureña 1921; Lipski 1994, 6; Zamora and Guitart 1982, 182 ff.), where pronominal rates above 30 percent are commonplace (cf. Cameron 1993; Orozco and Guy 2008; Otheguy and Zentella 2007, 2012; Ortiz López 2009; among others). A comparison with the pronominal rate of 35.7 percent in Orozco and Guy (2008) suggests a methodological implication: A dataset of approximately 1,000 tokens suffices to establish a reliable pronominal rate. That is, the overt SPP rate in Barranquilla is not significantly different from that of the pilot study despite using here a dataset almost two thousand tokens larger.

The pronominal rate by grammatical person (table 2.1) corroborates the conclusion drawn from the results of previous studies that singular SPPs occur more frequently as overt subjects than their plural counterparts (Abreu 2009, 2012; Bayley and Pease-Alvarez 1997; Bentivoglio 1987, 36; Carvalho and Child 2011; Claes 2011; Erker and Guy 2012; Flores-Ferrán 2002, 2004, 2007, 2009; Otheguy and Zentella 2007, 2012; Otheguy, Zentella, and Livert 2007; Posio 2011, this volume; Prada Pérez 2009; Ortiz López 2011; among others). Despite comprising less than one percent of the data, second person plural subjects have a much higher overt pronoun occurrence (38.9 percent) than the other plural grammatical persons. This may be due to the need to disambiguate between *ustedes* 'you (plural)' and *ellos* 'they,' which have identical verbal morphology in all tenses.

In general, the multivariate analyses results reveal a complex pattern of linguistic and social forces with ten constraints (eight internal and two external) reaching statisti-

Table 2.1 Distribution of overt and null SPPs by grammmatical person

Grammatical Person	Pronominal Rate	Overt SPPs	Null Subjects	% data
1st singular	44.5%	565	705	42.2%
2nd singular	32.5%	76	158	7.8%
3rd singular	39.6%	300	458	25.2%
1st plural	12.8%	43	293	11.2%
2nd plural	38.9%	7	11	0.6%
3rd plural	9.9%	39	354	13.1%
All pronouns	**34.2%**	1,030	1,979	100.0%

cal significance. The selection order with either dataset configuration—discussed above (see the envelope of variation and the analysis on page 20)—largely coincides with the range values. For instance, in both cases SPP person and number is selected first and has the highest range value. Contrariwise, clause type is selected last regardless of analytical configuration. Internal constraints, with higher order of selection and range values, appear to condition SPEs more strongly than social factors. These results are largely commensurate with those of Otheguy, Zentella, and Livert (2007). They are also consonant with Otheguy and Zentella's (2007, 276) affirmation that either the same or very similar factors constrain SPPs across the board, that is, in Caracas (Bentivoglio 1987), Puerto Rico (Enríquez 1984), Madrid (Cameron 1993, 1995), New York (Otheguy and Zentella 2007, 2012), Los Angeles (Silva-Corvalán 1982, 1997), inter alia. The discussion of internal constraints follows.

INTERNAL CONDITIONING

The internal conditioning on SPE reveals the significant effect of eight constraints: One of them, clause type, is clause-related. Three constraints pertain to the verb: TMA, lexical content, and verb class. The remaining four—priming, prior subject's person and number, switch reference, subject's grammatical person and number—fall within the subject-related category. I have divided my discussion of internal constraints into three parts, according to the groups of constraints presented previously, that is, clause-, verb-, and subject-related constraints.

Clause-Related Constraints

The results show clause type as the only clause-related constraint that conditions SPP usage. The other clause-related constraint analyzed, discourse style (whether a clause is in a narrative or is a response to a question or comment), was not selected by Goldvarb as statistically significant.

Clause Type

I initially coded the data using the same six factors as Otheguy, Zentella, and Livert (2007, 798) that is, independent, conditional, coordinate, relative, argument, and other subordinate. Preliminary results, congruent with those of Otheguy and Zentella (2012,

268), showed three different types of subordinate clauses (argument, relative, other subordinate) to follow similar tendencies. Thus, I conducted all subsequent analyses with the three types of clause shown in table 2.2 (subordinate, independent, coordinate). All probability values reported here are significant [$p < 0.05$]. Individual statistical probabilities closer to one favor the occurrence of an overt subject, while those closer to zero disfavor it. Subordinate clauses favor overt pronominal subjects with a statistical weight of .54 while independent clauses (statistical weight .50) have a neutral effect. On the other hand, coordinate clauses exert a favorable effect on null subjects with a value of .47, a tendency that also occurs in New York City (cf. Otheguy and Zentella 2012; Shin and Montes Alcalá 2014; Orozco 2012) and in the Uruguay–Brazil border region (Carvalho and Bessett, this volume). The example in (2), where a coordinate clause with a null subject precedes a subordinate clause with an overt subject, illustrates the tendencies exhibited by both coordinate and subordinate clauses, respectively.

(2) *... y **{Ø} HA RECIBIDO** hijos de las personas que **ELLA RECIBIÓ**, o sea nietoh, cómo quien dice.* [BF07116-117]

‘... and [she] **HAS DELIVERED** children of the people that **SHE DELIVERED**, that is grandchildren, we could say.’

Table 2.2 Clause type

Factor	Prob.	%	N	% data
Subordinate	.54	38.3%	274/715	23.8%
Independent	.50	34.5%	503/1457	48.5%
Coordinate	.47	30.0%	250/834	27.7%
Range	*7*			

Although clause type significantly conditions overt SPP usage in Costeño Spanish, its effect is at best marginal. Its factors exert modest favorable and unfavorable pressures resulting in a low-range value of 7; thus, it barely reaches statistical significance. One difference that emerges when comparing these results with those of Otheguy, Zentella, and Livert (2007) is the stronger effect of clause type in New York City. Clause type is selected either fourth or fifth in a field of ten constraints, among the four different NYC speaker groups they studied. In general, the conditioning effect of clause type on SPPs in Costeño Spanish is consonant with findings in various other corners of the Hispanic World including Madrid (Enríquez 1984, 256–58), Oaxaca, Mexico (Shin and Erker, this volume), New Jersey (Flores-Ferrán 2009), NYC (Flores-Ferrán 2009; Otheguy and Zentella 2012; Shin and Erker, this volume) and Rivera, Uruguay (Carvalho and Bessett, this volume). However, as occurs in the Spanish of Puerto Ricans (Abreu 2009, 125) and NYC Colombians (Orozco 2012), clause type is at the bottom of the selection order and exerts a rather week effect on the occurrence of overt SPPs. Concurrently, clause type does not condition SPP use in other communities (cf. Carvalho and Child 2011; Claes 2011, 198; Prada Pérez 2009, 97, this volume; Torres Cacoullos and Travis 2011, 254, 258). Thus, clause type appears to defy the tendency exhibited by most other constraints on SPP expression (cf. Erker and Guy 2012; Otheguy and Zentella 2012; Shin and Erker, this volume) to consistently condition this linguistic variable. This state of affairs calls for further research on the effects of this constraint on pronominal usage in other speech communities to provide more definitive answers regarding the universality of its conditioning effect on overt pronominal expression or lack thereof. My discussion of verb-related constraints follows.

VERB-RELATED CONSTRAINTS

Three of the five verb-related constraints probed condition SPE in Barranquilla. TMA has the strongest effect, followed by verb class and lexical content, respectively. Neither preceding verb TMA nor verb regularity conditions pronominal usage significantly.

LEXICAL CONTENT OF VERB (LEXICAL CONTENT)

As with Otheguy and Zentella (2012, 265), I initially divided verbs according to the four categories used by Enríquez (1984): mental activity, estimative, external activity, and stative. Preliminary results showed mental activity and estimative verbs to follow similar tendencies. Thus, as done by Erker and Guy (2012, 535) and Shin and Erker, this volume, among others, I amalgamated these two categories under mental activity to conduct this analysis. Results (table 2.3) indicate that stative verbs promote overt pronominal subjects (statistical weight .56) and so do, though modestly, mental activity verbs with a probability value of .52. Conversely, external activity verbs disfavor overt subjects with a weight of .47. That is, there is a general polarizing tendency with external activity verbs favoring null subjects and all other verbs favoring overt SPPs. This overall tendency, consistent with findings reported by Enríquez (1984, 240) and Erker and Guy (2012, 541), is more easily noticeable by looking at the overt pronominal rates presented in table 2.3 (mental activity 46 percent, stative 41 percent, external activity verbs 29 percent). Further, the results of a distributional analysis revealed that, similarly to Madrid (Enríquez 1984, 241), stative and mental activity verbs occur more frequently with *yo* and *tú* than external activity verbs do. I used the alternate data set configuration addressed above in my discussion of the envelope of variation (see page 20) to probe deeper into verb semantics by exploring the effects of verb class, the discussion of which follows.

VERB CLASS

To explore this constraint, I adapted the classification used by Bentivoglio (1987). The results in table 2.3 show perception verbs exerting the strongest favorable pressure on overt pronominal subjects with a probability of .63. Copulative, speech, and cognition verbs also favor overt SPPs with respective values of .61, .57, and .51. Contrariwise, verbs in the 'all other' and motion categories favor null subjects with values of .48 and .43, respectively. Further analysis using the same configuration for this constraint as Travis (2005b, 2007) uncovered tendencies identical to those in New Mexico and Cali, Colombia (Travis 2007, 115): Copulative (.61/47 percent SPE), speech (.57/38 percent), and psychological, that is, cognition and perception, (.56/46 percent) verbs favor overt SPPs whereas 'all other' (.47/31 percent) and motion (.42/26 percent) verbs favor null subjects. The favorable effect of psychological verbs on overt SPPs also concurs with the findings of Bentivoglio (1987, 60), Enríquez (1984, 240), Otheguy and Zentella (2012, 164), Silva-Corvalán (1994, 162), and Torres Cacoullos and Travis (2011, 250), inter alios. The finding that copulatives promote overt subjects is further consistent with those of Enríquez (1984, 240) and Ashby and Bentivoglio (1993, 65), respectively. Moreover, these results provide evidence that the effect of verb class is fairly consistent across languages, dialects, and speech genres.

Although the results for lexical content and verb class concur with those of previous studies, confirming that verb semantics condition SPE, they do not considerably

Table 2.3 Verb-related constraints

Factor	Prob.	%	N	% data
Lexical Content of Verb				
Stative	**.56**	41.4%	307/741	24.6%
Mental Activity	**.52**	46.0%	180/391	13.0%
External Activity	**.47**	28.9%	543/1877	62.4%
Range	*9*			
Verb Class				
Perception	**.63**	48.8%	99/203	6.7%
Copulative	**.61**	46.5%	147/316	10.5%
Speech	**.57**	38.0%	104/274	9.1%
Cognition	**.51**	42.6%	112/263	8.7%
Other	**.48**	30.8%	362/1174	39.0%
Motion	**.43**	26.4%	206/779	25.9%
Range	*20*			
TMA Form of Verb				
Imperfect Indicative	**.59**	38.5%	352/914	30.4%
Perfect Forms & Conditional	**.51**	36.5%	38/104	3.5%
Present Indicative	**.50**	38.0%	348/916	30.4%
Preterite Indicative	**.46**	29.4%	235/799	26.6%
Subjunctives, Futures, Imperative	**.32**	20.7%	57/276	9.2%
Range	*27*			

inform our knowledge beyond what we already know. By dividing verbs into the categories traditionally used to explore lexical content in SPE studies, we continue to use a classification that has been considered somewhat problematic (Posio 2011, 780)[2] while failing to address Orozco and Guy's (2008, 77) call for more definite information as to the effect of verb semantics on pronominal usage. At the same time, the results for verb class do not provide a much better alternative. For instance, copulatives favoring overt pronouns and 'all other' verbs favoring null subjects would both fall within the stative category of lexical content. In view of this, among other things, I present another take of the effects of verb semantics on subject pronoun expression.

A subsequent multivariate analysis testing the most frequent verbs in each lexical content category as independent factors reveals the findings presented in table 2.4. The order of selection for lexical category, as well as the statistical tendencies for all other constraints and factors, remains the same as in the original run. Results uncover divergences between one or more verbs and those remaining within each lexical content category, that is, stative, mental and external activity. For instance, *decir* 'say, tell' and *ir* 'go' both favor overt SPPs while most other external activity verbs favor null subjects. These results provide a more detailed account of how verbs condition SPE as follows.

Table 2.4 Lexical content of verb (another take)

Factor	Prob.	%	N	% data
Ser 'be'	**.677**	51.2%	83/162	5.4%
Stative Verbs (all others)	**.563**	38.6%	88/228	7.6%
Estar 'be'	**.529**	40.1%	55/137	4.6%
Tener 'have'	**.495**	37.9%	81/214	7.1%
Creer 'believe'	**.729**	75.5%	37/49	1.6%
Saber 'know'	**.540**	52.2%	48/92	3.1%
Mental Activity Verbs (all others)	**.478**	38.0%	95/250	8.3%
Decir 'say, tell'	**.596**	42.3%	88/208	6.9%
Ir 'go'	**.530**	36.8%	46/125	4.2%
Hacer 'do, make'	**.511**	27.1%	26/96	3.2%
Venir 'come'	**.479**	33.3%	18/54	1.8%
External Activity Verbs (all others)	**.442**	26.2%	365/1394	46.3%
Range	*283*			

Whereas most stative verbs favor overt SPPs, *tener* 'have,' the most frequent stative verb, has a rather neutral effect. Within stative verbs, the favoring effect of *ser* 'be' (.68) on overt subjects is significantly stronger than that of *estar* 'be' (.53). At the same time, both *creer* 'think, believe' and *saber* 'know' favor overt pronominal subjects while all other mental activity verbs favor null subjects. In fact, *creer* and *saber* appear to account for the favorable effect of mental activity verbs on overt SPPs (cf. Erker and Guy 2012; Otheguy and Zentella 2012, 164; Torres Cacoullos and Travis 2011). For that matter, not all external activity and motion verbs have similar tendencies. Results (table 2.4) indicate that whereas *ir* favors overt SPPs, *venir* 'come' disfavors them. In Costeño Spanish, *decir* 'say, tell,' *ir* 'go' and *hacer* 'do, make' favor pronominal expression while all other external activity verbs favor null subjects. In sum, these results, taken together with those of Travis (2005b, 2007), Posio (2011) and Erker and Guy (2012), strongly suggest that we need to further explore the effects of verb semantics on SPE using an approach that takes into account the configuration of the corpus at hand, the characteristics of different verbs, and, most importantly, lexical frequency.

Verbal Tense, Mood, and Aspect (TMA)

As done by Erker and Guy (2012), Orozco and Guy (2008), and Otheguy and Zentella (2012, 253) among others, I initially tested the effects of ten TMA forms—(1) present indicative, (2) imperfect indicative, (3) preterite indicative, (4) perfect paradigms, (5) conditional, (6) morphological future, (7) periphrastic future, (8) subjunctive paradigms, (9) imperatives, and (10) other paradigms. Preliminary results revealed similar tendencies for (a) perfect tenses and the conditional, and (b) subjunctives, futures, and imperatives. Thus, I conducted all subsequent analyses using the five factors in table 2.3: imperfect indicative, perfect forms and conditional, present indicative, and subjunctives futures and imperative. Results show that the imperfect indicative favors overt subjects with a weight of .59. The perfect tenses and the conditional with a value of .51 and the present indicative with a value of .50 have only a neutral effect on SPP usage.

The preterite indicative modestly favors null subjects (.46). The subjunctives, futures, and the imperative, acting as a single factor, clearly favor null subjects with a statistical weight of .32.

These findings coincide with those reporting the conditioning effect of TMA on pronominal variation in both monolingual (Abreu 2009, 2012; Bentivoglio 1987, 45; Cameron 1993; Claes 2011; Prada Pérez 2009; Travis 2005b, 2007; among others) as well as in bilingual (Bayley and Pease-Alvarez 1996, 1997; Erker and Guy 2012; Flores-Ferrán 2002, 2004, 2009; Hochberg 1986; Hurtado 2005a; Otheguy and Zentella 2007, 2012; Otheguy, Zentella, and Livert 2007; Shin and Montes-Alcalá 2014) communities. Moreover, these results support the premise that morphologically ambiguous verbal paradigms such as the imperfect tense promote more pronoun use than unambiguous forms. Both the favorable effect of the imperfect indicative on overt subjects and the favorable effect that imperatives exert on null subjects are congruent with what occurs in other speech communities including Oaxaca, Mexico (Shin and Erker, this volume), and New York City (Erker and Guy 2012; Otheguy and Zentella 2012, 164; Shin and Erker, this volume). TMA in Costeño Spanish largely reflects the same tendencies found in other communities. That is, unlike clause type, there is uniformity of effects across speech communities.

In general, verb-related constraints exert stronger conditioning pressures than clause-related constraints on SPP usage. The effect of TMA follows the same tendencies found across the board. On the surface, the same appears to be true for lexical content of verb. The importance of verb semantics as a SPE predictor is undeniable since it is frequently found to be a significant constraint in SPP studies as well as in investigations pertaining to other linguistic variables. Although both lexical content and verb class inform our knowledge, both groupings appear to obscure important differences between verbs in a single category. Classifying verbs according to their semantic commonalities in exploring how they condition SPPs, and perhaps, other linguistic variables, may leave important differences uncovered. Instead, we might increase our understanding by means of a multipronged approach that incorporates lexical frequency, among other criteria. Consequently, we need to find a more reliable alternative to explore the effect of verb semantics on SPE. I will turn next to the effect of subject-related constraints.

Subject-Related Constraints

Four of the five subject-level constraints explored condition pronominal usage significantly: (1) priming, (2) prior subject's person and number, (3) switch reference, and (4) person and number of the subject. SPPs are not conditioned by distance from previous coreferential subject. As discussed earlier (see the envelope of variation and the analysis, page 20), switch reference and prior subject's person and number were run separately to avoid factor interactions.

Priming

Results (table 2.5) show that a prior overt SPP promotes the occurrence of overt SPPs with a statistical weight of .62. A preceding NP subject has a neutral effect (.49) while a previous null subject favors the occurrence of another null subject with a probability of .45. That is, one specific type of subject promotes the occurrence of subjects of the

Table 2.5 Subject-related constraints

Factor	Prob.	%	N	% data
Priming				
Preceding Overt SPP	**.62**	44.0%	298/677	22.5%
Preceding Noun Phrase	**.49**	38.0%	277/728	24.2%
Preceding Null Subject	**.45**	28.3%	452/1599	53.2%
Range	*17*			
Prior Subject's Person & Number				
Different Person	**.63**	44.6%	610/1369	45.6%
Same Person Different Number	**.46**	22.5%	55/244	8.1%
Same Person & Number	**.38**	25.9%	361/1392	46.3%
Range	*25*			
Switch Reference				
Complete Change in Subject	**.67**	45.9%	571/1244	41.4%
Partial Change in Subject	**.50**	32.3%	120/372	12.4%
Same Subject (coreferent with prior subject)	**.35**	24.2%	336/1387	46.2%
Range	*32*			
Person & Number of the Subject				
1st singular (*yo*)	**.62**	44.5%	565/1270	42.2%
3rd singular (*el, ella, uno*)	**.61**	39.6%	300/758	25.2%
2nd singular (*tú*)	**.52**	32.5%	76/234	7.8%
All plural (*nosotros, ustedes, ellos*)	**.21**	11.9%	89/747	24.8%
Range	*41*			

same type with overt pronominal subjects promoting overt subjects and null subjects promoting null subjects. The examples below illustrate these tendencies.

(3) *… o sea,* ***ÉL ESTABA ACOSTUMBRADO*** *como a llevarme al parque, y* ***YO*** *siempre me le* ***EHCONDÍA*** … [BF11129-130]
… that is, **HE WAS USED** like to taking me to the park, and **I** always **WOULD HIDE** from him.

(4) *O sea noh guhtaba hablar, o sea* ***{Ø} HABLÁBAMOH*** *bahtante.* ***{Ø}*** *noh* ***CONTÁBAMOH*** *todo ahí en el colegio. Ya dehpuéh que* ***{Ø} SALIMOH****, del colegio no noh,* ***{Ø}*** *no noh* ***VOLVIMOH A VER*** *máh.* [BM10010-013]
That is, [we] liked to talk; that is [**we**] **TALKED** a lot. [**We**] **TOLD** each other everything there at school. Then, after [**we**] **LEFT** school, [we] **DIDN'T SEE** each other again.

In (3) we find two successive overt pronominal subjects while in (4) we find a succession of null subjects. The successive occurrence of overt subjects in (3) illustrates a change in reference from the preceding clause with an overt pronoun promoting another overt pronoun with the same grammatical person. At the same time, (4) highlights how a preceding null subject promotes the occurrence of null subjects. The observed priming effect is congruent with tendencies found in other varieties of Spanish (cf. Cameron 1995; Flores-Ferrán 2002; Cameron and Flores-Ferrán 2004; Travis 2005b, 2007). It also illustrates how SPE in Costeño Spanish is conditioned by priming, a phenomenon that extends well beyond SPP usage (Cameron 1995).

Prior Subject's Person and Number

The results (see table 2.5) reveal two patterns. In the first, prior subjects of a different grammatical person, regardless of number, favor overt subjects with a probability of .63. In the second pattern, a prior subject of the same person promotes null subjects. Specifically, null subjects are favored by prior subjects of the same person and different number (.46) and more so by prior subjects with the same person and number with a value of (.36). The examples above also illustrate these tendencies. In (3) the subject changes from the third person (*él*) to the first (*yo*), resulting in two consecutive overt subjects. In (4) we find successive instances of a null subject preceded by another null subject of the same person and number. These results indicate that the presence of one form or structure correlates with subsequently higher frequencies of the same forms or structures (Cameron and Schwenter 2013, 476). These findings also further inform our knowledge of the effects of priming as well as those of switch reference since the occurrence of a change in grammatical subject is often a consequence of a referential switch.

Switch Reference

Switch reference conditions SPE more strongly than priming and prior subject's person and number, respectively, according to both order of selection and range values. Results (see table 2.5) corroborate the probability weights and the three levels of continuity of reference found by Orozco and Guy (2008, 74) as follows. Overt SPPs are favored by a complete change in subject with a probability of .67; this tendency is illustrated in examples (3) and (5). In contrast, null subjects are favored by subjects that are coreferent with those of the previous clause with a value of .35; this tendency is illustrated in (4) above. At the same time, a partial change in subject has a neutral effect with a statistical weight of .50. The range value of 32 indicates that switch reference exerts the strongest conditioning effect of those constraints that explore subject continuity. The favoring effect of a complete referential switch on overt SPPs can be interpreted as a functional effect (Hochberg 1986, 618) since pronouns appear to be overtly expressed to disambiguate change of reference. Interestingly, the statistical probabilities found are quite similar to those reported for other varieties of Spanish including Puerto Rico, Madrid, Caracas, East Los Angeles, and NYC, among others (cf. Abreu 2012; Bentivoglio 1987; Enríquez 1984; Cameron 1995; Flores-Ferrán 2002; Otheguy, Zentella, and Livert 2007; Otheguy and Zentella 2012; Silva-Corvalán 1982). Thus, these results provide further evidence that "the influence of switch reference is systematic, and patterns alike" across varieties of Spanish (Cameron 1995, 11). That is, a switch of reference exerts a consistent effect on the frequency of SPP occurrence for all grammatical persons and numbers, and there is grammar uniformity acting throughout the different subject-related constraints.

(5) *Si {Ø}* ***HACÍAMOH*** *algo,* ***ÉL*** *se* ***QUEDABA*** *ahí …* [BM11004-005]
If **{WE} DID** something, **HE WOULD STAY** there …

Grammatical Person and Number of the Subject

These results (table 2.5), as those for prior subject's person and number, also adhere to two main tendencies prevalent across the board: Singular pronouns favor overt subjects and plural pronouns disfavor them. First, third and second person singular pronouns favor overt subjects with statistical weights of .62, .61 and .52, respectively. In contrast, plural SPPs as a whole strongly disfavor overt subjects, with a probability of .21. It appears that since the conditioning effect of SPP person and number affects virtually all varieties of Spanish, we are dealing with a general tendency that has a universal linguistic explanation. The results for this constraint are consonant with previous findings (Otheguy, Zentella, and Livert 2007; Otheguy and Zentella 2012, among others) that show grammatical person and number of the subject exerting the strongest conditioning effect on SPE. The low rate of use of the plural pronouns is consistent with findings for Puerto Rican speakers in Boston (Hochberg 1986, 613) and both Caribbean and Mainlander speakers in NYC (Otheguy and Zentella 2007, 2012). The disfavoring effect of plural SPPs on overt subjects could arguably stem from the frequent occurrence of fixed expressions with null subjects such as *vamos* and *nos vemos*. At the same time, Costeño speakers, by favoring the use of overt singular SPPs, appear to follow language-specific patterns characteristic of the grammar of Spanish (see examples in (3), (4) and (5)).

Subject-related constraints in Barranquilla largely follow widespread pan-Hispanic tendencies, with person and number of the subject exerting the strongest conditioning effect. Moreover, the results for subject-related constraints emerge as those that most strongly condition SPE in Costeño Spanish, and the present analysis provides a more detailed view of priming and its effects. It is clear that the internal conditioning is mainly driven by subject-related constraints. I discuss the external conditioning on SPE in the next section.

EXTERNAL CONDITIONING

Two social constraints significantly affect variable pronominal expression in Barranquilla: conversation conditions and the combined effect of speaker's sex and age. Neither education nor socioeconomic status conditions SPE significantly.

Conversation Conditions

The effects of conversation conditions, presented in table 2.6, show that one-on-one conversations favor overt subjects with a statistical value of .54 while the presence of members of the consultants' social networks favors null subjects with a weight of .46. If the lower incidence of overt pronominal subjects among younger Barranquilleros reported in Orozco and Guy (2008, 78) indicates an innovation, then these results would suggest that the presence of others contributes to more vernacular, informal speech. Judging by the fact that the presence of others favors the use of the periphrastic future—associated with informality—in Costeño Spanish (Orozco 2007b, 107), we can assume that, in this speech community, the presence of third parties promotes spontaneity and informality in people's linguistic behavior. These tendencies are congruent with the conceptualization of a sociolinguistic interview as a discursive event in which the presence of multiple participants contributes to the optimal conditions for the production of more spontaneous and natural speech (cf. Moreno Fernández 2012, 191 ff.).

Speaker's Sex/Age

Since Orozco and Guy (2008) report that age conditions SPP usage, I initially explored age and sex as separate constraints. Preliminary results uncovered a gender gap effect that shows women favoring overt SPPs with a probability of .53 and men promoting null subjects with .46. Preliminary findings also revealed interaction between age and sex. So, to gain additional insight into the social forces constraining SPE, I explored the combined effects of age and sex as a complex constraint carefully controlling the distribution of both tokens and consultants in each multivariate cell. In this way, some interesting differences between speakers on either side of age forty emerged. The results (see table 2.6) show women born before 1960 favoring overt SPPs with a statistical weight of .55. Conversely, men born after 1960 favor null subjects, with a Goldvarb weight of .45. At the same time, women born after 1960 and men born before 1960 have a neutral effect with probabilities of .50 and .49, respectively. Differences in the sociolinguistic behavior of speakers on either side of age forty have already been reported in this community regarding the expressions of futurity (Orozco 2007b) and possession (Orozco 2009, 2010). Such differences have also been found in the expression of futurity in Castellón, Spain (Blas Arroyo 2008, 112). Further research will hopefully determine whether we are in the presence of a widespread phenomenon or a mere coincidence.

Table 2.6 External constraints

Factor	Prob.	%	N	% data
Conversation Conditions				
One on One Conversation	**.54**	37.4%	562/1501	49.9%
Others Present	**.46**	31.0%	468/1508	50.1%
Range	*8*			
Intersection of Speaker's Sex & Age				
Women Born before 1960	**.55**	40.3%	329/816	27.1%
Women Born after 1960	**.50**	33.2%	226/680	22.6%
Men Born before 1960	**.49**	30.6%	244/797	26.5%
Men Born after 1960	**.45**	32.3%	231/716	23.8%
Range	*10*			

The favoring effect that older women in Barranquilla have on overt SPPs is congruent with women's favoring overt SPPs in Santo Domingo, Dominican Republic, and Mexico City, Mexico, reported in this volume by Alfaraz and Lastra and Martín Butragueño, respectively. In Barranquilla, older women's SPE clearly differentiates them from the rest of the community. They constitute the only segment of the population that favors overt SPPs, having both the highest pronominal rate (40.3 percent) and probability value (.55). This tendency directly opposes that of younger males who, with a probability value of .45, favor null subjects. Half a century of variationist research on the effects of age, recognized as the principal social correlate of language change (Chambers 2002, 349), shows that younger speakers consistently promote linguistic innovations (Labov 2001, 437). Given the evolutionary tendency from Latin being a null pronoun language to the Romance languages gradually becoming non-pro-drop (e.g., French, Brazilian Portuguese), the trend exhibited by Barranquilla's young men appears to be an instance of retrograde movement (cf. Labov 2001, 75) toward lower overt pronominal usage in Costeño Spanish. Surprisingly, such a counter-directional trend would eventually make this variety less Caribbean and more *Cachaco*, that is, mainlander. These results could be a reflection of the increased influence of the *Cachaco* variety on those of the coastal regions. Further study of the effects of age shall help determine, among other things, whether we are witnessing a case of permanent retrograde movement or simply an interim evolutionary detour.

DISCUSSION AND CONCLUSIONS

The results of this study contribute to the formation of a data baseline for further inquiry on SPE. Answering our first research question, the overall pronominal rate for Costeño Spanish (34.2 percent) places it squarely within the Caribbean varieties. Future research shall determine whether the lower incidence of second person subjects (7.8 percent singular, 0.6 percent plural, respectively) is due to speech genre differences or to other factors. The answer to the second research question confirms that the conditioning effects on overt SPP usage are mainly similar to those throughout the Hispanic World. That is, the conditioning is mainly internal with eight linguistic and two social constraints significantly affecting SPE in Barranquilla. These results also support the main hypothesis tested here that *the constraints and individual factor tendencies conditioning overt SPP usage in Spanish largely reflect uniformity across different varieties of Spanish despite differences in overt pronominal rates with SPP usage being more strongly conditioned by subject-related constraints*. The functional usage of overt pronouns appears evident. The discourse connection pattern found here is arguably functional at the discourse level. Syntactic and semantic constraints on overt SPP use are also evident.

I divided the analysis of internal constraints into three categories: clause-, verb-, and subject-related constraints. Judging by both the number of significant constraints within each category, as well as by their order of selection and range values, SPP usage is more strongly conditioned by subject- and verb-related constraints. Results show that although verb semantics and pragmatics constitute important predictors of pronominal usage, they are also very complex ones. Consequently, the most frequent classifications used to study the effects of verbs on SPE do not provide conclusive information. Instead, concurring with Erker and Guy (2012), Posio (2011) and Travis (2005b, 2007), we could increase our understanding by means of a multipronged approach that incorporates lexical frequency, among other criteria.

The effects of social constraints answer my third research question. Despite reports that social constraints do not significantly constrain SPE in monolingual varieties (Bayley and Pease-Alvarez 1997; Bentivoglio 1987; Cameron 1992, 1994; Flores-Ferrán 2002; Martínez-Sanz 2011), this study concurs with Ávila-Jiménez (1995), Alfaraz (this volume), and Lastra and Martín Butragueño (this volume) in finding that external constraints indeed affect pronominal expression. The general effect of age in Barranquilla is similar to that in Mexico City with younger individuals using fewer overt pronouns than their elders. In Puerto Rican Spanish, on the other hand, the opposite trend prevails (Ávila-Jiménez 1995). Although younger Barranquilla speakers use fewer overt SPPs, we have no evidence to determine whether what we currently observe may be a function of broader social change rather than an emergent change in progress. The Colombian national normative institutions are dominated by the more prestigious dialect of the highlands, which is a low-SPP dialect. Thus, expansion of internal mobility, national mass communication, and education, which have occurred in recent generations in Colombia, may be spreading characteristics of the *Cachaco* dialect to the coastal regions.

In its evolutionary trajectory, Latin appears to be changing toward becoming a non-pro-drop language (cf. Richards 1958, 56). Modern French and Haitian Creole are non-pro-drop languages, and Brazilian Portuguese is considered a semi-pro-drop language (cf. Erker and Guy 2012, 531). What are some of the possible ramifications of this for Spanish? The frequent occurrence of verbal periphrases to replace inflections in Spanish discussed by Fleischman (2009, 31), Orozco (2007a), and Schwegler (1990) may develop into the need to use an overt subject which is currently dispensable in Spanish (Fleischman 2009, 116 ff.). A particular linguistic change, rather than occurring in a vacuum, goes hand in hand with other changes. Thus, these developments appear to be a manifestation of a larger series of diachronic changes toward fixed SV syntax that has been proposed for Spanish (Givón 1971; Green 1976; Schwartz 1975). A consequence of such change would be a proliferation of overt SPP usage. In fact, the high incidence of overt SPPs in Dominican Spanish has been associated with this apparent change in progress (Alfaraz, this volume; Jiménez Sabater 1975; Lunn 2002; Morales 1989, 1997; Shin and Otheguy 2013; Toribio 2000). Therefore, a trend toward reduced SPP usage in Costeño, a Caribbean Spanish variety, would constitute a case of external constraints impacting natural evolution.

In general, the results of this study identify the constraints that significantly condition variable SPP expression in Colombian Costeño Spanish. These results are, for the most part, consistent with the findings of numerous other investigations with internal factors playing a crucial role in pronominal usage. Despite differences in pronominal rates between different varieties of Spanish, the constraints conditioning SPE and their individual factor effects are essentially uniform. In conclusion, the results of this analysis provide additional evidence regarding the status of SPE in Costeño Spanish. Some of the questions generated by this study have to do with how to more appropriately explore verb semantics and pragmatics. Some others pertain to the direction of language evolution in connection with SPE; that is, whether Costeño Spanish is on its way to becoming more *Cachaco* and less Caribbean. Further study shall provide more definite answers in that regard as well as augment our collective knowledge regarding the effects of social constraints on the variable occurrence of SPPs.

ACKNOWLEDGMENTS

I am thankful to Gabriela Alfaraz, Pekka Posio, Naomi Shin, and two anonymous reviewers for their insightful comments and valuable suggestions. All remaining infelicities are my sole responsibility.

This research was supported in large part by the *Awards to Louisiana Artists and Scholars (ATLAS)* grant # LEQSF(2011-12)RD-ATL-05, and by a 2013 LSU Manship Summer Research Award. I am grateful to my research assistants Maritza Nemogá and Bailey Nunez for their valuable contributions to this project. Most of all, I thank the speakers who provided the data for this study.

NOTES

1. The codes that accompany the examples, that is, [BM07016], provide the following information. B stands for Barranquilla, the second letter (M or F) identifies the consultant's sex, the first two digits (07) the consultant number. The last three digits correspond to the token number in the present analysis.
2. Posio (2011, 708) states that
   a. "the same verb can be included in two categories, depending on its meaning";
   b. "the categories are defined on the basis of very heterogeneous criteria"; and that
   c. "it is also unclear to what extent the frequency of pronominal subject expression varies among verbs included in one category."

REFERENCES

Abreu, Laurel. 2009. "Spanish subject personal pronoun use by monolinguals, bilinguals and second language learners." Doctoral diss., University of Florida.

———. 2012. "Subject pronoun expression and priming effects among bilingual speakers of Puerto Rican Spanish." In *Selected Proceedings of the 14th Hispanic Linguistics Symposium*, edited by Kimberly Geeslin and Manuel Díaz-Campos, 1–8. Somerville, MA: Cascadilla Proceedings Project.

Ashby, William, and Paola Bentivoglio. 1993. "Preferred argument structure in spoken French and Spanish." *Language Variation and Change* 5:61–76.

Ávila-Jiménez, Bárbara I. 1995. "A sociolinguistic analysis of a change in progress: Pronominal overtness in Puerto Rican Spanish." *Cornell Working Papers in Linguistics* 13:25–47.

Barrenechea, Ana María, and Alicia Alonso. 1977. "Los pronombres personales sujetos en el español de Buenos Aires." In *Estudios sobre el español hablado en las principales ciudades de América,* edited by Juan M. Lope Blanch, 333–349. Mexico City: Universidad Nacional Autónoma de México.

Bayley, Robert, and Lucinda Pease-Alvarez. 1996. "Null and expressed subject pronoun variation in Mexican-descent children's Spanish." In *Sociolinguistic variation: Data, theory, and analysis,* edited by Jennifer Arnold, Renee Blake and Brad Davidson, 85–99. Stanford, CA: Center for the Study of Language and Information.

———. 1997. "Null pronoun variation in Mexican-descent children's narrative discourse." *Language Variation and Change* 9(3):349–371.

Bentivoglio, Paola. 1987. *Los sujetos pronominales de primera persona en el habla de Caracas*. Caracas: Universidad Central de Venezuela, Consejo de Desarrollo Científico y Humanístico.

Blas Arroyo, José Luis. 2008. "The variable expression of future tense in Peninsular Spanish: The present (and future) of inflectional forms in the Spanish spoken in a bilingual." *Language Variation and Change* 20(1):85–126.

Cameron, Richard. 1992. "Pronominal and null subject variation in Spanish: Constraints, dialects, and functional compensation." PhD diss., University of Pennsylvania.

———. 1993. "Ambiguous agreement, functional compensation, and non-specific *tú* in the Spanish of San Juan, Puerto Rico and Madrid, Spain." *Language Variation and Change* 5:305–334.

———. 1995. "The scope and limits of switch reference as a constraint on pronominal subject expression." *Hispanic Linguistics* 6/7:1–27.

———. 1996. "A community-based test of a linguistic hypothesis." *Language in Society* 25:61–111.

———. 1998. "A variable syntax of speech, gesture, and sound effect: Direct quotations in Spanish." *Language Variation and Change* 10:43–83.

Cameron, Richard, and Nydia Flores-Ferrán. 2004. "Preservation of subject expression across regional dialects of Spanish." *Spanish in Context* 1:41–65.

Cameron, Richard, and Scott Schwenter. 2013. "Pragmatics and variationist sociolinguistics." In *The Oxford handbook of sociolinguistics,* edited by Robert Bayley, Richard Cameron, and Ceil Lucas, 464–483. Oxford and New York: Oxford University Press.

Carvalho, Ana M., and Michael Child. 2011. "Subject pronoun expression in a variety of Spanish in contact with Portuguese." In *Selected Proceedings of the 5th Workshop on Spanish Sociolinguistics*, edited by Jim Michnowicz and Robin Dodsworth, 14–25. Somerville, MA: Cascadilla Proceedings Project.

Chambers, J. K. 2002. "Patterns of variation including change." In *The handbook of language variation and change,* edited by J. K. Chambers, Peter Trudgill, and Natalie Schilling-Estes, 349–372. Oxford: Blackwell.

Claes, Jeroen. 2011. "¿Constituyen las Antillas y el Caribe continental una sola zona dialectal? Datos de la variable expresión del sujeto pronominal en San Juan de Puerto Rico y Barranquilla, Colombia." *Spanish in Context* 8:191–212.

Enríquez, Emilia V. 1984. *El pronombre personal sujeto en la lengua española hablada en Madrid.* Madrid: Consejo Superior de Investigaciones Científicas.

Erker, Daniel. 2005. "Functional compensation for morphological ambiguity in New York Spanish." Master's thesis, City University of New York.

Erker, Daniel, and Gregory R. Guy. 2012. "The role of lexical frequency in syntactic variability: Variable subject personal pronoun expression in Spanish." *Language* 88:526–557.

Fleischman, Suzanne. 2009. *The future in thought and language: Diachronic evidence from Romance.* New York: Cambridge University Press.

Flores-Ferrán, Nydia. 2002. *A sociolinguistic perspective on the use of subject personal pronouns in Spanish narratives of Puerto Ricans in New York City.* Munich: Lincom-Europa.

———. 2004. "Spanish subject personal pronoun use in New York City Puerto Ricans: Can we rest the case of English contact?" *Language Variation and Change* 16:49–73.

———. 2007. "Los Mexicanos in New Jersey: Pronominal expression and ethnolinguistic aspects." *Selected Proceedings of the Third Workshop on Spanish Sociolinguistics*, edited by Jonathan Holmquist, Augusto Lorenzino, and Lotfi Sayahi, 85–91. Somerville, MA: Cascadilla Proceedings Project.

———. 2009. "Are you referring to me? The variable use of *UNO* and *YO* in oral discourse." *Journal of Pragmatics* 41:1810–1824.

Givón, Talmy. 1971. "Historical syntax and synchronic morphology: an archaeologist's field trip." *Papers from the Seventh Regional Meeting of the Chicago Linguistic Society, April 16–18*, 394–415. Chicago, IL: University of Chicago.

Green, John N. 1976. *How free is word order in Spanish? Romance syntax: Synchronic and diachronic perspectives.* Salford: University of Salford.

Henríquez Ureña, Pedro. 1921. "Observaciones sobre el español en América." *Revista de Filología Española* 8:357–390.

Hochberg, Judith. 1986. "Functional compensation for /s/ deletion in Puerto Rican Spanish." *Language* 62(3):609–621.

Hurtado, Luz Marcela. 2001. "La variable expresión del sujeto en el español de los colombianos y colombo–americanos residentes en el condado de Miami-Dade." PhD diss., University of Florida.

———. 2005a. "El uso de *tú, usted* y *uno* en el español de los colombianos y colombo–americanos." In *Contactos y contextos lingüísticos: el español en los Estados Unidos y en contacto con otras lenguas,* edited by Luis Ortiz López and Manel Lacorte, 187–200. Madrid/Frankfurt: Iberoamericana/Vervuert.

———. 2005b. "Condicionamientos sintáctico-semánticos de la expresión del sujeto en el español colombiano." *Hispania* 88:335–348.

Jiménez Sabater, Maximiliano. 1975. *Más datos sobre el español en la República Dominicana.* Santo Domingo: Ediciones Intec.

Labov, William. 1972. *Sociolinguistic patterns.* Philadelphia: University of Pennsylvania Press.

———. 2001. *Principles of linguistic change, volume 2: Social factors.* Malden, MA: Blackwell.

Lipski, John M. 1994. *Latin American Spanish.* London and New York City: Longman.

Lunn, Pat. 2002. "Tout se tient in Dominican Spanish." In *Structure, meaning, and acquisition in Spanish*, edited by James F. Lee, Kimberly L. Geeslin, and J. Clancy Clements, 65–72. Somerville, MA: Cascadilla Press.

Martínez-Sanz, Cristina. 2011. "Null and overt subjects in a variable system: The case of Dominican Spanish." PhD diss., University of Ottawa.

Morales, Amparo. 1980. "La expresión de sujeto pronominal primera persona en el español de Puerto Rico." *Boletín de la Academia de la Lengua Española,* 8(3):91–102.

———. 1989. "Hacia un universal sintáctico del español del caribe. El orden SVO." *Anuario de Lingüística Hispánica,* 5:139–152.

———. 1997. "La hipótesis funcional y la aparición de sujeto no nominal: el español de Puerto Rico." *Hispania* 80(1):153–165.

Moreno Fernández, Francisco. 2012. *Sociolingüística Cognitiva: Proposiciones, escolios y debates.* Madrid/Frankfurt: Iberoamericana/Vervuert.

Orozco, Rafael. 2007a. "The impact of linguistic constraints on the expression of futurity in the Spanish of New York Colombians." In *Spanish in contact: Educational, social, and linguistic inquiries,* edited by Kim Potowski and Richard Cameron, 311–328. Philadelphia, PA: John Benjamins.

———. 2007b. "Social Constraints on the Expression of Futurity in Spanish-Speaking Urban Communities." In *Selected Proceedings of the Third Workshop on Spanish Sociolinguistics,* edited by Jonathan Holmquist, Augusto Lorenzino, and Lotfi Sayahi, 103–112. Somerville, MA: Cascadilla.

———. 2009. "La influencia de factores sociales en la expresión del posesivo." *Lingüística* 22:25–60.

———. 2010. "Variation in the expression of possession in *Costeño* Spanish." *Spanish in Context* 7(2):194–220.

———. 2012. "Variable pronominal usage in two Colombian communities." Paper presented at the 6th International Workshop on Spanish Sociolinguistics, Tucson, AZ. April 13.

Orozco, Rafael, and Gregory Guy. 2008. "El uso variable de los pronombres sujetos: ¿Qué pasa en la costa Caribe colombiana?" In *Selected Proceedings of the Fourth Workshop on Spanish Sociolinguistics,* edited by Maurice Westmoreland and Juan Antonio Thomas, 70–80. Somerville, MA: Cascadilla Proceedings Project.

Ortiz López, Luis. 2009. "Pronombres de sujeto en el español (L2 vs L1) del Caribe." In *El español en Estados Unidos y otros contextos de contactos: sociolingüística, ideología y pedagogía,* edited by Manel Lacorte and Jennifer Leeman, 85–110. Frankfurt Main/ Madrid: Vervuert/Iberoamericana.

———. 2011. "Spanish in contact with Haitian Creole." In *The handbook of Spanish sociolinguistics,* edited by Manuel Díaz-Campos, 418–445. Malden, MA: Wiley-Blackwell.

Otheguy, Ricardo, and Ana Celia Zentella. 2007. "Apuntes preliminares sobre el contacto lingüístico y dialectal en el uso pronominal del español en Nueva York." In *Spanish in contact: Policy, social and linguistic inquiries,* edited by Kim Potowski and Richard Cameron, 275–295. Amsterdam/ Philadelphia: John Benjamins.

———. 2012. *Spanish in New York: Language contact, dialectal leveling, and structural continuity.* Oxford: Oxford University Press.

Otheguy, Ricardo, Ana Celia Zentella, and David Livert. 2007. "Language contact in Spanish in New York toward the formation of a speech community." *Language* 83:770–802.

Posio, Pekka. 2011. "Spanish subject pronoun usage and verb semantics revisited: First and second person singular subject pronouns and focusing of attention in spoken Peninsular Spanish." *Journal of Pragmatics* 43:777–798.

Prada Pérez, Ana de. 2009. "Subject expression in Minorcan Spanish: Consequences of contact with Catalan." PhD diss., Pennsylvania State University.

Richards, John F. 1958. *Essentials of Latin.* New York: Oxford University Press.

Schwartz, Arthur. 1975. "Verb-anchoring and verb-movement." In *Word order and word order change*, edited by Charles Li, 439–462. Austin, TX: University of Texas Press.

Schwegler, Armin. 1990. *Analyticity and syntheticity: A diachronic perspective with special reference to Romance languages.* New York: Mouton de Gruyter.

Shin, Naomi, and Cecilia Montes Alcalá. 2014. "El uso contextual del pronombre sujeto como factor predictivo de la influencia del inglés en el español en Nueva York." *Sociolinguistic Studies* 8:85–110.

Shin, Naomi, and Ricardo Otheguy. 2013. "Social class and gender impacting change in bilingual settings: Spanish subject pronoun use in New York." *Language in Society* 42:1–24.

Silva-Corvalán, Carmen. 1982. "Subject expression and placement in spoken Mexican–American Spanish." In *Spanish in the United States: Sociolinguistic aspects,* edited by Jon Amastae and Lucía Elías-Olivares, 93–120. New York: Cambridge University Press.

———. 1994. *Language contact and change: Spanish in Los Angeles.* New York: Oxford University Press.

———. 1997. "Avances en el estudio de la variación sintáctica: La expresión del sujeto." *Cuadernos del Sur* 27:35–49.

Tagliamonte, Sali. 2006. *Analysing sociolinguistic variation.* Cambridge and New York: Cambridge University Press.

Toribio, A. Jacqueline. 2000. "Setting parametric limits on dialectal variation in Spanish." *Lingua* 10:315–341.

Torres Cacoullos, Rena, and Catherine E. Travis. 2011. "Testing convergence via code-switching: Priming and the structure of variable subject expression." *International Journal of Bilingualism* 15:241–267.

Travis, Catherine E. 2005a. *Discourse markers in Colombian Spanish: A study in polysemy* (Cognitive Linguistics Research). New York: Mouton de Gruyter.

———. 2005b. "The yo-yo effect: Priming in subject expression in Colombian Spanish." In *Theoretical and experimental approaches to Romance linguistics: Selected papers from the 34th Linguistic Symposium on Romance Languages, 2004,* edited by Randall Gess and Edward J. Rubin, 329–349. Amsterdam / Philadelphia: John Benjamins.

———. 2007. "Genre effects on subject expression in Spanish: Priming in narrative and conversation." *Language Variation and Change* 19:101–135.

Travis, Catherine E., and Rena Torres Cacoullos. 2012. "What do subject pronouns do in discourse? Cognitive, mechanical and constructional factors in variation." *Cognitive Linguistics* 23:711–748.

Zamora Munné, Juan C., and Jorge Guitart. 1982. *Dialectología Hispanoamericana: Teoría, descripción, historia.* Salamanca, Spain: Ediciones Almar.

3

Subject Pronoun Expression in Oral Mexican Spanish

**Yolanda Lastra and
Pedro Martín Butragueño**

Research exploring presence versus absence of subject personal pronouns (SPPs) in Spanish rests on a solid foundation. The seminal works—Barrenechea and Alonso (1977) on Buenos Aires Spanish, Silva-Corvalán (1982) on Mexican–American Spanish in West Los Angeles (WLA), Morales (1982) on Puerto Rican Spanish, Bentivoglio (1980, 1987) on Caracas Spanish—examined some of the variables commonly tested in most subsequent studies: switch reference, ambiguity, verb type, among others. Moreover, the advent of regression analyses helped establish comparisons between frequencies and statistical probabilities since the 1970s. While subject pronoun expression (SPE) research has been abundant, it has traditionally explored two types of data: 1) data from Caribbean populations, as a means of exploring the high rates of overt SPPs and their implications for the functional compensation hypothesis (e.g., Hochberg 1986); 2) data from language contact situations, especially with English, primarily to explore the impact of non-pro-drop on pro-drop languages (e.g., Amastae et al. 2000; Bayley et al. 2012; Flores-Ferrán 2007; Hurtado 2005; Otheguy and Zentella 2012; Torres Cacoullos and Travis 2011). By contrast, studies on monolingual and Mainland dialects have been less common. In the particular case of Mexican Spanish, the scarcity of research in monolingual settings is striking (but see Cantero Sandoval 1978, 1986; Amastae et al. 2000). Also, social factors have had limited relevance in most earlier studies, especially in monolingual settings. In multilectal and multilingual settings, nevertheless, things are different, as Otheguy and Zentella (2012) and Shin and Otheguy (2013, on the effect of social class and gender in New York City) reveal.

The present study is part of a larger investigation devoted to explore, describe, and analyze syntactic variation in Mexico City (MC) Spanish (cf. Lastra and Martín Butragueño 2010, 2012); we seek to offer a quantitative account of spoken Mexican

Spanish at the turn of the 21st century. Since what we know today of Spanish SPE is derived mostly from contact situations, a monolingual point of reference is necessary for future inquiry. Our monolingual data offer some evidence of social variation, linked to age (and partially to educational level and gender). We also interpret our findings within a dynamic and realistic point of view about linguistic and social factors (Martín Butragueño and Vázquez Laslop 2002; Martín Butragueño 2014) and in terms of Kroch's (1989) Constant Rate Hypothesis (CRH).

METHODOLOGY

In this section, we address the characteristics of the data, the envelope of variation, the working hypotheses, and the factor groups explored.

The Corpus, Informants, and Data Set

Our data constitute a sub-sample of the *Corpus sociolingüístico de la Ciudad de México* (CSCM), collected between 1997 and 2007 (see Martín Butragueño and Lastra 2011, 2012, forthcoming, for a detailed description). The CSCM consists of approximately 500 hours of recorded interviews and sociolinguistic questionnaires with more than 320 speakers in the Metropolitan area of Mexico City (inhabited by twenty million speakers). The Corpus is divided into a number of sections: non-immigrants, immigrants, children and adolescents, marginal people, and group recordings.[1] Our sub-sample for this study consists of 18 speakers from the non-immigrant module, organized by educational level (low = six years of school or less; medium = between seven and twelve years of school; high = more than thirteen years—but usually sixteen or more); age (20–34 years; 35–54 years; 55 years and older); and gender (male and female).

The Envelope of Variation and Data Selection

As with the other studies throughout this volume, the envelope of variation employed in our analysis adheres to the parameters advanced by Silva-Corvalán (1982). We included in the dataset only those clauses with ascertainable animate pronominal subjects containing a conjugated verb where the overt/null subject alternation is clearly possible. Thus, all tokens constitute one of two possible ways of saying the same thing. In selecting our data, first we collected 200 utterances including subject slots + VPs from the beginning of each interview, for a total of 3,600 utterances from 18 speakers. Second, we selected those cases with variable alternation between a null subject and a subject personal pronoun (SPP), resulting in a total of 2,040 tokens.

Hypotheses

Our study of SPE in Mexico City tests two main hypotheses.

a. *The strength of linguistic constraints on SPE is similar to what has been found in most other Spanish-speaking communities.*

b. *Social factors do not significantly affect SPE in Mexico City Spanish.*

Our first hypothesis is based on the Constant Rate Hypothesis (Kroch 1989), previously employed to explore SPE by Cameron (1993), and our second hypothesis is based on the results of the great majority of previous SPP studies.

Variables Examined

In selecting the predictor variables to be examined in this study, we took into account: *i)* the results of key previous studies; *ii)* the PRESEEA *Guía de codificación* (Bentivoglio, Ortiz and Silva-Corvalán 2011); and *iii)* Otheguy and Zentella's (2012) coding manual. We selected the following independent linguistic variables for our analysis.

a. Person and number of the SPP,
b. Specificity,
c. Verbal mood,
d. Verb tense, progressive aspect, and verbal morphology,
e. Verb class (cf. Bentivoglio, Ortiz and Silva-Corvalán 2011),
f. Morphological ambiguity (cf. Silva-Corvalán 1982, 109; 2001, 154–169),
g. Enunciative type,
h. Co-reference,
i. Textual genre,
j. Conversational style, and
k. Pronoun position.

The limited significance of social variables in the distribution of overt SPPs is a recurrent observation in the Spanish sociolinguistic literature (but see Orozco and Guy 2008; Shin and Otheguy 2013). To test that this is also the case in Mexico City, we examine three social variables: educational level, age, and gender.

RESULTS

First, the pronominal rate in Mexico City is considered in relation to other urban settings; second, the role of internal and social factors is established.

Pronominal Rate

Table 3.1 presents the rate of overt subject pronoun expression in MC Spanish as well as pronominal rates from 15 other studies.

The pronominal rate in MC (21.7 percent) is one of the lowest found anywhere (see table 3.1). It is very similar to the 22 percent for NYC Mexicans (Otheguy and Zentella 2012, 72), the 18.7 percent for Mexican newcomers to NYC (Otheguy and Zentella 2012), as well as to the rates found in other Mexican communities (cf. Bayley and Pease-Alvarez 1996; Silva-Corvalán 1994; Flores-Ferrán 2007; Bayley et al. 2012; Michnowicz, this volume). On the other hand, the MC SPP rate is very different from most Caribbean pronominal rates reported: 44.8 percent in San Juan (Cameron 1993, 306), 42.3 percent in Santo Domingo (Alfaraz, this volume), 34.2 percent in Barranquilla (Orozco, this volume). Thus, MC Spanish is clearly a Mainland variety (in the sense of Otheguy and Zentella 2012), exhibiting a relatively low overt pronominal rate. Concurrently, results show that overt SPPs occur, for the most part, in pre-verbal position (85.6 percent, 379/443). In general, it is accepted that post-verbal subjects are marked in Spanish, and quantities suggest that our data are no exception. Only 64 tokens contain post-verbal overt subjects (14.4 percent, 64/443).

Table 3.1 Rates of overt SPPs, by percentage

Speech Community	%
San Juan, Puerto Rico (Cameron 1993)	44.8
WLA Mexican–Americans (Silva-Corvalán 1982)	42.5
Barranquilla, Colombia (Orozco, this volume)	34.2
LA Mexican–Americans (Silva-Corvalán 1994)	28.9
NYC Latino Communities (Otheguy & Zentella 2012)	34.0
Castañer, Puerto Rico (Holmquist 2012)	28.0
San Antonio Mexican-background speakers (Bayley et al. 2012)	27.0
Mexican immigrants in New Jersey (Flores Ferrán 2007)	24.0
NYC Mexicans (Otheguy & Zentella 2012)	22.0
Mexico City (this paper)	21.7
Northern California Mexican immigrant and Chicano children (Bayley & Pease Álvarez 1996)	20.0
Madrid, Spain (Cameron 1993)	20.9
Yucatan Spanish overall (Michnowicz, this volume)	19.7
NYC Mexican newcomers (Shin & Otheguy 2013)	18.7
Monolingual Yucatan Spanish (Michnowicz, this volume)	16.0
Mexico children from Querétaro and Oaxaca (Shin 2012)	6.3

Internal Factor Groups

The results from a Goldvarb binary logistic regression appear in table 3.2.

Eight constraints significantly condition SPE in Mexico City. They are presented in table 3.2 in descending order of strength according to their range values. Grammatical person and number exerts the strongest, and style the weakest, conditioning pressures on SPE. The order of selection of the most statistically significant constraints, including the strongest influence of grammatical person and number, are congruent with findings in all varieties of Spanish, including Puerto Rico (Cameron 1993), Yucatan (Michnowicz, this volume), Barranquilla, Colombia (Orozco and Guy 2008; Orozco, this volume), and New York City (Otheguy and Zentella 2012, 160; Otheguy, Zentella, and Livert 2007), to name a few. Below we discuss the conditioning effects of linguistic factors on SPE in Mexico City in the same order in which they are presented in table 3.2.

Grammatical Person and Number

The main tendencies found indicate that singular persons clearly favor pronoun expression more than plural persons do. First and third singular persons propitiate overt SPPs (fws = .58, .57), with similar proportions (approximately 25 percent). All other grammatical persons disfavor overt SPPs. The disfavoring effect on overt SPPs is strongest for the plural grammatical persons: The third person plural registers a probability value of .33, and the first person plural has the most disfavoring effect on overt subjects with a weight of only .26.

Table 3.2 Linguistic constraints on overt SPPs in Mexico City (in order of range)

Constraints	Factor weight (FW)	%	N overt/Total N
a) Grammatical person and number			
1st sg	**.58**	24.7%	232/939
3rd sg	**.57**	27.1%	122/450
2nd sg	**.40**	16.6%	49/296
3rd pl	**.33**	11.9%	21/176
1st pl	**.26**	10.6%	19/179
Range = 32			
b) Co-reference			
Change in reference	**.70**	32.7%	182/556
Object	**.54**	22.8%	69/303
Subject	**.39**	16.3%	192/1181
Range = 31			
c) Verbal mood			
Indicative	**.52**	22.6%	433/1916
Non-indicative	**.23**	8.1%	10/124
Range = 29			
d) Enunciative type			
Affirmative	**.54**	23.5%	410/1741
Non-affirmative	**.31**	11.0%	33/299
Range = 23			
e) Textual genre			
Argumentation	**.66**	28.7%	105/366
Description	**.55**	27.2%	70/257
Dialogue	**.48**	16.9%	76/449
Narrative	**.43**	19.8%	192/968
Range = 23			
f) Verb Tense			
Imperfect	**.60**	31.4%	153/488
Present	**.50**	21.1%	187/888
Preterit	**.44**	15.5%	86/556
Other tenses	**.40**	15.7%	17/108
Range = 20			
g) Ambiguity			
Ambiguous	**.61**	36.1%	127/352
Non-ambiguous	**.48**	18.7%	316/1688
Range = 13			
h) Style			
Second part	**.54**	23.2%	236/1016
First part	**.46**	20.2%	207/1024
Range = 8			

Note: Log likelihood = –938.190, significance= .018, input= .181.

The favorable effect of first and third person singular subjects on overt pronominal expression is a general trend that consistently occurs throughout the Hispanic World. The same is true for plural grammatical persons promoting null subjects (Cameron 1993; Hochberg 1986; Michnowicz, this volume; Orozco and Guy 2008; Otheguy, Zentella, and Livert 2007, 2012; Shin 2012, inter alios). Cameron (1993, 306) suggests a convincing explanation to account for these tendencies: "If we conceive of plural subjects as sets, we find that discourse is typically structured so that the great majority of plural subjects occur in contexts where their set members are either explicitly or inferably present within the immediately preceding discourse. Such contexts favor null subject expression. Therefore, plural subjects are frequently null overall" (1993, 328, n. 2).

Nevertheless, the fact that the second person singular favors null subjects in our data contradicts the general tendency for singular pronouns and reveals some interesting features, especially when we divide specific and nonspecific *tú*. An example of non-specificity is provided in (1), in which the speaker addresses a specific second person, but later changes to a non-specific *tú* (*Tú te encontrabas todavía canales*).

(1) ***[Ø] acuérdate que en las litografías** eh/ del pasado// ya no mucha distancia/ hace cien años/ por decir**te** algo/ que suena muy lejano/ pero que históricamente/ es un segundo// hace cien años/ **tú te encontrabas todavía/ canales**// con/ piraguas de verduras en// en Jamaica.* (ME-294-33H-07, turn 39)

In our study, specific *tú* reaches 14 percent (14/103), and non-specific *tú* rises to 18.1 percent (35/193). In contrast with the low rates in MC, Cameron (1993, 325) finds 60 percent of *tú* in Puerto Rico and 25 percent in Madrid. Furthermore, the similar rates for specific and nonspecific *tú* in our data contrast with other studies, which have found that rates vary depending on specificity of the referent. For example, in monolingual Yucatan Spanish (YS), the SPE rate for specific *tú* is 32 percent, while for nonspecific *tú* it is 8 percent (Michnowicz, this volume). With respect to non-specific *tú*, MC is different from San Juan but similar to Madrid (69 percent in San Juan, 19 percent in Madrid and 18 percent in MC). On the other hand, with respect to specific *tú*, MC is different from both Madrid and San Juan: only 14 percent in MC versus 40 percent in Madrid and 48 percent in San Juan (Cameron 1996, 89). If we compare probability values, however, our data turn out to be closer to Puerto Rico than to Madrid: Caribbean data show .72 for non-specific *tú* and .86 for non-specific *uno* (respectively .50 and .72 in Madrid), versus .75 of overall non-specificity in MC. Regarding specific *tú*, Puerto Rico offers .51 (.72 in Madrid) versus .47 of overall specificity in MC.

These results call for further scrutiny of the use of second person singular SPPs, perhaps using additional data from the *Corpus sociolingüístico de la ciudad de México*. An expanded analysis shall provide more conclusive information regarding the differences between specific and non-specific pronominal usage.

Co-reference

With a range value of 31, co-reference exerts the second strongest influence on SPE in Mexico City. Change in reference, a factor that includes absence of previous reference, as well as cases with a previous mention at medium or long distance, or with only a contextual reference (fw = .70, pronominal rate = 32.7 percent) strongly favors the occurrence of overt pronominal subjects. Co-reference with object (fw = .54, rate = 22.8 percent) also favors overt SPPs. On the other hand, co-reference with the subject of the previous main clause favors null subjects (fw = .39, rate = 16.3 percent). Our results are congruent with those of other studies (e.g., Cameron 1993, 315; Michnowicz, this volume; Orozco and Guy 2008, 74; Silva-Corvalán 1982, 104; 1994, 157–158), indicating the following general trend: A switch in reference and longer distance from previous reference are contexts that favor overt SPPs. When the subject is co-referent with the object of the previous clause, overt pronoun expression is still favored, but only slightly. Finally, overt pronominal expression is disfavored with co-referent subjects (i.e., same referent, same function).

A question that arises has to do with the large number of co-referent subjects in our sample, constituting 57.8 percent of the cases, most likely due to the role of the subject in topical discursive continuity. Discursive interpretation is conditioned by both co-reference and textual ambiguity. Although most cases can be easily interpreted, there are a number where it is necessary for interlocutors to use all tools at their disposal, including general knowledge of the situation. For example, in (2) it is crucial to know that the speaker is referring to a female writer's life, especially when she introduces the role of the writer's mother.

(2) *entonces/* ***ella***$_i$ *es de una// familia/ en donde el matriarcado se hace efectivo//* ***su madre***$_j$ *una/ pues muj-/* ***una mujer***$_j$ */// digamos eh// no común en su ... [...] para su época// eh mm/* ***hija***$_j$ *de un/ señor que/ pues* ***la***$_j$ *quiere complacer y* ***[Ø]***$_j$ *está segura de que/ de que* ***su***$_j$ ***hija***$_i$ */ pues está bien que* ***[Ø]***$_i$ *haga lo que le gusta/ ¿no?// ¡y!/* ***ella***$_j$ *tiene varios hijos/ [Ø] no me acuerdo si [Ø] son siete pero/ de distinto padre todos// y* ***ella***$_j$ *¡los registra!/ como hijos* ***suyos***$_j$ */ naturales/ con toda la libertad/ con toda la/ tranquilidad// y/ ¡pues eso implica! tener ya un/ un modelo/ especial/ ¿no?/ parece que* ***[Ø]***$_i$ *tiene ¡muy buena relación! con* ***ella***$_j$ *// aunque/ se percibe por* ***su***$_i$ *poesía/ y por lo que* ***ella***$_i$ *dice de* ***ella***$_j$ *// que* ***[Ø]***$_i$ *no tuvo una// relación ¡física! cercana.* (ME-264-33M-05, turns 1–3)

From a syntactic perspective, it is not possible to establish who the mother of *varios hijos* is in (2), or who *ella* is in *lo que ella dice de ella*. Discursive resources help. In one interpretation, the co-referent of *ella* in *ella tiene varios hijos* is Ø in *está bien que Ø haga lo que le gusta*, based on the argument of short distance between first and second subject. Nevertheless, we do not expect the presence of a personal pronoun in the second occurrence, precisely because of the short distance between them. After listening to the recording that contains this interview passage, it is evident that there is no prosodic peak. So, the alternative interpretation is that *ella* is the same person initially introduced as *su madre*. But this, of course, is only an interpretation suggested afterwards by the assertion that *¡pues eso implica! tener ya un <~un:>/ un modelo/ especial* (under the belief that one can expect a mother to be a model for a child, more than the other way around). This is not to suggest that reference assignment is a difficult task. In fact, there are many cases easily interpreted despite their complexity.

Verbal Mood

Our main finding for verbal mood is that non-indicatives disfavor overt SPPs (all non-indicatives: fw = .23). The indicative mood had no effective role on pronoun expression (fw = .52). The imperative mood categorically occurred without SPPs in our data. If we further examine pronoun rates in these moods according to clause types, and we consider only the indicative and subjunctive moods, we find evidence that the subjunctive disfavors pronoun expression. Overt SPP rates with subjunctive forms are *always* lower in all types of clauses: 10 percent in main clauses (1/10), 13 percent in subordinate clauses (8/62), and 8 percent in coordinate clauses (1/12). In contrast, indicative forms present a virtually equal number of overt SPPs in main (24 percent, 220/917) and in subordinate clauses (25 percent, 111/452). In coordinate clauses, however, the rate decreases to 19 percent (105/551). The disfavoring effect of the subjunctive on pronoun expression is consistent with this mood's usual subordinate function and, consequently, the likely short distance of co-referring previous noun phrases.

Enunciative Type

Results for enunciative type show a clear difference between affirmative and non-affirmative (i.e., negative and interrogative) forms. As probabilistic weights reveal, affirmative statements favor the presence of an overt SPP (.54); non-affirmative cases disfavor overt SPPs (fw = .31). Example (3) illustrates affirmative statements occurring with overt SPPs. Examples (4) and (5) provide contexts showing the effects of negation. In example (4) there is one isolated negated clause that occurs with an overt pronoun. But in fact, examples like (4), where the negation occurs in isolation, were infrequent in our data. We found many more cases like (5), in which a series of negative statements cluster together. This clustering could explain the low occurrence of overt subjects with negation; that is, if negated clauses cluster together, it is possible that co-reference across these negated clauses contributes to their disfavoring effect on overt SPPs. Interactions between co-reference and negation should be explored in future studies.

(3) ***yo creo** mi mamá ya no me quería tener ahí no sé qué pero a la/ mi hermana mi m- la mayor/ este [Ø] le pidió que [Ø] me llevara a Pachuca a trabajar/ y yo pues ahí yo eh la persona con la que [Ø] trabajaba/ este no me daba bien de comer/ [Ø] no me daba este/ jabón para ¡bañarme!/ **yo estaba** muy sucia y / pues / **ella salía**/ [Ø] no sé dónde/ porque [Ø] casi nunca estaba ahí/ **yo me quedaba sola** y/ pues **yo sufría mucho**.* (ME-313-13M-07, turn 13)

(4) *y pues yo la verdad/ **yo tampoco no me aguanté** o sea/ [Ø] estaba/ como tú ahorita.* (ME-252-31M-05, turn 7)

(5) *[Ø] empecé a ter-/ bueno/ [Ø] empecé otra vez la carrera// pues sí/ sí [Ø] la terminé/ ya/ ahí en la Sep/ **[Ø] ya no pude aguantar** o sea/ ya era así de que/ **[Ø] ya no quería ir**// **[Ø] ya no quería**/ o sea nomás [Ø] me acord-/ "¡chin!/ [Ø] ya me tengo que ir a trabajar"// **no**/ **[Ø] no quería ir**/ a veces pues (risa) **[Ø] ya ni iba**/ ¿no?/ mejor [Ø] me iba a mi casa.* (ME-257-32H-05, turn 40)

Textual Genre

Textual genre appears fifth in the model. Argumentation (including explanation) favors overt SPPs most strongly (.66), and description (.55) slightly favors overt SPPs. In contrast, dialogic and narrative genres disfavor overt pronouns (.48 and .43, respectively). This tendency appears to be motivated by the necessity of fixing points of view and underscoring one's own and others' opinions as in (6). It is likely that textual genre, verb tense, and verbal function all share a common thread. As Silva-Corvalán (1997) observed, a correspondence exists between verb tense and function. Reported speech favors overt subjects, due to the need to clarify who the speaker is; (7) shows a dynamic narrative where the informant talks to two different persons and reports the dialogue between them and herself, putting the resources provided by presence and absence of pronouns into practice. By contrast, echo-interrogatives in dialogue as in (8) do not especially favor explicit subjects if we consider the nature of the interviews we have analyzed, where usually it is not necessary to establish the referents of *tú* and *yo*.

(6) *mucho muy distinto a l/ los tiempos de ahora//* ***yo pienso que mi vida*** *[Ø]* ***he vivido demasiado/ demasiado yo/ doy gracias a la vida/*** *por darme esa oportunidad de vivir/ fracasos [sufrimientos]/ desventuras/ todo.* (ME-283-23M-06, turn 116)

(7) *entonces /* ***[Ø] le dije a la muchacha*** *"ay/* ***¿qué crees [Ø]?*** *que/ pues* ***yo me quiero ir de aquí/*** *pero* ***[Ø] no tengo a nadie*** *" entonces* ***[Ø] dice "yo conozco a una señora*** *que es partera/* ***si [Ø] gustas/ [Ø] vete con ella" [Ø] le digo*** *"sí"/* ***yo le dije a la señora/*** *"* ***[Ø] me voy a ir" [Ø] dice*** *"pero ¿por qué?"/* ***[Ø] le digo*** *"porque pues es que* ***yo/ yo ya no quiero estar*** *"/ "pero* ***si tú no tienes familia*** *"/ "no pero este/* ***[Ø] voy a ver*** *si/* ***[Ø] me voy*** *a mi fa-/ con mi familia" y* ***[Ø] dice*** *"pues no/* ***[Ø] no te vayas" [Ø] dice*** *"aquí* ***nosotros te pagamos*** *tu/ tu cama/ y el bebé que* ***[Ø] tengas/*** *pues* ***si [Ø] quieres [Ø] nos lo regalas*** *"/ y* ***[Ø] le digo*** *"no/ es que/ este/ mi* ***compañerita este/ conoce este/ a mi familia*** *y* ***yo me voy a ir.*** *"* (ME-313-13M-07, turn 19)

(8) *¿qué* ***hacía [Ø]*** *?/ limpieza de oficinas.* (ME-307-11M-07, turn 14)

Verb Tense

The tendencies for verb tense reveal the Imperfect (or Co-preterit indicative) as the only tense that promotes overt SPPs (.60). The Present has a neutral influence on pronominal usage (.50). Conversely, the Preterit disfavors overt SPPs (.44). The other verb tenses, grouped as "other tenses," disfavor overt SPPs (.40). Further scrutiny uncovers that more than half of all occurrences of the Imperfect are morphologically ambiguous. Focusing on these ambiguous occurrences of the Imperfect, we find that the overt SPP frequency rises to approximately three fourths of the sample (72.5 percent, 111/153). This remarkable difference could suggest a functional compensation effect (Hochberg 1986). The example in (9) illustrates an accumulation of overt SPPs with the Imperfect.

(9) *porque* ***yo agarraba*** *y/* ***yo veía*** *a mis compañeros* ***que*** *en ocasiones* ***ellos agarraban*** *y [Ø] se subían a los trenes/ y* ***yo*** *también* ***lo trataba de hacer/*** *al principio [Ø] me dio mucho trabajo/ pero y después [Ø] lo dominaba a la perfección.* (ME-283-23M-06, turn 76)

Our findings for verb tense concur with those for verbal mood (see above) that have already revealed the disfavoring character of non-indicative forms for overt SPPs. Our results also confirm that the Morphological Future is scarce in MC (cf. Lastra and Martín Butragueño 2010), as in the rest of the Spanish-speaking world. The overall tendencies for verb tense are in line with those among Mexican–Americans in Los Angeles (Silva-Corvalán 1997, 126; 2001, 161) and with those in Oaxaca, Mexico (Shin and Erker, this volume). They are also consonant with findings in Barranquilla, Colombia (Orozco, this volume), NYC (Erker and Guy 2012; Otheguy and Zentella 2012, 164; Shin and Erker, this volume), and other communities. In general, the findings for verb tense suggest universal effects by being consistent across the board (cf. Bayley and Pease-Álvarez 1996; Erker and Guy 2012; Hochberg 1986; Otheguy, Zentella, and Livert 2007, 2012; Orozco this volume, and references therein).

Morphological Ambiguity

Our findings for morphological ambiguity reveal that despite the level of textual ambiguity being extremely low, the factor group is significant with morphological ambiguity favoring overt SPPs (.61). MC overt pronoun rates are very similar to rates reported for "less distinctive" and "more distinctive" verb tenses/moods in Yucatan Spanish, (17 percent and 35 percent for monolinguals and bilinguals combined, and 31 percent and 14 percent for monolinguals only; Michnowicz, this volume). It is likely that low discursive ambiguity is the direct result of the presence of overt SPPs with ambiguous morphological verb forms. For instance, in (10) *podía* could have a co-referent as a subject *yo* (the speaker) or *ella* (the speaker's mother). Probably, the unmarked interpretation would be *ella* due to the short distance and the absence of a contrastive focus (*yo*), but certainly the ambiguity is not resolved.

(10) *mi este/ mi mamá trabajaba en el correo// y ella empezó a /// a ver si me [Ø] **podía** meter/ ¿no?/ pues [Ø] ya empecé a ir al sindicato/ a pasar listas/ a que/ me conocieran/ casi un año/ de estar yendo// y mientras pues a tu casa a hacer el aseo y todo/ ¿no?// hasta que ya/ [Ø] entré a trabajar/// [Ø] voy a cumplir/ en este/ primero de julio/ treinta años de servicio/ trabajando.* (ME-274-22M-06, turn 43)

Our results show probabilistic weights very similar to those offered by Blanco Canales (1999) in her study of first person SPPs in Alcalá de Henares: .64 for ambiguous and .49 for non-ambiguous (versus .61 and .48 in MC). Cameron sees the effects of morphological ambiguity "not as independent constraints [...] but as effects that interact with switch reference, the central constraint" (1993, 307). Our data reveal this same tendency. In a cross-tabulation of *overall* data, ambiguous verbs with overt SPPs are more frequent with change in reference: 54 percent versus 43 percent (co-reference with an object) and 29 percent (with a subject). Nevertheless, both effects are at least partially independent. The same logic can be applied to the relation between ambiguity and verb tense. In our *overall* dataset, overt SPPs linked to morphological ambiguity are concentrated in the Imperfect (39 percent, 111/283); percentages of overt/ambiguous in other verbal tenses rest in few data points (8/37 for Present, 2/12 for Preterit, 6/20 for other tenses). A link between the Imperfect, ambiguity and switch/same reference with overt SPPs is not evident. If we isolate contexts in which there is a change in reference, Imperfects show the highest rate of overt SPPs (45 percent), followed by the Present (31 percent), the Preterit (26 percent), and finally, other tenses (19 percent). The same trend emerges when we isolate contexts in which there is co-reference with an object: Imperfect (45 percent) > Preterit (19 percent) > Present (18 percent) > other (1 percent). So too, when we isolate contexts in which there is co-reference with the previous subject, the Imperfect still has the highest pronominal rate (23 percent), followed by other tenses (17 percent), the Present (16 percent), and then the Preterit (11 percent).

Style

This constraint appeared in eighth position in the order of selection. In our analysis, first-part style is defined as a section of the interview in which there are a number of introductory turns. Second-part style includes a higher quantity of long turns by the interviewee, as well as a higher proportion of argumentation and reported speech. Our results show that second-part style favors overt SPPS (.54) more than first-part style (.46). Only a few studies have considered style, but in very different senses. Silva-Corvalán (1982, 118) compared written Spanish and spoken Mexican–American Spanish and the percentages of overt subjects were very similar (45 percent and 43 percent, respectively). Blanco Canales (1999) encountered .56 in formal register versus .44 in informal register. Due to her study being limited to the first person, it is possible that the formal register included a higher proportion of argumentative-like style tokens. Shin (2012, 136) shows significant overt SPP expression differences by speech context: 3.3 percent in picture book, 3.9 percent in story from memory, and 11.5 percent in sociolinguistic interviews. Travis (2007) compares conversation with narratives and finds the mirror opposite of what we find here: a higher rate of pronoun expression in the former than the latter. Her study focuses on first person singular *yo* alone, which may account for the differences between her study and ours. The interaction between grammatical person and style is worth exploring in future research.

Social Factors

Out of the three social factor groups included in our analysis, speaker's age significantly conditions SPE while educational level and gender do not. This shows that in Mexico City, as in most other monolingual speech communities, the conditioning effects on SPE are mainly linguistic.

The results for age presented in table 3.3 show that older speakers (over the age of 55) favor overt SPPs with a probability value of .61. All other speakers favor null subjects. The youngest speakers favor null subjects the most in this community with a probability weight of .42. Thus the results show a pattern of SPP rates decreasing with age, in both frequency (29.6 > 20.0 > 16.4 percent) and factor weights (.61 > .48 > .42). We propose here that our data, coupled with those from other studies, reveal a *floor effect* for pronoun expression. We posit that the lowest pronoun rates that we find among the younger people in MC (which range from 10 to 15 percent) represent the minimum amount—the *floor*—of overt SPPs that adults will use in Spanish (cf. the child language in Shin 2012). This floor effect is the counterpart of the ceiling effect proposed by Shin and Otheguy (2013, 431), who argue that Spanish speakers' pronoun rates generally do not rise above 45 percent because past that ceiling, the reference-tracking function of pronoun expression will be lost.

Table 3.3 Social distribution of overt SPPs (by age)

Age	Factor Weight	%	N expressed/total N
Older than 55	**.61**	29.6%	190/641
35–54 years	**.48**	20.0%	130/650
20–34 years	**.42**	16.4%	123/749
Range = 19			

Note: Log likelihood = –1049.361, significance = .000, input = .212.

The clear significance of age in our study (p = .000) warrants further attention to determine whether these results indeed reflect an age effect or a change in progress (Labov 1994, 77 ff.). A similar pattern whereby younger speakers express fewer pronouns obtains in Barranquilla, with different percentages, but almost identical statistical weights (groups by age are not exactly equivalent): speakers 50 and older (41 percent, fw = .60) > 20–50 years old (33 percent, fw = .49) > adolescents (32 percent, fw = .40) (Orozco and Guy 2008, 78). If our findings for Mexico City Spanish indeed reflect a change in progress, then that change is a particularly strong example of what Labov (2001) calls "retrograde movement" (75). That is, the change goes against the expected evolution towards increasing rates of occurrence, which has been the norm in varieties of Romance. As Erker and Guy (2012) write, "from this perspective lower SPP rates are archaic" (531).

Despite not reaching statistical significance, the results for education and sex suggest that there might be some social value attached to SPE. The frequencies for education tell us that people with low educational level produce the highest SPP rate (24.2 percent, 161/666), followed by medium-level (20.9 percent, 157/752) and high-level (20.1 percent, 125/622). The descending percentages suggest a (albeit weak) correlation between overt SPPs and lower education, which might indicate that pronoun omission carries more prestige. The frequencies for speaker's sex show women favoring overt SPPs (23.6 percent) at a slightly higher rate than men (19.8 percent). Interestingly, the same pattern appears in every age group: 31 versus 28 percent for 55 and older; 23 versus 18 percent for 35–54 years; and 17 versus 16 percent for 20–34 years. Such a gender effect whereby women use pronouns more often than men do is congruent with several other studies (Bayley and Pease-Álvarez 1996; Otheguy and Zentella 2012, 117–121; Shin 2013; Shin and Erker, this volume; Shin and Otheguy 2013). One of our intuitions was that some older women produced a higher number of overt SPPs, especially in the case of *yo*. In fact, out of all the SPPs produced in the data, women generally use even more pronouns than men in a majority of the cases, as 54.7 percent were produced by women and 45.3 percent by men. Interestingly, if we isolate the cases of expressed first-person singular *yo*, the gender effect is even more apparent, as 60.7 percent of all cases of *yo* were produced by women. Gender differences deserve more attention in future research, especially in contexts where there might be a change in progress.

DISCUSSION

Two issues are especially significant, both related to the initial hypotheses: the relatively expected effect of the Constant Rate Hypothesis and the unexpected effect of social variables.

The Constant Rate Hypothesis Question

Our empirical Mexico City SPE analysis partially validates the Constant Rate Hypothesis (Kroch 1989). That is, the internal conditioning on pronominal expression is consistent with previous findings throughout the Hispanic World showing strong effects for grammatical person and number and co-reference. Additionally, other constraints such as verbal mood have emerged as significant. The probabilistic tendencies of the factors included in some groups (e.g., person and number, co-reference, and ambiguity) are virtually identical to those reported in previous research. These facts lend validity to the CRH, taking dialects as witnesses of apparent time (or real geography), and underlining the similar behavior of linguistic constraints within them. Nevertheless, a number of particular features, such as a low pronominal rate for specific *tú*, differentiate MC from other varieties. Morphological ambiguity and switch reference are at least partially independent, and the same can be said about ambiguity and verb tense. Also, we find not only an overall low overt SPP rate, but also a low rate of post-posed overt SPPs, contrary to Cameron's (1993) prediction. These aspects seem to weaken the CRH. Regardless, MC would not be engaged in a change in the direction "more free overt SPPs position" > "pre-V overt SPPs," as has been proposed for Caribbean Spanish, as a fragment of a more general solidification of SVO order. One question that arises as a result of this study of SPE in MC is why the overt SPP rate is decreasing in apparent time. Considering the relatively stable behavior of linguistic factors (in the probabilistic comparison with other dialects), it is necessary to look even more in depth at social factors so that clearer profiles of the community's high versus low pronoun users can be established.

Social Variation

The results have disproven our hypothesis regarding social constraints, as we predicted that social factors would not impact SPE. In particular, we found that speaker's age significantly conditions SPE. Thus, our results raise the question of whether the decreasing pronoun rate in MC represents a change in progress, an age-specific tendency, or a combined model (Cheshire 2005; Cameron 2011). Given that Orozco (this volume) and Orozco and Guy (2008) have also found a similar age effect in Barranquilla, the possibility that some Latin American varieties are experiencing such retrograde movement is worth exploring.[2] To that end, we examine the pronoun rates produced by individual speakers, as well as the rates among subgroups divided by gender and educational level. The role of individual speakers is essential in considering an ongoing change scenario and establishing who the leaders in the change are (Labov 2001, part C). Table 3.4 shows every individual speaker, speaker's age, absolute overt SPP frequency (F), and (percent) overt SPPs rate per speaker, going from 11.6 percent to 50 percent.[3] These data reveal important differences among informants: 23M, the speaker with the highest number of SPPs, shows a figure more than three times higher than that of 32H (first in the column), with only 13 cases; the same can be said about rate. Although there are important differences among speakers, these differences rise gradually without extreme outliers, perhaps with the exception of 13H (ten speakers stay under the overall rate, 21.7 percent, and eight are over the overall rate).

If we observe the extremes of the series (Martín Butragueño 2006, 2014), we can divide the list of informants into thirds and assign a low, a medium, and a high value to each segment. Among the six lowest rates, there are four men (in fact, three men have the lowest rates), four young speakers, and two people of each educational level. In the high extreme, there are the same number of male and female speakers, four older people and three well-educated speakers.[4] A crosstab between age and gender reveals that older women have the highest percentage of SPPs at 31 percent (versus 28 percent for their male peers), almost ten points over the mean (21.7 percent).

Regarding a possible ongoing change, this would be a retrograde movement promoted by the younger, mainly male, speakers with lower overt SPP rates—the same exact tendency uncovered in Barranquilla (Orozco, this volume). That is, older people's traditional speech patterns contain higher SPP usage. It is true that the same process is taking place with other linguistic variables in Mexican Spanish (such as vowels and rhotics; Martín Butragueño 2006, 2014), but the leaders of change in those processes are mostly self-made women with a personal history of social rise, in line with the description of leaders by Labov (2001). Thus, if we have a change in progress in SPP expression, it would be necessary to explain why younger men are the leaders (if they are) and why they have this social effect. If indeed pronoun rates are changing across generations, perhaps this has to do with the fast ongoing change in many Mexican cities, and particularly in MC, in relation to forms of address (see Hummel, Kluge and Vázquez Laslop 2009), especially the reduction in the use of *yo*, *usted*, and *uno*. But this is a hypothesis that will have to be explored subsequently.

In the previous observations, age has been taken as a discrete variable, divided in three generations. We now consider age as a continuous variable and further investigate the effect of it on subject pronoun expression via linear regression analyses. In order to do this, we created a continuous dependent variable called *Pronoun Rate* (the rate of

Table 3.4 Overt SPPs per speaker in Mexico City

Speaker	Gender	Educational Level	Age	F	Rate (%)
Lowest pronoun rates					
32H	Male	High	45	13	11.6
31H	Male	High	29	14	11.8
23H	Male	Medium	59	16	12.5
21M	Female	Medium	27	19	14.8
11H	Male	Low	27	19	16.0
11M	Female	Low	21	19	16.5
Medium pronoun rates					
22H	Male	Medium	40	24	18.0
21H	Male	Medium	20	29	19.7
12M	Female	Low	37	24	20.2
31M	Female	High	21	24	20.2
22M	Female	Medium	51	23	23.5
13M	Female	Low	78	33	24.1
Highest pronoun rates					
32M	Female	High	40	23	24.5
12H	Male	Low	52	24	25.3
33H	Male	High	72	21	27.6
33M	Female	High	58	31	31.0
23M	Female	Medium	56	46	38.3
13H	Male	Low	73	41	50.0

expressed pronouns out of all possible contexts), which was calculated for each participant (as displayed in table 3.4). Results from the linear regressions confirm the statistical tendencies, as we observe the effect of age on Pronoun Rate in subgroups of participants divided by gender and educational level (similar to Labov 1994, Ch. 3). In the results below we report R^2, which indicates the total variance accounted for by all of the variables in the regression. We also report F_{ANOVA} and Standardized β values, which tell us the predictive power associated with each independent variable (Hernández Campoy and Almeida 2005, 240–248).

a. Age.
   Overall data: rate (%) = .311*age + 8.595, R^2 = .355.
   [F_{ANOVA} = 8.803, p = .009; Standardized β = .596, p = .009].
b. Age and gender.
   Men: rate (%) = .397*age + 2.972, R^2 = .397.

[F_{ANOVA} = 4.610, p = .069; Standardized β = .630, p = .069].
Women: rate (%) = .240*age + 13.308, R^2 = .402.
[F_{ANOVA} = 4.702, p = .067; Standardized β = .634, p = .067].

c. Age and educational level.
Low: rate (%) = .378*age + 7.207, R^2 = .505.
[F_{ANOVA} = 4.079, p = .114; Standardized β = .711, p = .114].
Medium: rate (%) = .194*age + 12.967, R^2 = .112.
[F_{ANOVA} = .506, p = .516; Standardized β = .335, p = .516].
High: rate (%) = .261*age + 9.571, R^2= .363.
[F_{ANOVA} = 2.282, p = .205; Standardized β = .603, p = .205].

The linear trend for the overall data confirms that age is a significant predictor of SPE expression. When the data are divided by gender, we see that age exhibits a similar effect among both men and women (R^2 = .397 and .407, respectively), and their ANOVA and Standardized β values approach significance (p = .067 and .069, for men and women, respectively). When the data are divided into subgroups of educational level, however, age is not significant.

What do these results mean? First, we have here further corroboration of the effect of age on SPE, with more pronoun expression among the older speakers and less among the youngest speakers. Second, men and women are basically parallel with respect to age: Older speakers produce higher pronominal rates and this is true for both men and women. Third, younger speakers with low education levels produce a higher rate of null subjects than the older low-education-level people do, although this difference does not reach statistical significance. At this juncture, we cannot conclusively determine whether we are witnessing an ongoing change in SPE. In the future it would be helpful to develop a model that includes stratification by age (and partially by gender and educational level), based on the development of a *different conversational style* through an individual's life span and ongoing change, based on the *floor effect*, which can be viewed as a type of economy principle.

CONCLUSION

The overall pronominal rate (21.7 percent) suggests that Mexico City Spanish is a conservative dialect. Linguistic factor groups that significantly predict subject pronoun expression in MC are grammatical person and number, co-reference, verbal mood, enunciative type, textual genre, verbal tense, ambiguity, and style. There are remarkable similarities between our findings and previous SPE studies, not only with respect to which factor groups are significant, but also with respect to probability weights associated with particular factors. Turning to the results for the social factors investigated, we found robust effects for age, which is significant as a discrete variable in logistic regression analysis, and as a continuous variable in linear regression analysis. Gender and educational level were not significant when subordinated to age in a linear regression analysis.

Our study also suggests a floor effect for SPE (the counterpart to Shin and Otheguy's 2013 ceiling effect). We propose that the lowest SPE rate that Spanish-speaking adults exhibit is around 10–15 percent, which is the rate produced by some MC speakers. Also, MC data support a weak version of the CRH, and offer evidence of age variation. Specifically, we found significantly lower overt SPP rates among younger speakers. Additional research is needed, however, in order to uncover the reason for this age effect. Whether there is a retrograde change in progress or there is age grading is a question we leave for future investigation.

ACKNOWLEDGMENTS

We would like to express thanks for Poncho Aispuro's search of exempla in CSCM, as well as the observations by different members of the Grupo de investigación sociolingüística (http://lef.colmex.mx). We are also very grateful to two anonymous evaluators, to Naomi Shin for her invaluable editorial input and suggestions, and to Rafael Orozco, whose comments have been fundamental in improving the analysis. Of course, remaining mistakes are ours.

NOTES

1. For more information, see http://lef.colmex.mx.
2. Interestingly, according to Shin (2012) and Shin and Erker (this volume), Mexican children produce very low overt SPP rates, with slightly higher rates among girls than boys. We do not propose a simplistic connection between these and our data (for age gender effects along the life span on SPPs, see Shin 2012, 138), but it is worthwhile to note that both observations are compatible.
3. Manjón-Cabeza et al. (2014) find a similar pattern in Granada, Spain. The speaker's label encodes the following information: first number, educational level (1, low; 2, medium; 3, high); second number, age (1, 20–34; 2, 35–54; 3, 55+); letter "H," male, and letter "M," female.
4. It is interesting to consider qualitatively some older people: 23M is a middle-class, 56-year-old woman with only a secondary education, plus a series of subsequent formative courses. She gives the impression of being a self-made woman. In the fragment we examined, she uses *yo* quite frequently (32 in 47 SPPs) when speaking about her childhood—e.g., *yo me peleaba*, *yo pienso*, *yo doy gracias a la vida*. Her profile fits quite well with the fact that some older Mexico City women reveal remarkable overt SPP coefficients. Concurrently, 13H would seem to be a partial exception as a male speaker. This uneducated 73-year-old man worked as a porter and had an especially hard life. His interview is halfway between a description of life in popular neighborhoods, and a more personal narrative of himself as a member of that landscape, but from the background, what converges with a medium level of *yo* (15/42) and especially of *uno* (18/42).

REFERENCES

Amastae, Jon, Betty Dajlala T., Xóchitl Díaz, Alberto Esquinca M., Saidah Yazmín Ochoa, Philip Porter, and María José Torres. 2000. "Ø Hablo: el uso del sujeto en el español fronterizo [El Paso, Juárez, Parral]." In *Memorias del V Encuentro Internacional de Lingüística en el Noroeste,* t. 2, edited by María del Carmen Morúa Leyva and Gerardo López Cruz, 219–232. Hermosillo: Universidad de Sonora.

Barrenechea, Ana María, and Alicia Alonso. 1977. "Los pronombres personales sujetos en el español hablado en Buenos Aires." In *Estudios sobre el español hablado en las principales ciudades de América,* edited by Juan M. Lope Blanch, 333–349. México: Universidad Nacional Autónoma de México.

Bayley, Robert, and Lucinda Pease-Alvarez. 1996. "Null and overt pronoun variation in Mexican-descent children's Spanish." In *Sociolinguistic Variation: Data, Theory, and Analysis,* edited by Jennifer Arnold, Renee Blake, and Brad Davidson, 85–99. Stanford, CA: Center for the Study of Language and Information.

Bayley, Robert, Lucinda Pease-Alvarez, Norma L. Cárdenas, Belinda Treviño Schouten, and Carlos Martín Vélez Salas. 2012. "Spanish dialect contact in San Antonio, Texas: An exploratory study." In *Selected Proceedings of the 14th Hispanic Linguistics Symposium,* edited by Kimberly Geeslin and Manuel Díaz-Campos, 48–60. Somerville, MA: Cascadilla Proceedings Project.

Bentivoglio, Paola. 1980. *Why* canto *and not* yo canto*? The problem of first-person subject pronoun in spoken Venezuelan Spanish*. MA thesis, University of California.

———. 1987. *Los sujetos pronominales de primera persona en el habla de Caracas.* Caracas: Universidad Central de Venezuela.

Bentivoglio, Paola, Luis A. Ortiz, and Carmen Silva-Corvalán. 2011. "La variable expresión del sujeto pronominal. Guía de codificación." In *PRESEEA – Grupo de análisis de expresión de sujetos*. Retrieved from http://preseea.linguas.net/Portals/0/Metodologia/guia_codificacion_sujetos_julio_2011.pdf.

Blanco Canales, Ana 1999. "Presencia/ausencia de sujeto pronominal de primera persona en español." *Español Actual* 72:31–39.

Cameron, Richard. 1993. "Ambiguous agreement, functional compensation, and non-specific *tú* in the Spanish of San Juan, Puerto Rico, and Madrid, Spain." *Language Variation and Change* 5 (3):305–334.

———. 1996. "A community-based test of a linguistic hypothesis." *Language in Society* 25(1):61–111.

———. 2011. "Aging, age, and sociolinguistics." in *The Handbook of Hispanic Sociolinguistics,* edited by Manuel Díaz-Campos, 207–229. Oxford: Wiley-Blackwell.

Cantero Sandoval, Gustavo. 1978. "Observaciones sobre la expresión innecesaria de los pronombres personales sujeto en el español de México." *Anuario de Letras* 16:261–264.

———. 1986. "Tipos de expresión obligatoria de los pronombres personales sujeto en español." In *Actas del V Congreso Internacional de la Asociación de Lingüística y Filología de América Latina*, 243–248. Caracas: Instituto de Filología Andrés Bello.

Cheshire, Jenny. 2005. "Age and generation-specific use of language." In *Sociolinguistics: An Introductory Handbook of the Science of Language and Society,* edited by Ulrich Ammon, Norbert Dittmar, Klaus Mattheier, and Peter Trudgill, 1552–1563. Berlin: Mouton de Gruyter.

Erker, Daniel, and Gregory R. Guy 2012. "The role of lexical frequency in syntactic variability: Variable subject personal pronoun expression in Spanish." *Language* 88(3):526–557.

Flores-Ferrán, Nydia. 2007. "Los Mexicanos in New Jersey: Pronominal expression and ethnolinguistic aspects." In *Selected Proceedings of the Third Workshop on*

Spanish Sociolinguistics, edited by Jonathan Holmquist, Augusto Lorenzino, and Lotfi Sayahi, 85–91. Somerville, MA: Cascadilla Proceedings Project.

Hernández Campoy, Juan Manuel, and Manuel Almeida. 2005. *Metodología de la investigación sociolingüística*. Málaga: Comares.

Hochberg, Judith G. 1986. "Functional compensation for /s/ deletion in Puerto Rican Spanish." *Language* 62(3):609–621.

Holmquist, Jonathan. 2012. "Frequency rates and constraints on subject personal pronoun expression: Findings from the Puerto Rican highlands." *Language Variation and Change* 24(2):203–220.

Hummel, Martin, Bettina Kluge, and María Eugenia Vázquez Laslop, eds. 2009. *Formas y fórmulas de tratamiento en el mundo hispánico*. México – Graz: El Colegio de México – Karl-Franzens-Universität.

Hurtado, Luz. 2005. "El uso de *tú*, *usted* y *uno* en el español de los colombianos y colombo–americanos." In *Contactos y contextos lingüísticos: el español en los Estados Unidos y en contacto con otras lenguas*, edited by Luis A. Ortiz López and Manel Lacorte, 185–200. Frankfurt/Madrid: Vervuert/Iberoamericana.

Kroch, Anthony 1989. "Reflexes of grammar in patterns of language change." *Language Variation and Change* 1(1):199–244.

Labov, William. 1994. *Principles of Linguistic Change*. Vol. 1: *Internal Factors*. Oxford: Blackwell.

———. 2001. *Principles of Linguistic Change*. Vol. 2: *Social Factors*. Oxford:Blackwell.

Lastra, Yolanda, and Pedro Martín Butragueño. 2010. "Futuro perifrástico y futuro morfológico en el *Corpus sociolingüístico de la ciudad de México*." *Oralia* 13:145–171.

———. 2012. "Aproximación al uso del modo subjuntivo en la ciudad de México." *Boletín de Filología* 47:101–131.

Manjón-Cabeza, Antonio, Francisca Pose, and Francisco J. Sánchez. 2014. "Primera aproximación a la variable presencia/ausencia de sujeto pronominal en el corpus PRESEEA de Granada (España). Variables semánticas, pragmáticas, sociales y dialectales." In *Actas del XVII Congreso Internacional de la Asociación de Lingüística y Filología de la América Latina, João Pessoa, Paraíba, Brazil.*

Martín Butragueño, Pedro. 2006. "Líderes lingüísticos en la ciudad de México." In *Líderes lingüísticos. Estudios de variación y cambio,* edited by Pedro Martín Butragueño, 185–208. México: El Colegio de México.

———. 2014. *Fonología variable del español de México*. Vol. I: *Procesos segmentales*. México: El Colegio de México.

Martín Butragueño, Pedro, and Yolanda Lastra 2011. *Corpus sociolingüístico de la ciudad de México*. Vol. 1: *Hablantes de instrucción superior*. México: El Colegio de México.

———. 2012. *Corpus sociolingüístico de la ciudad de México*. Vol. 2: *Hablantes de instrucción media*. México: El Colegio de México.

———. Forthcoming. *Corpus sociolingüístico de la ciudad de México*. Vol. 3: *Hablantes de instrucción baja*. México: El Colegio de México.

Martín Butragueño, Pedro, and María Eugenia Vázquez Laslop 2002. "Variación y dinamismo lingüístico: problemas de método." *Lexis* 26:305–344.

Morales, Amparo. 1982. "La perspectiva dinámica oracional en el español de Puerto Rico." In *El Español del Caribe: Ponencias del VI Simposio de Dialectología,* edited by Orlando Alba, 203–219. Santiago de los Caballeros: Universidad Católica Madre y Maestra.

Orozco, Rafael, and Gregory Guy. 2008. "El uso variable de los pronombres sujetos: ¿qué pasa en la costa Caribe colombiana?" In *Selected Proceedings of the 4th Workshop on Spanish Sociolinguistics,* edited by Maurice Westmoreland and Juan Antonio Thomas, 70–80. Somerville, MA: Cascadilla Proceedings Project.

Otheguy, Ricardo, Ana C. Zentella, and David Livert. 2007. "Language and dialect contact in Spanish in New York: Towards the formation of a speech community." *Language* 83(4):770–802.

Otheguy, Ricardo, and Ana C. Zentella. 2012. *Spanish in New York: Language Contact, Dialectal Leveling, and Structural Continuity.* Oxford: Oxford University Press.

Shin, Naomi Lapidus. 2012. "Variable use of Spanish subject pronouns by monolingual children in Mexico." In *14th Hispanic Linguistics Symposium*, edited by Kimberly Geeslin and Manuel Díaz-Campos, 130–141. Somerville, MA: Cascadilla Proceedings Project.

———. 2013. "Women as leaders of language change: A qualification from the bilingual perspective." In *Proceedings of the 6th International Workshop on Spanish Sociolinguistics*, edited by Ana Maria Carvalho & Sara Beaudrie, 135–147. Cascadilla Proceedings Project.

Shin, Naomi Lapidus, and Ricardo Otheguy. 2013. "Social class and gender impacting change in bilingual settings: Spanish subject pronoun use in New York." *Language in Society*, 42:429–452.

Silva-Corvalán, Carmen. 1982. "Subject variation in spoken Mexican–American Spanish." In *Spanish in the United States: Sociolinguistic Aspects,* edited by Jon Amastae and Lucía Elías-Olivares. New York: Cambridge University Press, 93–120.

———. 1994. *Language Contact and Change*. Oxford: Oxford University Press.

———. 1997. "Variación sintáctica en el discurso oral: problemas metodológicos." In *Trabajos de sociolingüística hispánica*, edited by Francisco Moreno Fernández, 115–135. Alcalá de Henares: Universidad de Alcalá.

———. 2001. *Sociolingüística y pragmática del español*. Washington: Georgetown University Press.

Torres Cacoullos, Rena, and Catherine E. Travis. 2011. "Testing convergence via code-switching: Priming and the structure of variable subject expression." *International Journal of Bilingualism* 15(3):241–267.

Travis, Catherine 2007. "Genre effects on subject expression in Spanish: Priming in narrative and conversation." *Language Variation and Change* 19:101–135.

4

Subject Pronoun Usage in Formulaic Sequences

Evidence from Peninsular Spanish

Pekka Posio

It is well known on the basis of previous research that the expression of Spanish subject personal pronouns (SPPs) shows different rates with different verb lexemes. For instance, mental verbs have been found to favor subject pronoun expression (SPE) in Peninsular Spanish (e.g., Enríquez 1984; Aijón Oliva and Serrano 2010; Posio 2011, 2013, 2014) as well as in American varieties (e.g., Morales 1997; Otheguy, Zentella, and Livert 2007; Travis and Torres Cacoullos 2012). The high rate of SPP expression has been attributed to the speakers' desire to emphasize the subjects of verbs "expressing opinions" or the allegedly recurrent use of mental verbs in contrastive contexts (e.g., Enríquez 1984; Fernández Soriano 1999). However, such explanations are problematic for various reasons. In practice, contrastive contexts are rare in discourse and even when they occur, they do not necessarily favor SPP expression (Travis and Torres Cacoullos 2012), not all mental verbs favor SPP expression (cf., e.g., Orozco, this volume; Posio 2014), and not all languages or language varieties behave similarly in this respect (Posio 2012c). In fact, the most frequently used mental verb tokens such as *creo* 'I believe/think'—rather than semantic verb categories—are associated with specific SPP expression patterns that are to a great extent responsible for the frequent subject expression within the category of mental verbs (Orozco, this volume; Posio 2013, 2014).

The present chapter explores the hypothesis that, in addition to being more sensitive to the factors generally affecting subject expression than less frequent verb forms

(Erker and Guy 2012), the most frequently occurring verb tokens are typically associated with discourse-pragmatic functions that may account for the idiosyncratic subject expression tendencies with those verb forms. Frequent verb tokens occurring with or without expressed SPPs, then, are assumed to be stored in the speaker's memory as formulaic (e.g., Wray 2002) or recurrent (e.g., Butler 2005) sequences, formulae or chunks (e.g., Ellis 2003) or prefabs (e.g., Erman and Warren 2000).

While linguistic theories—especially in the generative framework—have traditionally been more interested in the productivity of language than in formulaic collocations or other non-productive aspects of language use, the role of formulaic language has gained prominence in usage-based theories (e.g., Hopper 1987; Bybee 2010). It has been estimated that more than half of all actual language use in English is formulaic as opposed to novel, that is, productively created by the speaker (Erman and Warren 2000). As for Spanish, Butler (1997, 65) remarks that recurrent sequences are especially common in spoken as opposed to written language. According to Butler's (1997) findings on English and Spanish, in both languages recurrent sequences typically serve an interpersonal or textual function; in essence, these sequences express the speakers' perspective or stance towards the representational contents of what is serving as structuring or cohesive elements in speech or text.

Although the notion of formulaic sequences or prefabs is an intuitively attractive one and has been around for a long time in functional linguistics, establishing a clear, operational definition of them is not an easy task (see Butler 2005 for a discussion). An oft-cited formulation by Wray (2002) defines formulaic sequence as "a sequence, continuous or discontinuous, of words or other elements, which is, or appears to be, prefabricated: that is, stored and retrieved whole from memory at the time of use, rather than being subject to generation or analysis by the language grammar" (9). Erman and Warren (2000), on the other hand, define a prefab as "a combination of at least two words favored by native speakers in preference to an alternative combination which could have been equivalent had there been no conventionalization" (32). Formulaic sequences may contain open slots where variation is possible; however, they differ from the notion of constructions (as used in Construction Grammar) in that all but one slot are lexically filled and present little or no variation or exchangeability (Erman and Warren 2000, 32).

While Wray's (2002) and Erman and Warren's (2000) definitions focus on aspects of storage and production of the sequences, in corpus-linguistic studies formulaic sequences are typically defined as strings of words occurring over a certain threshold of frequency in a given corpus, for instance, more than 10 times (Butler 1997, 65). The definitions need not contain a functional component: In principle, any frequently repeated combinations of items (such as *and the*) may be considered a formulaic sequence. However, in practice, formulaic sequences are often discernible because they regularly serve specific functions in discourse. For instance, Spanish *yo creo que* 'I think that' is used to express the speaker's epistemic stance in a similar way as the sequence *I think* in English (e.g., Thompson and Mulac 1991; Aijón Oliva and Serrano 2010, Van Bogaert 2011, Posio 2011, 2013, 2014). In the present study, formulaic sequences are defined as strings of two or more words occurring at a certain frequency in the corpus (see Data and Methodology below) and serving a regular pragmatic function in discourse that can be determined by a qualitative analysis. Although these sequences are assumed to form single units in the speaker's memory, it is obvious that the way speakers store and access these units cannot be taken as a definitional criterion in a corpus-based study, but rather as a hypothesis to be confirmed by psycholinguistic research.

High frequency of use is related to formulaicity but does not constitute a necessary definitional criterion: Many idioms and proverbs are not particularly frequent although they are clearly formulaic. However, they are salient items in discourse because of their unexpected form–function correspondences. It appears that speakers are more conscious of the existence of idioms with non-compositional meaning (e.g., *kick the bucket* for 'die') than of the frequently repeated ones with more-or-less compositional meaning (e.g., *yo creo que* 'I think that') whose idiosyncratic properties can only be discovered through corpus-based frequency analyses (see Posio, 2014).

Recent studies on variable subject pronoun expression in Spanish (Erker and Guy 2012; Posio 2012b) and Portuguese (Travis and Silveira 2009; Silveira 2011; Posio 2012c) have highlighted the role of frequency effects (Bybee and Thompson 1997) in accounting for variable subject expression. Erker and Guy (2012) argue that the high frequency of certain verb tokens has an amplifying effect with regard to the factors conditioning SPP expression. In their data from Mexican and Dominican speakers residing in New York City, the factor groups verb type, grammatical person and regular versus irregular morphology only show a significant effect with frequently occurring verb tokens (defined as those which make up at least 1 percent of the totality of the data). The factors tense/mood/aspect and same/switch reference show a significant effect with all verb tokens, but the effect is stronger with the frequently occurring tokens. Thus, frequency amplifies the effect of predictors of SPP presence, although it is not a significant factor on its own.

While frequency of use undoubtedly allows for the collocational patterns to emerge and become entrenched, attributing the low or high rates of subject pronoun expression to frequency of verb forms alone is not a fully satisfying explanation, given that SPP expression varies considerably among the highly frequent verb forms. For instance, in Erker and Guy's (2012, 539) data, the lowest rate of subject expression is 12 percent attested with *digo* 'I say' and the highest is 92 percent with *sabes* 'you know'. Such differences between high-frequency verbs cannot be attributed entirely to contextual factors such as same versus switch reference but rather represent idiosyncratic properties of the verb tokens (Posio 2013, 284). This observation raises three questions:

1. What functions do the frequently occurring verb tokens have in spoken discourse?
2. Is there a regular link between the pragmatic or grammatical function of the verb form (or the sequence containing it) and its SPP expression pattern?
3. What (if any) differences can be found between different varieties of Spanish with regard to the frequently occurring verbs and their patterns of SPP expression?

The present chapter attempts to provide answers to the first two questions by examining the most frequently occurring verb tokens in a corpus of spoken Peninsular Spanish. Providing a fully satisfactory answer to the third question would require cross-dialectal analysis of comparable data that is not possible in the scope of this chapter. However, comparison of the results obtained from Peninsular Spanish data with other studies in this volume suggests that the formulaic sequences are partially similar, but also partially dependent on the dialect in question.

DATA AND METHODOLOGY

The corpus consists of part of the subsection *Conversaciones* of the *COREC* (*Corpus de referencia del español contemporáneo*, Marcos-Marín 1992). This selection of transcribed speech contains relatively informal conversations between two or more speakers, recorded at different locations in Spain in the early 1990s. It includes data from informal, face-to-face communicative settings as well as radio and television debates.[1] The limited size of the corpus—59,060 words—permits the manual examination of the verb tokens in their contexts of occurrence, taking into account their discourse-pragmatic functions that have been overlooked in previous quantitative studies.

While usage-based studies claim that frequency effects can be observed above a certain threshold, it is difficult to establish such a threshold independently of the data to be observed. Erker and Guy (2012) and Silveira (2011) consider verb forms making up at least 1 percent of the totality of the data as "frequent." Erker and Guy (2012, 549) test the feasibility of other frequency thresholds and come to the conclusion that as far as their data is concerned, the 1 percent limit is where the cut-off point between sufficiently frequent and not sufficiently frequent verb forms is located. Following their results, the 1 percent threshold was also adopted in the present study. Given that the corpus contains 7,773 finite verb forms, this means that only tokens occurring more than 42 times in the corpus were considered frequent. The most frequently occurring form is *es* 'be-3SG' that alone makes up 16 percent of all verb tokens in the corpus. In total, the 34 most frequent verb forms occurring above the 1 percent threshold make up 62 percent of all finite verbs in the data.

Since the focus of the present study is on variable SPP expression, third person forms with non-human referents were discarded from the data, as the use of SPPs for non-human referents is extremely rare in Peninsular Spanish (according to Enríquez 1984, 177, it occurs only with 0.015 percent of third person verb forms). Table 4.1 shows the final selection. The most frequent verb forms are predominantly first and third person singular forms; second person plural forms are not among them (the most frequent second person plural form *tenéis* 'have-2PL' occurs only 15 times).[2]

The list of frequent verb forms in table 4.1 contains several occurrences of the grammatical auxiliary *haber* 'have'. Given that the auxiliary *he* does not express lexical contents *per se*, one might argue that the perfect forms should rather be classified according to the main verb (e.g., *he visto* 'I have seen'; see the section on this topic later in the chapter). However, if frequency effects are understood to be caused by mechanical repetition of items in speech rather than by the semantic contents of these items, such effects should occur independently of the semantic contents (cf. Erker and Guy 2012). For this reason, the auxiliary forms are classified on par with the lexical verbs.

ANALYSIS AND RESULTS

The following subsections present the results of the analysis. The findings for each grammatical person are discussed separately.

First Person Singular

Table 4.2 presents the numbers of null and expressed subjects and the pronominal expression rate for each first person singular verb form. The average SPP expression rate among the verb forms included in the analysis is 27 percent, which is very close to the rates reported for first person singular in previous studies on Peninsular Spanish (e.g., 31.89 percent by Enríquez 1984, 348; 31 percent by Cameron 1992, 233). The differences in subject pronoun frequency between the verb forms are statistically significant.[3]

The following subsections analyze the sequences where the first person singular verb forms are found. The analysis is based on a qualitative scrutiny of the verb tokens in their context of occurrence, paying special attention to the pragmatic and/or grammatical functions of the tokens (or the sequences in which they are contained). The

Table 4.1 Frequent verb forms with human subject referents

Verb form	Raw frequency	Proportion of all verb forms
sé know-1SG	247	3 %
he AUX-1SG	167	2 %
vamos go-1PL	128	2 %
ha AUX-3SG	127	2 %
dice say-3SG	127	2 %
digo say-1SG	116	1 %
tengo have-1SG	114	1 %
voy go-1SG	106	1 %
mira look-2SG.IMPERATIVE	94	1 %
es be-3SG	88	1 %
han AUX-3PL	88	1 %
creo think-1SG	88	1 %
tienes have-2SG	88	1 %
tiene have-3SG	84	1 %
oye hear-2SG.IMPERATIVE	83	1 %
sabes know-2SG	72	1 %
estoy be-1SG	68	1 %
hemos AUX-1PL	50	1 %
has AUX-2SG	50	1 %
vas go-2SG	44	1 %
tenemos have-1PL	42	1 %
Total	*2071*	*27 %*

Table 4.2 Subject expression in first person singular

Verb form	Null subjects	Expressed subjects	Total	Subject expressed
voy go-1SG	90	16	106	15%
sé know-1SG	206	41	247	17%
estoy be-1SG	73	15	88	17%
digo say-1SG	93	26	119	22%
he AUX-1SG	112	54	166	33%
tengo have-1SG	74	40	114	35%
creo think-1SG	36	51	87	59%
Total	*611*	*228*	*839*	*27%*

Note: Pearson's chi-squared test: $\chi^2 = 78.881$, df = 6, p < 0.0001 (*****).

tokens *estoy* 'I am,' *voy* 'I go,' and *tengo* 'I have' were not found to occur in any recognizable formulaic sequences in the data. Table 4.3 summarizes the formulaic sequences identified in first person singular.

Table 4.3 Formulaic sequences with 1SG verb forms

	No SPP	With SPP	Total	SPP expression rate
Sequences with sé *'I know'*				
no sé (parenthetical) 'I don't know'	105	1	106	1%
no sé + CLAUSE 'I don't know'	84	8	102	8%
sé + CLAUSE 'I know'	17	7	24	29%
qué sé yo / yo que sé 'how would I know'	0	25	23	100%
Total	*206*	*41*	*255*	*16%*
Note: Pearson's chi-squared test with simulated p-value: $\chi^2 = 151.266$, $p < 0.001$ (***).				
Sequences with digo *'I say'*				
quotative *digo*	51	13	64	20%
pseudo-quotative *digo*	34	10	44	23%
corrective *digo*	7	1	8	14%
other uses	1	1	2	–
Total	*93*	*25*	*118*	*21%*
Note: Pearson's chi-squared test with simulated p-value: $\chi^2 = 1.448$, $p = 0.683$ (not significant).				
Sequences with creo *'I think'*				
creo que 'I think that' + clausal complement	28	46	74	62%
epistemic/evidential parenthetical *creo*	8	5	13	38%
Total	*36*	*51*	*87*	*59%*
Note: Pearson's chi-squared test with Yates' continuity correction: $\chi^2 = 1.677$, df = 1, $p = 0.195$ (not significant).				
Sequences with he *'I have'*				
he visto 'I have seen'	12	15	27	56%
other perfect forms	100	39	139	28%
Total	*112*	*54*	*166*	*33%*
Note: Pearsons chi-squared test with Yates' continuity correction: $\chi^2 = 6.586$, df = 1, $p < 0.05$ (**).				

SÉ 'I KNOW'

The verb form *sé* occurs most often in the parenthetical (i.e., syntactically unattached) epistemic downtowner *no sé* 'I don't know,' nearly always with a null subject (see example 1a). Another frequent use of the verb form is in negative clauses with a clausal complement; in this use as well, SPP expression is rare (see example 1b). Both constructions serve to express that the speaker is not taking full responsibility for the propositional contents or that the information comes from an indirect source.[4]

(1a) *Tengo un amigo que estuvo hace poco en Co ... en Costa Rica, y justo en ese restaurante se encontraron con ... con algún conocido; no ...* ***no sé****, con algún amigo o algo así. Que allí van mucho los europeos, ¿no?*

'[I] have a friend who was some time ago in Costa Rica, and precisely in that restaurant [they] met ... some acquaintance, [I] don't ... **I don't know**, some friend or something like that. The Europeans go there a lot, don't they?'

(1b) *Pues ...* ***no sé que te diga****, macho. Yo creo que estas navidades casi no voy a tener vacaciones.*

'Well, **[I] don't know what to say to you**, pal. I think this Christmas [I]'ll hardly have any vacation at all.'

In addition to subject expression patterns, another characteristic that differentiates *sé* from other first person singular forms is that it occurs most of the time negated (208 occurrences of 247, that is, 84 percent). In negative clauses, the rate of subject expression is only 4 percent (i.e., 9/208), as opposed to 35 percent (9/26) in clauses with positive polarity (see example 2a). In the formulaic sequences *yo qué sé ~ qué sé yo* 'how would I know' (see example 2b) there is no variation in SPP expression: It is always present.[5]

(2a) *Y* ***yo sé*** *lo que es aprender alemán. Y aprender alemán es irte a Alemania ... dos o tres años, vamos, no es ...*

'And **I know** what it means to learn German. And to learn German is to go to Germany ... for two or three years, you see, it's not ...'

(2b) <s1> *¿Y qué va a pasar?*

'And what's going to happen?'

<s2> ***Yo qué sé****. Yo creo que no va a pasar nada.*

'**How would I know**. I think nothing's going to happen.'

In conclusion, SPP expression patterns with the verb form *sé* 'I know' are strongly dependent on the polarity and the pragmatic function of the clause in the Peninsular Spanish data under analysis. Such a connection between polarity and SPP presence is not found with any other verb form in the data (cf. Travis and Torres Cacoullos 2012, 737, 740, on the effects of negative polarity on SPP expression).

DIGO 'I SAY'

All sequences containing the verb form *digo* have a relatively low rate of overt SPP expression; the differences between the categories in table 4.3 are not significant. *Digo* occurs most often in quotative sequences whose function is to mark the following item as constructed dialogue (see Tannen 1989). In this function, the verb form occurs most of the time without SPP and precedes the stretch of constructed dialogue without a complementizer as in example (3).

(3) ***Siempre digo*, *digo*** *"Es que eres igual que mi tío Lorenzo" y como no lo conoce ... dice "Mira, yo no sé tu tío Lorenzo ... ," cuando me meto en plan con él,* ***le digo que es un muermo*, *digo*** *"Igual que mi tío Lorenzo."*

'**[I] always say, [I] say** 'The thing is that [you]'re just like my uncle Lorenzo' and because [he] doesn't know him ... [he] says 'Look, I don't know your uncle Lorenzo ...', when [I] want to pick on him **[I] tell him that he's a crashing bore, [I] say** 'Just like my uncle Lorenzo.''

The quotative *digo* can be considered a grammaticalizing discourse marker that has lost its morphosyntactic productivity. It occurs systematically in the present indicative even when the context is in the past and the quoted sequence is not introduced by the complementizer *que* (Posio 2013, 272). Some speakers in the corpus systematically insert the quotative *digo* before the stretch of constructed dialogue even if the verb *decir* 'say' has already been used to introduce the quoted sequence (see the underlined occurrences of *digo* in example 3). This repetition suggests that *digo* as a quotative marker has, to a certain extent, been lexicalized and is detached from the productive verbal uses of the same form.

The constructions labeled pseudoquotative in table 4.3 differ from actual quotatives in that the speakers do not use them to introduce constructed dialogue but rather to draw the interlocutor's attention to what is being said. In this function, the verb takes a clausal complement introduced by the complementizer *que.* This is the case in example (4) where the whole underlined sequence has a formulaic character.

(4) *¿Tú sabes una cosa que te digo ... ? Es un segundo, mira. Eh ... en un libro, en un libro relacionando el sexo y el deporte ...*

'Do **you know one thing [I] say to you?** Just a second, look. Er ... in a book, in a book relating sex with exercise ...'

The **corrective** use of *digo* occurs, as in example (5), in contexts where the speaker corrects a slip-of-tongue. In this function, the SPP is generally not expressed.

(5) <s1> *¿Y otros modelos?*

'And other models?'

<s2> *Y otros modelos que también haya de tu talla, verás.*

'And other models that we have in your size, [you]'ll see.'

<s1> *No, ese color no me gusta.*

'No, I don't like this color.'

<s2> *¿Larga?,* ***digo****, ¿blanca? Bueno.*

'Long? **[I] mean**, white? Well.'

An exceptional characteristic of the quotative and pseudoquotative *digo,* in comparison with other verb forms, is that they favor subject expression in the postverbal position. In total, 13 of the expressed SPPs (i.e., 52 percent) are postverbal. An example of postverbal *yo* is found in (6).

(6) (The speaker tells about a bus company he has found that offers a trip from Madrid to Vigo for 2,700 pesetas.)

Joe, pues sí … Sí, eso es muy poco. ***Digo yo*** *como no estoy muy bien de dinero, y todo el que tengo … me es poco para lo que voy a hacer …*

'Yeah, that's right. It's very little. **I say**, as [I]'m not very well off, and all the money I have … is too little for what [I] want to do.'

The sequence *digo yo* also has a regular pragmatic function in discourse: It explicitly marks the previously uttered proposition as representing the speaker's personal view as opposed to a commonly accepted opinion or a view shared with the interlocutors (see Posio 2012a, 172). The low expressed SPP rate with *digo* appears to be characteristic of Peninsular Spanish but not necessarily of other varieties. In Orozco's Colombian data (this volume), the verb *decir* actually favors overt SPP expression.

CREO 'I THINK'

Creo 'I think' is the verb form with the highest SPP expression rate in the data. This form has been found to strongly favor SPP expression in other studies on different varieties of Spanish (e.g., Travis and Torres Cacoullos 2012, Erker and Guy 2012, Aijón Oliva and Serrano 2010; Posio, 2014; Orozco, this volume). Although cognitive verbs are more likely to occur in switch reference contexts than other verbs and the SPP expression rate is sensitive to same/switch reference, they maintain a significantly higher rate of expressed SPPs even in same reference contexts (Travis and Torres Cacoullos 2012, 735).

The form *creo* occurs in two kinds of contexts in the data: as a complement-taking mental predicate followed by a clausal complement (ex. 7a), and as an epistemic/evidential parenthetical that can occur at different positions in the utterance (ex. 7b). Although the two uses differ with regard to SPP expression rate, the difference is not statistically significant.

(7a) (speaking about the size of beverages in Mexico, compared to Spain)

<s1> *Pero te ponen … las cervezas, tío, son de … de 35 … centilitros. Y … y las coca-colas y … todo son … son también.*

'But [they] give you … the beers, pal, are 35 centilitres. And … and Cokes and … everything, they as well.'

<s2> *Es que* ***yo creo*** *que en todos sitios las coca-colas son grandes.*

'It's that **I think** that in all places Cokes are big.'

(7b) <s1> *Tere, y si te acuerdas tráeme … un libro que tienes mío,* ***creo****, de Italo Calvino.*

'Tere, and if you remember bring me … a book of mine that [you] have, **[I] think**, by Italo Calvino.'

<s2> *Tengo dos libros.* […] *Uno de cuentos … Ah, el de "Los amores difíciles,"* ***creo****, y el otro no me acuerdo.*

'[I] have two books. One with short stories … the one called 'Difficult Loves', **[I] think**, and the other one [I] don't remember.'

The high expression rate of the pronoun *yo* clearly sets *creo* apart from other frequently occurring verb forms. In fact, the sequence (*yo*) *creo que* resembles in many ways the English expression *I think* that has grammaticalized from a complement-taking mental predicate into an epistemic parenthetical (Thompson and Mulac 1991;

Aijmer 1996; Van Bogaert 2011; Posio 2011, 785; 2014). The high rate of expressed SPPs can be regarded as evidence of internal fixation of the sequence.

Aijón Oliva and Serrano (2010) suggest that the sequences *creo* and *yo creo* are in fact functionally differentiated. They argue that *yo creo* is related to the expression of subjective or argumentative contents, whereas *creo* without the SPP would convey objective or epistemic meanings (cf. Davidson 1996). Although the distinction is not easy to operationalize for the purposes of a quantitative analysis, it is supported by the qualitative examination of individual examples. For instance, in (7a) the speaker has personal experience with the size of beverages in Mexico and thus presents his opinion about a fact that he is certain about, using *yo creo*. In (7b), on the other hand, the speaker is not sure about the information and mitigates his position by the use of *creo*. Using the mitigating *creo* in a possibly face-threatening context (as in the first line of (7b), where the first speaker asks the second one to return a book she has borrowed) may also be considered a politeness strategy (Stewart 2003).

HE 'I HAVE'

The perfect auxiliary *he* has a relatively high overall rate of subject expression. However, a closer look at the occurrences reveals that this is caused by the high SPP expression rate with the most frequent perfect form in the data, that is, *he visto* 'I have seen'. This sequence occurs 27 times, 15 times with an expressed subject pronoun (i.e., 56 percent).[6] Example (8) illustrates a typical context of occurrence of the sequence *he visto* to indicate the source of knowledge.[7]

(8) (Two female friends are talking on the phone about the tennis skills of an acquaintance.)

<s1> *¿Ves? Dice "¡Idiota!," y le dice Alberto, "Idiota, ¿por qué se lo dices?" Dice "Ya no quiere jugar conmigo." Digo, "No, ya no quiero jugar contigo, porque juegas muy bien"* <laughs>

'[You] see? [He] says '[You] idiot!', and Alberto says to him, '[You] idiot, why do you say that to her?' [He] says, '[He] doesn't want to play with me anymore.' [I] say, 'No, [I] don't want to play with you anymore because [you] play very well.' <laughs>

<s2> *Y ... ¿efectivamente juega bien?*

'And ... [he] really plays well?'

<s1> *Y efectivamente juega bien.* ***Le he visto ... yo****, cuando han estado jugando ellos en la pista de abajo, y bueno, vamos, me manda a mí una pelota y tardo un año en cogerla.*

'And [he] really plays well. **I ... have seen him**, when [they] were playing in the lower court, and well, I mean, [he] sends me a ball that takes me a year to catch.'

The perfect tense in general refers to past actions that are somehow relevant at the time of speech and its use is therefore a cross-linguistically common strategy for the expression of non-first-hand evidentiality (Aikhenvald 2004, 112). However, in the data under survey, the sequence *yo he visto* rather indicates that the speaker does have first-hand evidence of the event. In this context, the presence of *yo* typically indicates strong speaker commitment to what is being said, as is the case with *yo creo* 'I think'.

Second Person Singular

The second person singular is characterized by a high presence of verb forms whose pragmatic function is to call for the interlocutor's attention: The imperatives *oye* 'listen', *mira* 'look', and, to a certain extent, *sabes* 'you know' serve this function. Table 4.4 shows the rates of different verb forms with null and expressed subjects.

Table 4.4 Subject expression in second person singular

Verb form	No SPP	With SPP	Total	SPP expression rate
oye hear-2SG.IMPERATIVE	83	0	83	0%
mira look-2SG.IMPERATIVE	93	1	94	1%
vas go-2SG	39	4	43	9%
tienes have-2SG	75	13	88	15%
has aux-2SG	39	10	51	20%
sabes know-2SG	53	18	71	25%
Total	*382*	*46*	*430*	*11%*

Note: Pearson's chi-squared test: $\chi^2 = 41.318$, df = 5, $p < 0.0001$ (*****). Pearson's chi-squared test excluding the imperatives *mira* and *oye*: $\chi^2 = 5.634$, df = 3, $p = 0.131$ (not significant).

The average SPP expression rate in second person singular is 11 percent if the imperative forms *oye* 'hear' and *mira* 'look' are included; without them, the rate increases to 18 percent and no significant differences emerge between the forms. Enríquez (1984, 348) and Cameron (1992, 233) report higher SPP expression rates for second person singular (25–26 percent). Apart from the imperatives, the only token that occurred in formulaic sequences is *sabes*. *Vas* 'you go' and *tienes, has* 'you have' are not attested in recognizable formulaic sequences in the data.

Mira 'Look', *Oye* 'Listen'

As can be observed in table 4.5, the differences in subject expression rates between second person singular verb forms are only significant if the imperative forms *mira* 'look' and *oye* 'listen'—with a subject expression rate close to zero—are included. The expression of subject pronouns is not ungrammatical in the imperative but it seems to pertain to certain fixed constructions (e.g., *fíjate tú*, that is, 'pay attention'). The two most frequent imperative forms *mira* and *oye*, however, are nearly always without a subject pronoun in the data.

Sabes 'You know'

The verb form *sabes* 'you know' occurs typically in interrogative contexts, either in rhetorical interrogative clauses (ex. 9a) or as a syntactically unattached discourse particle uttered with a rising intonation (ex. 9b).[8] The third most frequent context is the sequence *ya sabes* 'you already know', exemplified by (9c).

(9a) (Talking about exchange students coming to Spain)

*¡Ah! ¿**sabes** lo que viene ahora? Americanos. A la facultad.*

'Oh, **[you] know** what's coming now? Americans. To the faculty.'

Table 4.5 Formulaic sequences with 2SG verb forms

Constructions with *sabes* 'you know'	No SPP	With SPP	Total	SPP expression rate
interrogative clauses	17	12	29	41%
interrogative particle *¿sabes?*	23	6	29	21%
ya sabes 'you already know'	12	0	12	0%
'you can' + INF	1	0	1	–
Totals	*53*	*18*	*71*	*25%*

Note: Pearson's chi-squared test with simulated p-value: $\chi^2 = 8.685$, $p < 0.05$ (**).

(9b) (Explaining the contents of a new job)

Y luego hace … informes … Eh … tarea de … contacto con el usuario, o de … mantenimiento … no sé … ***¿sabes?***

'And then [she] does … reports. Er … task of … contact with the user, or … maintenance, [I] don't know. **[You] know?**

(9c) (Two research assistants talking about the possibility of using funds to buy books)

Y si pides presupuesto a Inés y te los compra, pues ***ya sabes****, me los pasas.*

'And if [you] ask Inés for a budget and [she] buys them for you, **well [you] know already**, [you] lend them to me.'

In Erker and Guy's (2012, 539) data from speakers of Mexican and Dominican origin, the verb form *sabes* 'you know' has an extremely high rate of subject pronoun usage (92 percent). Assuming that *sabes* is used for similar purposes in those varieties and Peninsular Spanish, it is difficult to suggest a functional explanation of the difference in subject expression rates. Rather, it seems that *tú sabes* 'you know' has reached formulaic status in the Latin American varieties represented by Erker and Guy's (2012) data whereas in the Peninsular data under survey the interrogative *sabes* occurs more often without SPP (see also Orozco, this volume).[9]

First Person Plural

SPP expression in first person plural is scarce, and no significant differences emerge between the three verb forms examined here (see table 4.6).

Table 4.6 Subject expression in first person plural

Verb form	Null subjects	Expressed subjects	Total	Subject expressed
vamos go-1PL	127	1	128	0%
hemos aux-1PL	55	1	56	0%
tenemos have-1PL	39	3	42	10%
Total	*221*	*5*	*226*	*0%*

Note: Pearson's chi-squared test: $\chi^2 = 5.978$, df = 4, p = 0.201 (not significant).

Previous studies including all verb forms found in the data have reported SPP expression rates ranging from 4.5 percent (Posio 2012b, 344) to 10.4 percent (Enríquez 1984, 384) or even 16.7 percent (Serrano 2011, 95). Thus it seems that the most frequent tokens *vamos, hemos,* and *tenemos* are even more likely to occur without SPPs than the other first person plural forms. However, the only first person plural form occurring in formulaic sequences in the data is *vamos* '[we] go' (table 4.7).

Table 4.7 Formulaic sequences with 1PL verb forms

Sequences with *vamos* 'we go'	**No SPP**	**With SPP**	**Total**	**SPP expression rate**
vamos used as a discourse particle	44	0	44	0%
future auxiliary	36	1	37	0%
vamos a ver 'let's see'	24	0	24	0%
'we go' + LOCATION	18	0	18	0%
'we speak about' + TOPIC	5	0	5	0%
Total	*127*	*1*	*128*	*0%*

Note: Pearson's chi-squared test with simulated p-value: $\chi^2 = 2.479$, $p = 0.648$ (not significant).

The form *vamos*, with only one expressed subject pronoun, occurs in five different types of constructions in the data. In two constructions, the presence of *nosotros* seems strictly impossible: the discourse-particle use as in (10a) and the expression *vamos a ver* 'let's see', found in (10b).

(10a) (Talking about a motorcycle helmet belonging to a common friend.)

<s1> *¿El Shoei ese que tenía?*

'The Shoei that he had?'

<s2> *¿Eh?*

'Huh?'

<s1> *Ese que tenía marca Shoei.*

'The one that [he] had whose make was Shoei.'

<s2> *No sé qué marca, pero* ***vamos****, era, era de puta madre.*

'[I] don't know which make it was, but **come on**, it was, it was really cool.'

(10b) (A dinnertime discussion between the members of a family; the 23-year-old daughter expresses her disagreement with the perspective of getting married, suggested by her parents.)

Pero ***vamos a ver****. No, pero es que no entiendo eso qué tiene que ver.* ***Vamos a ver.*** *Yo es que … nunca te he oído a decir: "Yo quiero que este chico se case y deje ya de estudiar tanto* […]"

'But **let's see**. No, but it's that [I] don't understand what it has to do with it. **Let's see.** I just … I've never heard you say 'I want that guy to marry and stop studying so much …'

The two uses of *vamos* exemplified by (10a) and (10b) can be considered as grammaticalized discourse particles. They do not permit morphosyntactic variation such as the presence of subject pronoun or tense-mood-aspect variation. Functionally, they invite the hearer to co-construct an interpretation on the basis of what is being or has been said. Inserting the SPP *nosotros* would cancel these functions and trigger the lexical meaning of the verb. Interestingly enough, while the use of *vamos* as a discourse particle is common in Peninsular Spanish, according to Cameron (1997, 34–35) it does not occur in Puerto Rican data.

Another frequent use of the form *vamos* is in constructions with a cohortative function, that is, encouraging the interlocutors to engage a joint action (Posio 2012b, 352, De Cock 2011, 2770). This is the case in most of the clauses where *vamos* occurs as a future auxiliary or with a locative complement; both uses are exemplified by (11a). The form *vamos* occurs also in the cohortative function in nominal contexts, as in example (11b) where it is followed by the NP *un aplauso* 'an applause'.

(11a) ***Vamos a ponernos*** *en un sitio más* [...] *accesible.* [...] ***Vamos a otra mesa*** ... *que se vea mejor la puesta de sol.*

'**Let's move** to a more ... accessible place. ... **Let's go to another table** ... where we could see the sunset better.'

(11b) *¿No ven los niños qué quietos han estado, qué buenos? ¡**Vamos**, **chicos**, un aplauso!*

'Don't you see how quiet the children have been, how good? **Let's go kids**, applause!'

In conclusion, the form *vamos* occurs typically in contexts where it encourages the interlocutors to participate in a joint action, such as constructing a new interpretation of what is being said (example 10) or engaging in a non-linguistic action (example 11). The expression of the SPP *nosotros* is extremely rare in all of these uses, as it is in the hearer-inclusive uses of the first person plural in general (Serrano 2011, 101; Posio 2012a, 347). It is possible that the pronoun *nosotros*—a result of the univerbation of the old personal pronoun *nos* with the emphatic word *otros* 'others' (see Eberenz 2000)—is sensed by the speakers as more restrictive and contrastive than other SPPs. This interpretation is supported by the rarity of its use as well as its strong tendency to occur with a hearer-exclusive referential reading (Posio 2012a).

Third Person Singular and Plural

Third person verb forms have low SPP expression rates—ranging from 2 percent to 11 percent—in comparison with first and second person singular. This is close to the average rate of 8 percent reported by Cameron (1992, 233) for SPP expression in the third person in Madrid Spanish; Enríquez (1984, 348) reports considerably higher rates (13.34 percent in 3SG and 14.12 percent in 3PL). However, the amount of all expressed subjects (i.e., noun phrases, proper names, interrogative and relative pronouns) is high compared to other persons.[10] The form *dice* 's/he says' is an exception, as it has a low rate of expressed pronominal and non-pronominal subjects (see table 4.8).

The only third person form that occurs in formulaic sequences in the data is *dice* 's/he says' (see table 4.9).

Similarly to the first person singular form *digo*, most of the occurrences of *dice* are in quotative constructions preceding constructed dialogue, either with no expressed subject (ex. 12a) or with a postverbal NP subject (ex. 12b). The complementizer con-

Table 4.8 Subject expression in third person

Verb form	Null subject	With SPP	With other subject (NPs, proper names, relative and indefinite pronouns)	Total	Rate of SPP expression	Rate of subject expression
dice say-3SG	105	5	17	127	4%	16%
ha AUX-3SG	64	4	59	127	3%	50%
es be-3SG	48	2	38	88	4%	45%
tiene have-3SG	36	9	39	84	11%	57%
han AUX-3PL	70	8	10	88	9%	20%
Total	*323*	*29*	*152*	*504*	*6%*	*36%*

Note: Pearson's chi-squared test with simulated p-value: $\chi^2 = 74.139$, $p < 0.001$ (***).

Table 4.9 Formulaic sequences with third person verb forms

Sequence with *dice* 's/he says'	Null subject	With SPP	With other subject	Total	SPP expression rate	Subject expression rate
quotative (*dice*)	72	1	17	90	1%	19%
dice que '(s)he says that'	20	0	0	20	0%	0%
other	13	4	0	17	24%	24%
Total	*105*	*5*	*17*	*127*	*4%*	*16%*

Note: Pearson's chi-squared test with simulated p-value: $\chi^2 = 27.061$, $p < 0.001$ (***).

structions differ from the quotative ones in that they introduce a paraphrase of what the other speaker has said rather than constructed dialogue (ex. 12c).

(12a) (The speaker is telling about a visit to a tailor's shop to buy a wedding suit for her fiancé, involving a rendering of the dialogue with the salesclerk.)

No sé si dijo "un traje de novio, un chaqué" y tal, y ***dice*** *"bueno y ... ¿cuándo se casa?" ... Y* ***dice Andrés*** *"el 14 de junio."* [...]. ***Dice*** *"¿cuándo ... ?"* ***dice*** *"Bueno, pues yo creo que a finales de mayo, y si no ... pues en junio,"* ***dice****, "pero llámeme."*

'[I] don't know if [he] said 'a wedding suit, a jacket' and so on, and [he] says 'well, and… when are you getting married'… and **Andrés says** 'the 14th of June'. [...] [**He**] **says** 'when?' **he says** 'well, I think that at the end of May and if not, then ... in June', [**he**] **says**, 'but call me.'

(12b) *Y ésta me* ***dice****, me* ***dice la Carmen****,* ***dice*** *"pues hija, no sé qué decirte."*

'And this one **says** to me, **Carmen says** to me, [**she**] **says** 'well girl, [I] don't know what to say to you."

(12c) (The speaker is telling about a car crash that he was involved in.)

> *... era un cruce de semáforos* [...] ***dice que*** *yo me lo salté y yo digo que él se lo saltó.*
>
> 'It was a crossroads with lights ... **[he] says that** I ran them and I say that he ran them.'

Note that in example (12a), once the participants in the constructed dialogue have been mentioned, their turns are marked by *dice* without explicit subjects. Similarly to the first person singular form *digo*, *dice* occurs as the present indicative form independently of the context being in the past. Another particularity of this verb form is that expressed subjects are postposed more often than not: In fact, all non-SPP subjects of quotative constructions occur in the postverbal position in the data. A possible functional explanation to this is that the postposition reduces the prominence of the subject while focusing more attention on the stretch of constructed dialogue (Posio 2011a, 171). However, since the postverbal placement is so common in this particular function, it can be considered an idiosyncratic property of the formulaic sequence rather than resulting from a productive choice made by the speaker.

CONCLUSIONS

The initial hypothesis of the study was that the most frequently occurring verb tokens present a tendency to occur in formulaic, prefabricated sequences and those sequences exhibit subject pronoun usage that deviates from the general tendencies. The examination of the most frequently occurring verb forms in a corpus of spoken Peninsular Spanish reveals that formulaicity indeed plays a role in accounting for the variable expression of SPPs, but not all frequently occurring verbs behave similarly. The most frequent verb tokens belong to either grammatical auxiliaries (e.g., *haber, ir*), copulas (e.g., *ser, estar*), or lexical verbs that are used for various discourse-pragmatic functions. In the data examined, only the verbs pertaining to the last category exhibit recognizable formulaic sequences where the presence and placement of the subject pronoun follow local, construction-specific patterns. These verb forms can be classified into epistemic/evidential markers (e.g., *no sé, creo, yo creo, yo he visto, digo yo*), quotative markers (e.g., *digo, dice, dice* + NP), attention-seeking markers (e.g., *mira, oye, ¿sabes?*) and interpersonal markers (e.g., *vamos, vamos a ver, vamos* + infinitive/NP). All of them exhibit local patterns of SPP expression and placement.

Given that the verb forms occurring in the above-mentioned sequences are among the most frequent ones in spoken discourse, accounting for the SPP usage in them is not a trivial task. Crucially, examining both the formulaic and productive SPP uses brings us closer to understanding the role of SPPs in discourse. The qualitative analysis focusing on the discourse-pragmatic functions of different verb forms suggests that frequency of use may not only amplify the effect of general constraints on SPP expression—as shown by Erker and Guy (2012)—but also permits the emergence of local patterns of SPP expression. This eventually leads to the development of formulaic sequences or particles deriving from verb forms used either with or without expressed subjects.

Although it may be futile to search for a uniform function of SPP expression or omission in all contexts, in the case of formulaic sequences we can speak of strong tendencies related with SPP expression. However, in most cases there is variation within the constructions, indicating different levels of fixedness. For instance, the uses of *vamos* discussed above categorically reject overt SPP expression while the uses of *creo* discussed above present variation between SPP expression and omission that may be functionally motivated. Given the lack of previous comparative studies focusing on different varieties of Spanish within the same research perspective, it is not clear to what extent these tendencies are common to all varieties of Spanish. Some of the formulaic sequences analyzed present significant differences between dialects, such as *sabes* 'you know' (see Erker and Guy 2012; Orozco, this volume). As the varieties of Spanish are also known to have different overall rates of SPP expression, future cross-dialectal studies are needed to find out to what extent the formulaic sequences differ between the varieties and what their contribution is to interdialectal differences in SPP usage.

CORPORA

COREC = Marcos-Marín, Francisco (1992): *Corpus oral de referencia del español contemporáneo*. Universidad Autónoma de Madrid. Available at http://www.lllf.uam.es/~fmarcos/index.html. Accessed on 1 November 2007.

Davies, Mark. (2002) "*Corpus del Español* (100 million words, 1200s–1900s)." Available at www.corpusdelespanol.org. Accessed on 5 February 2012.

NOTES

1. Eventual differences in SPP expression between the data coming from these two situation types are not within the scope of the present chapter.
2. This may be in part due to the type of data included in the corpus, as in most of the conversations there are only two participants and thus little need for 2PL verb forms. However, other studies on Peninsular Spanish discourse have also registered low frequencies of 2PL verbs (e.g., Vázquez Rozas and García-Miguel 2006).
3. The Pearson's chi-squared test in R was used to calculate the statistical significance of all tables, using Yates' continuity correction in four-cell tables and simulated p-value (based on 2000 repetitions) in tables with low cell values. The p-values are rated as follows: $p > 0.05$ (not significant), $p \leq 0.05$ (*), $p \leq 0.01$ (**), $p \leq 0.001$ (***), $p \leq 0.0001$ (*****). Note that in tables comparing different constructions with the same verb token, a p-value above the 0.05 limit means only that the constructions do not differ significantly from each other with regard to SPP expression, not that there would be no significant difference between the verb token in question and other tokens.
4. In (1b), the whole expression *no sé qué te diga* 'I don't know what to say to you' is a formulaic sequence, according to the dictionary of the Real Academia used "to indicate mistrust or uncertainty of what is being said to someone" (RAE 2001:2001).
5. A reviewer notes that sequences presenting no variation in SPP usage should not be analyzed on a par with variable contexts. While sequences such as *que sé yo* would not enter the 'envelope of variation' in a variationist study, in the present theoretical perspective there is no reason to exclude non-variable contexts from the analysis. Rather, lack of variability is seen as one end of the continuum between fully variable and non-variable contexts. The existence of non-variable sequences with some of the most frequently used verb tokens presents evidence of a high degree of entrenchment.
6. In order to check whether the high frequency of *he visto* and its high rate of expression are just a particularity of the data under survey, I confirmed the result by ana-

lyzing the occurrences of first person singular perfects in *Corpus del Español* (Davies 2002). In the 1900s data of the *Corpus del Español*, *he visto* is the most frequent first person singular perfect form, occurring 675 times when the total number of first person singular perfects is 7,090. The part of the corpus containing spoken Peninsular Spanish has 128 occurrences of *he visto:* 72 (i.e., 56 percent) have the subject pronoun *yo* expressed. These results thus echo the ones obtained with the present selection of data.

7. Note that example (9) also contains quotative uses of *digo* and *dice* in the first turn and an occurrence of *vamos* in the last turn (see the sections on First Person Singular and First Person Plural).
8. Indicated by question marks in the COREC transcription.
9. However, note that Lastra and Butragueño (this volume) observe that interrogative clauses in general favor non-expressed SPPs.
10. This is to be expected, given that third person referents are not necessarily present in the communicative situation and therefore require the use of more informative referring expressions than first and second person referents.

REFERENCES

Aijmer, Karin. 1996. "*I think*: An English modal particle." In *Modality in Germanic Languages - Historical and Comparative Perspectives,* edited by Toril Swan and Olaf Jansen Westvik, 1–47. Berlin: Mouton de Gruyter.

Aijón Oliva, Miguel Ángel, and María José Serrano. 2010. "El hablante en su discurso: expresión y omisión del sujeto de *creo*." *Oralia* 13:7–38.

Aikhenvald, Alexandra Y. 2004. *Evidentiality.* Oxford University Press.

Butler, Christopher S. 1997. "Repeated word combinations in spoken and written texts: some implications for functional grammar." In *A Fund of Ideas: Recent Developments in Functional Grammar,* edited by Christopher S. Butler, J.H. Connolly, R.A. Gatward and R.M. Vismans, 60–77. Amsterdam: IFOTT.

———. 2005. "Formulaic language. An overview with particular reference to the cross-linguistic perspective." In *The Dynamics of Language Use. Functional and Contrastive Perspectives,* edited by Cristopher S. Butler, María de los Ángeles Gómez González, and Susana M. Doval Suárez, 221–242. Amsterdam/Philadelphia: John Benjamins.

Bybee, Joan. 2010. *Language, Usage and Cognition.* Cambridge: Cambridge University Press.

Bybee, Joan, and Sandra A. Thompson. 1997. "Three frequency effects in syntax." *Berkeley Linguistics Society* 23:378–388.

Cameron, Richard. 1992. "Pronominal and null subject variation in Spanish: Constraints, dialects, and functional compensation." PhD diss., University of Pennsylvania at Philadelphia.

———. 1997. "Accessibility theory in a variable syntax of Spanish." *Journal of Pragmatics* 28:29–67.

Davidson, Brad. 1996. "'Pragmatic weight' and Spanish subject pronouns: The pragmatic and discourse uses of '*tú*' and '*yo*' in spoken Madrid Spanish." *Journal of Pragmatics* 26(4):543–565.

De Cock, Barbara. 2011. "Why *we* can be *you*: The use of 1st person plural forms with hearer reference in English and Spanish." *Journal of Pragmatics* 43(11):2762–2775.

Eberenz, Rolf. 2000. *El español en el otoño de la edad media. Sobre el artículo y los pronombres*. Gredos, Madrid.

Ellis, Nick. 2003. "Constructions, chunking, and connectionism: The emergence of second language structure." In *Handbook of Second Language Acquisition,* edited by Catherine J. Doughty and Michael E. Long, 62–103. Oxford: Blackwell.

Enríquez, Emilia V. 1984. *El pronombre personal sujeto en la lengua española hablada en Madrid.* Madrid: Instituto Miguel de Cervantes.

Erker, Daniel, and Gregory Guy. 2012. "The role of lexical frequency in syntactic variability: Variable subject personal pronoun expression in Spanish." *Language* 88(3):526–557.

Erman, Britt, and Beatrice Warren. 2000. "The idiom principle and the open choice principle." *Text* 20:29–62.

Fernández Soriano, Olga. 1999. "El pronombre personal. Formas y distribuciones. Pronombres átonos y tónicos." In *Gramática descriptiva de la lengua española. Volumen 1: Sintaxis básica de las clases de palabras*, edited by Ignacio Bosque and Violeta Demonte, 1209–1273. Madrid: Espasa Calpe.

Hopper, Paul J. 1987. "Emergent grammar." *Berkeley Linguistics Society* 13:139–57.

Morales, Amparo. 1997. "La hipótesis funcional y la aparición de sujeto no nominal: el español de Puerto Rico." *Hispania* 80(1):153–165.

Otheguy, Ricardo, Ana Celia Zentella, and David Livert. 2007. "Language and dialect contact in Spanish in New York: Toward the formation of a speech community." *Language* 83(4):770–802.

Posio, Pekka. 2011. "Spanish subject pronoun usage and verb semantics revisited: First and second person singular subject pronouns and focusing of attention in spoken Peninsular Spanish." *Journal of Pragmatics* 43(3):777–798.

———. 2012a. "The functions of postverbal pronominal subjects in spoken Peninsular Spanish and European Portuguese." *Studies in Hispanic and Lusophone Linguistics* 5(1):149–190.

———. 2012b. "Who are 'we' in spoken Peninsular Spanish and European Portuguese? Expression and reference of first person plural subject pronouns." *Language Sciences* 34(3):339–360

———. 2012c. "Subject pronouns in Peninsular Spanish and European Portuguese: Semantics, pragmatics, and formulaic sequences." PhD diss., University of Helsinki.

———. 2013. "Expression of first person singular subjects in spoken Peninsular Spanish and European Portuguese: Semantic roles and formulaic sequences." *Folia Linguistica* 47(1):253–292.

———. 2014. "Subject expression in grammaticalizing constructions: The case of *creo* and *acho* 'I think' in Spanish and Portuguese." *Journal of Pragmatics*. 63:5–18.

Real Academia Española. 2001. *Diccionario de la lengua española. Vigésima segunda edición*. Madrid: Real Academia Española.

Serrano, María José. 2011. "'Otras personas y yo': Variación socioestilística de la expresión/omisión del sujeto pronominal nosotros en las conversaciones espontáneas." In *Variación Variable*, edited by María José Serrano, 93–126. Almería: Círculo Rojo; Ministerio de Ciencia e Innovación.

Silveira, Agripino de Souza, 2011. "Subject expression in Brazilian Portuguese: Construction and frequency effects." Unpublished PhD diss., University of New Mexico.

Stewart, Miranda. 2003. "'Pragmatic weight' and face: Pronominal presence and the case of Spanish second person singular subject pronoun *tú*." *Journal of Pragmatics* 35(2):191–206.

Tannen, Deborah. 1989. *Talking voices: Repetition, dialogue, and imagery in conversational discourse*. Cambridge: Cambridge University Press.

Thompson, Sandra, and Anthony Mulac. 1991. "A quantitative perspective on the grammaticalization of epistemic parentheticals in English." In *Approaches to Grammaticalization*, edited by Elizabeth Closs Traugott and Bernd Heine, 313–339. Amsterdam: John Benjamins.

Travis, Catherine, and Agripino Silveira. 2009. "The role of frequency in first-person plural variation in Brazilian Portuguese: *Nós* vs. *a gente*." *Studies in Hispanic and Lusophone Linguistics* 2(2):347–376.

Travis, Catherine, and Rena Torres Cacoullos. 2012. "What do subject pronouns do in discourse? Cognitive, mechanical and constructional factors in variation." *Cognitive Linguistics* 23(4):711–748.

Van Bogaert, Julie. 2011. "*I think* and other complement-taking mental predicates: A case of and for constructional grammaticalization." *Linguistics* 49(2):295–332.

Vázquez Rozas, Victoria, and José María García-Miguel. 2006. "Transitividad, subjetividad y frecuencia de uso en español." In *Actes del VII Congrès de Lingüística General*, 1–20. Barcelona: Universidad de Barcelona. Retrieved from http://webs.uvigo.es/weba575/jmgm/public/VazquezRozas-GarciaMiguel_CLG7.pdf.

Wray, Alice. 2002. *Formulaic Language and the Lexicon*. Cambridge: Cambridge University Press.

PART II

Subject Pronoun Expression in Spanish in Contact with Other Languages

5

Foundations for the Study of Subject Pronoun Expression in Spanish in Contact with English

Assessing Interlinguistic (Dis)similarity via Intralinguistic Variability

Rena Torres Cacoullos and Catherine E. Travis

Subject expression has been considered a paradigmatic case for grammatical convergence in studies of US Spanish, as bilinguals are thought to associate Spanish and English subject pronouns. The overwhelming preference for expressed subjects in English is thus predicted to boost the rate of expressed subjects in contact-Spanish varieties. But is Spanish subject expression an appropriate linguistic variable to ascertain convergence? A "prerequisite" to analyzing contact-induced change, as Weinreich (1968, 2) stressed, is that "the differences and similarities between the languages in contact [...] be exhaustively stated." In this chapter, we offer such a statement of interlinguistic grammatical comparability, by probing the conditioning of Spanish and English first person singular (1sg) subject expression.

A statement of Spanish–English (dis)similarity must distinguish cross-linguistically valid patterns from particular ones pertaining to the language pair. Subject expression patterns are said to be shaped cross-linguistically by cognitive factors, such as discourse cohesion and activation or accessibility (Ariel 1988, 79; Givón 1983; Levinson 1987, 384), alongside more interactional or pragmatic factors, related to the kind of action the utterance performs (Fox 1987; Oh 2005; Ono and Thompson 2003, inter alia). Quantitative analyses have confirmed accessibility effects (e.g., Nagy et al. 2011; Paredes Silva 1993), and have also revealed the mechanical factor of priming, or the perseveration of the same syntactic structure across utterances (Cameron and Flores-Ferrán 2003, 50–54; Travis 2007, 120–121), as well as a role for frequent lexically particular constructions (Travis and Torres Cacoullos 2012, 738–741; cf. Erker and Guy 2012).

We focus this first comparison of Spanish and English subject expression on 1sg because it has yet to be empirically shown that subject pronouns constitute a single category; third person, for example, has different information status from first and second person, and first person, as a reference to the speaker, has also had attributed to it particular pragmatic functions.

We begin by motivating the value of intralinguistic variation patterns for establishing interlinguistic grammatical (dis)similarity. We then review the results for Spanish *yo* expression, specifically, the effect of cognition verbs (which we show is a construction effect); of subject continuity (which we reconfigure as Human Switched Reference, an accessibility effect); and of priming (which modulates subject continuity). Finally, we consider these same effects for English *I* expression, identifying similarities and differences which provide a basis for testing for convergence in contact varieties.

LINGUISTIC CONDITIONING AS A CHARACTERIZATION OF THE GRAMMAR OF SUBJECT EXPRESSION

The Uninformativeness of Overall Rate Comparisons

Figure 5.1 shows rates of 1sg subject expression in Spanish across a range of studies as well as in English. This figure confirms that, at over 95 percent, the rate of English *I* (versus an unexpressed 1sg subject), in the right-most bar, is approximately two to four times greater than the rate of Spanish *yo*, in the bars to the left. The near-categorical rate of subject expression in English has been the basis of the prediction that US Spanish varieties will evince higher rates of subject expression than non-contact varieties. Yet we observe here that reported rates of Spanish 1sg subject expression also have a wide range from about 25 percent to 50 percent. A difference in rate of use between contact and non-contact varieties of Spanish, alone, then, is insufficient to claim influence from English, as the threshold for qualifying as a 'high(er)' rate remains unknown: Statistically significant rate differences need not translate into grammatically relevant differences. Subject expression frequency differences in and of themselves do not permit an inference of change in progress (as Cameron 1994, 24, n. 6 cautions).

Indeed, despite differences in overall rate, variable subject expression in Spanish displays widely replicated uniformity in *linguistic conditioning*, both across dialects (e.g., Cameron 1993, 1994) and genres (Travis 2007). Numerous reports on Spanish subject expression, including those in this volume, have arrived at homologous multivariate models of contextual effects on speakers' use of expressed versus unexpressed subject pronouns in both contact and non-contact varieties (see Silva-Corvalán [2001, 154–169] for a review and Otheguy and Zentella [2012] for a recent, detailed treatment). By the criterion of linguistic conditioning, then, the grammar is the same across Spanish varieties.

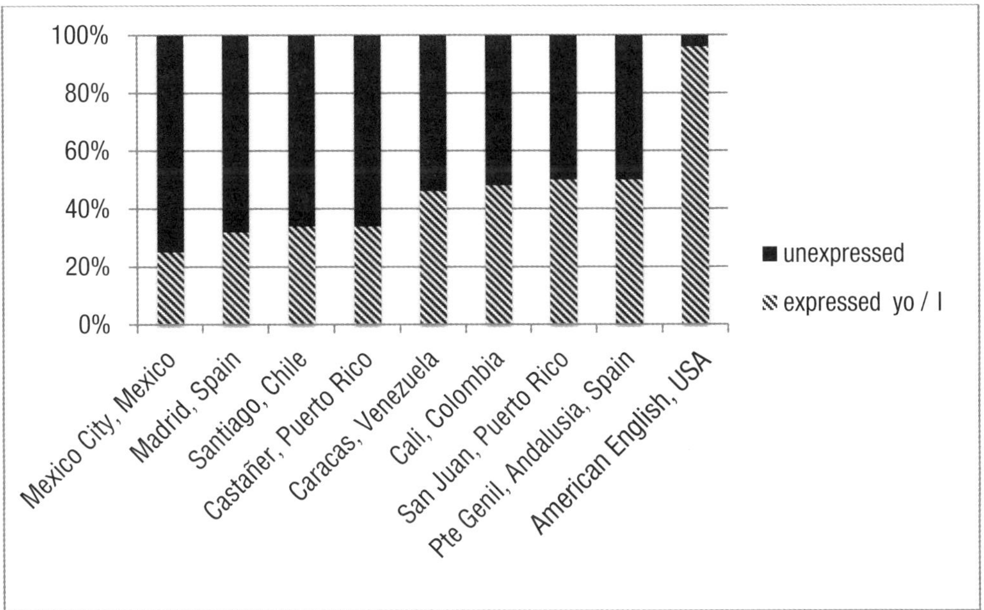

Figure 5.1 Comparison of overall rates of occurrence of 1sg subject pronoun: Spanish *yo** and English *I*
*Source:*Mexico City (N=234) Lastra & Butragueño, this volume; Madrid, Spain (N=10,185) (Enríquez 1984) and Santiago, Chile (N=2,238) (Cifuentes 1980–1981), as reported in Silva Corvalán (1994, 153); Castañer, Puerto Rico (N=1,527) (Holmquist 2012, 211); Caracas, Venezuela (N=721) (Bentivoglio 1987, 36); Cali, Colombia (N=878) (Travis 2007, 113); San Juan, Puerto Rico (N=949) (Cameron 1992, 233); Puente Genil, Andalusia, Spain (N=307) (Ranson 1991, 135, 138); American English, USA (Travis and Torres Cacoullos 2014, 22).

What has yet to be discovered, however, is whether Spanish grammar is similar to the grammar of English in regard to subject expression. That is, it is unknown whether in the rare instances when *I* is left unexpressed in English, the conditioning factors coincide with, or differ from, those that are operative in Spanish. It is only once this has been established that a true test of convergence can be conducted, and it can be determined whether the contact variety evinces English-specific properties, with (non-) expression rates that are higher (or lower) in the same *linguistic subcontexts* as they are in English.

Variationist Comparative Method for Establishing Grammatical (Dis)similarity

A thorough empirical statement of grammatical (dis)similarity is obtained from comparisons of the linguistic conditioning of variant choice. (On the variationist comparative method, see Poplack and Levey 2010; Poplack and Meechan 1998; Torres Cacoullos and Travis, to appear). Our premise is the following:

> In discourse, interlinguistic similarity is assessed via intralinguistic variability, by comparing the effects of contextual factors contributing to the selection of a given variant: Parallel favoring effects of factors operationalizing putative shared constraints or functions indicate grammatical similarity.

Table 5.1 Two independent variable-rule analyses of factors contributing to the selection of 1sg subject pronoun: *yo* (vs. unexpressed) in conversational Colombian Spanish (CCCS) and *I* (vs. unexpressed) in conversational American English (SBCSAE) (non-significant factor group within [ ])

	Yo		***I* (IU-initial, non-coordinated)**	
N	1,020		262	
Corrected mean (input)[a]	.48		.29	
	Prob	**N**	**Prob**	**N**
Verb class				
Cognition	.66	134/201	[.52]	53/71
Other	.46	363/819	[.49]	133/191
Priming: Realization of previous co-referential 1sg subject[b]				
Expressed *yo / I*	.58	209/372	.53	103/143
Unexpressed	.41	112/330	.35	17/32
Subject continuity: Human switched reference				
Intervening hum subj present	.56	283/519	.60	87/111
Intervening hum subj absent	.42	144/365	.42	90/137
Tense				
Imperfect[c]	.62	71/116	N.A.	
Present	.48	287/573	.52	71/99
Preterit / Past Tense	.48	86/186	.48	91/139

Note: Non-significant factor groups in both analyses: Polarity, Turn Position; also included for *yo*-expression: realization of subject of immediately preceding clause (pronouns favor).

a. The corrected mean (input) indicates the overall likelihood that the variant (expressed *yo*, *I*) will occur in the variable context as defined. Comparison of input values here is not meaningful, as for *I* expression only a sample of the expressed variant was taken (see subsection on the variable context of English subject expression below).

b. Realization of previous co-referential 1sg subject up to two intervening human subjects. The bulk of these are at 0 or 1 intervening human subjects (86%, 602/702 for *yo*, 98%, 171/175 for *I*).

c. Includes other syncretic forms, that is, Pluperfect, Present Subjunctive (N Imperfect=83).

Table 5.1 shows two independent variable-rule analyses (Sankoff, Tagliamonte and Smith 2012) of factors contributing to choice of 1sg subject expression: Spanish expressed *yo* (vs. unexpressed) drawn from the Corpus of Conversational Colombian Spanish (CCCS) (Travis 2005); and English expressed *I* (vs. unexpressed) drawn from the Santa Barbara Corpus of Spoken American English (SBCSAE) (Du Bois et al. 2000–2005). Variable-rule analysis uses logistic regression to perform binomial multivariate analysis for a choice between two variants. The results for Spanish (in the left-hand pair of columns) and English (in the right-hand pair of columns provide probabilities (factor weights) with values closer to 1 indicating favoring effects on expressed *yo* and expressed *I*.[1] A factor (level of a predictor variable) *favors* a variant when its frequency relative to its alternative is higher in the presence of the contextual feature represented by the factor, which itself operationalizes a hypothesis about speaker choices. We first review the linguistic conditioning shown here for Spanish and then go on to consider that for English.

OPERATIONALIZING (CROSSLINGUISTIC) CONSTRAINTS OR FUNCTIONS

The results for Spanish given in table 5.1 correspond with those that are reported in this volume and numerous prior studies of Spanish subject expression (cf. Torres Cacoullos and Travis, to appear). *Yo* is favored with cognition verbs, when the previous co-referential 1sg subject is also realized as *yo*, in (human) switched reference contexts and with imperfective tense-aspect. Here we present a reconsideration of these amply reported contextual factors.

Cognition Verbs: Identifying Particular Constructions

For Spanish 1sg subject expression, an observation beginning with, as far as we know, Bentivoglio (1987, 50–54), is that *yo* is favored by cognition (or mental activity) verbs—most frequently here *creer* 'think/believe', *saber* 'know', and *pensar* 'think'. This effect is also found in the present data, as seen in table 5.1. Moreover, these verbs display not only a higher rate of expression, but also distinct linguistic conditioning, as revealed by independent multivariate analyses of cognition versus other verbs (Travis and Torres Cacoullos 2012, 734–737). Only cognition verbs are subject to a turn-position effect (cf. Bentivoglio 1987, 38–40): *yo* is favored in turn-initial position with cognition verbs, but no such turn taking effect is found with other verbs (as in line 3 in (1)).[2] We take this divergence in subject expression patterns as evidence for a class of cognition verbs, defined by the verb slot in a (*yo*) + COGNITION VERB$_{1sg}$ construction.

(1) (*yo*) + COGNITION VERB$_{1sg}$

1.	Santi:	... *Están rescatando los valores [familiares],*	'they are going back to [family values].'
2.	Ángela:	*[Hm],*	'[Hm],
3.		***Yo creo** que es que por ahí.*	**I think** that that's where.
		Es que hay que empezar.	There's where you've got to start.'

(CCCS, Almuerzo: 1736–1739)[3]

There is growing recognition that particular expressions mold the structure of variation (e.g., Poplack, Lealess and Dion 2013; Torres Cacoullos and Walker 2009). In usage-based models (e.g., Bybee 2010; Goldberg 2006), speakers have available a number of stored constructions of differing levels of schematicity. Particular constructions may be identified in a replicable way by token and relative frequency, by unithood indices and, once again, by the linguistic conditioning of variants (Bybee and Torres Cacoullos 2009; Torres Cacoullos and Walker 2011).

Yo creo 'I think' is a strong candidate for a lexically particular construction within the cognition verb class, as evidenced in (1) the high token frequency of the *yo creo* string; (2) the high proportion it comprises of all occurrences both of the lexical type *creer* and of the pronoun *yo*; and (3) in independent multivariate analysis of (*yo*) *creo*, the absence of a subject continuity effect, with a tendency toward a higher *yo* rate in same reference contexts, that is, contrary to the predicted direction of effect (Travis and Torres Cacoullos 2012, 739–741). At the same time, the favoring effect of co-referential subject priming observed for other verbs remains significant for cognition verbs including *yo creo*. Particular constructions thus both contribute to and deviate from more general variation patterns and clearly merit analysts' attention.

A New Subject Continuity Measure: Human Switched Reference

Widely replicated is the effect of 'switch reference', defined by Silva-Corvalán as the context in which "the subject referent of the preceding finite verb [...] is different from the referent of the [...]" subject of the target finite verb (1982, 104). Such an effect is consistent with the notion of accessibility, whereby cross-linguistically more coding material (here, an expressed subject) is said to correspond to contexts of lesser accessibility—such as when the referent has not been recently mentioned—and less coding material (here, an unexpressed subject) to correspond to contexts of greater accessibility (Givón 1983, 18).

As a refinement of the clause-based notion of switch reference, Travis and Torres Cacoullos (2012, 726–729) proposed 'Human Switched Reference,' which considers the presence of subjects with specific human referents intervening between co-referential subject mentions.[4] The two measures largely overlap; in the CCCS database most 1sg tokens of switch reference are also Human Switched Reference (87 percent, 519/595). The difference is illustrated in the following example: While *te digo* '(I) will tell you' (line 3) occurs in what would be considered a co-referential (same reference) context according to a clause-based measure, *lo miro* '(I) will look at it' (line 5) and *te aviso* '(I) will let you know' (line 8) would both be considered switch reference. But in both cases the subjects intervening between co-referential mentions are inanimate (and in a subordinate clause) and hence, by the measure of Human Switched Reference, do not count as disrupting subject continuity.

(2)

1.	Santi:	*Yo me averiguo,*	'I'll find out,
2.		*y,*	and,
3.		*Y **Ø** te digo si hay algún apartamento,*	And **(I)**'ll tell you if there's an apartment,
4.		*Entonces,*	So,
5.		***Ø** lo miro,*	**(I)**'ll look at it,
6.		*.. si tiene alcoba del servicio,*	.. if it has a service room,
7.		*.. entonces te --*	.. so --
8.		*.. **Ø** Te aviso.*	.. **(I)**'ll let you know.'

(CCCS, Pizza: 1332–1339)

Human Switched Reference provides a more discerning account of variable *yo* expression than does clause-based switch reference, as shown in table 5.2: When there are no intervening human subjects between co-referential mentions (the top row), the difference between same and switch reference contexts vanishes (with rates of expres-

Table 5.2 Rate of expressed *yo* according to intervening clauses and intervening human subjects (Human Switched Reference) (N=884) (adapted from Travis and Torres Cacoullos 2012, 738, table 3)

Human Switched Reference	Same Reference (0 interven. clauses)	Switch Reference (1+ interven. clauses)
Intervening human subject absent (0)	39% (113/289)	41% (31/76)
Intervening human subject present (1+)	No cases	55% (283/519)

sion of 39 percent and 41 percent, respectively). On the other hand, within switch reference contexts (the rightmost column), there is a significantly higher rate of *yo* expression in contexts of Human Switched Reference (55 percent vs. 41 percent, $p = .03$, by Fisher's exact test).

Co-referential Subject Priming: Interaction with Subject Continuity

Near-ubiquitous in language variation is structural priming, or perseveration effects, reported in the sociolinguistic literature as early as Poplack (1980) and Wiener and Labov (1983). *Co-referential subject priming* is seen in the tendency to repeat the form of the previous co-referential 1sg subject: A previous *yo* favors a subsequent *yo*, as in (3), and a previous unexpressed mention favors a subsequent unexpressed mention, as illustrated in lines 5 and 8 of (2) above. Co-referential subject priming is of specifiable duration, operating in the CCCS for previous mentions at distances of two or fewer intervening human subjects (Travis and Torres Cacoullos 2012,730).

(3)

Angela: ***yo*** *ahorita no estoy trabajando.*	'Right now **I**'m not working.
… Entonces,	… So,
Es de ahorros.	It's from savings.
… de unos ahorritos que ***yo*** *tengo,*	… from some savings that **I** have,'

(CCCS, Insurance: 687–690)

Priming and subject continuity interact, having non-independent effects (even though the factors themselves are distributionally independent) (on interaction, see Sankoff 1988, 986). Figure 5.2 depicts the rate of subject expression in contexts of Same Reference versus Human Switched Reference, according to the realization of the previous co-referential 1sg subject.

First, the strength of the co-referential subject priming effect is moderated by subject continuity: Priming is greater in same reference contexts (no intervening human subjects), as also observed by Cameron and Flores-Ferrán (2003, 49). This is seen in the larger gap between the lines in Same Reference (to the left) as opposed to Human Switched Reference contexts (to the right): In the former, the rate of *yo* expression is twice as high with a previous *yo* than with a previous unexpressed mention (52 percent,

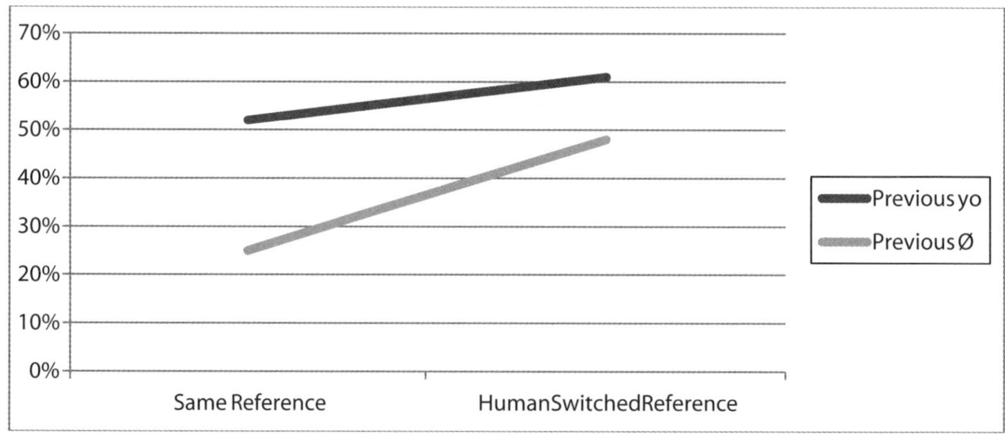

Figure 5.2 Rate of subject expression in Human Switched Reference vs. Same Reference (presence vs. absence of intervening human subjects) (N=883), according to the realization of the previous co-referential 1sg subject

N=192 vs. 25 percent, N=173), whereas in the latter the difference between 'Previous *yo*' and 'Previous Ø' narrows (61 percent, N=266 vs. 48 percent, N=252).[5]

Second, the strength of subject continuity is moderated by co-referential subject priming. This is seen in the steeper slope of the 'Previous Ø' line, which tells us that Human Switched Reference has a greater effect when the previous co-referential 1sg subject was unexpressed. In this context, the rate of *yo* goes up from 25 percent under Same Reference to nearly double, 48 percent, in the presence of one or more intervening human subjects. But when the previous mention was *yo*, the increase in the rate of *yo* is smaller, from 52 percent under Same Reference to 61 percent under Human Switched Reference.[6]

In fact, what we have is a lower rate of *yo* with a previous unexpressed mention in a co-referential context (25 percent), on one side, and on the other, similarly high rates in all three other cells (48 percent–61 percent). Thus, subject continuity operates when the preceding subject is unexpressed but is neutralized by *yo-yo* priming, while *yo-yo* priming operates in continuous contexts but is neutralized in non-continuous contexts (Travis and Torres Cacoullos 2012, 729–733).

Elusive Tense Effects

As seen in table 5.1, the Imperfect favors *yo*. Although favoring by the Imperfect and other tenses with person syncretism has been interpreted as supporting an ambiguity-resolving function for subject pronouns, true ambiguity may be uncommon (Ranson 1991) and instead relevant may be tense-aspect-mood discourse function (Silva-Corvalán 1997, 2001). Furthermore, tense may be more pertinent in narrative than in conversation (cf. Travis 2007, 119) and for third person than for first (Travis and Torres Cacoullos 2012, 734) and may interact with other predictors (subject continuity [Cameron 1994, 33–38] or verb class [Torres Cacoullos and Travis 2011, 253]). It is hoped that further (crosslinguistic) exploration will elucidate tense-aspect effects.

Summary: Reconsidering Constraints on Subject Expression

In sum, the study of subject expression will benefit from a reconsideration of the widely invoked factors influencing this variability, namely:

(1) The verb class effect as one of particular constructions.

The [(*yo*) + COGNITION VERB$_{1sg}$] construction, a frequent instance of which is *(yo) creo* 'I think', is distinguished by its linguistic conditioning, with turn-initial position favoring *yo* expression with cognition, but not other, verbs.

(2) The cognitive factor of subject continuity as an operationalization of referent accessibility.

The intervening human subjects–based measure (Human Switched Reference) provides a more discerning account of *yo* expression than does the clause-based measure (switch reference).

(3) Mechanical priming effects in conjunction with subject continuity.

Established here is co-referential subject priming—the realization of the previous co-referential mention as subject, which, importantly, interacts with subject continuity.

Are these candidates for crosslinguistic constraints or are they particular to Spanish? Below we test these factors for English 1sg subject expression.

UNEXPRESSED ('NULL') SUBJECTS IN ENGLISH

As seen in figure 5.2 above, while Spanish rates of 1sg expression range from approximately 25 percent to 50 percent, English rates are above 95 percent. A more telling difference, however, lies in the variable context for *I* expression, which is found to be more limited than for Spanish *yo* expression (as discussed in Torres Cacoullos and Travis 2013).

THE VARIABLE CONTEXT OF ENGLISH SUBJECT EXPRESSION

A first circumscription of the variable context of English subject expression is to declarative main clauses, as in lines 2 and 3 in (4). Initial analysis revealed no cases of unexpressed *I* in interrogatives or subordinate clauses outside of instances with *and*-coordination (as in *if I go out and Ø ask for it* (17 Jim: 7)). In contrast, in Spanish, main (as opposed to subordinate) clauses have been reported either to have no significant effect (Travis 2007, 115) or to favor subject expression (Shin and Montes-Alcalá 2014; Cuadro 6, 98).

(4)
1. Angela: ... (TSK) (H) and **I** put some onion powder ... in the mayonnaise,
2. .. (H) and **Ø** put it on some .. boiled eggs.
3. ... **Ø** Opened em up,
4. (H) and **I** didn't stuff the eggs.
5. (H) **I** just put that (H) mayonnaise on top.

(SBCSAE, 11 This retirement bit: 759–763)

The variable context for *I* expression must further leave aside discourse markers: collocations *I mean*, *I guess*, *I think*, *I (don't) know*, *I remember*, and *I'm sure* when produced prosodically independently from other clausal material or when appearing as parentheticals (between the subject and verb or following the verb). Not only is *I* invariably expressed but, with the exception of *I don't know*, it is generally unstressed in these collocations when they are used as discourse markers, indicative of their formulaic status (cf. Travis and Torres Cacoullos, 2014, 363–365). Likewise, *say*, *be like*, *go* and *think* when used as quotatives pattern like discourse-marker formulas in disfavoring stress on *I* and appear with unexpressed *I* only in *and*-coordinated constructions (for example, *I phoned her and Ø said* (11 Angela: 954)).

Finally, also outside the variable context are contracted forms of auxiliaries *be, will, have, had,* and *would,* which did not once appear in the absence of expressed *I* (i.e., there were no cases of *'m,'ll,'ve,'d*). These three sets of contexts together represent nearly half of all instances of ***I*** (155/320 in a random sample).

This meticulous circumscription of the variable context allows us to follow the *principle of accountability,* according to which occurrences and non-occurrences of a given variant are to be counted (Labov 1982, 30). The following analyses are based on all 151 unexpressed 1sg subjects occurring in the SBCSAE (compared with approximately 9,000 tokens of expressed *I*) and, following the methodology applied in Leroux and Jarmasz (2005), a sample of approximately twice as many expressed *I*, constituted by the closest preceding and following co-referential token falling within the envelope of variation.[7] For example, for the unexpressed 1sg subject in line 4 in (5) below, we extract the closest following *I* produced by the speaker which is in line 9, but skip over the closest preceding in line 2 as it occurs in a subordinate clause and extract the token in line 1. In cases of sequences of two or more unexpressed, we went to the next closest previous and following eligible tokens.[8] This protocol yielded 446 tokens, in which the *I* expression rate is (an artificial) 66 percent, which then allows us to compare the frequency of the variants in sets of linguistic subcontexts in order to determine the linguistic conditioning.

(5)
1. Alan: **I** keep a diary,
2. ... when I,
3. ... go out of the country.
4. ... **Ø** Still got em in here.
5. .. Otherwise,
6. (H) my problem is,
7. ... and it's a lot easier to do it that way,
8. but I,
9. ... **I** keep a diary when I go out of the country,

(SBCSAE, 60 Shaggy dog story: 757–765)

Further analysis of these 446 tokens leads to additional refinement of the variable context. Table 5.3 depicts rates of the expressed 1sg subject pronoun in English and Spanish according to coordination and position in the prosodic unit, here, the Intonation Unit (IU) ("a stretch of speech uttered under a single coherent intonation contour" [Du Bois et al. 1993, 47], transcribed on a single line).

In terms of *and-* and *y*-coordination, English and Spanish show the same tendency: For both languages (seen in lines 2 and 4 in (4) for English and line 3 in (2) for Spanish), *and-* and *y*-coordinated verbs have the lowest rates of expression. In terms of position in the prosodic unit, however, the languages differ. For English, outside the context of *and*-coordination, *unexpressed* 1sg subjects occur virtually only in absolute initial position, as in line 4 in (5).

Though the English initial-position constraint for unexpressed subjects has been characterized in terms of an undefined notion of the sentence (cf. Napoli 1982, 99; Roberts and Holmberg 2010, 5), it is not a syntactic constraint, but a prosodic one (Torres Cacoullos and Travis 2014, 29).

As can be seen in table 5.3, in non IU-initial position expressed *I* is near categorical.[9] In contrast, in Spanish, in non-IU-initial position the rate of expressed *yo* is lower than in initial position. Here, then, we have a 'conflict site' according to which the grammar, as instantiated in the structure of variability, is clearly different for Spanish and English 1sg subject expression, beyond patent overall rate differences.

We discuss the two loci of variability of English *I* expression in turn below: *and*-coordinated verbs and, elsewhere, IU-initial position.

Table 5.3 Rate of expressed 1sg subject pronoun by coordination and according to position in prosodic unit (Intonation Unit, IU)

	English – SBCSAE	**Spanish – CCCS**
	% *I* (vs. Ø) **N= 446** **Overall sample: 34%[a]**	**% *yo* (vs. Ø)** **N=913** **Overall sample: 49%**
and/*y*-coordinated co-referential V[b]	24% (24/98)	26% (9/27)
Non-coordinated verbs		
Non-IU-initial V	99% (85/86)	45% (106/238)
IU-initial V	71% (186/262)	55% (353/645)

a. Gross overall rate of English *I* (not considering the variable context) is > 95%.
b. As defined in the next section.

And-Coordinating Constructions: Debunking VP Conjunction

As seen in table 5.3 *and*-coordination very strongly favors unexpressed *I* in the second conjunct, where the rate of expression is 24 percent (24/98), compared with 78 percent (271/348) elsewhere. We define *and*-coordinated clauses narrowly as clauses with co-referential subjects (that is, no intervening human subjects) conjoined with *and*, as in lines 1–2 and 3–4 in (4) above, and in (6) below.[10] This is the pertinent delimitation of *and*-coordination, because the rate of expression of *I* in non-co-referential contexts in clauses introduced with *and* is near the overall rate (19/20). Furthermore, though other conjunctions have been included in this set in past treatments of English null subjects (e.g., Quirk et al. 1985, 910), not only are conjunctions other than *and* much less frequent with 1sg clauses (e.g., *but* occurs just 11 times and *or* does not occur at all), they show no indication of having the same tendency as *and* of favoring unexpressed *I* (5 of 6 *but*-clauses in co-referential contexts have expressed *I*).

(6)

Alina: .. <u>I went</u> and **Ø saw** their house the other night.

(SBCSAE, 06 Cuz: 1474)

Besides the lower rate of *I* expression, co-referential clauses conjoined with *and* are distinguished in tending to occur with positive polarity (95 percent, 93/98 of *and*-coordinated vs. 83 percent, 218/262 elsewhere), and in the Past rather than Present tense (75 percent, 70/93, vs. 58 percent, 139/238). Furthermore, *I* expression here is not subject to priming (as it is in other contexts, see the next section). Thus, we conclude that 1sg co-referential clauses conjoined with *and* represent a distinct schematic construction, depicted as [I VERB_{1sgi} *and* Ø VERB_{1sgi}].

It has been proposed that instances without a subject pronoun in the second conjunct of verbs conjoined with *and* (as in (6)) are best analyzed as 'VP-conjunction', involving a single clause with two predications, rather than two clauses with an unexpressed subject in the second (e.g., Huddleston 2002, 238 (section 3.1); Quirk et al. 1985, 942 (section 13.44)). Reliable criteria for identifying VP-conjunction, however, have been lacking.

Here we consider not only the absence of an expressed subject, but take into account morphosyntactic, semantic, and prosodic criteria, considered to be more tightly linked clauses that have the same tense, refer to the one event, and occur on the same Intonation Unit; material occurring on one IU tends to have a tighter syntactic relationship than material occurring across IUs (Chafe 1994, Ch. 9; Croft 1995; Torres Cacoullos and Travis 2015). This prosodic criterion holds true for the [I VERB_{1sgi} *and* Ø VERB_{1sgi}] construction: when *and*-coordination occurs across IUs the rate of non-expression for the second conjunct is lower than when both conjuncts appear on the same IU (42/66 across IUs, 32/32 on the same IU in our sample, though see (9) below for an illustration of an expressed subject in this context).

In (6), the morphosyntactic, semantic, and prosodic criteria all converge with the unexpressed subject in the second conjunct: Both verbs occur in the same tense, the acts of *going* and *seeing* could be considered part of the one event, and they appear in the one IU. However, we also find very similar examples spread across IUs, and even with intervening material, as in lines 4–6 in (7), where *look* and *make sure* have the same tense and occur simultaneously. And in (8), the two parts of the conjunct refer to distinct events (the first making mayonnaise, the second putting that mayonnaise on the eggs), but here also we retain the unexpressed subject. Finally, we note that even when these features coincide, we do occasionally find expressed subjects, illustrated in line 7 in (9) (as compared with line 1, of which it is a near repetition, but where the subject is left unexpressed). These examples counter the notion of a discrete category of 'VP-conjunction'. Rather, we seem to have a continuum, from two verbs that are very tightly associated (as in (6)), which favor unexpressed subjects more, to those that are less so (as in (8)), which favor unexpressed subjects less.

(7)
1. Fred: … (H) I look at my bank sta- .. bank statements.
2. And,
3. Wess: Mhm.
4. Fred: … Ø look through my checks.
5. When they come in.
6. .. And **Ø make** sure that it's fine.

(SBCSAE, 59 You baked: 754–756)

(8)
Angela: … (TSK) (H) and I put some onion powder … in the mayonnaise,
.. (H) and **Ø put** it on some .. boiled eggs.

(SBCSAE, 11 This retirement bit: 759–760)

(9)
1. Walt: then I go and **Ø talk**,
2. <VOX oh he's gonna say this and,
3. (H) he's gonna say that and,
4. (H) he's gonna be in my face and,
5. da-na-da-na-da-na-da-na= VOX>.
6. ... And I'm like,
7. ... and then I go and **I talk to him**.

(SBCSAE, 21 Fear: 1092–1098)

Within the same-IU co-referential coordinating construction [I Verb$_{1sgi}$ and Ø Verb$_{1sgi}$], we find two lexically specific constructions, which together make up 88 percent (28/32) of its instances. These are with a quotative as the second verb, [I Verb$_{1sgi}$ *and* Ø Verb-of-speech$_{1sgi}$], for example, *I phoned her and Ø said* (11, Angela: 954), and with a motion verb as the first verb, [I go/ Verb-of-motion$_{1sgi}$ *and* Ø Verb$_{1sgi}$], for example, *That's why I went out and Ø bought the coffee.* (49, John: 1176) (see Torres Cacoullos and Travis 2014, 31, for more discussion of these constructions).

To return, then, to the question of crosslinguistic equivalencies, we note that it is false to assert that English differs from so called null-subject languages in a syntactic structure of VP-coordination. Rather, English, like Spanish, demonstrates a disfavoring of expressed subjects in co-referential *and*-coordinated constructions. This may be a candidate crosslinguistic constraint, being also reported for Finnish (Helasuvo, forthcoming) and Russian (Nagy et al. 2011, 142).

Prosodic-Initial Position: Identifying a Conflict Site

As was seen in table 5.3, variability in *I* expression outside *and*-coordinated constructions is restricted to absolute IU-initial position. The multivariate analysis for this context is shown on the right of table 5.1 above. This indicates that, unlike Spanish, there is no cognition-verb effect in English. However, as for Spanish *yo*, significant factor groups are subject continuity (Human Switched Reference) and co-referential subject priming.

First, the priming effect seen here is that unexpressed subjects are favored when they are preceded by another unexpressed co-referential subject (with a probability of .35). That is, unexpressed *I* is rare, but when it does occur, it tends to do so in clusters, as in (10). The example in (11) (from the same conversation) illustrates a similarly structured narrative excerpt, this time all with expressed *I*.

(10)
1. Tom3: (TSK) (H) **Ø** Graduated from there,
2. ... u=m,
3. ... b- **Ø** got rea=l homesick for this part of the country.
4. (H) ... **Ø** ... Came back out here,
5. **Ø** went through law school at the University of New Mexico,

(SBCSAE, 32 Handshakes all around: 1654–1658)

(11)
1. Tom2: **I** stayed in the merchant navy,
2. u=m,
3. .. (H) my first trip was around the world out to the Middle East,
4. uh=,

5. Tom1: (H)
6. Tom2: **I** came back,
7. **I** went to school for a few months,

(SBCSAE, 32 Handshakes all around: 320–326)

Second, table 5.1 indicates that English shares with Spanish the effect of subject continuity, an obvious candidate for a crosslinguistic constraint on subject expression. Though there are cases of unexpressed 1sg in non-co-referential contexts (as in line 9 in (12)), it is disfavored, and Human Switched Reference is an environment strongly propitious to expressed *I*.

(12)
1. Alan: .. Had a pouch,
2. like,
3. sorta like you've got.
4. I carried it around.
5. Well any rate,
6. ... (H) my wife had fallen in lo=ve,
7. ... with a,
8. ... Mexican artist by the name of ... Nierman.
9. ... **Ø** Forgot his first name.

(SBCSAE, 60 Shaggy dog story: 104–112)

However, the subject continuity effect on *I* expression is at least in part dependent on the priming effect, as can be seen by the cross-tabulations in table 5.4. This shows the rate of expressed *I* by previous realization (co-referential subject priming) and Human Switched Reference (subject continuity).

Table 5.4 Rate of expressed *I* in Human Switched Reference vs. Same Reference (presence vs. absence of an intervening human subject) according to the realization of the previous co-referential 1sg subject, for IU-initial (non-*and*-coordinated) verbs (N=173[a])

	Realization of previous co-referential 1sg subject					
	Unexpressed (N=31)		Expressed (*I*) (N=142)		Total	
Subject continuity						
Same Reference	40%	10/25	71%	80/112	66%	90/137
Human Switched Ref		6/6	73%	22/30	77%	27/35
Total	52%	16/31	72%	102/142		

a. Excluded are 2 tokens for which, due to unclear speech, it is not possible to determine if there is 0 or 1 intervening subject.

Though the data are sparse, in the aggregate (seen in the Total columns), the tendency for subject continuity is the predicted one, with a lower rate of expressed *I* in same reference, or co-referential contexts (66 percent), than in Human Switched Reference, or non-co-referential (77 percent) contexts. But within same reference contexts (on the first row), 1sg is more likely to be expressed if the previous realization was also expressed (71 percent) than if it were unexpressed (40 percent) ($p = 0.0046$ by Fisher's exact test). Further, most cases (25/31) of a previous unexpressed subject occur in co-referential contexts. On the other hand, when the previous realization was expressed *I* (in the second column), subject continuity makes no difference, with a rate of expression of 71–73 percent in both Human Switched Reference and same reference contexts. Thus, the subject continuity effect in English is bound to unexpressed-to-unexpressed priming, which tends to occur with co-referential subjects, thus lowering the rate of expressed 1sg subjects in this context. Recall that in Spanish, similarly, subject continuity (Human Switched Reference) is moderated by priming, with a weakened effect under *yo*-to-*yo* priming.

In summary, the two loci of variable *I* expression are co-referential *and*-coordination and prosodic-initial position. A parallel favoring of non-expression in *y*-coordinated verbs applies to Spanish *yo*, while prosodic-initial position qualifies as a conflict site between the two languages. Within the variable context of prosodic-initial position, the favoring effect of cognition verbs replicated here for *yo* is absent for English *I* expression. However the comparison indicates parallel effects in Spanish and English for subject continuity (again, replicating an effect found in virtually every study of Spanish subject expression) and for priming (which thus far has received little attention).

CONCLUSION

Despite disparate rates of expression, 1sg subject pronouns in Spanish and English are conditioned similarly by the candidate crosslinguistic constraints of 'and'-coordination, subject continuity, and priming. For both Spanish *yo* and English *I*, the subject continuity effect is one of Human Switched Reference (in terms of intervening human subjects from the previous co-referential subject). As concerns priming, we find an effect for co-referential subject priming (that is, the realization of the previous co-referential subject), which, as demonstrated, modulates the subject continuity effect. Differences are also observed. The well-known favoring effect of cognition verbs on *yo* is confirmed here for Spanish (and is interpreted as an effect of particular constructions), but is absent for English *I* expression. And, crucially, a prosodic constraint exists for English only, such that outside of *and*-coordinating constructions, unexpressed 1sg subjects virtually only occur in prosodic initial position. This prosodic constraint thus provides an ideal test for convergence.

These findings allow us to answer the question of whether Spanish subject expression in Spanish–English bilingual speech is an appropriate linguistic variable to ascertain convergence. Having distinguished candidate crosslinguistic patterns from language-specific ones, we can answer 'yes', since the linguistic conditioning of *I* expression presents identifiable differences from that of *yo* expression, especially the prosodic-initial position constraint.

The analysis of intralinguistic variability has allowed us to distinguish superficial from structural interlinguistic similarity, and calls into question assumptions of blanket equivalence (or incommensurability) of English and Spanish subject expression. Beyond 'higher' or 'lower' overall rates, the conflict sites in the linguistic conditioning of variant choice identified via systematic quantitative analysis will enable analysts to gauge grammatical (dis)similarity (Torres Cacoullos and Travis, to appear).

APPENDIX: TRANSCRIPTION CONVENTIONS (DU BOIS ET AL. 1993)

.	final intonation contour	- truncated word
,	continuing intonation contour	= lengthening
?	appeal intonation contour	[ ] speech overlap
--	truncated intonation contour	(H) in-breath
..	short pause (about 0.5 seconds)	(TSK) click
...	medium pause (> 0.7 seconds)	<VOX VOX> marked voice quality

ACKNOWLEDGMENTS

The order of authors is alphabetical. Both contributed equally to this work. We acknowledge the support of the National Science Foundation (BCS 1019112/1019122 [2010–2013], http://nmcode-switching.la.psu.edu/). We thank Ana Maria Carvalho and the anonymous reviewers for their insightful comments.

NOTES

1. The corrected mean (input) indicates the overall likelihood that the variant (expressed *yo*, *I*) will occur in the variable context as defined. Comparison of input values here is not meaningful, as for *I* expression only a sample of the expressed variant was taken (see section on unexpressed subjects in English below).
2. The turn-position effect is independent from subject continuity; while most turn-initial tokens occur in non-continuous contexts, within such contexts the *yo* rate remains higher with turn-initial than non-turn-initial cognition verbs. Turn-initial are tokens anywhere in the first prosodic unit (IU) of a speaker's turn (or the second IU following minimal responses such as *hm* with continuing intonation, represented with a comma, as in (1)). Cognition verbs are more likely to occur in absolute IU-initial position than 'other' verbs ((90 percent, 177/197 vs. 65 percent, 466/716 respectively), including in turn-initial IUs (94 percent, 65/69, vs.74 percent, 160/216)). The difference in *yo* rate is maintained in absolute (IU-initial) turn-initial position: 85 percent, 55/65 for cognition versus 45 percent, 72/160 for 'other'.
3. Examples are reproduced verbatim from the transcripts (see Appendix for transcription conventions), aside from the bolding and underlining, and the addition of zeroes in the original and parentheses around *I* in the corresponding translation to ease identification of unexpressed subjects. Codes in parentheses following examples refer to corpus, transcript name, and line numbers.
4. We develop the subject continuity measure of intervening human subjects for variable 1sg expression, building on Givon's (1983,14) Potential Referential Interference measure, which counts semantically compatible referents.
5. We find a similar narrowing from same to switch reference contexts according to the clause-based measure: the rate of *yo* expression is 52 percent (N=153) with a previous *yo* versus 25 percent (N=137) with a previous unexpressed mention in same reference contexts but 59 percent (N=348) versus 46 percent (N=321) in switch reference contexts.

6. Again, we find a similar difference for clause-based switch reference, with an increase from 25 percent to 46 percent in the context of a previous unexpressed mention, but only from 52 percent to 59 percent in the context of a previous *yo*.
7. We obtain similar results from a sample constituted by only one preceding token of expressed *I* for each unexpressed (Torres Cacoullos and Travis 2013). We thank Matthew Callaghan for help with the extraction and coding of additional tokens.
8. In the few cases where there was no preceding or following instance (for example, when the unexpressed subject is at the start of a transcript), we looked in the other direction (i.e., to following tokens if there were none preceding); for one unexpressed token there was no expressed *I* meeting our extraction criteria in the transcript, and for a further five there was only one such token. We skipped over *I*s occurring in quoted speech or *I*s in a separate Intonation Unit from the verb (as in line 2 in (5)) (inapplicable to unexpressed mentions). Because we skip *I*s outside the variable context, the proportion of 1sg tokens occurring in co-referential contexts following this extraction method is akin to that when 1sg tokens are exhaustively extracted, at approximately 50 percent (comparing with a subset of this same corpus for a study of stressed *I*, Travis and Torres Cacoullos 2014).
9. Non-IU initial tokens are preceded most frequently by *so* (N=19), *(and) then* (N=11, as in line 7 in (9), *oh* (N=7), *well* (N=6), and a variety of adverbials (e.g., *first of all* (N=7)). There was just one token of an unexpressed *I* in this environment (*So I sat over here, . . . before we went over to Diane's, and Ø explained the recipe to em*, 43 Alice: 486). This token is preceded by *and* in the IU and has one intervening human subject in a subordinate clause, and thus could be considered a case of coordination in a broader definition than that which we apply here (cf. Torres Cacoullos and Travis 2014: 26). Not included in the count for IU position are cases (N=51) with an unexpressed subject in which the verb is preceded in the IU only by an adverbial which the expressed subject variably precedes or follows (most frequently *ya* (N=30) and *ahor(it)a*) (N=12)). Also excluded are interrogatives (N=19), and where *yo* occurs in a different IU from the verb (N=37).
10. We include *and* with minimal other material, such as *and um*, but not with more substantial material, such as *and then*.

REFERENCES

Ariel, Mira. 1988. "Referring and accessibility." *Journal of Linguistics* 24(1):65–87.

Bentivoglio, Paola. 1987. *Los sujetos pronominales de primera persona en el habla de Caracas*. Caracas: Universidad Central de Venezuela.

Bybee, Joan. 2010. *Language, usage and cognition*. Cambridge: Cambridge University Press.

Bybee, Joan, and Rena Torres Cacoullos. 2009. "The role of prefabs in grammaticization: How the particular and the general interact in language change." In *Formulaic language, vol. 1: Distribution and historical change*, edited by Roberta L. Corrigan, Edith Moravcsik, Hamid Ouali, and Kathleen Wheatley, 187–217. Amsterdam: John Benjamins.

Cameron, Richard. 1992. "Pronominal and null subject variation in Spanish: Constraints, dialects, and functional compensation." PhD diss. (unpublished), University of Pennsylvania.

———. 1993. "Ambiguous agreement, functional compensation, and nonspecific tú in the Spanish of San Juan, Puerto Rico, and Madrid, Spain." *Language Variation and Change* 5(3):305–334.

———. 1994. "Switch reference, verb class and priming in a variable syntax." *Papers from the Regional Meeting of the Chicago Linguistic Society: Parasession on variation in linguistic theory* 30(2):27–45.

Cameron, Richard, and Nydia Flores-Ferrán. 2003. "Perseveration of subject expression across regional dialects of Spanish." *Spanish in Context* 1(1):41–65.

Chafe, Wallace. 1994. *Discourse, consciousness and time: The flow and displacement of conscious experience in speaking and writing.* Chicago: University of Chicago Press.

Croft, William. 1995. "Intonation units and grammatical structure." *Linguistics* 33:839–882.

Du Bois, John W., Wallace L. Chafe, Charles Myer, Sandra A. Thompson, Robert Englebretson, and Nii Martey. 2000–2005. *Santa Barbara corpus of spoken American English, Parts 1–4.* Philadelphia: Linguistic Data Consortium.

Du Bois, John W., Stephan Schuetze-Coburn, Susanna Cumming, and Danae Paolino. 1993. "Outline of discourse transcription." In *Talking data: Transcription and coding in discourse*, edited by Jane Edwards and Martin Lampert, 45–89. Hillsdale, NJ: Lawrence Erlbaum Associates.

Erker, Daniel, and Gregory R. Guy. 2012. "The role of lexical frequency in syntactic variability: Variation subject personal pronoun expression in Spanish." *Language* 88(3):526–557.

Fox, Barbara. 1987. *Discourse structure and anaphora: Written and conversational English.* Cambridge: Cambridge University Press.

Givón, T. 1983. "Topic continuity in discourse: An introduction." In *Topic continuity in discourse: A quantitative cross-linguistic study*, edited by T. Givón, 1–41. Amsterdam: John Benjamins.

Goldberg, Adele E. 2006. *Constructions at work: The nature of generalization in language.* Oxford: Oxford University Press.

Helasuvo, Marja-Liisa. Forthcoming. "Searching for motivations for grammatical patternings." In *Pragmatics Special Issue on "Approaches to Grammar for Interactional Linguistics,"* edited by Elizabeth Couper-Kuhlen, Ritva Laury, and Marja Etelämäki.

Holmquist, Jonathan. 2012. "Frequency rates and constraints on subject personal pronoun expression: Findings from the Puerto Rican highlands." *Language Variation and Change* 24(2):203–220.

Huddleston, Rodney. 2002. "The clause: Complements." In *The Cambridge grammar of the English language*, edited by Rodney Huddleston and Geoffrey K. Pullum, 213–322. Cambridge: Cambridge University Press.

Labov, William. 1982. "Building on empirical foundations." In *Perspectives on historical linguistics*, edited by Winfred P. Lehmann and Yakov Malkiel, 17–92. Amsterdam: John Benjamins.

Leroux, Martine, and Lidia-Gabriela Jarmasz. 2005. "A study about nothing: Null subjects as a diagnostic of the convergence between English and French." *University of Pennsylvania Working Papers in Linguistics* 12(2):1–14.

Levinson, Stephen C. 1987. "Pragmatics and the grammar of anaphora: A partial pragmatic reduction of binding and control phenomena." *Journal of Linguistics* 23(2):379–434.

Nagy, Naomi G., Nina Aghdasi, Derek Denis, and Alexandra Motut. 2011. "Null subjects in heritage languages: Contact effects in a cross-linguistic context." *University of Pennsylvania Working Papers in Linguistics* 17(2):Article 16.

Napoli, Donna Jo. 1982. "Initial material deletion in English." *Glossa* 16:85–111.

Oh, Sun-Young. 2005. "English zero anaphora as an interactional resource." *Research on Language and Social Interaction* 38(3):267–302.

Ono, Tsuyoshi, and Sandra A. Thompson. 2003. "Japanese (w)atashi/ore/boku 'I': They're not just pronouns." *Cognitive Linguistics* 14(4):321–347.

Otheguy, Ricardo, and Ana Cecilia Zentella. 2012. *Spanish in New York: Language contact, dialectal leveling, and structural continuity.* Oxford: Oxford University Press.

Paredes Silva, Vera Lucia. 1993. "Subject omission and functional compensation: Evidence from written Brazilian Portuguese." *Language Variation and Change* 5(1):35–49.

Poplack, Shana. 1980. "The notion of plural in Puerto Rican Spanish: Competing constraints on (s) deletion." In *Locating language in time and space*, edited by William Labov, 55–67. New York: Academic Press.

Poplack, Shana, Allison Lealess, and Nathalie Dion. 2013. "The evolving grammar of the subjunctive." *Probus* 25(1), 139-195.

Poplack, Shana, and Stephen Levey. 2010. "Contact-induced grammatical change: A cautionary tale." In *Language and space: An international handbook of linguistic variation, vol. 1: Theories and methods*, edited by Peter Auer and Jürgen Erich Schmidt, 391–419. Berlin: Mouton de Gruyter.

Poplack, Shana, and Marjory Meechan. 1998. "Introduction: How languages fit together in codemixing." *International Journal of Bilingualism* 2(2):127–138.

Quirk, Randolph, Sidney Greenbaum, Geoffrey Leech, and Jan Svartvik. 1985. *A comprehensive grammar of the English language.* London: Longman.

Ranson, Diana L. 1991. "Person marking in the wake of /s/ deletion in Andalusian Spanish." *Language Variation and Change* 3(2):133–152.

Roberts, Ian, and Anders Holmberg. 2010. "Introduction: Parameters in minimalist theory." In *Parametric variation: Null subjects in minimalist theory*, edited by Theresa Biberauer, Anders Holmberg, Ian Roberts, and Michelle Sheehan, 1–57. Cambridge / New York: Cambridge University Press.

Sankoff, David. 1988. "Variable rules." In *Sociolinguistics: An international handbook of the science of language and society, vol. 2*, edited by Ulrich Ammon, Norbert Dittmar and Klaus J. Mattheier, 984–997. Berlin / New York: Walter de Gruyter.

Sankoff, David, Sali Tagliamonte, and Eric Smith. 2012. "Goldvarb LION: A variable rule application for Macintosh." University of Toronto. Retrieved from http://individual.utoronto.ca/tagliamonte/goldvarb.htm.

Shin, Naomi Lapidus, and Cecilia Montes-Alcalá. 2014. "El uso contextual del pronombre sujeto como factor predictivo de la influencia del inglés en el español en Nueva York." *Sociolinguistic Studies* 8(1):85–110.

Silva-Corvalán, Carmen. 1982. "Subject expression and placement in Mexican–American Spanish." In *Spanish in the United States: Sociolinguistic aspects*, edited by Jon Amastae and Lucía Elías Olivares, 93–120. New York: Cambridge University Press.

———. 1994. *Language contact and change: Spanish in Los Angeles.* Oxford: Clarendon Press.

———. 1997. "Avances en el estudio de la variación sintáctica: La expresión del sujeto." *Cuaderno del Sur: Letras, Homenaje a Beatriz Fontanella de Weinberg* 27:35–49.

———. 2001. *Sociolingüística y pragmática del español.* Washington, DC: Georgetown University Press.

Torres Cacoullos, Rena, and Catherine E. Travis. 2011. "Using structural variability to evaluate convergence via code-switching." *International Journal of Bilingualism* 15(3):241–267.

———. 2013. "Prosody, priming and particular constructions: The patterning of English first-person singular subject expression in conversation." *Journal of Pragmatics* 63:19–34.

———. 2015. "Gauging convergence on the ground: Code-switching in the community." *International Journal of Bilingualism.*

———. To appear. "Two languages, one effect: Structural priming in code-switching." *Bilingualism: Language and Cognition* (Special issue edited by Margaret Deuchar).

Torres Cacoullos, Rena, and James A. Walker. 2009. "The present of the English future: Grammatical variation and collocations in discourse." *Language* 85(2):321–354.

———. 2011. "Chapter 18: Collocations in grammaticalization and variation." In *The handbook of grammaticalization*, edited by Bernd Heine and Heiko Narrog, 225–238. Oxford: Oxford University Press.

Travis, Catherine E. 2005. *Discourse markers in Colombian Spanish: A study in polysemy.* Berlin / New York: Mouton de Gruyter.

———. 2007. "Genre effects on subject expression in Spanish: Priming in narrative and conversation." *Language Variation and Change* 19(2):101–135.

Travis, Catherine E., and Rena Torres Cacoullos. 2012. "What do subject pronouns do in discourse? Cognitive, mechanical and constructional factors in variation." *Cognitive Linguistics* 23(4):711–748.

———. 2014. "Stress on I: Debunking unitary contrast accounts." *Studies in Language* 38(2):360–392.

Weiner, E. Judith, and William Labov. 1983. "Constraints on the agentless passive." *Journal of Linguistics* 19(1):29–58.

Weinreich, Uriel. 1968. *Languages in contact.* The Hague: Mouton.

6

Subject Pronoun Expression in Contact with Maya in Yucatan Spanish

Jim Michnowicz

The Spanish of Yucatan has been consistently identified in the literature as a distinct variety of Mexican Spanish, primarily based on phonetic differences (Lope Blanch 1987; Michnowicz, in press). Many of these features have been attributed, rightly or wrongly, to contact with an indigenous language, Yucatec Maya (Michnowicz, in press; Klee 2009). Morphosyntactic properties in Yucatan Spanish, including subject pronoun expression (SPE), have been much less studied (Michnowicz, in press; Solomon 1999 is an important exception). As is widely known, Spanish is classified as a pro-drop language; the phrases *él vive* and *ø vive* 'he lives' are both possible syntactic forms, and the use of an overt subject pronoun is dependent on a variety of language-internal and discourse factors (see Otheguy and Zentella 2012, among others, for a detailed overview). The present study seeks to contribute to the general body of literature pertaining to SPE by 1) providing an analysis of SPE in Yucatan Spanish overall and 2) specifically examining the SPE patterns in both Maya–Spanish bilingual and Spanish monolingual speakers. As a contact situation between Spanish and Maya (a pro-drop indigenous language in Latin America), Yucatan Spanish presents a unique opportunity for studying the possible role of bilingualism and language contact on SPE. It will be shown that Yucatan Spanish overall coincides with SPE patterns reported for the rest of Mexico, but that bilingual (Maya–Spanish) speakers employ significantly higher rates of overt pronouns (overt pro), and their patterns of usage indicate distinct underlying grammatical constraints with respect to co-reference and definiteness.

SPE is one of the most studied morphosyntactic features in Spanish, and has been examined in a wide variety of dialects, both monolingual and in contact varieties (Abreu 2012; Barnes 2010; Bayley and Pease-Alvarez 1996; Cameron 1992, 1993;

Carvalho and Child 2011; Prada Pérez 2009; Erker and Guy 2012; Flores-Ferrán 2004, 2007; Orozco and Guy 2008; Otheguy and Zentella 2012; Otheguy, Zentella, and Livert 2007; Shin and Otheguy 2009; Silva-Corvalán 1994; Torres Cacoullos and Travis 2010, 2011; Travis 2007, among others). Specifically, the use of overt pronouns, both in overall rate and in underlying grammatical constraints, has been shown to vary across dialects of Spanish, with 'highland' dialects generally showing lower rates of overt subject pronouns than some 'lowland' (particularly Caribbean) varieties (Otheguy and Zentella 2012; Otheguy, Zentella, and Livert 2007; Orozco and Guy 2008, among others).

Language-internal constraints are the major factor in subject pronoun expression, and most studies of monolingual populations have not found a consistent role for social factors (Silva-Corvalán 2001). Some studies of bilingual speech, however, have reported an effect for several social factors, such as level of bilingualism, time in the bilingual environment, and gender (Otheguy, Zentella, and Livert 2007; Otheguy and Zentella 2012; Abreu 2012; Shin 2013, among others). In particular, many studies report an increased rate of overt pro and/or a different ranking of grammatical constraints when Spanish is in contact with a non-pro-drop language, such as English, presumably due to crosslinguistic influence (Otheguy and Zentella 2012; Otheguy, Zentella, and Livert 2007, among others). In contrast, other researchers argue that varieties of Spanish in contact with other languages do not differ from monolingual varieties in terms of SPE patterns (Flores-Ferrán 2004; Travis 2007; Torres Cacoullos and Travis 2010, 2011). Even among those researchers who do find that bilingualism results in a change in SPE, there is debate regarding the reasons for that change. On the one hand, several scholars have interpreted the increase in overt pronoun rates and/or differences in underlying constraints as (indirect) transfer from the contact language to Spanish (Silva-Corvalán 1994; Otheguy and Zentella 2012; Shin and Otheguy 2009, 2013; Shin 2013; among others). Other scholars, however, have argued that increased pronoun rates and changes in underlying grammar are evidence of simplification processes that are triggered by bilingualism itself, whereby bilingual speakers lessen the cognitive load via the simplification of grammatical or discourse constraints (see Sorace 2004, 2005). Other studies distinguish simplification from convergence, a process by which two languages in contact become more similar (Prada Pérez 2009, 4).

The study of contact between two null subject languages, where presumably transfer of the pro-drop setting from one language to another is not a factor, can help to shed light on the processes at work in bilingual SPE patterns. In particular, in situations where two null subject languages are in contact, explanations based on simplification or convergence make different predictions (Prada Pérez 2009). Specifically, a simplification explanation predicts an increase in SPE rates and/or a weakening of pragmatic constraints on SPE, while convergence predicts rates and patterns of usage that fall somewhere in between the two contact languages (Prada Pérez 2009, 55). Some studies on SPE among bilinguals of two null subject languages, such as Spanish in contact with Greek (Margaza and Bel 2006) or Italian (Bini 1993), have found an increased use of overt pronouns suggestive of simplification. Other studies, consistent with convergence, have not reported an increase in pronoun rates, but have found differences in constraint rankings between monolinguals and bilinguals in areas where the two source languages differ (Prada Pérez 2009 for Spanish–Catalan bilinguals). Regardless of the explanation of either simplification or convergence, the underlying syntax of Spanish, which already allows both null and overt subject pronouns, is not altered. Instead, bilingual speakers may show a weakening or differences in the hierarchy of the pragmatic constraints on SPE, in particular sensitivity to co-reference

(Silva-Corvalán 1994; Bayley and Pease-Alvarez 1996; Otheguy and Zentella 2012; Shin and Otheguy 2009; Shin 2013). The present study, which quantitatively studies SPE in two null subject languages, can contribute to the discussion on the role of bilingualism in SPE.

PRO-DROP IN YUCATAN SPANISH AND MAYA

Despite considerable work on SPE in general, very little research has focused specifically on the contact situation in Yucatan. Solomon (1999) presents results from 12 young speakers from Valladolid, Yucatan, who displayed a rate of 19 percent overt pro, not substantially different from rates in other mainland varieties (see Otheguy, Zentella, and Livert 2007; Otheguy and Zentella 2012; table 6.3 below, for a cross-dialectal comparison). Significant factors conditioning the use of overt pro in Valladolid were ambiguous verb forms; singular verbs; switch reference; lower education; and female gender (Solomon 1999, 250). Solomon also found the type of narrative to be an important predictor, with conflict or contrast narratives promoting increased use of explicit pronouns (234). Solomon (1999) did not include language background as a factor, but she did report the results of an earlier study (Solomon 1996) in which bilingualism was not a significant factor with respect to SPE, although she notes that constraint rankings were "not investigated systematically" (225) and were based on a small number of subjects and tokens. Following recent methods in the study of language variation (e.g., Tagliamonte 2012; Torres Cacoullos and Travis 2010), the present investigation will provide a more detailed examination of bilingual constraints and patterns of underlying grammar.

Yucatec Maya (along with other Mayan languages) is a pro-drop language in which independent personal pronouns optionally appear in emphatic or contrastive contexts, such as topic or focus (Solomon 1999; Gutierrez-Bravo 2011; Skopeteas and Verhoeven 2012). In addition, Mayan languages also display two sets of person-agreement markers, traditionally referred to as Set A and Set B (Bolles and Bolles 1996; Norcliffe 2009a, 2009b; Skopeteas and Verhoeven 2012). As is common in ergative languages, Maya distinguishes between transitive subjects (marked with Set A) and intransitive subjects and direct objects (marked with Set B) (Norcliffe 2009a, 2009b). Set A markers are preverbal clitics. Before a vowel-initial verb, a glide is epenthesized (noted in parentheses in table 6.1). Set B markers are verbal suffixes (Norcliffe 2009a, 13). The agreement markers are obligatory in most cases, except in some instances of agent focus (Skopeteas and Verhoeven 2012; see also Andrade 1955), while a co-referent noun phrase may optionally occur.

Table 6.1 Dependent agreement markers and independent personal pronouns in Maya. Adapted from Norcliffe (2009a, 13, 71)

	Dependent Agreement Markers				Independent Pronouns	
	Set A		Set B			
	Singular	Plural	Singular	Plural	Singular	Plural
1st person	in(w)	k(…-o'n)	-en	-o'n	tèen	to'n
2nd person	a(w)	a(w)…-e'x	-ech	-e'x	t'eech	te'x
3rd person	u(y)/y	u(y)…-o'b	ø/-ih	-o'b	leti'	leti'o'b

In the following example adapted from Solomon (1999, 225), it can be seen that the independent personal pronouns are optional, while the agreement markers (marked as 'erg') are generally obligatory.

Overt	*Ts'o'ok*	*u*	*k'uchul*	*leti'*
	perf	erg3	arrive	she
Null	*Ts'o'ok*	*u*	*k'uchul*	∅
	perf	erg3	arrive	

"(She) has arrived."

Overt and null subject pronouns in Maya. Example adapted from Solomon (1999, 225).

The existence of optional, independent tonic pronouns to mark emphasis, topic, or focus has led most scholars to classify Maya as pro-drop.[1] In fact, Maya displays very low rates of overt personal pronouns (less than 1 percent in Solomon 1999, 225, although with a very small pilot sample of 105 tokens). This number, however, is in line with studies of other Mayan languages (Dubois 1987; Quizar 1994). Thus, any increase in SPE rates among bilingual speakers in Yucatan is not likely to be due to direct transfer from Maya to Spanish (see the discussion).

Based on previous research, the principal research questions for the study are as follows:

1. What are the overall patterns of SPE in Yucatan Spanish (both the rate of explicit pronoun expression and the grammar underlying its use)?
2. Are there differences in SPE patterns between Spanish monolinguals and Maya–Spanish bilinguals? If so, how do differences pattern vis-à-vis previous studies on SPE in contact situations?

METHODOLOGY

The following sections outline the data coding procedures, speaker backgrounds, and type of quantitative analysis undertaken in order to answer the research questions outlined above.

Coding and the Envelope of Variation

The first 100 tokens per speaker that were included within the envelope of variation were extracted from the corpus and coded for analysis, for a total of 1,985 tokens.[2] The envelope of variation included all finite verbs that *could* appear with an overt subject pronoun, whether or not a subject pronoun was actually present. Verbs in contexts where a subject pronoun would not be possible were excluded from analysis (see Otheguy and Zentella 2012 for details). Since the primary goal of this chapter is to analyze possible differences in SPE among monolingual and bilingual speakers of Yucatan Spanish, no attempt was made to address every possible factor reported in previous studies. Instead, the most common and/or important factors from previous studies were chosen. These include five language-internal/discourse factors (person/number of the verb; tense, mood, and aspect of the verb (TMA); reflexivity; verb class; and coreference); and three language-external (social) factors (language group, age, and gender). Factors were generally coded following Otheguy and Zentella (2012), with some modifications as noted below.

Language-internal/discourse factors:

1. *Person/number of the verb*: Studies have consistently shown that person and number, as well as definiteness (for 2sg forms), are significant factors in SPE (Abreu 2012; Prada Pérez 2009; Bayley and Pease-Alvarez 1997; Cameron 1993; Otheguy and Zentella 2012, among many others). In general, singular forms favor pronoun expression, while plural forms disfavor overt pronouns. Dialects differ with respect to definiteness in 2sg forms. For example, Cameron (1993) found that while 2sg-indefinite favors overt pronouns in Puerto Rico, in Madrid the same form prompts a null pronoun. Following these previous studies, verb tokens were coded for person (1st, 2nd, 3rd), number (singular, plural), and definiteness (definite, indefinite) (Otheguy and Zentella 2012, 252–253). Preliminary analyses showed low token counts of *usted/ustedes* forms, causing these forms to behave erratically in the Rbrul runs. Therefore, *usted/ustedes* forms were excluded from the final analysis. Finally, the distinction between definite and indefinite forms was only coded for 2sg forms (Otheguy and Zentella 2012, 255).
2. *TMA*: Some previous studies have argued for a functional effect for TMA, whereby increased ambiguity in verbal conjugations is compensated for by increased pronoun rates (see Hochberg 1986), but more often the result is mixed (Orozco and Guy 2008). Verbs were initially coded as one of ten TMA possibilities: present indicative, preterit indicative, imperfect indicative, periphrastic future, future indicative, conditional, present subjunctive, past subjunctive, commands, and perfect forms. In preliminary analyses, low token counts for many of the TMA designations as well as similar patterning among some TMA classes led to the final analysis collapsing these categories into *more distinctive* vs. *less distinctive*, based on shared identity between 1sg and 3sg forms. Thus verbs in the imperfect, conditional, present subjunctive, and past subjunctive were coded as *less distinctive*; all other verbs were coded as *more distinctive* (see Orozco and Guy 2008).
3. *Reflexivity*: Previous studies have found reflexivity to influence SPE, with reflexive verbs co-occurring less frequently with overt pronouns (Abreu 2012; Carvalho and Child 2011; Otheguy and Zentella 2012). This effect is presumably due to the extra referential information encoded by the reflexive pronoun that makes disambiguation by an overt pronoun less necessary. Verbs were coded as *reflexive* or *non-reflexive*. As in Otheguy and Zentella (2012, 253–254), both semantic reflexives (*me baño* 'I bathe') and structural (non-semantic) reflexives (*me voy* 'I am leaving') were coded as *reflexive*.
4. *Verb class*: Following the simplified classification in Erker and Guy (2012, 535), verbs were coded as *stative*, including verbs that express non-dynamic states (*ser, estar,* and *tener*); *mental* verbs, including both verbs of mental activity (*pensar, entender,* and *aprender*) as well as estimative verbs (*creer, considerar*); or as *external activity* verbs, including all verbs that do not fit in the other categories (*estudiar, ir, salir, comprar*). Previous studies have generally found that *mental* verbs favor more overt pronoun expression than *external activity* verbs, and some studies have also found a significant effect for *stative* verbs (Orozco and Guy 2008). Based on initial analyses that showed no

significant differences between *mental* and *stative* verbs, these two categories were combined.

5. *Co-reference*: Previous research has found a strong effect for co-reference, with overt pronouns being favored in cases of a switch in reference from the previous verb. Following a simplification of the categories in Otheguy and Zentella (2012, 259), tokens were coded as *No Switch* when the target verb had the same referent as the trigger verb, as in " ... *[Ø] no me voy. [Ø] Me quedo aquí* ... " " ... [I] don't go. [I] stay here ..." (231F). In the initial analyses, two levels of switch reference were distinguished: *Complete Switch* when the referent of the target verb was different from that of either the subject or object of the preceding verb, as in " ... *[Ø] me di cuenta de que no solamente [Ø] no ha hecho casi nada* ..." "[I] realized that not only has [he] done almost nothing ..." (232M); and *Co-referent with Object* (*CoObject*) when the subject of the target verb was the same as the object of the trigger verb (direct object, indirect object, or object of a preposition), as in " ... *ayer [Ø] les dijo a los muchachos que ellos comían 'mac' [vorazmente; con las manos]* ..." " ... yesterday [he] told the boys that they were eating 'mac' (voraciously; with their hands) ..." (225F). In the overall analysis, however, the difference between *Complete Switch* and *CoObject* was not significant, and therefore was combined as *Switch* for the analysis. There were important differences, however, when the language groups were run separately, as seen in table 6.6 below. Finally, verbs were coded as *First Token* when no previous referent could be identified.

External (social) factors:

1. *Language group*: Participants were coded as either monolingual Spanish-speakers or bilingual Maya–Spanish speakers. Care was taken to select only speakers that could reasonably be considered fluent in Maya, based on self-reporting, family background, and the language(s) spoken by their parents.
2. ***Age:*** Age has occasionally been shown to have an effect on SPE (Orozco and Guy 2008). In the present study, speaker age was coded and run as a continuous variable.
3. ***Gender:*** As speaker gender has been shown to affect SPE in some varieties (Bayley and Pease-Alvarez 1997; Carvalho and Child 2011; Otheguy and Zentella 2012; Shin 2013), this factor was also coded as an independent variable.

Speakers

Data for the present study come from a corpus of sociolinguistic interviews of Yucatan Spanish, collected by the author. From that corpus, 20 speakers that best represented a balance between monolingual Spanish-speakers and *fluent* bilingual Maya-speakers were chosen for this initial analysis, with 10 fluent Spanish–Maya-speakers and 10 monolingual Spanish-speakers.[3] The subject pool overall is also balanced for gender, although within language groups perfect balance was not achievable, given the primary concern in the present study with language background. For the same reason, speaker age groups are not well differentiated, and age ranges from 19–76, with a mean age of 47. Speaker details are given in table 6.2.[4]

Table 6.2 Speaker demographic information

Maya–Spanish Bilinguals				Spanish Monolinguals			
Speaker	Age	Gender	Occupation	Speaker	Age	Gender	Occupation
231	24	Female	Domestic	221	22	Female	Student
215	24	Female	Domestic	233	37	Female	Administration
222	57	Female	Domestic	227	49	Female	Lawyer
213	65	Female	Housewife	228	53	Female	Housewife
234	19	Male	Domestic	235	69	Female	Housewife
106	40	Male	Maintenance	225	72	Female	Housewife
226	44	Male	Anthropologist	230	25	Male	Business
211	50	Male	Maintenance	219	42	Male	Lawyer
210	54	Male	Construction	232	67	Male	Retired business
220	65	Male	Maintenance	224	76	Male	Business

Data Analysis

The data were analyzed by means of a mixed effects logistic regression with 'speaker' as a random factor, fitted to the data with Rbrul (Johnson 2012). Rbrul is a front end for R (R Core Team 2012) that provides Varbrul-type analyses while addressing some of the shortcomings of that software. Specifically, Rbrul allows for continuous variables (as in the factor *age,* here) and mixed-effects models, with both fixed factors and random factors. For the statistical analysis, the binary dependent variable was *presence or absence* of an overt subject pronoun. Independent variables were the linguistic and social factors outlined in the subsection on internal and external factors above. As indicated, 'speaker' was included as a random factor in the model. A mixed-effects model with 'speaker' as a random factor "can still capture external effects, but only when they are strong enough to rise above the inter-speaker variation" (Johnson 2009, 365). Especially with a smaller subject pool, the mixed-effects analysis provides extra confidence that the results are not due to one or two extreme outliers skewing the data (Drager and Hay 2012).[5]

RESULTS

After recoding to remove invariant cases, 1,940 tokens were left for the analysis. In the present study, an overt subject pronoun was expressed in 19.7 percent (382/1,944) of all possible cases. Of those explicit pronouns, 88 percent (337/382) appear in preverbal position, with only 12 percent (45/382) occurring post-verbally. Given the overwhelming preference for pre-verbal pronouns in the present data, the rest of the analysis will focus only on "overt" vs. "null," without taking into account the position of the pronoun with respect to the verb.

The explicit pronoun rate of 19.7 percent places Yucatan Spanish firmly in line with other mainland varieties, with a rate virtually identical to that of Mexican speakers in other studies (both in Mexico City and New York City [NYC]), as well as that reported in Solomon (1999) for Yucatan Spanish. Despite the presence of substantial phonetic/phonological differences in Yucatan Spanish (Lope Blanch 1987; Michnowicz,

Table 6.3 Percent overt pronouns across varieties

Country/Region	% Overt pronouns
San Juan, Puerto Rico (Cameron 1993)	45%
Dominicans in NYC (Otheguy, Zentella, and Livert 2007)	41%
Barranquilla, Colombia (Orozco and Guy 2008)	36%
Chipilo, Mexico (Veneto–Span bilinguals) (Barnes 2010)	26%
Colombians in NYC (Otheguy, Zentella, and Livert 2007)	24%
Mexico City (Lastra & Butragueño this volume)	22%
Madrid (Cameron 1993)	21%
Yucatan overall (present study)	**20%**
Yucatan (Solomon 1999)	**19%**
Mexicans in NYC (Otheguy, Zentella, and Livert 2007)	19%

in press), it is interesting to note that overall Yucatan patterns with the rest of Mexico with respect to SPE.

Comparing rates of pronoun expression can be useful, but SPE rate is also affected by a variety of factors that make direct comparisons across studies difficult. Therefore, numerous researchers have indicated the usefulness of comparing the relative importance of each factor across varieties—i.e., the constraint hierarchy, which represents the underlying grammar (See Tagliamonte 2012; Poplack and Tagliamonte 2001; Silva-Corvalán 2001; Prada Pérez 2009; Torres Cacoullos and Travis 2010). Table 6.4 presents the significant factors for various studies. For ease of comparison, I have only included factors common to all studies.[6]

Table 6.4 A comparison of significant constraint hierarchies across varieties

Mainland speakers in NYC (Otheguy, Zentella, and Livert 2007)	Barranquilla, Colombia (Orozco and Guy 2008)	San Juan, Puerto Rico (Claes 2011)	Yucatan speakers (present study)
1. Person/number	1. Person/number	1. Person/number	1. Person/number
2. Co-reference	2. TMA	2. TMA	2. TMA
3. TMA	3. Co-reference	3. Co-reference	3. Co-reference
4. Reflexivity			4. Reflexivity

The order of importance for linguistic factors has been found to be largely consistent across studies and dialects, as seen in table 6.4. All of the studies shown found the person and number of the verb to be the primary factor, followed by either co-reference or TMA. Reflexivity ranks low in the two studies that included this factor. This consistency across studies and regions has been argued to indicate that, while surface realizations of pronoun rates may differ, the grammar underlying SPE in each of these varieties is essentially the same (Cameron 1993; Travis 2007; Torres Cacoullos and Travis 2010).

Table 6.5 Results of Rbrul mixed-effects one-level multivariate analysis; factors favoring overt pro; all speakers; speaker as random factor

Factor	Factor Weight	Tokens	% Overt	p-value	Range (fw)
Person/Number				2.87e-30[a]	54
1s	0.74	872	28%		
2s - definite	0.63	80	21%		
3s	0.62	281	21%		
3p	0.50	213	15%		
2s - indefinite	0.33	136	8%		
1p	0.20	358	5%		
TMA				6.01e-13	30
Not distinctive	0.65	239	36%		
Distinctive	0.35	1701	17%		
Co-reference				3.72e-08	19
Switch	0.59	948	23%		
First token	0.51	33	18%		
No switch	0.40	959	17%		
Language				0.00689	16
Maya–Spanish	0.58	947	23.5%		
Spanish only	0.42	993	16%		
Reflexivity				0.0188	12
Non-reflexive	0.56	1709	20.5%		
Reflexive	0.44	231	14%		
Gender				0.527	4
Male	[ns]	971	22%		
Female		969	18%		
Verb class				0.515	2
Mental/Stative	[ns]	729	22%		
External		1211	18%		
Age				0.727	
Continuous +1	[ns]				
Speaker (random) Std. Dev. 0.374					
Deviance: 1675.9745 df: 15 intercept: –1.568 grand mean: 0.197					

a. These p-values are presented in scientific E notation. Thus 2.87e-30 = 0.00000000000000000000000000000287.

Following is the best complete multivariate mixed-effects model as produced by Rbrul. The analysis found a total of five factors that significantly constrain SPE in Yucatan Spanish: person/number, TMA, co-reference, reflexivity, and language background. For purposes of space and comparison across studies, only factor weights (rather than log-odds, also produced by the software) are reported here. The factor weights reflect the relative favoring/disfavoring of overt pro for a given factor, with weights over .5 generally favoring overt pro, weights below .5 generally disfavoring, and weights around .5 being relatively neutral. Taking the internal linguistic factors in order of importance, we will now examine each factor group separately.

Internal Factors

Person/Number

The same pattern as in previous studies is evident here; we see that singular verbs co-occur with expressed pronouns 19.5 percent of the time, versus only 10 percent average for plural verbs. First person plural verbs were accompanied by an expressed pronoun the least (4.7 percent), while pronouns accompanying 1st person singular occurred the most (28.2 percent). Finally, 2sg-indefinite (8 percent overt) contrasts with 2sg-definite (21 percent overt). Solomon (1999, 250) also found that indefinite *tú* contexts disfavored overt pronoun expression in Valladolid, Yucatan (factor weight = 0.36).

TMA

Lending general support to functional explanations of SPE, verb tenses/moods that can be considered "less distinctive" were produced with more overt pronouns (36 percent average), compared to the "more distinctive" tenses/moods, which averaged 17 percent overt pro. A more detailed analysis of the intersection of TMA and person/number is required to comment further on questions of functional compensation in Yucatan Spanish.

Co-reference

Consistent with previous studies (Otheguy and Zentella 2012; many others), in the present data a switch in subject favored higher rates of overt SPE (22.8 percent), while continuity of reference (*No switch*) produced lower rates of overt pro (16.7 percent). First tokens also showed similar low rates of overt SPE (18.2 percent).

Reflexivity

As in previous studies, reflexive verbs significantly disfavor overt pro (14 percent vs. 20.5 percent overt for non-reflexives).

Verb Class

While not a significant factor in the present study, results are consistent with other studies, with speakers using higher rates of overt pro with stative and mental verbs (22.1 percent), compared with lower rates for external action verbs (18.2 percent).

Social Factors

Gender

Men produced higher rates of SPE than women, although this factor was not significant in the multivariate mixed model. This result conflicts with the findings of Shin (2013) and Otheguy and Zentella (2012), who found that women were leading the increase in overt pro in NYC, as well as Solomon (1999), who found that women used more overt pro in Valladolid, Yucatan. Possible explanations for this discrepancy will be addressed in the discussion.

Age

Regarding speaker age, no real pattern of overt pro is discernible, and age was not a significant factor in the analysis.[7] Individual speaker pronoun rates range from a low of 8 percent (22-year-old, female, Spanish monolingual) to a high of 37 percent (19-year-old, male, Maya–Spanish bilingual).

Language Group

Language group does play a significant role in determining SPE, with Maya–Spanish bilinguals producing significantly more overt pronouns than Spanish monolinguals. It is important to note, however, that both language groups produced overt pronoun rates that do not differ greatly from previous reports on Mexican Spanish (Lastra and Martín-Butragueño, this volume; Otheguy, Zentella, and Livert 2007; Otheguy and Zentella 2012). Instead, what we see here is that within the norm of pan-Mexican Spanish, Maya-speakers produced overt pro at the higher end of the range, while monolingual Spanish-speakers produced overt pro at the lower end. Interestingly, the Maya-speakers produced overt pro at a rate approaching that of the Veneto bilinguals in central Mexico, another situation of contact between two pro-drop languages (Barnes 2010; see table 6.5).

Given that language group was a significant factor in the overall mixed model detailed above, separate analyses were conducted for each language group, including only the factors found to be significant in the overall model. The results of these analyses are presented in table 6.6. As noted previously, initial analyses distinguishing *Complete Switch* and *CoObject* did find significant differences based on language group. Therefore, these two levels are kept separate in the individual language analyses. First, with the exception of reflexivity (only significant for Maya-speakers), each language group shares the same set and order of significant factors, with person/number being the strongest factors in constraining SPE for both groups. There are, however, differences in the relative importance of other factors across language groups. For Spanish monolinguals, TMA and co-reference are approximately equal with respect to their influence on SPE (ranges of 32 and 31, respectively). On the other hand, for Maya speakers TMA is substantially more important than co-reference (range of 28 vs. 17, respectively). Thus Maya-speakers are not attributing the same importance to co-reference as do Spanish-speakers, suggesting that these bilinguals and monolinguals may not share all of the pragmatic constraints on SPE. Additionally, reflexivity was not a significant factor for the Spanish group, while the Maya group did assign it lesser importance compared to other factors (range of 14).

An examination of the constraint ranking, that is, the order of factors within a factor group (see Tagliamonte 2012), reveals additional differences. First, one of the areas shown to vary across varieties of Spanish is the treatment of 2nd person singular definite versus indefinite pronouns (Cameron 1993). Here, both groups disfavor overt pro with 2sg-indefinite (8 percent and 10 percent, for Spanish- and Maya-speakers, respectively), but differ with respect to 2sg-definite. For Spanish-speakers, 2sg-definite favored more overt pro (32 percent), while for Maya-speakers, 2sg-definite disfavored explicit pronouns (13 percent), behaving very similarly to 2sg-indefinite. Thus, definiteness in 2sg is an important factor for Spanish monolinguals, but not for the bilingual group, representing a possible simplification in the bilingual grammar.[8]

The other major difference between language groups is found in the constraint ranking for co-reference. For Spanish-speakers, the order of constraints is CompleteSwitch > NoSwitch > CoObject.[9] NoSwitch and CoObject, both cases of continuity, behave similarly in disfavoring overt pro. For Maya-speakers, however, the

Table 6.6 Results of separate Rbrul runs by language group; speaker as random factor. All factors significant at $p < 0.05$

Spanish monolinguals factor	fw	N	%	R	Maya–Spanish bilinguals factor	fw	N	%	R
Person/Number				57	*Person/Number*				53
2s - definite	0.74	37	32		1s	0.77	414	35.5	
1s	0.71	442	21		3s	0.62	143	22	
3s	0.63	138	20		3p	0.56	129	18	
3p	0.44	81	10		2s - definite	0.49	30	13	
2s - indefinite	0.35	77	8		2s - indefinite	0.32	51	10	
1p	0.17	180	3		1p	0.24	172	6	
TMA				32	*TMA*				28
Not Distinctive	0.66	130	31		Not Distinctive	0.64	107	41	
Distinctive	0.34	825	14		Distinctive	0.36	832	21	
Co-reference				31	*Co-reference*				17
Complete Switch	0.69	462	21		CoObject	0.57	65	32	
No Switch	0.42	441	11		Complete Switch	0.55	359	25	
CoObject	0.38	52	10		No Switch	0.40	515	21	
Reflexivity (NS)				10	*Reflexivity*				14
Non-reflexive	[ns]	847	17		Non-reflexive	0.57	823	25	
Reflexive	[ns]	108	12		Reflexive	0.43	116	15.5	
Speaker (random) Std. Dev. 0.326					Speaker (random) Std. Dev. 0.372				
Deviance: 745.814 df: 11 intercept: −1.825 grand mean: 0.163					Deviance: 905.959 df: 11 intercept: −1.438 grand mean: 0.236				

order is CoObject > CompleteSwitch > NoSwitch. The two factors that favor overt pro for bilinguals, CoObject and CompleteSwitch, differ in their discourse continuity, and the Maya group employs infelicitous overt pronouns 32 percent of the time when the subject is co-referent with an immediately preceding object, as in … "*cuando* ***[Ø]*** *estás con* ***la mamá*** *o* ***un papá*** *así,* ***ellos*** *hablan en maya*" " … when [you] are with a mother or a father, they speak Maya" (speaker 234). Thus, while it appears that the bilingual Maya-speakers have fully acquired the fundamental distinction in Spanish between CompleteSwitch and NoSwitch, they fail to apply the pragmatic rules disfavoring overt pro in the presence of a co-referential object. In fact, an examination of the frequency for CoObject suggests that a large part of the bilinguals' overuse of overt pro stems from the failure to follow monolingual pragmatic constraints in this context—although they also produced almost twice as many overt pronouns in cases of NoSwitch as did monolinguals. This finding supports research by Shin and Otheguy (2009) and Shin (2013) that reports that shifting bilingual speakers in New York can lose their sensitivity to pragmatic constraints on co-reference. This possibility will be further addressed in the discussion.

DISCUSSION

First, as a whole, Yucatan Spanish does not differ greatly from other mainland varieties, including the rest of Mexico, with regard to either rates or underlying constraints. The significant constraints are primarily language-internal, and include person/number and TMA of the verb, co-reference, and reflexivity, with the patterns for each factor largely agreeing with the findings of previous work.

Regarding social factors, language group was the only significant constraint, with Maya-speakers producing higher rates of overt pro than monolingual Spanish-speakers (23.5 percent vs. 16 percent). Thus the present results lend weight to studies that have found an effect for bilingualism on SPE (Otheguy et al. 2007; Otheguy and Zentella 2012; Shin and Otheguy 2009; among others). In particular, following the distinction between simplification and convergence outlined in Prada Pérez (2009), the significant increase in overt pro for bilinguals can be interpreted as supporting a simplification strategy on the part of bilinguals (Sorace 2004, 2005), rather than a transfer per se from one language to another or convergence between the two languages.[10]

Two findings in the present data deserve further comment. First is the difference in sensitivity to co-reference between the two language groups. As discussed above, co-reference as a whole appears to be more active for monolinguals than for bilinguals. A comparison of ranges indicates that co-reference is only a little more than half as strong a constraint for the Maya bilinguals (range of 17 vs. 31 for Spanish monolinguals). So, while co-reference is a significant factor for both groups, it is attributed much greater importance by the monolingual group. Likewise, within co-reference, monolingual speakers essentially treat any co-reference as the same, regardless of whether the target is co-referent with a preceding subject (NoSwitch) or a preceding object (CoObject)—both conditions significantly disfavor overt pro. Bilingual speakers, on the other hand, treat CoObject as if it were a complete switch.

In failing to recognize the co-reference provided by a preceding object, the Maya bilingual speakers demonstrate a decreased sensitivity to co-reference, a result also found for Spanish–English bilinguals in NYC (Shin and Otheguy 2009; Shin 2013). Shin and Otheguy (2009, 128–130), while not distinguishing between complete and partial switches, found that New York–born speakers produced significantly higher pronoun rates in some situations of continuity than did recent immigrants. Shin and Otheguy (2009) refer to this as the loss of sensitivity to co-reference on the part of bilingual speakers in NYC, where the target of language shift is English, a language that does not have the same syntactic or pragmatic constraints on SPE as Spanish. In the case of Yucatan, where the target of language shift is Spanish, it seems more appropriate to talk about this as a failure to completely acquire the same sensitivity to co-reference as monolinguals. Shin (2006, 2012) found that sensitivity to co-reference takes a long time to master in L1 child acquisition of Spanish. It seems reasonable, therefore, to propose that the fluent Maya speakers in the present study—who likely acquired Spanish (at least early on) from other L1 speakers of Maya—have not acquired the same pragmatic constraints regarding co-reference as monolingual speakers. A similar argument has been made for the persistence of contact-induced traits in Yucatan Spanish phonology (Michnowicz 2009, 2011, 2012, in press; Michnowicz and Carpenter 2013). Here, the pattern for co-reference among bilinguals could be taken as evidence of simplification, both in the sense of Sorace (2005) as well as in the sense of tendencies toward overgeneralization common in (Spanish) second language acquisition (see

Lubbers Quesada 2014 for an overview), with overt pronouns appearing more often when the subject is not co-referent specifically with a preceding subject.

Likewise, Shin (2013) found that women are leading the change toward increased pronoun use in NYC, and attributes this finding to both social network ties and the general trend for women to show increased sensitivity to language change. In Yucatan, while gender was not a significant predictor, the trend is reversed. Men produced more overt pro than women, a result that also differs from Solomon (1999). This difference may be due to the number of speakers/tokens analyzed or possibly to differences between Valladolid and western Yucatan. Likewise, the result that men produce more overt pro, which at first blush seems to contradict Shin (2013), is likely due to the different contexts in which bilinguals in NYC and in Yucatan exist. In NYC, the trend is toward *more* pronoun use, in keeping with the patterns of the language to which speakers are shifting (target = English). In Yucatan, on the other hand, although speakers are shifting from one pro-drop language to another, the target is a monolingual variety of Spanish, and it is the pragmatic constraints of that language that must be learned by shifting bilinguals. Therefore, although the specific position of women with respect to overt pro differs in the two communities, the trend of women leading the change in SPE patterns is the same. Women in Yucatan produce less overt pro because the target variety of monolingual Spanish has a lower rate. In other words, it is the *target* that differs (more pronouns in NYC; fewer pronouns in the monolingual variety in Yucatan), not the trend for women to lead in the move towards that target.

SUMMARY AND CONCLUSIONS

The present study investigated SPE among monolingual and bilingual speakers in Yucatan, Mexico. Of the factors analyzed, a total of five were found to significantly constrain SPE: person/number of the verb, TMA, reflexivity, co-reference, and language group. For the linguistic/discourse factors, results support the findings of previous studies. Monolingual and bilingual speakers were found to differ significantly with respect to overall pronoun rate, and also regarding the importance attributed to co-reference. Maya–Spanish bilinguals gave less importance to co-reference and definiteness overall and differed from monolinguals specifically in how they treated co-reference with a preceding object (CoObj) and in the patterns of definite *tú*. It was proposed that bilinguals have failed to acquire monolingual pragmatic/semantic norms regarding co-reference and definiteness, and instead have simplified the discourse rules that govern the use of overt pronouns.

The subject pool for this study was relatively small. Although the results for language group were robust with the mixed-effects model employed giving us additional confidence in the results, future studies should incorporate more speakers. In particular, transitional speakers (i.e., passive Maya speakers representing the next phase in the shift to Spanish) should be included, to better understand the ways in which constraints on SPE are acquired in cases of shift to Spanish. Likewise, SPE should be studied in more bilingual contexts in which Spanish (or another null subject language) is the target, as one would expect different patterns for social factors depending on the direction of shift.

ACKNOWLEDGMENTS

I wish to thank the editors, two anonymous reviewers, and the audience at NWAV 42 for their helpful feedback. Special thanks to Naomi Shin for engaging discussions on SPE methods and for sharing her encyclopedic knowledge of the SPE literature, and to

David Mora-Marín for clarifying my questions on Maya grammar. All errors in fact or interpretation remain my own.

NOTES

1. Norcliffe (2009a, 2009b) argues that the obligatory Set A agreement markers can function as resumptive pronouns, which could argue against a traditional pro-drop analysis in certain contexts. Either way, the importance for the present discussion lies in the fact that overt, tonic pronouns function in much the same way in both Maya and Spanish— to indicate contrast or emphasis.
2. One speaker, 226, only produced 85 tokens of possible SPE in his interview, due to the topics of discussion. A majority of his finite verbs were impersonal *se* constructions, and therefore excluded from study.
3. Based on self-identification and family history; most of these speakers also show second language features in their Spanish, such as the lack of gender agreement, suggesting that Maya was their first language (see Michnowicz 2012). Speakers identified as passive Maya-speakers were excluded from this study.
4. The two anonymous reviewers point out that the inclusion of one Maya speaker with higher education (speaker 226) could have an effect on the results. This speaker produced an overt pronoun rate of 22.4%, very close to the overall average for Maya-speakers in the study (23.9%—see table 6.5). In this case, education does not seem to have had a significant effect on SPE for this speaker.
5. In the present data, a fixed effects analysis produced the same results, but with a smaller p-value for *Language Group*.
6. Note that different studies employ different methods to establish constraint hierarchies. Otheguy, Zentella, and Livert (2007, 789) employed Wald coefficients, Orozco and Guy (2008) used the order of selection in Varbrul, and Claes (2011) and the present study both used factor weight range. The comparability of these methods across studies clearly warrants further investigation, but what is striking is the overall similarity in hierarchy regardless of method. Thanks to Naomi Shin for her advice regarding methods and comparisons.
7. Speaker age was also not found to be significant in additional analyses with speakers divided into distinct age groups (18–39; 40–60; 60+).
8. Detailed study of 2nd person definiteness in Maya is required to distinguish between simplification and transfer from Maya. To my knowledge, this research does not yet exist.
9. Due to low token counts for *First Token* once the data was split for language group, this level was removed from these analyses.
10. Although following Norcliffe's (2009a, 2009b) argument that the Set A markers are indeed pronouns, identifying the process at work becomes less clear, and could in that case be considered (partial) transfer and/or convergence. Future study on the Maya pronominal system as well as the acquisition of Spanish by Maya speakers is needed. For now, most of the evidence points towards simplification resulting in a weakening of discourse-pragmatic constraints.

REFERENCES

Abreu, Laurel. 2012. "Subject pronoun expression and priming effects among bilingual speakers of Puerto Rican Spanish." In *Selected Proceedings of the 14th Hispanic Linguistics Symposium*, edited by Kimberly Geeslin and Manuel Díaz-Campos, 1–8. Somerville, MA: Cascadilla Proceedings Project.

Andrade, Manuel José. 1955. *A Grammar of Modern Yucatec*. Chicago: University of Chicago Library.

Barnes, Hilary. 2010. "Subject pronoun expression in bilinguals of two null subject languages." In *Romance Linguistics 2008: Interactions in Romance: Selected Papers from the 38th Linguistic Symposium on Romance Languages (LSRL)*, edited by Karlos Arregi, Zsuzsanna Fagyal, Silvina A. Montrul, and Annie Tremblay, 9–22. Amsterdam: John Benjamins.

Bayley, Robert, and Lucinda Pease-Alvarez. 1996. "Null and expressed pronoun variation in Mexican-descent children's Spanish." In *Sociolinguistic Variation: Data, Theory, and Analysis,* edited by Jennifer Arnold, Renee Blake, and Brad Davidson, 85–99. Stanford: Center for the Study of Language and Information.

———. 1997. "Null pronoun variation in Mexican-descent children's narrative discourse." *Language Variation and Change* 9:349–71.

Bini, Milena. 1993. "La adquisición del italiano: más allá de las propiedades sintácticas del parámetro pro-drop." In *La lingüística y el análisis de los sistemas no nativos*, edited by Juana Liceras, 126–139. Ottawa: Dovehouse.

Bolles, David, and Alejandra, Bolles. 1996. *A Grammar of the Yucatecan Mayan Language*. Labyrinthos: Lancaster, CA.

Cameron, Richard. 1992. "Pronominal and Null Subject Variation in Spanish: Constraints, Dialects, and Functional Compensation." PhD diss., University of Pennsylvania.

———. 1993. "Ambiguous agreement, functional compensation, and nonspecific tú in the Spanish of San Juan, Puerto Rico, and Madrid, Spain." *Language Variation and Change* 5:305–34.

Carvalho, Ana M., and Michael Child. 2011. "Subject pronoun expression in a variety of Spanish in contact with Portuguese." In *Selected Proceedings of the 5th Workshop on Spanish Sociolinguistics*, edited by Jim Michnowicz and Robin Dodsworth, 14–25. Somerville, MA: Cascadilla Proceedings Project.

Claes, Jeroen. 2011. "¿Constituyen las Antillas y el Caribe continental una sola zona dialectal?: Datos de la variable expresión del sujeto pronominal en San Juan de Puerto Rico y Barranquilla, Colombia." *Spanish in Context* 8:191–212.

Drager, Katie, and Jennifer Hay. 2012. "Exploiting random intercepts: Two case studies in sociophonetics." *Language Variation and Change* 24(1):59–78.

Du Bois, John W. 1987. "The Discourse basis of ergativity." *Language* 63:805–55.

Erker, Daniel, and Gregory R. Guy. 2012. "The role of lexical frequency in syntactic variability: Variable subject personal pronoun expression in Spanish." *Language* 88:526–57.

Flores-Ferrán, Nydia. 2004. "Spanish subject personal pronoun use in New York City Puerto Ricans: Can we rest the case of English contact?" *Language Variation and Change* 16:49–73.

———. 2007. "Los Mexicanos in New Jersey: Pronominal expression and ethnolinguistic aspects." In *Selected Proceedings of the Third Workshop on Spanish Sociolinguistics*, edited by Jonathan Holmquist, Augusto Lorenzino, and Lotfi Sayahi, 85–91. Somerville, MA: Cascadilla Proceedings Project.

Gutiérrez-Bravo, Rodrigo. 2011. "External and internal topics in Yucatec Maya." In *Representing language: Linguistic essays in honour of Judith Aissen*, edited by Rodrigo Gutiérrez-Bravo, Line Mikkelsen and Eric Potsdam, 105–119. Lexington, KY: Linguistics Research Center.

Hochberg, Judith G. 1986. "Functional compensation for /s/ deletion in Puerto Rican Spanish." *Language* 62:609–21.

Johnson, Daniel E. 2009. "Getting off the GoldVarb Standard: Introducing Rbrul for mixed-effects variable rule analysis." *Language and Linguistics Compass* 3:359–83.

———. 2012. Rbrul Version 2.05 http://www.danielezrajohnson.com/Rbrul.R.

Klee, Carol A. 2009. "Migrations and globalization: Their effects on contact varieties of Latin American Spanish." In *Español en Estados Unidos y otros contextos de contacto: Sociolingüística, ideología y pedagogía*, edited by Manel LaCorte and Jennifer Leeman, 39–66. Madrid: Vervuert/Iberoamericana.

Lope Blanch, Juan M. 1987. *Estudios sobre el español de Yucatán.* Mexico City: Universidad Nacional Autónoma de México.

Lubbers Quesada, Margaret. 2014. "Subject pronouns in second language Spanish." In *The Handbook of Spanish Second Language Acquisition*, edited by Kimberly L. Geeslin, 253–269. Malden, MA: John Wiley and Sons.

Margaza, Panagiota, and Aurora Bel. 2006. "Null subjects at the syntax–pragmatics interface: Evidence from Spanish interlanguage of Greek speakers." In *Proceedings of the 8th Generative Approaches to Second Language Acquisition Conference (GASLA 2006)*, edited by Mary Grantham O'Brien, Christine Shea, and John Archibald, 88–97. Somerville, MA: Cascadilla.

Michnowicz, Jim. 2009. "Intervocalic voiced stops in Yucatan Spanish: A case of contact induced language change?" In *Español en Estados Unidos y en otros contextos de contacto,* edited by Manel LaCorte and Jennifer Leeman, 67–84. Madrid: Vervuert/Iberoamericana.

———. 2011. "Dialect standardization in Merida, Yucatan: The case of (b d g)." *Revista Internacional de Lingüística Iberoamericana* 18:191–212.

———. 2012. "The standardization of Yucatan Spanish: Family case studies in Izamal and Mérida." In *Selected Proceedings of the Hispanic Linguistics Symposium 2010*, edited by Kimberly Geeslin and Manuel Díaz-Campos, 102–115. Somerville, MA: Cascadilla Proceedings Project.

———.In press. "Maya–Spanish contact in Yucatan, Mexico: Context and sociolinguistic implications." In *New Perspectives on Hispanic Contact Linguistics in the*

Americas, edited by Sandro Sessarego and Melvin González Rivera. Madrid: Iberoamericana/Vervuert.

Michnowicz, Jim, and Lindsey Carpenter. 2013. "Voiceless stop aspiration in Yucatan Spanish: A sociolinguistic analysis." *Spanish in Context* 10(3):410–437.

Norcliffe, Elisabeth. 2009a. "Head Marking in Usage and Grammar: A Study of Variation and Change in Yucatec Maya." PhD diss., Stanford University.

———. 2009b. "Revisiting agent focus in Yucatec." *New Perspectives in Mayan Linguistics* 59:135–56.

Orozco, Rafael, and Gregory Guy. 2008. "El uso variable de los pronombres sujetos: ¿qué pasa en la costa Caribe colombiana?" In *Selected Proceedings of the 4th Workshop on Spanish Sociolinguistics*, edited by Maurice Westmoreland and Juan Antonio Thomas, 70–80. Somerville, MA: Cascadilla Proceedings Project.

Otheguy, Ricardo, and Ana Celia Zentella. 2012. *Spanish in New York: Language Contact, Dialectal Leveling, and Structural Continuity*. Oxford University Press: New York.

Otheguy, Ricardo, Ana Celia Zentella, and David Livert. 2007. "Language and dialect contact in Spanish in New York: Toward the formation of a speech community." *Language* 83:770–802.

Poplack, Shana, and Sali Tagliamonte. 2001. *African American English in the Diaspora*. Oxford: Blackwell.

Prada Pérez, Ana de. 2009. "Subject Expression in Minorcan Spanish: Consequences of Contact with Catalan." PhD diss., Pennsylvania State University.

Quizar, Robin. 1994. "Split ergativity and word order in Ch'orti'." *International journal of American linguistics* 60:120–38.

R Core Team. 2012. R: "A language and environment for statistical computing." http://www.R-project.org/.

Shin, Naomi Lapidus. 2006. "The Development of Null vs. Overt Subject Pronoun Expression in Monolingual Spanish-Speaking Children: The Influence of Continuity of Reference." PhD diss., City University of New York.

———. 2012. "Variable use of Spanish subject pronouns by monolingual children in Mexico." In *Selected Proceedings of the 2010 Hispanic Linguistics Symposium*, edited by Kimberly Geeslin and Manuel Díaz-Campos, 130–141. Somerville, MA: Cascadilla Proceedings Project.

———. 2013. "Women as leaders of language change: A qualification from the bilingual perspective." In *Selected Proceedings of the 6th Workshop on Spanish Sociolinguistics,* edited by Ana M. Carvalho and Sara Beaudrie, 135–147. Somerville, MA: Cascadilla Proceedings Project.

Shin, Naomi Lapidus, and Ricardo Otheguy. 2009. "Shifting sensitivity to Continuity or reference: Subjet pronoun use in Spanish in New York City." In *Español en Estados Unidos y otros contextos de contacto: Sociolingüística, ideología y pedagogía*, edited by Manel LaCorte and Jennifer Leeman, 111–136. Madrid: Iberoamericana.

———. 2013. "Social class and gender impacting change in bilingual settings: Spanish subject pronoun use in New York." *Language in Society* 42(4):429–52.

Silva-Corvalán, Carmen. 1994. *Language Contact and Change: Spanish in Los Angeles.* Clarendon: Oxford.

———. 2001. *Sociolingüística y pragmática del español.* Georgetown: Georgetown University Press.

Skopeteas, Stavros, and Elisabeth Verhoeven. 2012. "Left-peripheral arguments and discourse interface strategies in Yucatec Maya." In *Contrasts and Positions in Information Structure*, edited by Ivona Kučerová and Ad Neeleman, 296–321. Cambridge: Cambridge University Press.

Solomon, Julie. 1996. "Subject expression in Yucatec Spanish: Accounting for similarities and differences in a contact variety." Paper presented at NWAVE-XXV, Las Vegas, Nevada, October 19–21, quoted in Julie Solomon 1999, "Phonological and Syntactic Variation in the Spanish of Valladolid, Yucatán." PhD diss., Stanford University: 225.

———. 1999. "Phonological and Syntactic Variation in the Spanish of Valladolid, Yucatán." PhD diss., Stanford University.

Sorace, Antonella. 2004. "Native language attrition and developmental instability at the syntax-discourse interface: Data, interpretations and methods." *Bilingualism Language and Cognition* 7:143–5.

———. 2005. "Selective optionality in language development." In *Syntax and Variation: Reconciling the Biological and the Social*, edited by Leonie Cornips and Karen Corrigan, 55–80. Amsterdam: John Benjamins.

Tagliamonte, Sali A. 2012. *Variationist Sociolinguistics: Change, Observation, Interpretation.* Wiley-Blackwell: Malden, MA.

Torres Cacoullos, Rena, and Catherine E. Travis 2010. "Variable yo expression in New Mexico: English influence?" In *Spanish of the U.S. Southwest: A Language in Transition*, edited by Susana Rivera-Mills and Daniel Villa, 185–206. Madrid: Iberoamericana/Vervuert.

———. 2011. "Testing convergence via code-switching: priming and the structure of variable subject expression." *International Journal of Bilingualism* 15:241–67.

Travis, Catherine E. 2007. "Genre effects on subject expression in Spanish: Priming in narrative and conversation." *Language Variation and Change* 19:101–35.

7

First Person Singular Subject Pronoun Expression in Spanish in Contact with Catalan

Ana de Prada Pérez

The study of subject personal pronoun expression (SPE) has attracted the attention of scholars from several subfields of linguistics. Syntactic theoretical accounts, dating back to Perlmutter (1971), differentiate between languages that require the presence of an overt subject (non-null subject languages), like English, and those that allow for an empty category (e.g., Spanish, Italian, Catalan, Greek, etc.), known as *pro-drop* (pronoun-dropping, or null subject) languages. The focus in these formal approaches lies on the parametric variation attested across languages regarding the availability of null pronominal subjects. However, the alternation between null and overt pronominal subjects, which is available only with thematic subjects, goes largely unexplored. Only one variable is considered to have an effect, discourse structure, whereby the referent of the target subject is either (a) the same as in the previous sentence (topic maintenance), favoring the use of a null subject, (b) different from the previous referent (topic shift), or (c) in contrast with another referent (contrastive focus), the last two favoring the use of overt pronominal subjects. As a consequence, this assumption is maintained in formalist studies of second and heritage language acquisition. The variationist endeavor, on the other hand, has considered a comprehensive number of variables that regulate this distribution, particularly in Spanish/English contexts (cf. Michnowicz on Spanish in contact with Maya; Carvalho on Spanish in contact with Portuguese, this volume). This project draws upon variationist methodologies to analyze first person singular subject expression in Spanish. It is innovative in the analysis of Catalan–Spanish bilinguals from Minorca as compared to Spanish produced by monolingual speakers from Valladolid,

Spain, and Catalan produced by Catalan-dominant speakers from Minorca. Two main conclusions are drawn from the analyses. First, regarding language-internal variables, bilinguals differ from the control groups for variables where Spanish and Catalan do not. Thus, the data presented in this chapter are interpreted as an example of *simplification*, which targets lower ranked variables to make them more salient (i.e., more significant) or to make them less predictive (i.e., not significant) so that the distribution approaches categorical behavior. Second, regarding language-external variables, the data were divided into language groups: There were the three groups of participants from Minorca, subgrouped according to language dominance and the language of the interview (Spanish-dominant Spanish data, Catalan-dominant Spanish data, and Catalan-dominant Catalan data). There was also a control group of Spanish monolingual speakers from Valladolid.

The chapter is organized as follows. The next section explains SPE in Spanish and Catalan. The following section discusses the methodology. After that, a section presents the results. Lastly, a final section offers some conclusions.

DISTRIBUTION OF NULL AND OVERT PRONOMINAL SUBJECTS IN SPANISH AND CATALAN

Numerous variationist studies have examined the variables that affect the distribution of null and overt pronominal subjects in Spanish (cf. Abreu 2012; Bayley and Pease-Alvarez 1996, 1997; Bentivoglio 1987; Cameron 1994, 1995; Cameron and Flores-Ferrán 2004; Casanova 1999; Enríquez 1984; Erker and Guy 2012; Flores-Ferrán 2004; Lapidus and Otheguy 2005a, 2005b; Lozano 2009; Margaza and Bel 2006; Morales 1997; Otheguy and Zentella 2012; Otheguy, Zentella, and Livert 2007; Ranson 1991; Shin 2012, 2013; Silva-Corvalán 1982, 1994; Torres-Cacoullos and Travis 2010, 2011; Travis 2005, 2007; among many others). Regarding grammatical PERSON, for instance, authors report a first person singular effect, where overt pronominal subjects occur more frequently than with other grammatical persons. The variable CO-REFERENTIALITY (or switch reference) explains the difference in use of overt pronominal subjects when the subject is co-referential with the preceding clause's subject versus when it is not. To cite one more example, when the verb form is morphologically ambiguous, overt pronominal subjects are used more than when the verb form is unambiguous. For Catalan, Casanova (1999) and Prada Pérez (2010) have examined both dialectal and contact variation. Prada Pérez (2010), in particular, compares Valladolid Spanish and Minorcan Catalan, indicating similar overall rates of overt pronominal subjects in both languages, but minor differences in variable and constraint rankings. Since that analysis was problematic due to collinearity, in the present chapter, fewer variables are examined.

In addition to language-internal variables, some external variables have been examined (see Flores-Ferrán 2007 for a review). In this project, the external variables examined are AGE, GENDER, and contact with Catalan (LANGUAGE GROUP). For these variables, a distinction needs to be made between monolingual and bilingual speech communities as GENDER and AGE are often times correlated with bilingual language use (Shin and Otheguy 2013). In monolingual communities, however, age and gender are considered as variables indicating linguistic change (e.g., Bailey's [2004] "apparent time" for age).

In monolingual varieties, AGE has been found to variably condition SPE. For instance, Cameron (1992) did not report an age effect while Ávila-Jiménez (1995) did, both examining the same variety and region. In bilingual contexts, age has not been reported as significant unless it is correlated with contact with English (Otheguy and Zentella's corpus).

For GENDER, two results have been attested: no effect (Holmquist 2012; Orozco and Guy 2008; Otheguy, Zentella, and Livert 2007), or a *women effect*, in which female participants are leading the change towards expressed pronouns in monolingual and bilingual varieties (Bayley and Pease-Alvarez 1996; Carvalho and Child 2011; Otheguy and Zentella 2012; Shin 2013; Shin and Otheguy 2013). In monolingual varieties, there is evidence beyond SPE that is interpreted as women leading linguistic change (Eckert and McConnell-Ginet 2003; Labov 2001: both cited in Shin and Otheguy 2013). In bilingual varieties, on the other hand, a *women effect* has been reported for first generation Mainlanders (Otheguy and Zentella 2012), first generation speakers from several regions (Shin 2012), and for innovative speakers (Shin and Otheguy 2013), which has been attributed to female bilinguals' increased contact with second-generation bilingual speakers (Shin 2013, Shin and Otheguy 2013). Beyond New York City, the *women effect* has been attested in the US Southwest (Bayley and Pease-Alvarez 1996) and Uruguay (Carvalho and Child 2011).

Lastly, the effect of contact with English has been widely researched, creating a division among scholars between those who report a bilingual effect (Lapidus and Otheguy 2005a, 2005b; Otheguy, Zentella, and Livert 2007; Otheguy and Zentella 2012; Shin 2013; Shin and Otheguy 2013; among others) and those who do not (Torres Cacoullos and Travis 2010). Shin and Otheguy (2013) propose, for instance, that the differences reported across studies might be due to the difference in network density between communities of Spanish speakers in the Northeast versus the Southwest. Since these external variables receive a local explanation, the identification of a *women*, age, or contact effect in Catalan–Spanish bilingual speakers in Minorca or in monolingual speakers in Valladolid will be contextualized within the local community. It is noteworthy that the Catalan–Spanish contact situation examined here also differs from previous research in the similarities that exist between subject expression in Spanish and Catalan, both null subject languages. This difference is important for language acquisition research as an existing proposal by Sorace (2011, 2012) predicts an increased use of overt pronominal subjects in bilingual speech, irrespective of language pairing. The prediction of this proposal (i.e., that there will be an increased use of overt pronominal subjects in Spanish in contact with Catalan) can therefore be tested with the data discussed here. The variables examined in the previous research (Abreu 2012; Bayley and Pease-Alvarez 1996, 1997; Bentivoglio 1987; Cameron 1994, 1995; Carvalho and Child 2011, Orozco and Guy 2008; Otheguy and Zentella 2012; Ranson 1991; Shin 2012, 2013; among many others) inform the design of the present study, which we describe in the following section.

METHOD

The aim of the present study is to both compare Spanish to Catalan and bilingual to monolingual varieties of Spanish. In particular, there are two aims guiding the research presented in this chapter. First, the chapter compares Catalan and Spanish data in order to examine what differences there are between these languages with respect to the rate of first person singular subject expression as well as the variables that are significant, their ranking, and the constraint rankings for each language. Second, the chapter investigates differences between Spanish and Catalan bilinguals in relation to each other and to Spanish monolinguals and Catalan-dominant bilinguals.

Participants

Participants were divided into four language groups: two control groups and two bilingual Spanish groups. The twelve Spanish controls (SC) were monolingual speakers from Valladolid while the twelve Catalan controls (CC) were Catalan-dominant speakers from villages in the center of Minorca, where Spanish is rarely spoken. The bilingual data comprised speech samples from twelve Catalan L1 bilinguals (CB) and eleven Spanish L1 bilinguals (SB). Each group comprised (roughly) the same number of male and female participants who were equally distributed into three age groups. The age group division takes into account the changes in education that the Franco regime imposed. Age group 1 (ages 13 to 35) was schooled during the democracy and had access to education in Catalan; age group 2 (ages 36 to 64) did not have access to education in Catalan, whereas age group 3 (65 and over) grew up with little to no education in either language. For the purposes of investigating the Minorca data, however, the division was simplified to two groups: age group 1, the group with schooling in Catalan (former age group 1) and age group 2, the group without schooling in Catalan (former age groups 2 and 3) while the three-way distinction was maintained for the Valladolid data.

In addition to language background, data were also collected on self-reported language proficiency (using a 1–7 Likert scale, where 1 referred to minimal abilities and 7 to native-like abilities), attitudes towards both languages (including a 7-point scale to rate the importance of both languages), and language use. CBs' self-reported proficiency in Spanish ranged from 4 to 7 (mean: 5.3) regarding speaking ability and from 6 to 7 with respect to listening proficiency (mean: 6.8). They unanimously rate the importance of their L1, Catalan, as 7, and the importance of Spanish for them ranges from 2 to 7 (mean: 5). Although participants are exposed to both languages every day, they vary in their production in each of the languages. They produce Catalan every day while Spanish is produced as much as every day (n=7) and as little as once or twice a month (n=1), with the rest of the participants producing it a few times a week (n=2) or once a week (n=2). SBs' self-reported speaking proficiency in Catalan ranges from 1 to 7 (mean: 4) and their listening proficiency from 5 to 7 (mean: 6.7). They almost unanimously rate the importance of Spanish as 7—one participant rates it as 6—and the importance of Catalan ranges from 1 to 7 (mean: 4.7). As in the case of CBs, SBs use both languages every day but vary in their production in each of the languages.

Materials

The oral interview included a language background questionnaire used for participant profiling, a sociolinguistic interview where the data for this chapter were extracted from, and a survey of language attitudes and ideologies. The sociolinguistic interview was based on Tagliamonte (2006) and adapted to the target culture. Participants were asked about their personal experiences as well as about their hometown, traditions, celebrations, typical dishes, etc. The interviews in Spanish were carried out by the author, a native of Valladolid.[1] The interviews in Catalan were performed by a native of Alaior, Minorca.[2] Participants were selected through snowball sampling (chain-referral sampling); therefore, some participants had a closer relationship with the interviewer than others, although there was always a maximum of one degree of separation.

Variables and Constraints

All the data were coded for SUBJECT FORM (lexical, overt, and null pronominal subjects), even though only null and overt pronominal subjects were included in the analysis provided in this chapter. To avoid collinearity, not all the language-internal variables coded for were included in the current analysis (see Prada Pérez 2009, 2010 for coding scheme). Since some of these variables were highly significant, they were controlled for by only including first person singular forms in topic continuation and broad focus contexts within main clauses, reducing considerably the greater than 14,000 tokens initially coded to the 4,466 included in the analysis. In this chapter, I examine CONNECT, VERB FORM AMBIGUITY, and SEMANTIC VERB TYPE. A subject was coded as more connected if it was co-referential with the previous subject and the tense-mood-aspect (TMA) of the verb was also the same as the TMA in the preceding verb. It could also be co-referential but a different TMA or non-co-referential. The predictions were largely guided by antecedent research, where more connected speech favored null subjects over less connected speech (Bayley and Pease-Alvarez 1996; Cameron 1996; Otheguy, Zentella, and Livert 2007; Otheguy and Zentella 2012; among others). A verb form was coded as ambiguous if it was morphologically ambiguous with another form (e.g., 1st and 3rd person imperfect and conditional, among other related forms). It was predicted that ambiguous forms would favor overt pronominal subjects more than unambiguous forms. Verbs were classified as stative, mental, or external (Enríquez 1984). In previous studies, stative and mental verbs favored overt pronominal subjects. Thus, the same distribution was expected in this study.

The external variables included in the final analysis were LANGUAGE GROUP (SC, CC, SB, CB), GENDER (male and female) and AGE GROUP ((1) 13 to 35; and (2) over 35). The only difference in the coding across groups was that for the Spanish monolinguals there were three age groups ((1) 13 to 35; (2) 36 to 64; and (3) 65 and over) as dividing them according to education in Catalan did not seem relevant.

Results

The total percentage of first person singular overt pronominal subjects was 20.5 percent (vs. 79.5 percent null forms). The groups' percentages ranged from 19.8 percent to 21.3 percent, a non-significant difference. Table 7.1 presents the data from all groups with LANGUAGE GROUP as a variable.

All linguistic variables were returned as significant. Regarding CONNECT, overt first person singular pronominal subjects were favored in non-co-referential contexts and disfavored in co-referential contexts [.34], even more so if the TMA was the same as in the previous predicate [.65]. With respect to VERB FORM AMBIGUITY, ambiguous verb forms favored overt first person singular pronominal subjects [.59] more than unambiguous ones [.48], as predicted. Regarding SEMANTIC VERB TYPE, mental and stative verbs favored overt first person singular pronominal subjects, [.55] and [.53] respectively, more than external actions [.48] (in line with Silva-Corvalán 1982; Otheguy and Zentella 2012).[3] The extra-linguistic variables GENDER and AGE GROUP were comprised of speakers from different communities. Therefore, the results in table 7.1 should be taken with caution and their discussion will be offered for each of the groups. In any case, for AGE GROUP, the older generation favors overt first person singular pronominal subjects [.55] while the younger generation disfavors them [.42]. This result is consonant with findings by Orozco and Guy (2008), for monolingual speakers from Barranquilla, Colombia, while it is contrary to what has been reported for Puerto Rico (e.g., Ávila-Jiménez 1995; Flores-Ferrán 2002; Lizardi 1993). Since the communities display age group differences, this variable is better examined within language groups (see below). The variable GENDER indicates that female speakers favor the use of overt first person singular pronominal subjects [.53] more than male speakers [.47]. Recall that previous research either finds no effect for gender (Holmquist 2012; Orozco and

Table 7.1 Results from all groups (multivariate regression analysis of the contribution of internal and external factors to the probability of producing an overt pronominal subject vs. a null subject; factor groups selected as significant in gray background)

	Factor weight	%	N
CONNECT			
Different referent	**0.65**	20.6	616
Same referent, different TMA	0.42	14.6	152
Same referent, same TMA	0.34	10.4	147
Range	*31*		
AGE GROUP			
2	**0.55**	23.9	654
1	0.42	15.1	261
Range	*13*		
AMBIGUITY			
Ambiguous	**0.59**	25.6	237
Unambiguous	0.48	19.1	678
Range	*11*		
VERB TYPE			
Mental	**0.55**	24.5	208
Stative	**0.53**	24.7	178
External	0.48	18.3	529
Range	*7*		
GENDER			
Female	**0.53**	22.5	521
Male	0.47	18.3	394
Range	*6*		
LANGUAGE GROUP			
Catalan L1 bilinguals	**0.51**	21.3	274
Catalan control	**0.50**	20.7	234
Spanish control	0.49	19.8	154
Spanish L1 bilinguals	0.49	19.9	253
Range	*2*		
Total N			4466
Corrected mean			.182
Log likelihood			–2098.615
Significance			.009

Guy 2008; Otheguy, Zentella, and Livert 2007) or a *women effect* (Shin 2013; Shin and Otheguy 2013). Therefore, this result is unsurprising. As with AGE GROUP, I will return to this variable in the analysis of each speaker group as this result is the compound of several communities and does not reach significance in every speaker group when they are examined separately. Lastly, the variable LANGUAGE GROUP shows that the odds ratio of producing an overt first person singular pronominal subject versus a null subject is equal in all the groups, against Sorace's (2011) prediction.

Spanish Controls

For the SC dataset, recall that a three-way distinction regarding AGE GROUP was maintained, as it was significant only when the three groups were distinguished. In this group of monolinguals, AGE GROUP is not correlated with knowledge of Spanish and is therefore interpreted as indicating a language-internal change. Overall, the SC group used overt first person singular pronominal subjects 19.8 percent of the time (vs. 80.2 percent null).

As shown in table 7.2, the variables selected as significant were CONNECT, AGE GROUP, and AMBIGUITY. The linguistic variables CONNECT and AMBIGUITY exhibit the same constraint ranking as in the previous analysis. The variable AGE GROUP, on the other hand, is slightly different. The middle-aged generation's (generation 2) odds ratio of producing overt first person singular pronominal subjects [.60] is higher than those of the youngest [.49] (generation 1) and oldest generations [.39] (generation 3). The results from generations 1 and 3 are consistent with findings in Puerto Rico (e.g., Ávila-Jiménez 1995; Flores-Ferrán 2002; Lizardi 1993) as the youngest generation has a larger factor weight, meaning that they favor overt first person singular pronominal subjects more than those in generation 3 who disfavor them. Generation 2, however, favors overt pronoun expression the most. Therefore, the increased odds ratio in generation 2 with respect to generation 3 does not extend to generation 1, as would be expected if the linguistic change was progressing (see, however, results in Orozco and Guy 2008, where the trend is towards a decrease in overt pronominal expression). More data and comparisons with other communities are warranted by this result, to which we will return in the Discussion section. Even though the variable ranking among Spanish monolinguals is the same as in the model with all groups included, VERB TYPE and GENDER did not reach significance in SC. The general trends for these variables, however, were still the same.

Catalan Controls

The CC data are presented next in order to facilitate the comparison between the two baselines before exploring bilingual Spanish. Participants produced overt first person singular pronominal subjects in Catalan 20.7 percent of the time (vs. 79.3 percent null).

The variable ranking in the Catalan control group is the same as the one among Spanish monolinguals, as seen in table 7.3. Even though VERB TYPE did not reach significance in either control group, the constraint ranking is different in Catalan in that external actions are within the favoring range and favor more overt first person singular pronominal subjects than mental processes do. Unlike in the SC dataset, in the CC data, GENDER reached significance. For the other variables, the constraint ranking is the same as in SC. AGE GROUP indicates a decrease in the use of overt first person singular pronominal subjects in the younger generation [.38], a result consistent with the trend reported in Orozco and Guy (2008) for Barranquilla, Colombia. For GENDER, females favored overt first person singular pronominal subjects [.54] while males disfavored them [.45], a pattern consonant with data from Mexican–American Spanish in San

Table 7.2 Results from Spanish controls (multivariate regression analysis of the contribution of internal and external factors to the probability of producing an overt pronominal subject vs. a null subject; factor groups selected as significant in gray background)

	Factor weight	%	N
CONNECT			
Different referent	**0.66**	29.3	114
Same referent, different TAM	0.40	12.6	22
Same referent, same TAM	0.30	8.4	18
Range	*36*		
AGE GROUP			
2	**0.60**	11.2	84
1	0.49	9.5	68
3	0.39	6.4	41
Range	*21*		
AMBIGUITY			
Ambiguous	**0.65**	28.4	40
Unambiguous	0.47	17.9	114
Range	*18*		
VERB TYPE			
Mental	**0.59**	25.9	35
Stative	**0.55**	23.1	30
External	0.46	17.3	89
Range	*13*		
GENDER			
Female	**0.54**	22.5	70
Male	0.47	18	84
Range	2		
Total N			778
Corrected mean			.170
Log likelihood			–348.136
Significance			.004

Table 7.3 Results from the Catalan control group (multivariate regression analysis of the contribution of internal and external factors to the probability of producing a first person singular overt pronominal subject vs. a null subject; factor groups selected as significant in gray background)

	Factor weight	%	N
CONNECT			
Different referent	**0.63**	27.9	234
Same referent, different TAM	0.47	18.3	53
Same referent, same TAM	0.30	9.8	29
Range	33		
AGE GROUP			
2	**0.58**	25.2	74.8
1	0.38	13.7	60
Range	20		
AMBIGUITY			
Ambiguous	**0.63**	29.4	75
Unambiguous	0.46	18.2	159
Range	17		
VERB TYPE			
Stative	**0.56**	24.9	46
External	**0.51**	21.3	140
Mental	0.44	16.7	48
Range	12		
GENDER			
Female	**0.54**	23.2	137
Male	0.45	18.0	97
Range	9		
Total N			1130
Corrected mean			.182
Log likelihood			–531.896
Significance			.021

Antonio, Texas, and other contact varieties (Bayley and Pease-Alvarez 1996; Carvalho and Child 2011; Otheguy and Zentella 2012; Shin 2012; and Shin and Otheguy 2013).

Spanish-Dominant Bilinguals

The SB data are now compared to both control groups in table 7.4. Since the control groups did not differ greatly, bilingual speakers were not expected to differ appreciably either. Similarly to the control groups, Spanish bilinguals produced overt first person singular pronominal subjects 19.9 percent of the time (vs. 80.1 percent null).

SBs present a similar variable hierarchy as the control groups. VERB TYPE, however, ranks higher than GENDER and is returned as significant. Recall that the variable VERB TYPE did not reach significance in the control group data. The result regarding AMBIGUITY, which is returned as not significant, is also unexpected, given the rankings for Spanish and Catalan. It, however, follows the same trend as both controls, as instantiated in the constraint ranking. Regarding the other variables, the constraint rankings are the same, except for GENDER, which is barely significant. Male speakers favor overt first person singular pronominal subjects [.54] while female speakers disfavor them [.47]. This trend has not been reported elsewhere in the literature and is not the case for the rest of the island, requiring an additional analysis. A one-way ANOVA revealed that there is no gender effect regarding speaking, $F(1,11) = 4.301$, $p = .07$, or listening proficiency, $F(1,11) = 3.889$, $p = .08$, or use of L1, $F(1,11) = .294$, $p = .60$, or L2, $F(1,11) = .343$, $p = .65$. As a consequence, the effect cannot be due to a correlation between gender and any of those variables. Since this constraint ranking is different from the ranking in both control groups and, as we will see below, in the CB data, it cannot be attributed to this group behaving like the groups in Minorca or the group from Valladolid; it is important to note, however, that with a range of 7 it is barely significant. Regarding the linguistic variables, the data indicate that SBs have similar grammars to SCs. Recall that Catalan and Spanish differed in terms of VERB TYPE, even though it did not reach significance for either. In these data, SB's grammar aligns with SC's regarding this variable. It does, however, reach significance for SB.

Catalan-Dominant Bilinguals

The CB data were compared to the data from the two controls groups as well as the SB group. The overall use of overt first person singular pronominal subjects is 21.3 percent (vs. 78.9 percent null).

As shown in table 7.5, the variables selected as significant were ranked as follows: CONNECT> GENDER> AGE GROUP> VERB TYPE. This hierarchy is the same as in the other speaker groups, except for GENDER, which is ranked higher in this dataset. For CBs, like for SBs, AMBIGUITY did not reach significance, even though the trend is in the same direction as in the other groups. As with other speaker groups, the variable CONNECT ranks first. Additionally, as in the SB group, VERB TYPE reaches significance, even though it did not in either control group. With this variable, however, CBs use the same grammar of Spanish as SCs do, where mental and stative verbs favor overt first person singular pronominal subjects, [.59] and [.55], respectively, while external action verbs disfavor them [.46]. Interestingly, CBs and SBs are linguistically identical as they pattern with Spanish where Spanish and Catalan differ in their VERB TYPE constraint rankings. At the same time, they are unlike both controls with respect to VERB FORM AMBIGUITY, which is not significant in the bilingual Spanish datasets while it is in the control datasets, and VERB TYPE, which is significant in the bilingual Spanish data but not in the control data.

Table 7.4 Results from Spanish L1 bilingual data (multivariate regression analysis of the contribution of internal and external factors to the probability of producing a first person singular overt pronominal subject vs. a null subject; factor groups selected as significant in gray background)

	Factor weight	%	N
CONNECT			
Different referent	**0.67**	32.2	165
Same referent, different TAM	0.42	13.5	40
Same referent, same TAM	0.35	10.4	48
Range	32		
AGE GROUP			
2	**0.57**	23.8	176
1	0.40	14.4	77
Range	17		
VERB TYPE			
Mental	**0.61**	28.2	53
Stative	**0.53**	24.6	52
External	0.47	17.0	148
Range	14		
GENDER			
Male	**0.54**	21.1	114
Female	0.47	19.0	139
Range	7		
AMBIGUITY			
Ambiguous	**0.54**	22.9	64
Unambiguous	0.49	19.1	189
Range	5		
Total N			1272
Corrected mean			.174
Log likelihood			–580.352
Significance			.046

Extra-linguistically, however, differences were found regarding GENDER. Catalan L1 speakers both in Catalan and Spanish display the same constraint ranking. For SBs, this variable was returned as significant, as it was for the CC and CB data and unlike SC data. Nevertheless, the constraint ranking, where males used overt first person singular pronominal subjects more than females, was different from all. Since this is an extra-linguistic variable, it is not surprising that Catalan L1 speakers speaking Spanish and Catalan L1 speakers speaking Catalan would pattern the same way.

Table 7.5 Results from Catalan L1 bilingual data (multivariate regression analysis of the contribution of internal and external factors to the probability of producing a first person singular overt pronominal subject vs. a null subject; factor groups selected as significant in gray background)

	Factor weight	%	N
CONNECT			
Different referent	**0.67**	32.8	185
Same referent, different TAM	0.40	13.3	37
Same referent, same TAM	0.35	11.7	52
Range	*32*		
GENDER			
Female	**0.57**	25.6	175
Male	0.43	16.4	99
Range	*14*		
AGE GROUP			
2	**0.55**	24.1	204
1	0.41	15.9170	77
Range	*14*		
VERB TYPE			
Mental	**0.59**	30.0	72
Stative	**0.55**	25.6	274
External	0.46	17.9	152
Range	*13*		
AMBIGUITY			
Ambiguous	**0.54**	23.4	58
Unambiguous	0.49	20.8	216
Range	*5*		
Total N			1286
Corrected mean			.186
Log likelihood			-606.360
Significance			.009

The results presented here indicate an interesting interplay between linguistic and extra-linguistic variables in SPE in Spanish in contact with Catalan in Minorca. These results are further discussed in the following section.

DISCUSSION: COMPARISON ACROSS GROUPS

The data presented in this chapter indicate striking similarities between Spanish and Catalan. The sole comparison of the percentage of use of overt first person singular pronominal subjects across samples is not as informative as a comparison of the variables that affect the distribution. In this study, however, comparing the percentages across groups is a necessary procedure to test Sorace's (2011, 2012) predictions. She predicts an increased use of overt pronominal subjects in bilingual speakers, irrespective of language pair, a prediction that does not bear out in our data. Additionally, these percentages are consonant with the regression result that the variable LANGUAGE GROUP was not significant. Lastly, the differences reported for the individual runs were minor, especially considering the differences attested across varieties of Spanish. This section further discusses the effects of linguistic and extra-linguistic variables as well as the implications for bilingual theories.

LINGUISTIC VARIABLES

The linguistic variables included in this study were CONNECT, VERB FORM AMBIGUITY, and VERB TYPE. As shown in table 7.6, CONNECT was found to be very influential in first person singular subject expression in all four groups and always reflected the same constraint ranking in both languages as well as in monolingual and bilingual Spanish. This variable, which was the highest ranked, was impervious to language contact. The other two linguistic variables ranked lower than CONNECT and were different in monolingual and bilingual Spanish. Specifically, VERB FORM AMBIGUITY was higher than VERB TYPE in the control groups while VERB TYPE was higher than VERB FORM AMBIGUITY in the bilingual groups. VERB FORM AMBIGUITY exhibited the same trend in all four groups. Neither of the bilingual Spanish groups, however, returned this variable as significant. Therefore, the result could be attributed to linguistic simplification, understood as a change in the range of constraints that results in the variable being more categorical either by becoming more significant or not significant (the case of VERB FROM AMBIGUITY here).[4] Lastly, VERB TYPE was not significant in either control group, which additionally displayed different trends. The bilingual groups showed the same trends as the SCs, where mental verbs favor overt first person singular pronominal subjects the most, followed by stative verbs. Conversely, external actions disfavored overt first person singular pronominal subjects. This trend, however, did reach significance in the bilinguals. Regarding intra-linguistic variables, thus, it can be concluded that SBs and CBs, when speaking Spanish, form a single community with respect to first person singular subject expression and the variables examined here, as they select the same variables as significant and the constraint ranking is the same in these two groups of bilinguals.

EXTRA-LINGUISTIC VARIABLES

The external variables included in the study were LANGUAGE GROUP, AGE, and GENDER. LANGUAGE GROUP was not significant, indicating that the grammars of all four groups were similar, a result further confirmed in the variable and constraint ranking comparisons.

AGE GROUP differences emerge within each speaker cohort, as the variable reaches significance across groups. Recall that the coding for age group was different for monolinguals than for bilinguals, as the bilingual and CC groups were coded into two groups according to language policy changes while the monolinguals were divided into three groups. As shown in table 7.7, middle-aged to older Minorcans (age group 2) and middle-aged Vallisoletanos ranked highest, while older Vallisoletanos ranked lowest. Differences across age groups may suggest an ongoing linguistic change, which, in the

Table 7.6 Group comparisons of internal variables (factor weights resulting from multivariate regression analyses of the contribution of internal factors to the probability of producing a first person singular overt pronominal subject vs. a null subject across the four groups; factor groups selected as significant in gray background)

	SC	CC	SB	CB
CONNECT				
Different referent	**0.66**	**0.63**	**0.67**	**0.67**
Same referent, different TAM	0.40	0.47	0.42	0.40
Same referent, same TAM	0.30	0.30	0.35	0.35
Range	*36*	*33*	*32*	
AMBIGUITY				
Ambiguous	**0.65**	**0.63**	**0.54**	**0.54**
Unambiguous	0.47	0.46	0.49	0.49
Range	*18*	*17*	*5*	*5*
VERB TYPE				
Mental	**0.59**	0.44	**0.61**	**0.59**
Stative	**0.55**	**0.56**	**0.53**	**0.55**
External	0.46	**0.51**	0.47	0.46
Range	*13*	*12*	*14*	*13*

case of SPE, has been assumed to be an increased rate of SPE. Flores-Ferrán (2007), for instance, refers to a higher rate of SPE as less conservative. Under these assumptions, younger speakers would be expected to use more overt pronominal subjects than middle- and older-aged speakers. The age effect for the three Minorcan groups was, nonetheless, in the opposite direction: Older speakers favored overt first person singular subjects more than the youngest group, a trend also reported for Barranquilla, Colombia (Orozco and Guy 2008), and Mexico City (Lastra and Martín Butragueño, this volume). If the assumption that using fewer overt pronominal subjects is more conservative is correct, the reason for the trend reported in Minorca requires an alternative explanation, therefore, entailing a comparison of both age groups regarding other confounding variables. The two age groups also differ in literacy, where younger Minorcans are literate in both languages and middle-aged and older participants only in Spanish. If we consider using fewer overt pronominal subjects a sign of a more conservative linguistic behavior, literacy in both languages may give access to more conservative forms. With a small sample of speakers, I leave this issue for further testing with a larger group. Crucially, however, the reported trend where younger participants use fewer overt pronominal subjects is reported in various parts of the Hispanic World and, thus, the assumption that the change is towards more overt subjects may need to be reconsidered. Additionally, the effect of age in the SC data does not follow the hypothesis that linguistic change in subject expression leads to more overt pronominal subjects either, whereby younger speakers would use the less conservative form (i.e., a

Table 7.7 Group comparisons of external variables (factor weights resulting from multivariate regression analyses of the contribution of external factors to the probability of producing a first person singular overt pronominal subject vs. a null subject across the four groups; factor groups selected as significant in gray background)

	SC	CC	SB	CB
AGE GROUP				
2	**0.60**	**0.58**	**0.57**	**0.55**
1	0.49	0.38	0.40	0.41
3	0.39			
Range	*21*	*20*	*17*	*14*
GENDER				
Female	**0.54**	**0.54**	0.47	**0.57**
Male	0.47	0.45	**0.54**	0.43
Range	*2*	*9*	*7*	*14*

higher use of overt pronominal subjects). Spanish monolingual speakers in this project reveal an increase in overt pronominal expression from the oldest generation (generation 3) to the middle age generation (generation 2) as predicted by the hypothesis. This change, however, is not sustained onto the youngest generation (generation 1), which shows a lower rate of overt pronominal subjects than middle-aged speakers. Unlike in the bilingual data, there is no obvious cofounding variable to offer an explanation. At this point, further research is necessary in order to determine if the ongoing change in Spanish is towards a lower use of overt pronominal subjects.

GENDER differences were found between the SC group and the other three groups in terms of the significance of the variable. Additionally, differences were also attested in the ranking of the constraints. Females favored overt first person singular pronominal subjects in all groups except the SB. The previous literature also reports contradictory results regarding gender (Shin 2013). At this time, there is no obvious difference between males and females in the different groups in Minorca that I can offer to explain this result. In the older generations, it is possible that females may have had less access to education than males. That, however, does not explain why SBs are different from the other groups or why the younger generations included in the analysis did not compensate for the trend. Thus, further research with larger groups of participants is necessary to understand the effect of this variable in Minorca and Valladolid.

Effects of Bilingualism

The effects of bilingualism discussed in this chapter are *convergence* and *simplification,* albeit with a different definition required in light of the data presented here. We follow Bullock and Toribio's (2004) definition of convergence as the enhancement of structural similarity between languages in contact, which I apply to variationist research extending Otheguy and Zentella's (2012) example to these data, whereby changes in variable and constraint ranking in bilingual, as compared to monolingual varieties, increase the similarity in the rankings of both languages/varieties. This change is not attested in these data, as the only differences between SC and CC were in the constraint ranking of the non-significant variable VERB TYPE and how both bilingual groups converge with the SC ranking while returning this variable as significant. Simplification, while being a controversial term, has been adopted in the last decade by Sorace and colleagues to denote a strategy bilinguals may use to compensate for the increased processing cost of bilingualism. In the case of subject expression, Sorace's understanding of simplification would affect the distribution of null and overt pronominal subjects by (a) increasing the use of overt pronominal subjects to avoid the cognitive cost of keeping a referent in mind and (b) losing the pragmatic content (i.e., switch reference variable) of the alternation. Crucially, though, Sorace's (2011, 2012) processing account predicts simplification to be necessary to alleviate the processing burden of bilingualism, irrespective of language pairing. Therefore, even in the data presented here, Sorace predicts an increase in overt pronominal subject use, a result that does not bear in these data. The data are consistent, however, with a change interpreted as a *simplification* in another sense.

Simplification is present in our data in lower ranked internal variables but not as envisioned by Sorace and colleagues, where the overuse of overt pronouns is considered a cognitive economy strategy in that the processing of the pragmatic content of the overt pronoun is suspended (Sorace 2004, 144). Here *simplification* is understood as a reduction (i.e., variable weakening) or increase (i.e., variable fortition) in the linguistic variables affecting SPE as they become more categorical (i.e., with weights further from .50). VERB FORM AMBIGUITY displays the same constraint ranking in bilingual as in monolingual Spanish but the influence of this variable becomes negligible in bilingual Spanish (i.e., weakened as a result of a decrease in the range in constraint ranking from 18 and 17 in SCs and CCs to 5 in SBs and CBs). VERB TYPE is a case of fortition; the constraint ranking, which is the same as in monolingual Spanish, exhibits an increase in range in bilingual Spanish, which is rather small in our data (range = 13 in SCs, 14 in CCs, 14 in SBs, and 13 in CBs). Nonetheless, the variable reaches significance only in SBs and CBs. I would like to suggest here, therefore, that both weakening and fortition are instances of economy, where the variable SPE system changes in bilingual speech by enhancing and simplifying trends. Enhancing a trend is economical if it makes the effect of a constraint on a variable distribution more categorical. It remains unclear, however, when weakening rather than fortition should possibly take place.

I propose here as well as elsewhere (Prada Pérez, in progress; Prada Pérez and Pascual y Cabo 2012) that bilingualism affects the lower ranked variables. Given the similarities between Spanish and Catalan, it is not surprising that the effects of bilingualism are minor but it is crucial to this proposal that they take place only in the lowest ranked variables. Notably, the highest ranked variable, which exhibits the most categorical distribution, CONNECT, does not exhibit any bilingualism effect (an effect that would be expected under Sorace's 2011 account). These results are important because they show that bilinguals are able to converge with syntax on the grammar of Spanish for properties at the lexico-semantic interface, like VERB TYPE, and properties at the discourse-pragmatics interface, like CONNECT. At the same time, our results support Sorace's (2011, 2012) findings, as *simplification* is readily attested in our bilingual data albeit with significant modification in its meaning. Where *simplification* might take place is not at the discourse-pragmatics interface, as Sorace suggests, but in lower ranked variables (i.e., less categorical distributions). This proposal warrants further research as it remains undetermined whether the difference between the bilingual and the monolingual grammar constitutes an increase in the range between constraints, making the variable more influential, or a decrease in constraint range, making the variable more superfluous. Both outcomes are witnessed in these data and the pulling and pushing forces remain unclear.

CONCLUSION

In this chapter, I examined first person singular subject expression in the Spanish of Catalan- and Spanish-dominant bilinguals in comparison to both Spanish and Catalan. Comparisons across groups revealed that the four groups use overt first person singular pronominal subjects at similar rates (19.8 percent in SCs, 20.7 percent in CCs, 19.9 percent in SBs, and 21.3 percent in CBs) and in similar ways, as LANGUAGE GROUP was not a significant variable. Comparisons of variable and constraint rankings among the four groups further confirmed this trend. Cases where Catalan- and Spanish-dominant bilinguals differed from both controls but not from each other are also attested in our data. This was particularly so in the variables VERB FORM AMBIGUITY, which was significant only in the control groups, and VERB TYPE, which was significant only in the Spanish of the bilingual groups. These differences were interpreted as examples of *simplification*, in the sense that those variables which less strongly condition SPE (i.e., those lower ranked) are more categorical in bilingual grammars, either through variable fortition (variables became significant and higher ranked in the bilingual grammar) or through variable weakening (variables were lower ranked and not significant in the bilingual grammar). This outcome would lend support to a processing account along the lines of Sorace's (2011) work where the burden of two active languages is alleviated by simplifying the distribution of null and overt pronominal subjects in Spanish or a linguistic change approach where ongoing changes might be accelerated in bilingual speech (however, see Silva-Corvalán 1993).

Sorace (2011) proposes that processing is the reason underlying language contact outcomes. While this result is consistent with Sorace (2011), her predictions go beyond a specific variable and anticipate a general overuse of overt pronominal subjects in Spanish irrespective of the language pairing, a result not attested here. Additionally, she predicts changes to take place at the syntax interface with other modules, which is not supported by our results regarding target-like behavior with respect to the variable CONNECT. The results presented here are better explained by bilingualism affecting variables that are less influential in the distribution (Prada Pérez, in progress). This hypothesis is substantiated by the fact that CONNECT, the most influential variable, remains the same across the four data sets examined here, while VERB FORM AMBIGUITY and VERB TYPE do not (however, see Orozco, this volume, for the need to explore verb semantics differently). One more observation that can be made about the data is that in cases where the variable is more significant or higher ranked in one language than in the other, the bilinguals seem to pattern with the language that has a more categorical distribution (e.g., in the case of VERB TYPE, where bilinguals pattern with Spanish), a result consistent with the Vulnerability Hypothesis (Prada Pérez, in progress), where more categorical distributions are less affected by bilingualism. This hypothesis is further supported by the lack of correlation with L1—Spanish L1 speakers are not patterning more with Spanish controls and Catalan L1 more with Catalan controls—as the relative importance of the variable in a language seems to override L1 influence in these data.

Therefore, in trying to find the source of crosslinguistic influence, a task undertaken in the formal generative as well as in the variationist tradition, the use of adequate linguistic analysis of the property, as in the variationist analysis of subject expression, provides a valuable tool for theorizing. Variationist analyses, then, allow us to quantify how categorical or variable forms are in very specific contexts, as determined by variable hierarchy, allowing us to test the hypothesis that the direction of convergence will be determined by the more categorical language. Additionally, it implies that phenomena vulnerable to crosslinguistic influence are variable and may not lie at a syntax interface with another component (Prada Pérez, in progress).

Further research is needed to test the Vulnerability Hypothesis, from which several questions emerge. It remains unresolved in this chapter what restricts the role that language similarity has or whether *convergence* or *simplification* will surface. Refining the Vulnerability Hypothesis, however, requires further testing of variable phenomena in bilingual speech, especially with other language pairings that may still be null subject languages but have greater differences in variable and constraint rankings (Michnowicz, this volume; Carvalho and Bessett, this volume).

Lastly, this chapter aligns with previous identifications of external variables as community-dependent. Comparing the Spanish of Minorca and Valladolid is, thus, unnatural in that they form two separate communities. Evidence that the Minorcan groups form a speech community and that the Catalan L1 groups form a sub-community is found with regards to AGE GROUP and the distribution of the variable GENDER, respectively. AGE GROUP was highly significant in all four speaker cohorts only when the division was into three age groups for SC and two groups for the Minorca data. The constraint ranking for AGE GROUP was the same across the Minorcan groups, indicating that regarding age group they form a single speech community, while Valladolid Spanish speakers form a different speech community. This result is unsurprising as Minorca residents, whether Spanish or Catalan L1, form rather tight social networks. GENDER, on the other hand, shows that the CC group and the CB group are part of the same community. It is, however, the only difference between CBs and SBs reported here. Therefore, GENDER indicates a subdivision within the Minorcan community with respect to Spanish L1 versus Catalan L1 groups. Linguistically speaking, though, Catalan and Spanish L1 speakers are indistinguishable. Therefore, the inclusion of language-external variables in research on bilingual behavior helps us understand our contact situation and, as a consequence, our data more fully.

ACKNOWLEDGMENTS

This work was partially funded by the NSF dissertation research improvement grant 0746748. Thanks to Osmer Balam, the editors of this volume, and two anonymous reviewers for their helpful comments, to my research assistants for their help transcribing the interviews, to Eva Florit for interviewing the participants in Catalan, and to César Giraldo and Araceli de Prada Espinel for their help recruiting participants. Finally, a special thanks to the participants of this study. All errors are my own.

NOTES

1. The author has family ties to Minorca and spent one month per year in Minorca from ages 0–18 and less regularly afterwards.
2. The interviewer had training in philological studies and worked for the language planning sector of the local government.
3. In this analysis, the percentages and factor weights for mental and stative predicates do not align and should, thus, be taken with caution. This issue, however, dissipated in the separate runs.

4. The term *simplification* is used throughout the chapter without a negative connotation. In particular, it is a change in the variables that affect the distribution, be it a weakening or a fortition of variables.

REFERENCES

Abreu, Laurel. 2012. "Subject pronoun expression and priming effects among bilingual speakers of Puerto Rican Spanish." In *Selected Proceedings of the 14th Hispanic Linguistics Symposium*, edited by Kimberly Geeslin and Manuel Díaz-Campos, 1–8. Somerville, MA: Cascadilla Proceedings Project.

Ávila-Jiménez, Bárbara. 1995. "A sociolinguistic analysis of a change in progress: Pronominal overtness in Puerto Rican Spanish." *Cornell Working Papers in Linguistics* 13:25–47.

Bailey, Guy. 2004. "Real and apparent time." In *The handbook of language variation and change*, edited by J. K. Chambers, Peter Trudgill, and Natalie Schilling-Estes, 312–32. Cambridge: Blackwell.

Bayley, Robert, and Lucinda Pease-Alvarez. 1996. "Null and expressed pronoun variation in Mexican-descent children's Spanish." In *Sociolinguistic variation: Data, theory, and analysis*, edited by Jennifer Arnold, Renée Blake, and Brad Davidson, 85–99. Stanford, Calif.: CSLI Publications.

———. 1997. "Null pronoun variation in Mexican-descent children's narrative discourse." *Language Variation and Change* 9:349–371.

Bentivoglio, Paola. 1987. *Los sujetos pronominales de primera persona en el habla de Caracas*. Caracas: Central University of Venezuela.

Bullock, Barbara, and Almeida Jacqueline Toribio. 2004. "Convergence as an emergent property in bilingual speech." *Bilingualism: Language and Cognition* 7:91–93.

Cameron, Richard. 1992. "Pronominal and null subject variation in Spanish: constraints, dialects, and functional compensation." PhD diss., University of Pennsylvannia.

———. 1994. "Ambiguous agreement, functional compensation, and nonspecific tú in the Spanish of San Juan, Puerto Rico, and Madrid, Spain." *Language Variation and Change* 5:305–34.

———. 1995. "The scope and limits of switch reference as a constraint on pronominal subject expression." *Hispanic Linguistics* 6/7:1–27.

———. 1996. "A community-based test of a linguistic hypothesis." *Language in Society* 25, 61–111.

Cameron, Richard, and Nydia Flores-Ferrán. 2004. "Perseveration of subject expression across regional dialects of Spanish." *Spanish in Context* 1:41–65.

Carvalho, Ana M., and Michael Child. 2011. "Subject pronoun expression in a variety of Spanish in contact with Portuguese." In *Selected Proceedings of the 5th Workshop on Spanish Sociolinguistics*, edited by Jim Michnowicz and Robin Dodsworth, 14–25. Somerville, MA: Cascadilla Press.

Casanova Seuma, Lourdes. 1999. "El sujeto en catalán coloquial." *Revista Española de Lingüística* 29(1):105–131.

Eckert, Penelope, and Sally McConnell-Ginet. 2003. *Language and gender.* Cambridge: Cambridge University Press.

Enríquez, Emilia. 1984. *El pronombre personal sujeto en la lengua española hablada en Madrid.* Madrid: Consejo Superior de Investigaciones Científicas.

Erker, Daniel, and Gregory R. Guy 2012. "The role of lexical frequency in syntactic variability: Variable subject personal pronoun expression in Spanish." *Language* 88:526–57.

Flores-Ferrán, Nydia. 2002. *A sociolinguistic perspective on the use of subject personal pronouns in Spanish narratives of Puerto Ricans in New York City.* Munich: Lincom-Europa.

———. 2004. "Spanish subject personal pronoun use in New York City Puerto Ricans: Can we rest the case for English contact?" *Language Variation and Change* 16:49–73.

———. 2007. "A bend in the road: Subject personal pronoun expression in Spanish after 30 years of sociolinguistic research." *Language and Linguistic Compass* 1/6:624–652.

Holmquist, Jonathan. 2012. "Frequency rates and constraints on subject personal pronoun expression: Findings from the Puerto Rican highlands." *Language Variation and Change* 24:203–20.

Labov, William. 2001. *Principles of linguistic change: Social factors.* Cambridge, MA: Blackwell.

Lapidus, Naomi, and Ricardo Otheguy. 2005a. "Contact induced change? Overt nonspecific ellos in Spanish in New York." In *Selected Proceedings of the 2nd Workshop on Spanish Sociolinguistics*, edited by Lotfi Sayahi and Maurice Westmoreland, 67–75. Somerville, MA: Cascadilla.

———. 2005b. "Overt nonspecific ellos in Spanish in New York." *Spanish in Context* 2:157–74.

Lizardi, Carmen Mercedes. 1993. "Subject position in Puerto Rican wh-questions: Syntactic, sociolinguistic and discourse factors." Ph.D. diss., Cornell University.

Lozano, Cristóbal. 2009. "Selective deficits at the syntax-discourse interface: Evidence from the CEDEL2 corpus." In *Representational Deficits in SLA: Studies in honor of Roger Hawkins (Language Acquisition and Language Disorders)*, edited by Neal Snape, Yan-kit Ingrid Leung, and Michael Sharwood-Smith. Amsterdam: John Benjamins, 127–166.

Margaza, Panagiota, and Aaurora Bel. 2006. "Null subjects at the syntax-pragmatics interface: Evidence from Spanish interlanguage of Greek speakers." *Proceedings of the 8th Generative Approaches to Second Language Acquisition Conference (GASLA 2006)*, edited by Mary Grantham O'Brien, Christine Shea, and John Archibald, 88–97. Somerville, MA: Cascadilla.

Morales, Amparo. 1997. "La hipótesis funcional y la aparición del sujeto no nominal: El español de Puerto Rico." *Hispania* 80:153–65.

Orozco, Rafael, and Gregory Guy. 2008. "El uso variable de los pronombres sujetos: ¿qué pasa en la costa Caribe colombiana?" In *Selected Proceedings of the 4th*

Workshop on Spanish Sociolinguistics, edited by Maurice Westmoreland and Juan Antonio Thomas, 70–80. Somerville, MA: Cascadilla Proceedings Project.

Otheguy, Ricardo, and Ana Celia Zentella. 2012. *Spanish in New York: Language contact, dialectal leveling, and structural continuity*. New York: Oxford University Press.

Otheguy, Ricardo, Ana Celia Zentella, and David Livert. 2007. "Language and dialect contact in Spanish in New York: Towards the formation of a speech community." *Language* 83:1–33.

Perlmutter, David M. 1971. *Deep and surface structure constraints in syntax*. New York: Holt, Rinehart, and Winston.

Prada Pérez, Ana de. 2009. "Subject expression in Minorcan Spanish: consequences of contact with Catalan." Phd diss. (unpublished), The Pennsylvania State University.

———. 2010. "Variation in subject expression in Western Romance." In *Romance Linguistics 2009: Selected papers from the 39th Linguistic Symposium on Romance Languages (LSRL)*, edited by Sonia Colina, Antxon Olarrea and Ana M. Carvalho, 267–284. Amsterdam: John Benjamins.

———. In progress. "The Vulnerability Hypothesis."

Prada Pérez, Ana de, and Diego Pascual y Cabo. 2012. "Interface heritage speech across proficiencies: Unaccusativity, focus, and subject position in Spanish." *Selected Proceedings of the 14th Hispanic Linguistics Symposium*, edited by Kimberly Geeslin and Manuel Díaz-Campos, 308–318. Somerville, MA: Cascadilla Proceedings Project.

Ranson, Diana L. 1991. "Person marking in the wake of /s/ deletion in Andalusian Spanish." *Language Variation and Change* 3(2):133–152.

Sankoff, David, Sali Tagliamonte, and Eric Smith. 2012. Goldvarb LION: A variable rule application for Macintosh. Retrieved from http://individual.utoronto.ca/tagliamonte/goldvarb.htm.

Shin, Naomi Lapidus. 2012. "Variable use of Spanish subject pronouns by monolingual children in Mexico." In *Selected Proceedings of the 2010 Hispanic Linguistics Symposium*, edited by Kimberly Geeslin and Díaz-Campos, Manuel, 130–141. Somerville, MA: Cascadilla Proceedings Project.

———. 2013. "Women as leaders of language change: A qualification from the bilingual perspective." In *Selected Proceedings of the 6th Workshop on Spanish Sociolinguistics*, edited by Ana M. Carvalho and Sara Beaudrie, 135–147. Somerville, MA: Cascadilla Proceedings Project.

Shin, Naomi Lapidus, and Ricardo Otheguy. 2013. "Social class and gender impacting change in bilingual settings: Spanish subject pronoun use in New York." *Language in Society* 42:429–452.

Silva-Corvalán, Carmen. 1982. "Subject expression and placement in Mexican–American Spanish." In *Spanish in the United States: Sociolinguistic aspects*, edited by Jon Amastae and Lucía Elías-Olivares, 93–120. Cambridge: Cambridge University Press.

———. 1993. "On the permeability of grammars: Evidence from Spanish and English contact." In *Linguistic perspectives on the Romance languages*, edited by W. Ashby, M. Mithun, G. Perissinotto, 19–43. Amsterdam: John Benjamins.

———. 1994. *Language contact and change: Spanish in Los Angeles*. Oxford: Oxford University Press.

Sorace, Antonella. 2004. "Native language attrition and developmental instability at the syntax-discourse interface: Data, interpretations and methods." *Bilingualism: Language and Cognition* 7:143–145.

———. 2011. "Pinning down the concept of 'interface' in bilingualism." *Linguistic Approaches to Bilingualism* 1(1)1–33.

———. 2012. "Pinning down the concept of interface in bilingual development: A reply to peer commentaries." *Linguistic Approaches to Bilingualism* 2(2):209–217.

Tagliamonte, Sali A. 2006. *Analysing sociolinguistic variation*. Cambridge: Cambridge University Press.

Torres Cacoullos, Rena, and Catherine E. Travis 2010. "Variable yo expression in New Mexico: English influence?" In *Spanish of the U.S. Southwest: A language in transition*, edited by Susana Rivera-Mills and Daniel Villa, 185–206. Madrid: Iberoamericana/Vervuert.

———. 2011. "Testing convergence via code-switching: Priming and the structure of variable subject expression." *International Journal of Bilingualism* 15:241–67.

Travis, Catherine. 2005. "The yo-yo effect: Priming in subject expression in Colombian Spanish." *Selected Papers from the 34th Linguistic Symposium on Romance Languages (LSRL), Salt Lake City, 2004* ed. by Randall Gess and Edward J. Rubin, 329–49. Amsterdam: John Benjamins.

———. 2007. "Genre effects on subject expression in Spanish: Priming in narrative and conversation." *Language Variation and Change* 19.101–35.

8

Subject Pronoun Expression in Spanish in Contact with Portuguese

Ana M. Carvalho and Ryan M. Bessett

It is generally believed that typologically similar languages in long-term contact situations tend to converge grammatically (Muysken 2000, 2006; Thomason and Kaufman 1988), because the more similar the sentence structures are, the easier it is to mix the two languages, which may promote the suppression of syntactic differences (Muysken 2006, 157). Spanish and Portuguese present abundant structural and lexical parallels, which in theory should lead to grammatical convergence in bilingual situations. The long-term coexistence of Spanish and Portuguese in bilingual communities in northern Uruguay along the Brazilian border offers an ideal context for testing this assumption from a variationist viewpoint, one that systematically observes language in context, entails comparisons with the source monolingual varieties, and seeks to carefully discern internally motivated features from contact-induced ones (Poplack and Levey 2010; Poplack, Zentz, and Dion 2011).

By quantitatively examining Portuguese and Spanish in this bilingual context, we hope to assess how contact has influenced the development of these border varieties, and to contribute to the debate over whether Uruguayan Portuguese should be classified as a mixed language or a variety of Portuguese with Spanish influence. Those scholars who assume that language contact in these communities has created a stable mixed language that renders separation of the two base languages impracticable have classified Uruguayan Portuguese as a "new language" (Lipski 2009, 5), as "portuñol" (Marcos-Marín 2001; Sturza 2004), as a "basilect" (Douglas 2004), or as a "mixed language" (Hickey 2010, 3; Lipski 2006, 2010), usually defined as "the result of the convergence, by a population of speakers, on a set of linguistic norms which are collectively different from previous norms" (Kerswill 2010, 230). On the other hand, variation studies that examine both Uruguayan Portuguese and border Uruguayan Spanish show that these dialects demonstrate continuities with their monolingual counterparts (for Portuguese: Carvalho 2003a, 2003b, 2004, 2014; Pacheco, forthcoming; for Spanish: Carvalho 2006a, 2006b, 2010b; Waltermire 2006, 2008, 2011), compounding a situation where true bilingualism exists (Carvalho 2010b; Waltermire 2012).

In this chapter we test one point of potential convergence: subject pronoun expression. This variable is a plausible tool for investigating contact-induced language change in this bilingual situation because in both Spanish and Portuguese, verbs may or may not be accompanied by a phonetically realized subject. Examples (1) and (2), elicited from the same speaker, illustrate variable pronoun expression during an interview in Spanish (1) and a later interview in Portuguese (2):

(1) yo pongo el arroz en la olla, [Ø] pongo el aceite [Ø] pongo sal

I put the rice in the pan, [I] put the oil [I] put the salt

(2) eu faço e [Ø] vendo os vestido e [Ø] levo fora

I make and [I] sell the dresses and [I] take them out (#12)

In these parallel constructions, the first verb is preceded by a first-person pronoun ('*yo*' in Spanish, '*eu*' in Portuguese), followed by two other co-referential verbs with no expressed pronoun. Overall, Spanish tends to favor null pronouns (see the volume introduction for a summary), while Brazilian Portuguese is in transition toward mandatory overt expression of pronominal subjects (e.g., Barbosa, Duarte, and Kato 2005; Duarte 1993, 1995, 2003; Kato and Negrão 2000). In consequence, while Spanish continues to be considered a prototypically pro-drop language, many consider Brazilian Portuguese to be a semi- (or partial) pro-drop system (Barbosa, Duarte, and Kato 2005).

We examine the production of subject pronouns in the speech of border-area bilinguals to assess to what extent they use different patterns when speaking Portuguese versus Spanish. Given that both languages share numerous structural features, including very similar verb paradigms and pronoun expression patterns susceptible to similar pragmatic, discourse, and syntactic constraints, we expect parallel structures to be reinforced at the expense of divergent ones (following Silva-Corvalán's [1994] principle that bilingual speakers tend toward linguistic economy). Thus, in a contact situation subtle differences would be neutralized, resulting in a single, unified system. By investigating crosslinguistic patterned variation we can explore whether bilinguals in situations where similar languages are in contact indeed utilize parallels to develop a single variable system.

The challenge in assessing the impact of contact between typologically similar languages is that highly cognate systems share much pre-contact parallel variability (e.g., Barnes 2010 on Spanish in contact with Veneto, and Prada Pérez, this volume, on Spanish in contact with Catalan), and conflict sites are more gradient than abrupt binary choices. Likewise, monolingual varieties of both Spanish and Portuguese share substantial structural similarities that need to be accounted for before bilingual varieties are analyzed, a difficulty Blas Arroyo (2011, 390) encountered when examining Spanish–Catalan interlinguistic influences. Portuguese and Spanish present abundant grammatical parallels due to crosslinguistic coincidence (Carvalho 2006a; Guy 2014; Posio 2012, 2013), creating a need to exhaustively delineate the differences and similarities between these languages in non-contact situations before assessing the impact of contact (see Torres Cacoullos and Travis, this volume), in order to detect conflict sites (Meyerhoff 2009; Poplack and Tagliamonte 2001; Tagliamonte 2003), or potential locus of contact-induced change.

To this end, several studies compare contact and non-contact dialects through various means: contrasting previous reports of monolingual varieties with bilingual speech using different generations of speakers (Bayley and Pease-Alvarez 1997; Silva-Corvalán 1994) or years of US residence (Flores-Ferrán 2002), or comparing the speech of recently arrived immigrants (for pre-contact patterns) with US-born counterparts (e.g., Lapidus and Otheguy 2005; Otheguy and Zentella 2012; Othegey, Zentella, and Livert 2007; Shin and Montes-Alcalá, 2014). Abreu (2012) and Travis (2007) base their comparisons on interviews conducted in monolingual and bilingual Spanish-speaking communities, ensuring a unified data collection and coding procedure for all data. Only recently, scholars have begun considering constraints in English to more reliably assess the impact of Spanish–English contact (Torres Cacoullos and Travis, this volume; Shin and Montes-Alcalá, 2014). These studies base their comparisons on monolingual English, leaving the English spoken by Spanish–English bilinguals unexamined. Thus a difference between previous studies and the current one is that here we examine both languages as they are spoken in the same bilingual community.

In the present study, a major challenge is the dearth of studies of monolingual Uruguayan Spanish that could provide a basis for comparison with Uruguayan border Spanish. Subject pronoun expression in Brazilian Portuguese, in contrast, has been extensively examined, but the use of different coding systems makes it difficult to compare these results to ours (e.g., Barbosa, Duarte and Kato 2005; Duarte 1993, 1995, 2003; Kato and Negrão 2000; Silveira 2012). To ensure cross-language comparability, we contrast the same speakers' pronoun use in each language, using the same data collection, handling, and coding procedures. Every speaker participated in two sociolinguistic interviews: The first was conducted in Spanish (the language typically used in first encounters with non-locals). A few weeks later, after developing a personal relationship with the speaker, the same interviewer conducted another interview in Portuguese. By examining subject pronoun expression patterns by the same speaker in different languages, we can reasonably assess whether or not these parallel pronoun systems have completely converged in these bilinguals' minds; if divergence persists, this would suggest a certain independence of codes, despite prolonged contact.

The larger inquiry investigated in the present study is twofold: (1) Are overall SPE rates influenced by contact, manifested as either Uruguayan border Spanish expressing more pronouns than surrounding dialects due to convergence toward Portuguese, or as Uruguayan Portuguese expressing fewer pronouns than Brazilian Portuguese due to convergence toward Spanish?, and (2) Are there differences in the factor groups constraining this variable or in the ranking of factors within these groups? Following the principles of comparative sociolinguistics (Meyerhoff 2009; Nagy et al. 2011; Poplack and Levey 2010; Tagliamonte 2003), we interpret any difference in the distribution of this variable across languages as diagnostic of differences in the speaker's variable grammars. Given the lexical, morphological, and syntactic similarities between Spanish and Portuguese, and based on the premise that contact between cognate languages promotes grammatical convergence, we expect bilinguals to capitalize on this variable and allow both languages to reach a structural common ground.

PORTUGUESE–SPANISH COMPARISONS

SPANISH

In Spanish, subject pronoun expression has been extensively studied from a variationist perspective. Despite cross-dialectal differences in overall SPE rates, ranging from 19 percent in

Mexican Spanish (Solomon 1999) to 45 percent in Puerto Rican Spanish (Cameron 1994), one set of unified constraints is believed to condition pronoun expression across all dialects; namely, discourse continuity, type and number of grammatical person, and tense, mood, and aspect (TMA). As described in the volume introduction, pronouns tend to be expressed more often when the referent is singular, whenever the referent changes, and when the verb is in the imperfect tense. These commonalities across Spanish dialects lead Torres Cacoullos and Travis (this volume) to assert that "by the criterion of linguistic conditioning, the grammar is the same across Spanish varieties."

Nevertheless, there are some cross-dialectal differences in the ways constraints are selected and ranked. Comparing Caribbean and mainland newcomers in New York City, Otheguy, Zentella, and Livert (2007, 789) find that although these dialects differ markedly in pronoun expression rates, the constraint hierarchies are similar but not identical. In both varieties, the first two factors conditioning pronoun expression are person followed by discourse connectivity, but verb tense and clause type have different degrees of influence. Moreover, presence of a reflexive and a set phrase are important factors among mainland but not Caribbean dialects. Differences are also found in formulaic/grammaticalized constructions by Posio (this volume), who shows that frequently used forms of *decir* disfavor subject expression in Peninsular Spanish but favor it in Colombian Spanish.

Comparing Madrid and Buenos Aires dialects, Soares da Silva (2006) similarly finds that the top two factors conditioning pronoun realization (person and switch reference) are the same, but subsequent factors differ in order of importance. In addition, some factors (e.g., clause type and verb form) are relevant for the Buenos Aires but not the Madrid dialect. Thus, uniformity of constraints across Spanish varieties points to cross-dialectal consistency reflecting a "similar linguistic tradition" (Otheguy, Zentella, and Livert 2007, 789), but the lack of total coincidence in variable constraints across varieties shows that there is no single, unified cross-dialectal grammar for subject pronoun expression that can be contrasted with bilingual ones. Thus, it would be inappropriate to rely solely on previous studies as source for comparison with Uruguayan border Spanish, because it would be assumed that there is a unified monolingual variable grammar that can be contrasted with bilingual ones.

Portuguese

Brazilian Portuguese is more unified than Spanish and differs substantially from European Portuguese. Regarding pronoun use, overall rates range from 56 percent in Kalunga, a community in the state of Goiás (Ferreira 2003), to 63 percent in Rio de Janeiro (Duarte 1995). These rates are considerably lower in Portugal (27 percent; Duarte 1995) and Mozambique (28 percent; Bravin dos Santos 2006, in Soares da Silva 2006). In terms of factor rankings, few variationist pronoun expression studies in Brazilian Portuguese are comparable to ours due to differences in coding and handling of the data, as well as a focus on discourse in written language (e.g., Paredes Silva 1993). Nevertheless, person, discourse continuity, and TMA, when included, are invariably found to be significant (Duarte 2003; Lira 1982; Silveira 2012), suggesting crosslinguistic parallels with Spanish.

Brazilian Portuguese has undergone a diachronic change toward overt pronoun expression in the last century (see Duarte's comparison of several time periods in Brazil; Duarte 1993, 1995), supposedly due to impoverishment of the inflectional verbal paradigm in Brazilian Portuguese. Although there is no evidence that pronouns will be expressed in cases where verbal morphology is not explicitly marked for person, overt subject pronoun expression is believed to have originated as a functional compensation for reduced agreement morphology.[1] Currently, however, pronoun use has increased across the entire paradigm independent of any person-specific loss in verbal morphological information (Duarte 1993; Roberts 1993). While Spanish continues to be regarded as a prototypical pro-drop language in general, the reduced frequency of unexpressed pronouns in Brazilian Portuguese has been seen as a move away from a prototypical pro-drop language toward a semi-pro-drop system (e.g., Barbosa, Duarte, and Kato 2005; Duarte 1993, 1995, 2003; Kato and Negrão 2000[2]). Under this theoretical framework, Kato (2000) summarizes empirical evidence showing an increase in other properties associated with parametric change toward a *pro* language, including increase in subject doubling, SVO order, and third-person expressed pronouns with inanimate referents. Nevertheless, a quantitative contrast exists between most dialects of Spanish and Brazilian Portuguese, allowing this variable to be examined as a potential locus for linguistic permeability on the Uruguayan border.

Portuguese–Spanish Comparisons

Portuguese and Spanish present remarkably similar verbal paradigms with nearly identical verb morphology (stem + tense/aspect/mood + person/number). The verb paradigms are accompanied by parallel pronoun systems marking first, second, and third persons in both singular and plural forms, though this system may be drastically reduced in popular Brazilian Portuguese.[3] However, few studies have compared pronoun expression in Spanish versus Portuguese. Using a corpus of European Portuguese and Spanish, Posio (2013) quantifies first person singular pronouns. He attributes the disparate rates (35 percent for Spanish; 49 percent for Portuguese) to the fact that Spanish continues to be a language that prefers to leave subject pronouns unexpressed while Portuguese tends toward expression. Furthermore, Spanish has kept the inversion of SV order, whereas the SV order has become more rigid in Portuguese. Despite this cross-linguistic typological difference, Posio finds that both languages favor first person singular pronoun expression in contexts of switch reference and when subjects are stative rather than agentive.

Regarding the expression of first person plural pronouns in spoken peninsular Spanish and Portuguese, Posio (2012) again finds a significant difference in overall rates across languages: 4.5 percent in Spanish versus 32.3 percent in Portuguese. In addition, he detects a different underlying structural constraint: While the expression of 'nosotros' (Spanish) is always hearer-exclusive in his corpus, 'nós' (Portuguese) is also used with hearer-inclusive and impersonal reference. A second difference is the grammaticalized use of the pronoun 'a gente' as an alternative to first person plural forms in Portuguese. Consequently, Posio concluded that these languages are divergent in these two respects.

Also based on data extracted from European Spanish and Portuguese, Amaral and Schwenter (2005) question the existence of contexts where the pronoun expression is truly obligatory. By drawing examples from both languages, the authors explore linguistic devices other than subject expression that carry out referential functions. Although the aim of their study is not to compare Spanish and Portuguese, the pragmatic equivalences that emerged from the examples are obvious.

Soares da Silva (2006) briefly compares his analysis of pronoun expression in Buenos Aires and Madrid Spanish with the overall tendencies found in previous studies for Brazilian and European Portuguese. He finds the languages not only have disparate overall rates, but behave differently in terms of pronoun expression with third person singular inanimate referents: Third person pronouns are sometimes (albeit rarely) expressed in Portuguese, but never expressed in the Buenos Aires and Madrid corpora analyzed by Soares da Silva. The author proposes that instead of a binary difference between pro-drop and pro languages, we should consider a continuum where on one extreme, Madrid Spanish represents a prototypical pro-drop language, followed by Buenos Aires Spanish, European Portuguese, and Brazilian Portuguese, which approximates a *pro* language.

In sum, previous studies of monolingual varieties of Portuguese and Spanish point to parallel variable grammars underlying pronoun expression. The few differences noted concern slightly different use of first person plural, especially with the novelty of '*a gente*' as a pronoun in Portuguese, and an increasing tendency to express pronouns that refer to inanimate entities in Portuguese but not Spanish. In addition, frequency of pronoun expression is clearly different between South American Spanish and Brazilian Portuguese, a difference which could, in theory, be neutralized in the speech of border bilinguals.

METHOD

Rivera, the border town where the data were collected, is characterized by societal bilingualism: Spanish is the official language used in most public domains, but Portuguese has been maintained as a subordinate language for the last two hundred years. Both qualitative (Behares 1984) and quantitative (Carvalho 2007, 2010a; Waltermire 2012) studies have shown that, despite a great deal of code-switching, speakers' language choices are conditioned by conversational topics, formality of speech, and/or interlocutors' social status.

Uruguayan Portuguese, the native language of most border residents, is a rural variety of Portuguese with heavy lexical borrowing from Spanish (Carvalho 2003a, 2010a; Elizaicín, Behares and Barrios 1987), although the urban middle classes tend to speak an urbanized variety much influenced by Brazilian Portuguese (Carvalho 2003b, 2004, 2014). Border Spanish has also showed leveling toward the monolingual varieties of Uruguayan Spanish spoken farther south (Carvalho 2006a, 2010b, Waltermire 2008, 2011), especially among middle-class and young speakers. Although it is possible to find Spanish-dominant speakers, the present corpus is based on interviews with bilinguals who experienced neither incomplete acquisition nor language attrition and used both languages in their daily lives.

The corpus was collected during five months of fieldwork in Rivera. For this study, we extracted from the larger corpus one interview in Spanish and one in Portuguese for 18 participants. All speakers except #16 were raised in homes where Portuguese was spoken. Spanish predominated in #16's home, and he learned to speak Portuguese mainly in the community, but his bilingual proficiency and linguistic behavior did not differ significantly from those of the other speakers. The interviewees were 9 men and 9 women, and 6 each were members of the working class, lower middle class, and mid-middle class. In addition, 6 represented the youngest age group of 15–28 years, 6 more 29–49 years, and 6 were in the 50–70 years age range.[4]

These sociolinguistic interviews contained 2,641 tokens with variable subject pronoun expression in Spanish, and 2,587 tokens in Portuguese, respectively. Following variationist methodology, we analyzed only those forms that had a counterpart; that is, verbs that could be expressed with or without a subject pronoun. Thus, we excluded subject-headed relative clauses, null subjects referring to meteorological conditions, explicit post-posed subjects, hesitations/repetitions, non-finite verbs, and tokens inside code-switches.[5]

All other cases were submitted to multivariate analysis using GoldVarb. The linguistic factor groups included in the analysis were grammatical person, TMA, co-referentiality, clause type, presence of a reflexive pronoun, and lexical content of the verb. The analyses explore whether the ways these bilinguals express subject pronouns varies according to the language. We expect pronoun use to be similar across both languages due to the effects of contact. Alternately, discrepant behavior in terms of frequency and constraint hierarchy would suggest that these bilinguals do not possess a converged pronoun expression system despite language contact. Moreover, in order to trace comparisons between border varieties and monolingual counterparts, references will be made to other dialects of Spanish and Portuguese.

RESULTS

In what follows, we present and compare the overall frequencies and conditioning forces underlying subject pronoun expression in both Uruguayan Border Spanish and Portuguese.

Overall rates

Among 2,641 tokens in Spanish, 658 (25 percent) were verbs with an expressed pronoun. Portuguese showed roughly double the Spanish rate, at 1,181 of 2,587 (46 percent) tokens. Table 8.1 shows cross-dialectal differences in overall rates in both languages.[6]

Table 8.1 Cross-dialectal differences in overall rates of pronoun expression in Spanish and Portuguese

Spanish		Portuguese	
Madrid	21%	Portugal	22%
Uruguay-border	**25%**	Mozambique	28%
Buenos Aires	29%	**Uruguay-border**	**46%**
Barranquilla	36%	Brazil (Kalunga)	56%
Dominican Republic	42%	Brazil (Fortaleza)	60%

Source: Madrid (Cameron 1993), Border Uruguayan Spanish (this study), Buenos Aires (Soares da Silva 2006), Barranquilla (Orozco and Guy 2008), Dominican Republic (Alfaraz, this volume), Portugal (Barbosa, Duarte, and Kato 2005, based on written corpus of interviews), Mozambique (Soares da Silva 2006), and Kalunga, Brazil (Ferreira 2003), and Ceará, Brazil (Silveira 2012).

Solely based on overall rates, results point to lack of convergence between the two languages: The Spanish rate is even lower than the 29 percent rate in Argentinean Spanish, a close monolingual variety. Uruguayan Portuguese shows a frequency rate that is 10 percent lower than the lowest attested for Brazilian Portuguese, but significantly higher than Mozambican and European Portuguese. Most importantly, the disparate overall rates point to a tendency for individual bilinguals to maintain divergent pronoun expression behavior in each language. This surprising result counters Sorace's prediction (2011) that bilinguals would show higher rates of pronoun usage, a hypothesis confirmed by several studies (Prada Pérez, this volume; Michnowicz, this volume; Barnes 2012). In fact, when speaking Portuguese, these bilinguals show an overall frequency lower than monolingual Brazilians, which could point to a subtle influence from Spanish or stagnation at an early stage of the change toward mandatory pronoun expression in Brazilian Portuguese.

Conclusions about the effect of contact based solely on comparisons of overall rates are problematic. First, overall rates vary significantly within the same language (see Torres Cacoullos and Travis, this volume), and sometimes even within the same dialect.[7] Second, the presence or absence of a variant can depend on various features of the situation being recorded (Tagliamonte 2003, 732). This is particularly relevant in Spanish pronoun expression, as Travis (2007) showed that a corpus taken from conversation had a higher pronoun frequency than an interview-based corpus, not because of dialect differences but because of differences in the communicative events. Lastly, frequency differences can result from differences in how data are handled and coded, particularly in what constitutes the envelope of variation.

Nevertheless, we consider our results relevant because the different frequencies are found in the same speakers. Furthermore, the corpora in both languages were obtained in very similar communicative events: sociolinguistic interviews. Finally, the data were handled and coded in exactly the same manner, rendering these samples optimal for comparison. Given that pronoun expression rates are subject to dialect leveling, as Otheguy, Zentella, and Livert (2007) demonstrate for Spanish speakers in New York, we interpret the differences in pronoun expression between border Spanish and Uruguayan Portuguese in the speech of bilinguals as a first indicator of lack of linguistic convergence. Thus, we agree with Shin and Erker (this volume) and Otheguy, Zentella, and Livert (2007) that a basic comparison of overall rates may indeed shed light on issues of language contact. We now supplement this evidence by discussing constraints patterns.

Factor Selection

Examination of which factor groups are significant for the output of the variable and how factors are ordered within the groups is valuable for assessing possible effects of language contact, because different constraint rankings would indicate different underlying grammars of variation (Meyerhoff 2009, 303). Crosslinguistic similarities should not, however, be immediately identified as contact-induced pattern replication without evidence that the constraint hierarchy is language specific and not due to coincidence between the two languages.

In both Spanish and Portuguese, studies following the same data-coding principles show that subject pronouns are usually expressed according to grammatical person, co-referentiality, then tense, mood, and aspect (see Shin and Erker, this volume; Michnowicz, this volume; Silveira 2012). Therefore, there is no clear evidence of radical differences in constraint rankings in monolingual varieties of Portuguese and Spanish. A similar hierarchy operates in border-area Portuguese–Spanish bilinguals as well (table 8.2).

The same factor groups operate in both languages in the same order of importance: grammatical person, TMA, and co-referentiality. The only constraint difference is that clause type was selected for Portuguese but discarded from the Spanish analysis, pointing to a divergent behavior. It would however be premature to conclude that this is evidence of convergence: Spanish in general presents this tendency (Shin and Erker, this volume; Michnowicz, this volume). In Brazilian Portuguese, the only study that followed similar coding criteria (Silveira 2012) finds that verb clause and clause type were the strongest factors, followed by person, TMA, and co-referentiality, in exactly the same order as presented for Uruguayan Portuguese. Given the tendency for this variable to be affected by grammatical person, co-referentiality, and TMA in monolingual varieties of both Spanish and Portuguese, the parallel results for both languages could represent either convergence of variable grammars or, alternatively, crosslinguistic coincidence.

Table 8.2 Comparison of constraint hierarchies in subject pronoun expression in Uruguayan border Spanish and Portuguese

Rank	Uruguayan Border Spanish	Range	Uruguayan Portuguese	Range
1	Grammatical person	.66	Grammatical person	.66
2	TMA	.52	TMA	.65
3	Co-referentiality	.28	Co-referentiality	.23
4	Clause type	[ ]	Clause type	.23
5	Age group	.19	Age group	.07
6	Socioeconomic group	.16	Socioeconomic group	0.1
7	Gender	[ ]	Gender	0.05
Log likelihood = –1249.921			Log likelihood = –1562.173	
Significance = 0.01			Significance = 0.04	

Note: Excluded from both analyses are reflexive pronouns and lexical content of the verb.

In fact, co-referentiality, grammatical person, and clause type are reportedly the top conditioners of subject pronoun expression in languages as typologically dissimilar as Mandarin Chinese (Li, Chen, and Chen 2012). Because there are strong universal constraints and few language-/dialect-specific tendencies, similar constraint hierarchies are problematic for diagnosing the influence of contact. A more detailed look at how variables are distributed in each factor group may be a more reliable way to evaluate for possible convergence. Among the linguistic constraints, grammatical person shows the clearest divergence between Uruguayan Portuguese and Uruguayan border Spanish.

Grammatical Person

Except for the fact that singular pronouns tend to be expressed more often than plural ones, there is a great deal of disparate ordering cross-dialectally in both Spanish and Portuguese, rendering the comparison between border dialects and pre-contact varieties difficult.

For example, for singular referents in Spanish, Otheguy and Zentella (2012) found among Caribbean newcomers a preference to express pronouns in the second person, followed by first and third persons, whereas mainland newcomers tended to express pronouns in the third person, followed by first and second, respectively. Colombian Spanish, in contrast, is ordered in first person, followed by third, then second (Orozco and Guy 2008). In Portuguese, the influence of singular person also varies considerably. Both Paredes Silva (2003) and Duarte (1993) report expressed pronouns are more common in second person singular than in third or first person. Silveira (2012) finds in his corpus data an order of first person, then second, then third. The inconsistencies in monolingual varieties of both languages make it difficult to compare grammatical person rankings in the varieties spoken by border bilinguals (table 8.3).

Table 8.3 shows that the patterns for border Uruguayan Spanish and Portuguese in this sample do not depart substantially from results reported for other varieties in previous studies. In the Spanish column, note that specific 'usted' has the highest probability weight (.75). This tendency was also found by Erker and Guy (2012), Flores-Ferrán (2002), and Soares da Silva (2006), who argued that 'usted' maintains its role as an

Table 8.3 Grammatical person and expression of subject pronouns in Uruguayan border Spanish and Uruguayan Portuguese[a]

Rank	Uruguayan Border Spanish	Weight	%	n	Uruguayan Portuguese	Weight	%	n
1					A gente	.74	74	31/42
2	'Usted' [+specific]	.75	56	22/39	Você/Tu [+specif]	.64	55	48/88
3	Yo	.62	32	414/1309	Você/Tu [-specif]	.62	51	43/84
4	Usted/Tú [-specific]	.58	26	48/188	Ele/a [+anim, +specif]	.61	49	164/333
5	Él/Ella [+anim, +specific]	.53	27	79/298	Eu	.57	50	754/1504
6	Tú [+specific]	.51	18	13/73	Vocês	.55	67	2/3
7	Nosotros/as	.45	21	42/197	Nós	.45	41	51/123
8	Ellos/as [+specific]	.25	11	35/328	Eles/as [+specif]	.34	34	64/188
9	Él/ Ella [-anim, + specific]	.08	2	2/125	Ele/a [-anim, +spec]	.15	14	13/91
10	Él/Ella [+anim, -specific]	.09	4	1/28	Ele/a [+anim, -spec]	.10	9	4/45
11	Ellos/as [-specific] (knock-out)	[ ]	0	0/33	Eles/as [-specif]	.08	9	7/82
Log likelihood = −1249.921 Significance = 0.01					Log likelihood = −1562.713 Significance = 0.04			

a. Although the presence of only a few tokens in some groups is not optimal for multivariate analysis, we believe that these exploratory results are a good first step for further investigation, while allowing for immediate crosslinguistic comparisons.

address form, so therefore is usually expressed. The second most common grammatical person to trigger an expressed pronoun in Uruguayan border Spanish is first person, a tendency likewise reported in several studies (Orozco and Guy 2008; Shin 2012). In third place is nonspecific second person singular. In referential specificity of second person singular, Uruguayan border Spanish aligns with Puerto Rican Spanish (Cameron 1994), since both dialects tend to express pronouns with nonspecific more often than with specific second person singular. This tendency is reversed in third person singular, where specificity increases the probability that the pronoun will be expressed. Finally, first and third person plural forms are unlikely to take expressed pronouns, a behavior seen cross-dialectally. The only deviation from previous accounts of this variable in other dialects of Spanish is the expression of pronouns with inanimate third person referents, a tendency not reported in previous studies. Although the probability of a pronoun being expressed when the referent is a thing is very low (.08, based on only 2 expressed pronouns out of 125), as discussed later, this may have implications for the contact hypothesis.

Uruguayan Portuguese (see the right-hand side of table 8.3) maintains the singular/plural dichotomy found in Spanish and in other Portuguese varieties, where singular referents are more likely than plural ones to trigger expressed pronouns. The order of frequency of singular pronouns is very similar to that attested for Kalunga Brazilian Portuguese in Brazil, revealing a great deal of similarity between these dialects (table 8.4).

Table 8.4 Subject pronoun expression with similar grammatical person in Kalunga and Uruguayan Portuguese

Kalunga Brazilian Portuguese	Weight	%	Uruguayan Portuguese	Weight	%
A gente	.77	87%	A gente	.74	74%
Você/tu	.53	75%	Você/tu	.64	55%
Eu	.50	64%	Ele	.61	49%
Ele	.48	52%	Eu	.57	50%

Source: Kalunga Brazilian Portuguese from Ferreira (2003); Uruguyan Portuguese from this study.

Another feature common to both Brazilian and Uruguayan Portuguese is the use of the pronoun 'a gente', an innovation that is gradually replacing '*nós*' (we) as the first person plural pronoun. This grammaticalized construction in Portuguese shows a clear contrast with Spanish (e.g., Posio 2012) and an indisputable affiliation between Uruguayan and Brazilian Portuguese, where it is used 2.5 times more frequently than '*nós*' (Naro, Görski, and Fernandes 1999). In Rivera, the oldest group of participants contributed only 3 percent of '*a gente*' tokens (2/58), the middle-aged group contributed 39 percent (23/59), and the youngest 51 percent (18/35). Pacheco (2013, 139) likewise identified a slight preference for '*a gente*' among bilingual adults in Aceguá, Uruguay, a fact she attributes to the tendency for adults to have more diffuse social networks, including more contact with Brazilians across the border. Thus, a linguistic change that began in Brazil crossed national borders, a movement similar to that demonstrated for the palatalization of dental stops (Carvalho 2004).

Comparing the distribution of grammatical person in Portuguese and Spanish among Rivera bilinguals (table 8.3) reveals both similarities and differences. The grammatical person that most strongly constrains pronoun expression differs quite significantly. For Portuguese, the strongest constraint is '*a gente*', a construction with no equivalent in Spanish. For Spanish, '*usted* [+specific]' is the top constraint, an option listed right after '*a gente*' for Portuguese. Third in frequency for Portuguese is 'second person singular [-specific]', whereas in Spanish 'first person singular' ranks third, followed by 'second person [-specific]' in fourth. Thus, first person singular in Portuguese ('*eu*') and Spanish ('*yo*') are also discrepant; in Spanish, '*yo*' is one of the most important factors conditioning pronoun expression (e.g., Flores-Ferrán 2002; Orozco and Guy 2008; Soares da Silva 2006), but it is much less influential in Portuguese, following patterns found in Rio de Janeiro (Duarte 2003; Paredes Silva 2003).

Despite ranking differences, all persons that show positive and negative probability (higher or lower than 0.50) coincide in both languages. The tendency for plural persons to show negative probability is expected, since this tendency is seen crosslinguistically. Thus, all plural persons favor unexpressed pronouns in both languages, both in Rivera and in monolingual communities. The same is true for nonspecific third person referents, a context known to trigger unexpressed pronouns in both Portuguese and Spanish, since results have shown that animate generic referents resist pronoun expression (Cameron 1994; Ferreira 2003; Paredes Silva 1993). This is another crosslinguistic coincidence, since non-specific third person will resist pronoun expression in partial null-subject languages, according to the typology proposed by Roberts and Holmbert (in Nagy et al. 2011)

Despite abundant crosslinguistic commonalities, a probable conflict site is found in the expression of subject pronouns with inanimate referents. Whereas in Brazilian

Portuguese it is possible to express an inanimate pronoun, a tendency believed to signal a parametric change toward the suppression of pro-drop status in a language (Kato and Negrão 2000; Toribio 2000), in Spanish, to the best of our knowledge, this tendency has only been discussed in a few studies on Dominican Spanish (Enríquez 1984; Martínez-Sanz 2011; Toribio 2000) and on Uruguayan Spanish in contact with Portuguese (Elizaincín 1995). Example (4) illustrates this usage in Uruguayan Portuguese, and example (5) illustrates the parallel construction in Spanish:

(4) '*Ele (um livro) é largo, ele (um livro) é longo*' (70B)
"He (a book) is long, he (a book) is long."

(5) '*Ø Tá guardada. Ella (una pistola) es protección de la casa*' (3A)
"(It) Ø is put away. She (a pistol) is protection for the house."

Figure 8.1 shows the impact of animacy on third person singular in Uruguayan Portuguese compared with other varieties of Portuguese. The tendency toward pronoun expression is highest in Rio de Janeiro (54 percent), followed by Kalunga (32 percent), Uruguay (14 percent),[8] and Portugal (7 percent).[9]

The 2 percent of pronoun expression found with inanimate referents in border Spanish shows a substantially lower occurrence compared to any Portuguese variety, signaling a resistance to overt expression. However, given the lack of quantitative data about pronoun expression with inanimate referents in Spanish, it is difficult to compare the behavior of Uruguayan border Spanish with non-contact varieties of Spanish. Qualitative evidence seen in the few previous studies that include such cases in various Spanish-speaking communities shows that expressed pronouns are possible with inanimate subjects in Caribbean and South American dialects (Bullock and Toribio 2009, 57; Butt and Benjamin, 2011, 133; Elizaincín 1995,117; Otheguy and Zentella 2012, 241). This is significant for using inanimate subject pronoun expression as a means of assessing the impact of Spanish–Portuguese contact, in that the presence of such occurrences would suggest not direct transfer from Portuguese, but instead accelerated use of a tendency already found in Spanish. The assertion that this is a contact-induced variant would have to be based on quantitative comparisons between border Spanish and non-contact varieties. Currently, to the best of our knowledge, variationist studies of pronoun expression in Spanish do not quantify inanimate subjects in their analyses, considering them outside the envelope of variation.[10]

In sum, the analysis of the effect of grammatical person on subject pronoun expression points to both differences and similarities between Spanish and Portuguese. The languages differ in their rankings of first, second, and third person singular referents, showing a clear divergence of systems in the minds of these bilinguals, but pronoun expression with plural forms and the impact of generic referents in third person singular show a great deal of crosslinguistic similarity. Whereas the differences offer evidence of code independence, the similarities cannot be attributed to contact influences, since clear differences between the present corpus and behavior found in non-contact varieties could not be established to rule out crosslinguistic coincidence.

Constraints Other than Grammatical Person

Maintaining the premise that Spanish and Portuguese will show independence when divergent behavior is detected, but that similar behavior may be coincidental unless previous studies about monolingual varieties show otherwise, we will now turn to the next factor groups on the constraint hierarchy: TMA, co-referentiality, parallelism,

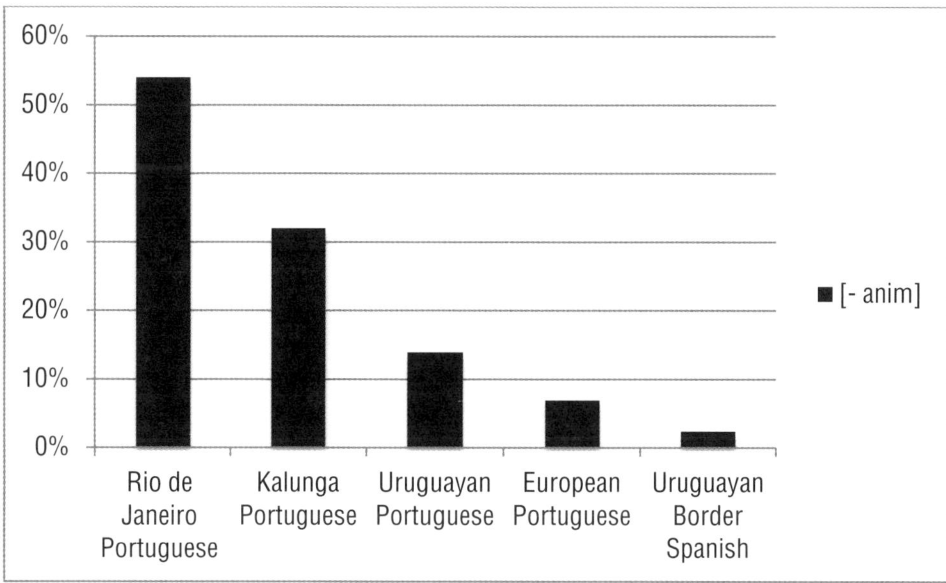

Figure 8.1 Frequency of subject pronoun expression with inanimate third-person singular referents in varieties of Portuguese and in Uruguayan Border Spanish
*Source:*Duarte 1995 (European and Kalunga Brazilian Portuguese); Duarte 2003 (Rio de Janeiro Portuguese).

clause type, and presence of a reflexive pronoun. Table 8.5 shows results for both languages.

The second factor group influencing pronoun expression is the tense, mood, and aspect of the verb. In Spanish, the imperfect tense has been found to most favor expression, while the imperative least favors it (e.g., Orozco, this volume; Posio, this volume; Shin and Montes-Alcalá, 2014; Shin and Erker, this volume). In Portuguese, there is no consensus that the imperfect tense is highest on the list of TMA factors. Silveira (2012) finds imperfect to favor expressed subjects among three broader categories (imperfect, preterit, and present), but Duarte (1995) finds that the present tense tops the list of factors in this group. Differences in coding procedures and tenses analyzed in these studies make comparison of TMA across monolingual varieties of Spanish and Portuguese difficult, but one could expect very similar behavior between the two languages. As table 8.5 shows, among bilingual speakers Portuguese and Spanish do show similarities in terms of the impact of TMA across factors, except for the imperfect, the only factor to demonstrate divergent behavior. Where in Spanish there is a positive probability of an expressed pronoun (.63), in line with findings of previous studies with other Spanish dialects, in Portuguese the probability is slightly negative (.46), in line with the present, imperfect, preterit order Duarte (1995) reports for Rio de Janeiro Portuguese.

Co-referentiality, the third most important factor for both languages, is one of the most important conditioners of subject personal pronoun expression in Spanish in general (e.g., Cameron 1993; Otheguy, Zentella, and Livert 2007; among others), in Portuguese (e.g., Duarte 1995, 2003; Paredes Silva 1993; Silveira 2012), and in other languages as well, such as Cantonese and Russian (Nagy et al. 2011). In this study, we coded the token according to its relationship to the immediately preceding verb. If the token referred to the same entity as the last verb, we marked it as co-referential; if it referred to the entity expressed by the object of the previous verb (either expressed or unexpressed), we marked it as co-referential to the object; in cases where the token did not refer to either

Table 8.5 Linguistic factors other than grammatical person contributing to subject pronoun expression in Uruguayan border Spanish and Uruguayan Portuguese

	Uruguayan Border Spanish			Uruguayan Portuguese		
Factor	**Weight**	**%**	**n**	**Weight**	**%**	**n**
TMA						
Conditional	.68	38%	10/26	.69	55%	17/31
Imperfect	.63	34%	98/287	.46	43%	146/341
Past subjunctive	.57	35%	9/26	.55	68%	17/25
Preterit	.51	29%	126/433	.43	41%	167/410
Present	.48	23%	369/1597	.54	48%	746/1569
Present subjunctive	.44	16%	4/25	.40	45%	10/22
Periphrasis	.30	28%	24/86	.49	47%	46/98
Perfective/Progressive	.28	19%	12/64	.56	55%	30/55
Imperative	.16	12%	5/41	.04	6%	2/32
Co-referentiality						
Complete switch	.64	33%	58/178	.63	59%	576/979
Switch with subject, core with object	.60	34%	388/1147	.7	60%	49/82
Co-reference with previous subject	.36	17%	211/1260	.40	37%	556/1522
Parallelism12						
E_	.65	27%	86/321	.67	57%	281/489
First token	.55	14%	19/133	.57	40%	90/227
N_	.42	12%	76/651	.31	18%	89/507
Clause type						
Main	[.53]	29%	150/510	.48	46%	473/1035
Subordinate	[.52]	28%	123/440	.62	60%	215/360
Relative	[.51]	30%	27/90	.69	65%	49/75
Coordinate	[.48]	23%	357/1545	.46	40%	444/1113
	Log likelihood = –1249.921			Log likelihood = –1562.713		
	Significance = 0.01			Significance = 0.04		

the subject or object of the previous verb, we marked it as a complete switch. Table 8.5 shows that in Spanish, as expected, a complete switch most often conditions pronoun expression (with a probability weight of .64); co-reference with the object is the factor with the highest weight in Portuguese (with a probability weight of .70). The same phenomenon is found among Maya–Spanish bilinguals in Mexico (Michnowicz, this volume), a fact the author attributes to a lack of understanding of pragmatic constraints among bilinguals, who treat co-reference with an object as if it were a complete switch.

However, given that monolingual varieties of Portuguese and Spanish are subject to the same constraints in terms of co-referentiality and that the percentage difference between them in Portuguese is only 1 percent, there is no clear evidence that Spanish–Portuguese bilinguals have in fact lost sensitivity to continuity of reference in Portuguese.

The other factor influencing this variable in both languages is priming, or the tendency of linguistic forms to occur together within a stretch of discourse. The tendency to produce parallel structures helps explain variation in co-referential contexts, where pronoun expression or omission is not explained by switch reference (Travis 2007, 107). Thus, assuming with Travis (see also Dumont 2006) that parallelism may affect the output of this variable, but mostly in contexts where co-referential tokens appear together, we coded only these contexts for this factor group. In order to avoid interaction with co-referentiality, we excluded the former before including priming in the analysis. The results in table 8.5 show both languages behaving as expected from previous studies: In contexts of co-reference, the expression of one pronoun leads to another expression, while the omission of one pronoun leads to another omission (e.g., Cameron and Flores-Ferrán 2004; Travis 2007). Meanwhile, the first token in this group presents essentially neutral probability (slightly higher than .50) in both languages. Abreu (2012) compares the role of priming as a factor influencing this variable among bilingual and monolingual Puerto Rican Spanish speakers, and finds that priming is indeed a universal process affecting both monolingual and bilingual speakers. Given that the constraints at work are universal, not language-specific, we conclude that parallelism does not constitute a good diagnostic tool to assess the role of language contact.

Finally, the last linguistic factor found to condition pronoun expression in Uruguayan Portuguese but not in Uruguayan border Spanish is clause type. Although the differences in probability weights in Spanish are not significant, both the weights and the percentages show very similar tendencies to those attested for Portuguese: Relative clauses top the hierarchy, followed by subordinate and main clauses. Coordinate clauses favor pronoun omission in both border dialects, in line with both monolingual Portuguese (Duarte 1995) and Spanish (e.g., Orozco and Guy 2008; Otheguy and Zentella 2012).

In sum, the ranking of factors within the linguistic groups shows both similarities and differences. As far as grammatical person is concerned, Portuguese and Spanish differ in the impact that singular person has on the variable, especially in the effect of first person singular, a top conditioner in Spanish but not in Portuguese. In addition, 'a gente' as a first person plural pronoun, an innovation in both Brazilian and European Portuguese, appears in Uruguayan Portuguese, diverging from its lexical equivalent in Spanish, 'la gente' (the people). Convergence of behavior can be hypothesized given the impact of plural person and third person singular [+specific] and [-animate]. Nevertheless, given tendencies attested in previous studies of non-contact varieties and the scarcity of occurrences in Spanish, there is insufficient evidence to affirm that these parallel behaviors are due to contact-induced change rather than pre-contact internal tendencies.

The other linguistic conditioners—TMA, co-referentiality, parallelism, and clause type—coincide for the most part, except for small differences in the ordering of factors affecting co-referentiality, the strength of the imperfect tense, and the conditioning power of clause type. Once again, a detailed comparison of bilingual tendencies reported in previous research on other Spanish and Portuguese varieties leads us to conclude that divergent behavior is indicative of independence of codes, or lack of convergence, whereas similar behavior is more likely due to internal tendencies.

CONCLUSION

In summary, analyses of the distribution of subject pronoun expression among Spanish–Portuguese bilinguals in Rivera, Uruguay, do not indicate completely divergent crosslinguistic behaviors. However, previous accounts of monolingual dialects of Spanish and Portuguese show abundant parallel variability in the two languages. This finding highlights the challenges of distinguishing language-specific properties from crosslinguistic tendencies in cognate languages, rendering the impact of contact difficult to identify. Nevertheless, some differences emerge and attest to the independence of the codes, counter to the expectation that both grammars would have merged. First, we presented evidence that in terms of overall rates of pronoun use, Uruguayan border Spanish parallels neighboring monolingual varieties of Spanish and shows no convergence toward Portuguese, countering the hypothesis that bilinguals would express more subject pronouns due to simplification (Sorace 2011). The fact that similar probabilistic grammars can generate significantly different outputs that mirror their monolingual counterparts points to the integrity of these languages' variable grammars in the minds of the bilinguals, countering the assertion that these languages have merged and formed a stable *new language* whose speakers cannot "switch to Portuguese" (Lipski, 2009, 5–7).

Second, dissimilarities among constraint rankings regarding the impact of grammatical person, especially with the use of grammaticalized '*a gente*' as the first person plural pronoun in Portuguese and the importance of '*yo*' as a major conditioner for pronoun expression in Spanish, show clear continuities with their monolingual counterparts and lack of crosslinguistic convergence. A possible site of conflict was detected for a larger tendency in Portuguese to express pronouns when the referent is inanimate in Spanish (albeit the lack of quantitative evidence). However, among these bilinguals, it is difficult to assert that Portuguese is influencing Spanish at all. First, only two occurrences in Spanish were found in the corpus, and second, as we point out, pronoun expression with this type of referent is possible in other Spanish dialects as well, rendering the assumption that contact is the sole cause of this phenomenon problematic. The influence of Spanish on Portuguese, on the other hand, may explain the lower rate of expressed pronouns in this category and should be the subject of further studies. The remaining linguistic factors, TMA, co-referentiality, parallelism, and clause type, present equivalent distributions that mirror monolingual varieties of Portuguese and Spanish, and, as such, cannot attest to contact. One exception is the positive probability that the imperfect tense will condition pronoun expression in Spanish, but not in Portuguese. While it is not a theoretical surprise that these grammars operate in parallel, what is relevant is the lack of complete coincidence in the distribution of this variable, which in our view contradicts the assumption that cognate languages like Spanish and Portuguese will merge into a single linguistic system among bilinguals. As claimed elsewhere (Carvalho, 2014), linguistic divergence is the result of social and ideological factors underlying diglossic dynamics on these border communities, where separation of linguistic systems is socially relevant. Thus, even though true hybridization does occur in unmonitored speech (such as the hybrid clusters analyzed by Elizaincín, Behares, and Barrios, 1987), Uruguayan Portuguese and border Spanish have not merged into a single mixed variety, as attested by the distribution of subject pronoun expression during sociolinguistic interviews where speakers were able to speak one of the languages in their repertoire and keep their variable grammars apart.

A natural follow-up to this line of inquiry is the expression of object pronouns in Uruguayan border Spanish and Portuguese, which presumably would be related to the tendency toward subject pronoun expression. Kato and Tarallo (1988) have also attributed the tendency toward omission of third person object pronouns in Brazilian Portuguese to the lessening of VS order, together with subject pronoun expression, as part of a larger divergence of the pronoun paradigm in Brazilian Portuguese from that of European Portuguese. It remains to be seen whether an examination of parallel variability in object pronoun expression between Spanish and Portuguese in these border varieties will show contact-induced changes or, alternatively, will constitute one more piece of evidence for the subtle separation of variable grammars in the minds of these bilinguals.

NOTES

1. For a similar discussion on the functional hypothesis that Caribbean Spanish may express more subjects to compensate for phonological erosion in the verb paradigm see Bayley and Pease-Alvarez (1997, 397), whose results do not support the hypothesis.
2. See Toribio (2000) for an alternative position, one that sees parametric distinctions between Dominican Spanish and standard Latin American Spanish.
3. Verbal agreement in Brazilian Portuguese is highly variable (for details, see Scherre and Naro, 2010; Naro and Scherre 2013, among others).
4. A discussion on the effects of social factors on the output of this variable is beyond the scope of this study and is discussed in Carvalho (2014).
5. Non-finite verbs headed by a pronoun are abundant in Uruguayan Portuguese, as illustrated in:

   (3) E ele não deixava eu fazer nada (12b)
   And he did not let me [I] do anything.

6. Frequency rate for Uruguayan Border Spanish reported by Carvalho and Child (2011) was 35 percent, based on 1,706 tokens extracted from 12 interviews. The inclusion of additional participants in the present study from the younger age group and middle class is responsible for the reduced overall rate of pronoun expression.
7. See Alfaraz (this volume), who reports three different overall rates of pronoun expression in Dominican Spanish.
8. Since most studies of Spanish pronoun expression exclude inanimate subjects because they consider that the incorporation of such tokens would skew the results, we included only inanimate subjects that were non-abstract (tangible), considering these to be the ones that are more likely to take an expressed pronoun. We excluded from our analysis inanimate subjects that were abstract (intangible), considering them to be very unlikely to take an expressed pronoun. Below are examples of abstract (intangible) inanimate subjects that were excluded from our analysis:
   (a) Ciudad (city): no **es** *(they city)* muy grande, pero **es** *(the city)* un pueblo un poco más chico que Rivera. (58A)
   (b) País (country): Yo pienso que tanto Brasil como Argentina son países muy desarrollados industrialmente y **pueden** *(the countries of Brazil and Argentina)* perfectamente en fin, manejarse a nivel de ellos y colmar todas las necesidade existente en estos países que están integrados. (62A)
   (c) UTO (an organization): UTO fue fundada oficialmente **empezó** *(the organization)* a funcionar el 24 de, perdón, perdón el 28 de agosto de 1924. 24. O sea que **tiene** *(the organization)*, ahora en agosto **va** *(the organization)* a

cumplir setenta y un año de existencia a nivel departamental. Muy antiguo. (62A)

(d) (the job market): Aunque a poquito **está mejorando** *(the job market)*, porque yo he visto que, visto que, **está mejorando** *(the job market)*, hay más jóvenes trabajando que antes. (21A)

(e) La vocación (vocation): si no hubiera ido, porque mi vocación era otra, no **era** *(vocation)* quedarme estacionada, **era** *(vocation)* evoluir. (57A)

(f) La vida (life): Sí, **ha quedado** más *(life)*, más poblada. (60A)

9. This context also has the highest probability for unexpressed pronouns (0.82) in the Portuguese spoken in Bahia (Gonçalves da Silva 2008).

10. In the Coding Manual Appendix to *Spanish in New York*, Otheguy and Zentella suggest including verbs with inanimate subjects only when there is an expressed pronoun and excluding other instances because the variation is minimal. Otheguy and Zentella make a valid point that we need to be careful not to include instances where variation exists, but in such a small degree that would skew our reporting and interpretations of the results. The presence of inanimate subject tokens in our data is evidence that there is variation. The fact that there are only two such cases in our Spanish data suggests that the variation is minimal, and thus would skew the results. However, when the inanimate tokens are included in Spanish there is only a one percent change in overall rates (25 percent (658/2641) with and 26 percent (655/2483) without). The data are very similar for Portuguese (46 percent (1181/2587) with and 47 percent (1168/2496) without). Furthermore, we have discussed in detail in this chapter that one possible place to measure possible influence of Portuguese on Spanish would be through the use of inanimate subject pronouns. Lacking in the literature is such data in Spanish monolingual communities, which would provide the needed comparison. If including inanimate tokens with unexpressed subjects does not skew the data, our argument here is that they should be reported.

REFERENCES

Abreu, Laurel. 2012. "Subject Pronoun Expression and Priming Effects among Bilingual Speakers of Puerto Rican Spanish." In *Selected Proceedings of the 14th Hispanic Linguistics Symposium*, edited by Kimberly Geeslin and Manuel Díaz Campos, 1–8. Somerville, MA: Cascadilla Proceedings Project.

Amaral, Patrícia Matos, and Scott A. Schwenter. 2005. "Contrast and the (Non-) Occurrence of Subject Pronouns." In *Selected Proceedings of the 7th Hispanic Linguistics Symposium*, edited by David Eddington, 116–127. Somerville, MA: Cascadilla Press.

Barbosa, Pilar, Maria Eugênia Duarte, and Mary Kato. 2005. "Null Subjects in European and Brazilian Portuguese." *Journal of Portuguese Linguistics* 4(2):11–52.

Barnes, Hilary. 2010. "Subject Pronoun Expression in Bilinguals of Two Null Subject Languages." *Amsterdam Studies in the Theory and History of Linguistic Science Series IV, Current Issues in Linguistic Theory* 313:9–22.

Bayley, Robert, and Lucinda Pease-Alvarez. 1997. "Null Pronoun Variation in Mexican-Descent Children's Narrative Discourse." *Language Variation and Change* 9:349–71.

Behares, Luis E. 1984. "Diglosia escolar en la frontera uruguaya con Brasil: Matriz social del bilingüismo." *Cadernos de Estudos Lingüísticos* 6:228–234.

Blas Arroyo, José Luis. 2011. "Spanish in Contact with Catalan." *The Handbook of Hispanic Sociolinguistics,* edited by Manuel Díaz-Campos, 374–394. Malden, MA: Wiley-Blackwell.

Bullock, Barbara E., and Almeida Jacqueline Toribio. 2009. "Reconsidering Dominican Spanish: Data from the Rural Cibao." *Revista Internacional de Lingüística Iberoamericana* 7:49–73.

Butt, John, and Carmen Benjamin. 2011. *A New Reference Grammar of Modern Spanish.* Abingdon, UK: Hodder Education.

Cameron, Richard. 1993. "Ambiguous agreement, functional compensation, and nonspecific *tú* in the Spanish of San Juan, Puerto Rico, and Madrid, Spain." *Language Variation and Change 5*(3): 305–334.

———. 1994. "Ambiguous agreement, functional compensation, and nonspecific tú in the Spanish of San Juan, Puerto Rico and Madrid, Spain." *Language Variation and Change* 5:305–334.

Cameron, Richard, and Nydia Flores-Ferrán. 2004. "Preservation of subject expression across regional dialects of Spanish." *Spanish in Context* 1(1):43–83.

Carvalho, Ana M. 2003a. "Rumo a uma definição do português uruguaio." *Revista Internacional de Lingüística Iberoamericana* 2:125–150.

———. 2003b. "The sociolinguistic distribution of (lh) in Uruguayan Portuguese: A case of dialect diffusion." In *Linguistic theory and language development in Hispanic Languages: Papers from the 5th Hispanic Linguistics Symposium and the 4th Conference on the Acquisition of Spanish and Portuguese*, edited by Silvina Montrul and Francisco Ordoñez, 30–44. Somerville, MA: Cascadilla Press.

———. 2004. ""I speak like the guys on TV": Palatalization and the urbanization of Uruguayan Portuguese." *Language Variation and Change* 16(2):127–151.

———. 2006a. "Políticas lingüísticas do século passado nos dias de hoje: O dilema da educação bilíngüe no Uruguai." *Language Problems and Language Planning* 30(2).49–171.

———. 2006b. "Nominal number marking in a variety of Spanish in contact with Portuguese." In *Selected Proceedings of the 8th Hispanic Linguistics Symposium*, edited by Timothy Face and Carol Klee, 154–166. Somerville, MA: Cascadilla Press.

———. 2007. "Diagnóstico sociolingüístico de comunidades escolares fronterizas en el norte de Uruguay." In *Portugués del Uruguay y educación bilingüe*, edited by Nicolás Brian, Claudia Brovetto, and Javier Geymonat, 49–98. Montevideo: ANEP.

———. 2010a. "¿Eres de la frontera o sos de la capital? Variation and alternation of second-person verbal forms in Uruguayan Border Spanish." *Southwest Journal of Linguistics* 29(1):1–23.

———. 2010b. "Contribuições da sociolingüística ao ensino de português em comunidades bilíngues do norte do Uruguai." *Pro-Posições* 21(3):45–66.

———. 2014. “Sociolinguistic continuities in language contact situations: The case of Portuguese in contact with Spanish along the Uruguayan–Brazilian border.” In *Portuguese/Spanish Interfaces*, edited by Patrícia Amaral and Ana M. Carvalho. 264–294. Amsterdam: John Benjamins.

Carvalho, Ana M., and Michael Child. 2011. “Subject pronoun expression in a variety of Spanish in contact with Portuguese.” In *Selected Proceedings of the 5th Workshop on Spanish Sociolinguistics*, edited by Jim Michnowicz and Robin Dodsworth, 14–25. Somerville, MA: Cascadilla Press.

Douglas, Kendra Lynne. 2004. “Uruguayan Portuguese in Artigas: Tri-dimensionality of transitional local varieties in contact with Spanish and Portuguese standards.” PhD diss., University of Wisconsin-Madison.

Duarte, Maria Eugênia. 1993. “Do pronome nulo ao pronome pleno: a tragetória do sujeito no português do Brasil.” In *Português Brasileiro: Uma viagem diacrônica*, edited by Ian Roberts and Mary Kato, 107–128. Campinas, Brazil: Universidade Estadual de Campinas.

———. 1995. “A perda do princípio ‘evite o pronome’ no português brasileiro.” PhD, diss., Universidade Estadual de Campinas.

———. 2003. “A evolução na representação do sujeito pronominal em dois tempos.” In *Mudança linguística em tempo real*, edited by Maria da Conceição A. de Paiva and Maria Eugênia Duarte, 115–128. Rio de Janeiro: FABERJ.

Dumont, Jenny. 2006. “Full NPs as subjects.” In *Selected Proceedings of the 9th Hispanic Linguistics Symposium*, edited by Nuria Sagarra and Almeida Jacqueline Toribio, 296–296. Somerville, MA: Cascadilla Press.

Erker, Daniel, and Gregory R. Guy. 2012. “The role of lexical frequency in syntactic variability: Variation subject personal pronoun expression in Spanish.“ *Language* 88(3):526–557.

Elizaincín, Adolfo. 1995. “Personal pronouns for inanimate entities in Uruguayan Spanish in contact with Portuguese.” In *Spanish in Four Continents: Studies in Language Contact and Bilingualism*, edited by Carmen Silva-Corvalán, 117–131. Washington DC: Georgetown University Press.

Elizaincín, Adolfo, Luis E. Behares, and Graciela Barrios. 1987. *Nós Falemo Brasilero. Dialectos portugueses del Uruguay.* Montevidéu: Amesur.

Enríquez, Emilia. 1984. *El pronombre personal sujeto en la lengua española hablada en Madrid.* Madrid: C.S.I.C.

Ferreira, Cinthia Carla. 2003. “A variação do pronome sujeito na fala da comunidade kalunga.” PhD diss., Universidade de Brasília, Brazil.

Flores-Ferrán, Nydia. 2002. Subject personal pronouns in Spanish Narratives of Puerto Ricans in New York City. Munich, Germany: LINCOM-Europa.

Gonçalves da Silva, Elisângela. 2008. “Condicionamentos linguísticos para a ocorrência do sujeito nulo em uma comunidade de fala.” In *Múltiplas Perspectivas em Linguística*, edited by José Sueli de Magalhães and Luis Carlos Travaglia, 1093–1105. Uberlândia: EDUFU.

Guy, Gregory. 2014. “Variation and change in Latin American Spanish and Portuguese.” In *Portuguese-Spanish Interfaces: Diachrony, Synchrony, and Contact*, edited by Patrícia Amaral and Ana M. Carvalho, 443–463. Amsterdam: John Benjamins.

Hickey, Raymond. 2010. "Language Contact: Reconsideration and Reassessment." In *The Handbook of Language Contact*, edited by Raymond Hickey, 1–28. Oxford: Wiley-Blackwell.

Kato, Mary, and Esmeralda Negrão. 2000. *Brazilian Portuguese and the Null Subject Parameter*. Frankfurt, Germany: Vervuert-Iberoamericana.

Kato, Mary A. 2000. "The partial pro-drop nature and the restricted VS order in Brazilian Portuguese." In *Brazilian Portuguese and the Null Subject Parameter*, edited by M. A. Kato and E. V. Negro, 223–258. Frankfurt: Vervuert/LatinoAmericana.

Kato, Mary, and Fernando Tarallo. 1988. "Restrictive VS syntax in Brazilian Portuguese and its relation to visible subjects and invisible clitics." Paper presented at the 1988 Georgetown Roundtable on Languages and Linguistics, Washington, D.C.

Kerswill, Paul. 2010. "Contact and new varieties." In *The Handbook of Language in Contact*, edited by Raymond Hickey, 230–251. Oxford: Wiley-Blackwell.

Lapidus, Naomi, and Ricardo Otheguy. 2005. "Overt non-specific *ellos* in Spanish in New York." *Spanish in Context* 2(2):157–174.

Li, Siaoshi, Siaoqing Chen, and Wen-Hsin Chen. 2012. "Variation of subject pronoun expression in Mandarin Chinese." *Sociolinguistic Studies* 6(1):91–119.

Lipski, John. 2006. "Too close for comfort? The genesis of 'portuñol/portunhol'." In *Selected Proceedings of the 8th Hispanic Linguistics Symposium*, edited by Timothy Face and Carol Klee. 1–22.

———. 2009. "Searching for the origins of Uruguayan *Fronterizo* dialects: Radical code mixing as 'fluent dysfluency.'" *Journal of Portuguese Linguistics* 8(1):3–44.

———. 2010. "Spanish and Portuguese in Contact." In *The Handbook of Language in Contact*, edited by Raymond Hickey, 550–580. Oxford: Wiley-Blackwell.

Lira, Solange De Azambuja. 1982. "Nominal, Pronominal and Zero Subject in Brazilian Portuguese." PhD diss., University of Pennsylvania.

Marcos-Marín, Francisco. 2001. "De lenguas y fronteras: el Spanglish y el portuñol." *Nueva Revista de Política, Cultura y Arte* 74:72–79.

Meyerhoff, Miriam. 2009. "Replication, Transfer, and Calquing: Using Variation as a Tool in the Study of Language Contact." *Language Variation and Change* 21:297–317.

Muysken, Pieter. 2000. *Bilingual speech: A typology of code-mixing*. Cambridge University Press: Cambridge.

———. 2006. "Two linguistic systems in contact: Grammar, phonology and lexicon." In *The Handbook of Bilingualism*, edited by Tej K. Bathia and William C. Ritchie, 147–168. Oxford: Wiley-Blackwell.

Nagy, Naomi, Nina Aghdasi, Derek Denis, and Alexandra Motut. 2011. "Null subjects in heritage languages: Contact effects in a cross-linguistic context." *University of Pennsylvania Working Papers in Linguistics* 17(2):135–144.

Naro, Anthony, Edair Görski, and Eulália Fernandes. 1999. "Change without change." *Language Variation and Change* 11(2):197–211.

Naro, Anthony, and Marta Scherre. 2013. "Remodeling the age variable: Number concord in Brazilian Portuguese." *Language Variation and Change* 25(1):1–15.

Orozco, Rafael, and Gregory Guy. 2008. "El uso variable de los pronombres sujetos: ¿Qué pasa en la costa Caribe colombiana?" In *Selected Proceedings of the 4th Workshop on Spanish Sociolinguistics*, edited by Maurice Westmoreland and Juan Antonio Thomas, 70–80. Somerville, MA: Cascadilla Proceedings Project.

Otheguy, Ricardo, and Ana Celia Zentella. 2012. *Spanish in New York: Language Contact, Dialect Leveling, and Structural Continuity*. Oxford: Oxford University Press.

Otheguy, Ricardo, Ana Celia Zentella, and David Livert. 2007. "Language and dialect contact in Spanish of New York: Toward the formation of a speech community." *Language* 83(4):770–802.

Pacheco, Cintia da Silva. 2013. "O Português brasileiro e o português uruguaio da fronteira Brasil–Uruguai (Aceguá)." Manuscript.

———. Forthcoming. "Primeiras reflexões sobre o português fronteiriço de Aceguá." *PAPIA: Revista Brasileira de Estudos Crioulos e Similares*.

Paredes Silva, Vera Lúcia. 1993. "Subject omission and functional compensation: Evidence from written Brazilian Portuguese." *Language Variation and Change* 5(1):35–49.

———. 2003. "Motivações funcionais no uso do sujeito pronominal: Uma análise em tempo real." In *Mudança linguística em tempo real*, edited by Maria da Conceição A. de Paiva and Maria Eugênia Duarte, 97–114. Rio de Janeiro: Contra Capa.

Poplack, Shana, and Stephen Levey. 2010. "Contact induced grammatical change: A cautionary tale." In *Language and space: An International Handbook of Linguistic Variation, Volume I,* edited by Peter Auer and Jürgen Erich Schmidt, 391–419. Berlin: Mouton De Gruyter.

Poplack, Shana, and Sali Tagliamonte. 2001. *African American English in the Diaspora*. Blackwell: Oxford.

Poplack, Shana, Lauren Zentz, and Nathalie Dion. 2011. "Phrase-final prepositions in Quebec French: An empirical study of contact, code-switching, and resistance to convergence." *Bilingualism: Language and Cognition* 15(2):203–225.

Posio, Pekka. 2012. "Who are 'we' in spoken Peninsular Spanish and European Portuguese? Expression and reference of first person plural subject pronouns." *Language Sciences* 34:339–360.

———. 2013. "The expression of first-person-singular subjects in spoken Peninsular Spanish and European Portuguese: Semantic roles and formulaic sequences." *Folia Linguistica* 47(1):253–292.

Roberts, Ian G. 1993. *Verbs and diachronic syntax: A comparative history of English and French*. Kluwer Academic Publishers: Dordrecht, the Netherlands.

Scherre, Marta, and Anthony Naro. 2010. Perceptual vs. Grammatical Constraints and Social Factors in Subject-Verb Agreement in Brazilian Portuguese." *University of Pennsylvania Working Papers in Linguistics* 16, 2.

Shin, Naomi Lapidus. 2012. Variable use of Spanish subject pronouns by monolingual children in Mexico. *Proceedings of the 2010 Hispanic Linguistics Symposium.* 130–141.

Shin, Naomi Lapidus, and Cecilia Montes-Alcalá. 2014. "El uso contextual del pronombre sujeto como factor predictivo de la influencia del inglés en el español en Nueva York." *Sociolinguistic Studies* 8: 85–110.

Silveira, Agripino. 2012. "Subject Expression in Brazilian Portuguese: Construction and Frequency Effects." PhD diss., University of New Mexico.

Soares da Silva, Humberto. 2006. "O parâmetro do sujeito nulo: Confronto entre o português e o espanhol." PhD diss., Universidade Federal do Rio de Janeiro.

Solomon, Julie. 1999. "Phonological and syntactic variation in the Spanish of Valladolid, Yucatán." PhD diss., Stanford University.

Sorace, Antonella. 2011. "Pinning down the concept of 'interface' in bilingualism." *Linguistic Approaches to Bilingualism* 1(1):1–33.

Sturza, Eliana Rosa. 2004. "Fronteiras e práticas linguísticas: um olhar sobre o portunhol." *Revista de Internacional de Lingüística Iberorománica* 1(3):151–160.

Tagliamonte, Sali. 2003. "Comparative Sociolinguistics." In *The Handbook of Language Variation and Change*, edited by J. K. Chambers, Peter Trudgill, and Natalie Schilling-Estes, 729–763. Oxford: Blackwell.

Thomason, Sarah Grey, and Terrence Kaufman. 1988. *Language contact, creolization, and genetic linguistics.* University of California Press: Berkeley.

Toribio, Almeida. 2000. "Setting Parametric Limits on Dialectal Variation in Spanish." *Lingua* 110(5):315–341.

Travis, Catherine E. 2007. "Genre effects on subject expression in Spanish: Priming in narrative and conversation." *Language Variation and Change* 19(2):101–135.

Waltermire, Mark. 2006. "Social and linguistic correlates of Spanish and Portuguese bilingualism on the Uruguayan–Brazilian border." PhD diss., University of New Mexico.

———. 2008. "Social stratification of language-specific variants of intervocalic /d/ along the Uruguayan–Brazilian border." *Sociolinguistic Studies* 2(1):31–60.

———. 2011. "Frequency effects on the morphological conditioning of syllable-final /s/ reduction in border Uruguayan Spanish." *Journal of Language Contact* 4:26–55.

———. 2012. "The differential use of Spanish and Portuguese along the Uruguayan–Brazilian border." *International Journal of Bilingual Education and Bilingualism* 15(5):509–531.

PART III

Subject Pronoun Expression in Contexts of Acquisition

9

The Emergence of Structured Variability in Morphosyntax

Childhood Acquisition of Spanish Subject Pronouns

Naomi Lapidus Shin and Daniel Erker

Spanish subject pronoun expression (e.g., *yo bailo* ~ *Ø bailo* 'I dance') has been so widely studied that Bayley et al. (2012) have recently called it the "showcase variable" of Spanish sociolinguistics. This description is due, in part, to the fact that the pronominal behavior of Spanish-speaking adults routinely demonstrates a hallmark feature of structured linguistic variation: While individuals and communities may vary widely in their overall rates of use of a particular variant—here, the use of a subject pronoun with a finite verb—patterns of usage reveal sensitivity to a shared set of conditioning factors (e.g., Cameron 1992, 1993; Carvalho and Child 2011; Claes 2011; Flores-Ferrán 2002; Holmquist 2012; Michnowicz, this volume; Orozco and Guy 2008; Otheguy and Zentella 2012; Otheguy, Zentella, and Livert 2007; Torres Cacoullos and Travis 2010, 2011). For example, throughout the Spanish-speaking world, subject pronouns are expressed more often a) when the referent of the verb is singular, b) when the referent of two consecutive grammatical subjects is different rather than the same, and c) with verbs conjugated in the imperfect rather than other TMA forms. Such trends in adult pronoun use are probabilistic in nature, and, from the perspective of variationist sociolinguistics, they are understood as the result of competing factors which contribute their relative weight to the likelihood that a pronoun will or will not be used in a variable context.

Despite the widespread demonstration that the variable linguistic behavior of adults is highly systematic (e.g., Labov 1994), it is not yet well understood when and how children converge on probabilistic components of grammar. There is growing evidence that young children are similar to adults with respect to phonological variation. For instance, both adults' and children's patterns of -t/-d deletion in English are constrained by many of the same factors (e.g., Roberts 1997; Smith, Durham, and Fortune 2009). Less is known about the emergence of structured variability in morphosyntax during childhood. Given the special status of subject pronouns in sociolinguistics and the remarkable extent to which this linguistic variable is understood, it is an optimal tool for exploring the acquisition of systematic variability in morphosyntax.

The data for the current study consist of 2,508 verbs extracted from sociolinguistic interviews with 24 monolingual Spanish-speaking children, ages six to eight, in Oaxaca, Mexico. The children's pronominal behavior is compared to that of 19 adult Mexican immigrants in New York City (NYC), each whom was selected from the *Otheguy-Zentella corpus of Spanish in NYC*.[1] Results reveal both differences and similarities between adults and children. A striking difference is that the children used far fewer pronouns than the adults. The lack of pronouns was especially prevalent among the boys. The girls produced significantly higher rates of pronouns than the boys did, nearing adult-like rates by age eight. This finding is in keeping with the large body of literature reporting that girls acquire language more quickly than boys do (e.g., Eriksson et al. 2012; Locke, Ginsborg, and Peers 2002; To, Cheung, and McLeod 2013; among others).

Despite the children's relatively infrequent use of pronouns, their behavior demonstrates systematic patterns of variation that reflect an adult-like sensitivity to certain linguistic constraints. The most robust predictors of pronoun use for the adults and children alike were (1) *person/number of the pronoun*, followed by (2) *switch reference*. While several other factors that clearly condition adult pronoun use fail to predict the behavior of the children—*semantic class of the verb*, *clause type*, and *reflexivity*—results do indicate an emerging sensitivity among the children to the tense, mood, and aspectual properties of verbs (TMA).

Taken together, these results—both the low rate of pronoun use and sensitivity restricted to only the most robust conditioning factors—reflect a conservative learning pattern, whereby children introduce new forms into their discourse in a constrained fashion (Boyd and Goldberg 2012; MacWhinney 2004; Tomasello 2003). Additionally, the results indicate that the acquisition of adult-like patterns of morphosyntactic variation proceeds in a predictable sequence: The stronger the pattern among adults, the earlier it emerges in children.

ADULT SPANISH SUBJECT PRONOUN USE: TRENDS IN GRAMMATICAL PATTERNING

Most corpora gathered in the Spanish-speaking world show that finite verbs appear with subject pronouns in 20 to 40 percent of variable contexts. The proportion of verbs that appear with pronouns in a given data set, often referred to as the *pronoun rate*, varies depending on dialect, with higher rates found in the speech of Caribbean speakers than in that of Mainland Latin Americans (e.g., Otheguy and Zentella 2012; Shin and Otheguy 2013). Among Mainlanders, Mexican adults, whose rate is typically around 20 percent, are among the least frequent users of pronouns (Lastra and Martín

Butragueño, this volume; Michnowicz, this volume; Shin 2012, 134; Shin and Otheguy 2013). Several scholars have argued that, by themselves, pronoun rates are not the best source of data for comparing groups of speakers because they can vary according to genre (Travis 2007) and conversation topic (Flores-Ferrán 2010). Nevertheless, there is abundant evidence that pronoun rates are valid indicators of pronoun use patterns. Indeed, it has been argued that frequency of use of linguistic elements has an impact on mental grammars in general (Bybee 2010) and on developing grammars in particular (Lieven 2010). In addition, high rates of pronoun use appear to promote the emergence of novel structures. In the Dominican Republic, for instance, particularly high rates are accompanied by patterns rarely found elsewhere, such as *ello llueve* 'it rains' (Toribio 2000). Also, in NYC increased pronoun rates among Spanish–English bilinguals are accompanied by a diminished sensitivity to constraints that condition pronominal behavior (Otheguy and Zentella 2012). Furthermore, investigations of rates have revealed how social factors impact usage (Otheguy and Zentella 2012; Shin and Otheguy 2013). Thus, in the current study we view the pronoun rate as a relevant measure to compare adults and children and also to examine the influence of social factors, such as speaker gender, on children's pronoun expression.

While we maintain that rates of pronoun use constitute an important and revealing measure for comparing varieties of Spanish, we agree that it also crucial to investigate *patterns* of pronoun use (see Otheguy and Zentella 2012; Poplack and Levey 2010; Poplack, Zentz, and Dion 2012; Torres Cacoullos and Travis 2010, 2011). We focus on the following five patterns that have been found in studies of adult speakers of Spanish.

Person/number: Singular pronouns (*yo, tú, vos, usted, él/ella*) are expressed significantly more often than plural pronouns (*nosotros/nosotras, ellos/ellas*).[2] Also, *yo* and *tú* are more likely to be expressed than *él/ella*, with *yo* emerging as the most commonly expressed pronoun in some studies (Enríquez 1984, 191; Claes 2011; Orozco and Guy 2008, 76; Shin 2012), and *tú* the most common in others (Abreu 2009, 99; Ávila-Jiménez 1995, 1996; Cameron 1992, 233; Carvalho and Child 2011, 19; Cifuentes 1980–1981, 748; Erker and Guy 2012; Flores-Ferrán 2002, 2004; Otheguy and Zentella 2012).

Reference: Pronouns are expressed significantly more often when the referent of two consecutive grammatical subjects is different (i.e., *switch reference*) than when it is the same (e.g., Bayley and Pease-Alvarez 1996, 1997; Bentivoglio 1987; Cameron 1993, 1995; Claes 2011; Erker and Guy 2012; Flores-Ferrán 2004; Holmquist 2012; Ortiz López 2011; Otheguy and Zentella 2012; Otheguy, Zentella, and Livert 2007; Shin and Cairns 2012; Shin and Otheguy 2009; Silva-Corvalán 1994; Torres Cacoullos and Travis 2011).[3]

Tense/mood/aspect (TMA) morphology: The TMA combination that occurs with the highest rate of pronoun expression is the imperfect indicative (e.g., *bailaba*), possibly due to the more ambiguous person-marking morphology in the imperfect than in, for example, the present indicative or the preterit. That is, while the imperfect form *bailaba* can mean 'I used to dance' or 'he/she/it/you-formal used to dance', the preterit *bailé* can only mean 'I danced.' Most studies have shown that verb forms with ambiguous person morphology, such as the imperfect and the conditional, promote pronoun use, while unambiguous forms, such as the preterit, disfavor pronoun use (Abreu 2009, 2012; Bentivoglio 1987, 45; Claes 2011; Erker 2005; Erker and Guy 2012; Flores-Ferrán 2002, 2004; Hochberg 1986; Holmquist 2012; Hurtado 2005; Otheguy and Zentella 2012; Otheguy, Zentella, and Livert 2007; Prada Pérez 2009; Shin 2014; Travis 2007, but also see: Bentivoglio 1987; Carvalho and Child 2011; Orozco and Guy 2008, 75; Ranson 1991).[4]

The imperative, in stark contrast, lies at the other end of the pronominal spectrum. Imperatives are often excluded from variationist studies of pronoun expression because linguists assume that they never occur with a subject pronoun (e.g., Claes 2011, 195). Out of 35 articles, we found only five in which results for imperatives were reported. Two studies that challenge the assumption that pronouns are categorically absent with imperatives are Enríquez's (1984, 201, 351) study of Spanish in Madrid and Carvalho and Child's (2011, 21) study of Spanish in Uruguay on the border with Brazil. In these studies, Spanish speakers expressed pronouns with imperatives at rates of 26 and 30 percent, respectively.[5] While the imperative indeed constitutes a variable context, that is, a context where either expression or omission is possible, three studies confirm the widespread impression that imperatives disfavor pronoun use more so than any other TMA form (Erker and Guy 2012, 540; Otheguy and Zentella 2012, 186; Shin and Montes-Alcalá 2014). To summarize, of all TMA combinations, the imperfect indicative is the strongest promoter of pronoun use, and the imperative the strongest promoter of omission.

Other linguistic predictors: Other variables that are known to influence pronoun expression include (a) clause type: coordinate clauses favor pronoun omission, while main clauses promote pronoun expression (Otheguy and Zentella 2012, Shin and Montes-Alcalá 2014); (b) semantic class: cognitive activity verbs like *creer* 'to believe' and *pensar* 'to think' favor pronoun use more than other types of verbs (Bentivoglio 1987, Otheguy and Zentella 2012, Posio 2011, Travis and Torres Cacoullos 2012), and (c) occurrence of reflexive pronouns: non-reflexive verbs promote pronoun expression more so than do verbs with reflexive pronouns (Abreu 2012; Bayley and Pease-Alvarez 1996, 1997; Carvalho and Child 2011; Otheguy and Zentella 2012).

Variable hierarchies: What is noteworthy beyond the findings that the same variables consistently impact adult subject pronoun expression is that the *hierarchy* of these variables is also often the same across communities. Such hierarchies rank the relative weight of conditioning factors in terms of their effect on the probability of pronoun use. The typical hierarchy of variables impacting adult Spanish subject pronoun expression is (1) *person/number*, followed by (2) *switch reference*, and (3) *TMA,* with other variables such as *semantic class* and *clause type* ranked lower (Abreu 2012, 5; Orozco and Guy 2008, 73; Otheguy and Zentella 2012; Prada Pérez 2009, 279; Torres Cacoullos and Travis 2011, 250).[6] This common hierarchy is depicted in figure 9.1.

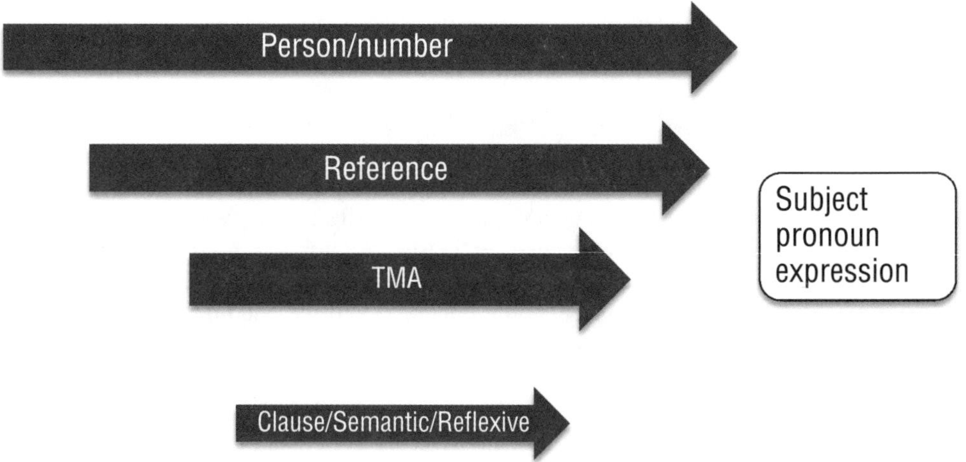

Figure 9.1 Hierarchy of linguistic predictors impacting adults' Spanish subject pronoun expression based on Otheguy and Zentella (2012, 160)

Figure 9.1 intentionally displays person/number as the most powerful constraint. It is followed by reference, then TMA, and then other variables such as clause, semantic, and reflexive. This particular hierarchy has been consistently demonstrated across communities, suggesting that it represents a pattern deeply entrenched in Spanish grammar: Adult speakers not only know that they can choose between expression and omission of subject pronouns, they also possess probabilistic knowledge that guides their choice and accounts for the specific distribution of forms in a given discourse. This knowledge can be characterized as "schemas," which Bybee (2001, 8, 40) describes as mechanisms guiding the use of forms and constructions in discourse. Schemas are not categorical, but are nonetheless systematic, and therefore result in clear, discernable patterns in usage (Bybee 2001, 64; Guy 2011, 2196).

In sum, the research on adult subject pronoun expression reveals consistent systematicity in probabilistic knowledge across communities, raising several questions for child language research.

1. Do children demonstrate the same systematicity in their variable use of subject pronouns?
2. What do similarities/differences between adults and children tell us about a) the grammar underlying subject pronoun expression and b) the development of variable morphosyntactic structures during childhood?

PREVIOUS RESEARCH ON GRAMMATICAL PATTERNING IN CHILD LANGUAGE

At present there is a dearth of research in language acquisition that examines the onset of structured variability in morphosyntax (cf. Kovac and Adamson 1981).[7] While this is largely true of Spanish subject pronouns, a preliminary picture has emerged. Most studies of child Spanish have focused on the alternation between overt (lexical and pronominal combined) and null subjects in the speech of children whose ages range from approximately one and a half to three years old (Austin et al. 1998, Bel 2003, Grinstead 2004, Paradis and Navarro 2003, Silva-Corvalán and Sánchez-Walker 2007). Children within this age range rarely produce subject pronouns; instead, their subjects tend to be lexical NPs or demonstratives. There is some evidence that pronoun expression increases between ages one and a half and three years (Bel 2003; Serratrice 2005; Valian and Eisenberg 1996), but even as late as early school age, children still produce many fewer pronouns than adults (Montrul and Sánchez-Walker, this volume; Ortiz López 2011, 432–437; Shin 2012). The scarcity of subject pronouns in young children's speech makes it difficult to assess the emergence of adult-like patterns of use. There is some indication that the person/number effect—where singular pronouns are favored over plurals—is operative in children's pronoun expression (Bayley and Pease-Alvarez 1996, 1997; Shin 2012). There is also evidence that Spanish–English bilingual children, ages eight to twelve, are similar to adults with respect to reference and TMA: Both switches in referent and verb forms with ambiguous TMA favor subject pronoun expression. Thus the pronoun use patterns of bilingual children, ages eight to twelve, appear to be constrained by person/number, reference, and TMA in much the same way that these variables constrain adult usage.

To summarize, we have evidence at this point that Spanish-speaking children's subject pronoun use displays some of the same trends that characterize adults' patterns. But little is known about the timing of the emergence of such patterns. Moreover, other factors known to affect adult pronoun expression, such as semantic class or clause type, have yet to be examined in a monolingual child language context. The current study seeks to address this lacuna in the literature and, in turn, increase our understanding of the acquisition of variable aspects of grammar.

THE CURRENT STUDY

In this section we outline our methodology, data, and results of multivariate analyses exploring the impact of linguistic constraints on pronoun use.

PARTICIPANTS

The participants in this study were 24 monolingual, Spanish-speaking children in Oaxaca, Mexico. We interviewed 10 boys and 14 girls, whose ages ranged from six to eight years old (average age = 7;4). For purposes of comparison, the study also included a control group of 19 adults (10 men, 9 women) selected from the *Otheguy-Zentella corpus of Spanish in NYC*. The 19 adults included in the present study were all first-generation Mexicans living in NYC at the time of their interview. Their average age was 33 years old, and their average age of arrival in the United States was 22 years old. As we will show in the subsection on results below, the adults' rate of pronoun expression was 21 percent. This rate is consistent with recent studies of adult Mexicans living in Mexico. Lastra and Butragueño (this volume) report a rate of 21.8 percent in Mexico City, and Michnowicz (this volume) reports a rate of 20 percent in Yucatan. The almost identical rates in NYC and Mexico suggest that pronoun use among the adult Mexicans in NYC is representative of adult Mexican pronoun use in general, a finding that bolsters our confidence that the NYC adult Mexicans constitute an appropriate control group for our study of Mexican children.

DATA: SOCIOLINGUISTIC INTERVIEWS AND VARIABLE SUBJECT PRONOUN EXPRESSION

Sociolinguistic interviews following procedures outlined by Labov (1984) were conducted with both the adults and children. In addition, the children were asked to retell their favorite stories, to make up original stories, and to narrate *Frog, where are you?*, a picture book often used in research on child language. Variable pronominal contexts—where the presence or absence of a pronoun is possible—were identified in the transcribed interviews.[8] To illustrate, consider example (1), produced by a Mexican girl, age 6;5. The absence of a pronoun is signaled by Ø in the Spanish excerpt and by pronouns in parentheses in the English gloss. Relevant contexts are in boldface.

(1) *... primero vino aquí mi hermano ... y, y luego yo porque* ***yo nací*** *hasta el último.* ***Ø Tengo*** *dos hermanos. 109*[9]

'... first my brother came here ... and, and later I because **I was born** last. **(I) have** two brothers.'

Example (1) includes two variable contexts, one in which the pronoun *yo* was expressed (*yo nací*), and the other in which it was not (*tengo*). Either option, expression or omission, is possible in both cases. In other words, the speaker could have said *porque nací*, leaving out *yo*. Likewise, the speaker could have said *Yo tengo dos hermanos.*

Not all contexts are variable like the ones in example (1). For instance, the use of subject pronouns referring to inanimate entities is so rare that it makes sense to exclude these cases. Similarly, overt subject personal pronouns do not typically appear with meteorological verbs (*llueve* 'it rains'), nor in subject-headed relative clauses (e.g., *Vi a la niña que estaba sentada al lado tuyo* 'I saw the girl that was sitting by your side' would rarely occur as *Vi a la niña que* ***ella*** *estaba sentada al lado tuyo* 'I saw the girl that she was sitting by your side.'). Contexts such as these, where there is little variation, were excluded from the study. For an in-depth discussion of contexts in Spanish that allow both pronoun expression or omission and those in which such variability is rare, see Otheguy and Zentella (2012, 45–67).

Unrecoverable Referents

In an effort to examine variable contexts only, cases in which the intended referent was unrecoverable were excluded from the study. Such unrecoverable referents are common in child language (See Barriga Villanueva 2002, 177). Consider example (2), in which a girl, age 7;4, retells the story of *The Beauty and the Beast.*

(2) *Y entonces la Bella estaba cantando así, y viene su caballo, y le dice "¿Qué pasó? ¿Dónde está papá?" Y s-, y, y él, y él, y ella este se f-,* ***se, Ø lo cargó****, y él se fue por el camino equivocado, y estaba en el castillo. Y le dije, y ella le dijo "Papá no obedeció." Y, y* ***Ø dejó*** *su sombrero allí en la puerta. Y entonces este,* ***Ø creyó*** *que se lo habían comido, y entró al castillo y todos la vieron y dijeron "qué bonita."* [203]

'And then Belle was singing like this, and her horse comes, and says "What happened? Where is papa?" And s- and, and he, and he, and she um lef-, Ø **carried him** and he went down the wrong path, and was in the castle. And I said, and she said "Papa didn't obey." And Ø **left** his?her? hat there at the door. And then um, Ø believed that they had eaten him, and entered the castle and everyone saw her and said "how pretty."'

The speaker's intended referent is unclear at several points in (2). Who carried whom? Did Bella carry the horse? And who left a hat at the door? The listener cannot be entirely sure of the referent. In our data set of children's speech there were a total of 361 such cases, and they were excluded from further analyses for two reasons. First, they demonstrate nearly categorical behavior; pronouns were omitted in 99 percent of the unrecoverable contexts. In other words, there were almost no cases of expressed subject pronouns with unidentifiable referents. The second reason is that we cannot code verbs with unrecoverable referents for the relevant predictor variables. For example, if the referent is unclear, it is impossible to code for a switch in referent. After excluding contexts of little to no variation, the data extraction process yielded a total of 2,150 verb tokens produced by the children. The control data set consisted of 8,319 produced by the adults.

Results: Pronoun Rates

Overall Pronoun Rates

As shown in table 9.1, the control group of adult Mexicans expressed subject pronouns at a rate of 21 percent, a rate that is commensurate with the range found in studies of Mexican adults in Mexico (Lastra and Martín Butragueño, this volume; Michnowicz, this volume). By comparison, the children, with a pronoun rate of 9 percent, produced pronouns very infrequently. Such a rate has never been reported for adult Spanish.

Table 9.1 Rates of SPP expression in Mexican adults and children

Adults (NYC)		Children	
N Vbs	% SPP	N Vbs	% SPP
8,319	21%	2,150	9%

Pronoun Rates and Sex

The data reveal a clear difference between boys and girls with respect to rates of pronoun use: The rates for the girls in the study are significantly higher, $t(2148) = 2.56$, $p < .01$.[10] Figure 9.2 illustrates this result below.

Given that the children in general have considerably lower pronoun rates than their adult counterparts, the girls' pronominal behavior can be viewed as more adult-like than that of the boys. This difference is consistent with a general trend in the language acquisition literature that girls outpace boys in terms of achieving adult-like linguistic behavior (e.g., Eriksson et al. 2012) In addition, and with respect to previous studies of pronoun use among Spanish speaking children, the results in figure 9.2 corroborate those reported by Bayley and Pease-Alvarez (1996, 1997) as well as Shin (2006). Each of these studies also observed higher rates of pronouns among girls.

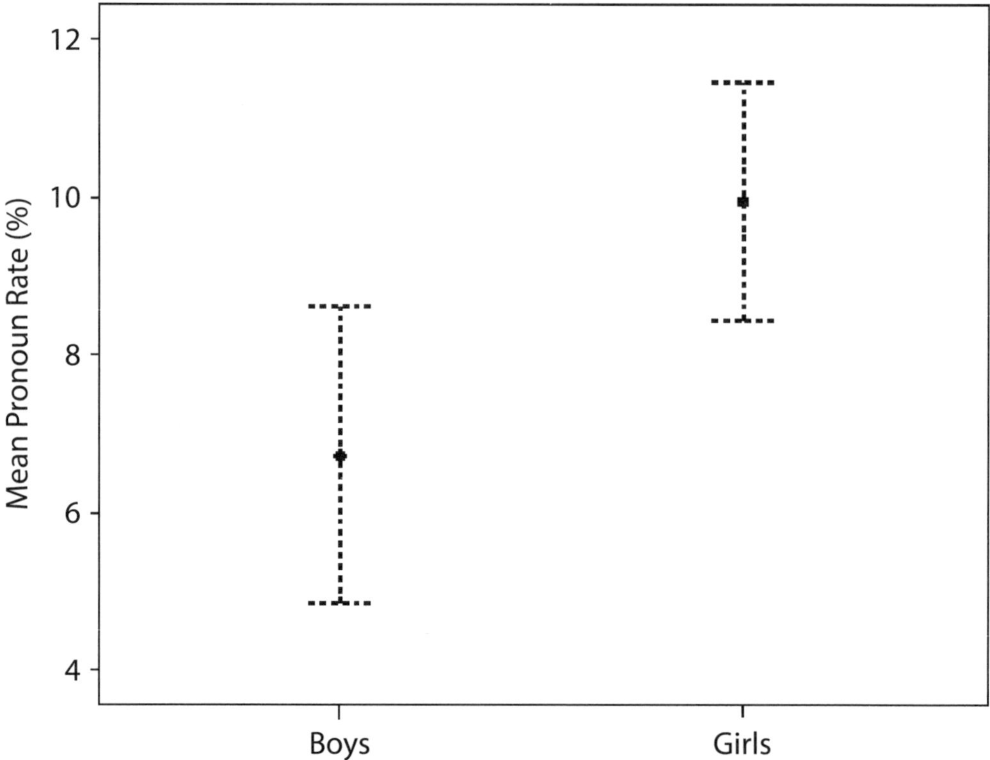

Figure 9.2 Mean pronoun rates by sex

Age and Sex

The results do not show evidence of a main effect for age, $F(3, 2147) = 1.4$ $p < .23$. However, a Repeated Measures Analysis of Variance (RM-ANOVA) reveals evidence of a significant interaction between age and sex, $F(5, 2145) = 6.5$, $p < .001$. Consider figure 9.3 below, which plots the mean pronoun rates for boys and girls by age group. It shows that in all three groups girls have higher pronoun rates than boys. However, while pronoun rates among the girls uniformly increase with age, this is not the case for the boys. Examining each age group separately, we find the following: The lowest rates of pronoun use for each sex are observed among the six-year-olds. In fact, among six-year-old boys, we observe the categorical absence of subject pronouns. Rates then increase among the seven-year-olds, with the boys shifting from categorical to variable behavior and the girls increasing their rates marginally. A substantial divergence then emerges among eight-year-olds. Whereas the girls continue to display an increase in pronoun rates alongside an increase in age—their rate of 16 percent brings them in close proximity to the 21 percent of the adults cited above—the eight-year-old boys demonstrate a *decrease* in their frequency of pronoun use compared to the seven-year-olds. In summary, the data demonstrate that pronoun rates steadily increase with age among the girls in the study. Among boys, while one might suggest that a shift from categorical to variable behavior coincides with an increase in age, it is not the case that rates continue to climb as the boys get older.

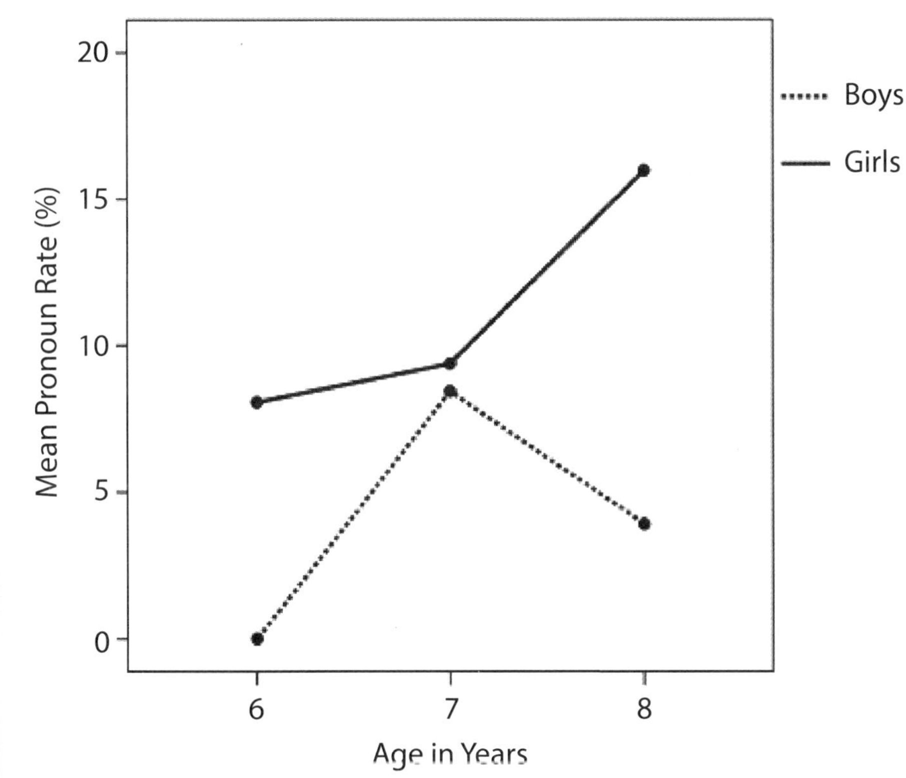

Figure 9.3 Mean pronoun rates by sex and age

SUMMARY OF PRONOUN RATE RESULTS

Results demonstrate that the children, ages six to eight, express far fewer subject pronouns than adults do. There is also evidence that girls advance more quickly than boys do towards adult-like behavior.

Results: Linguistic Constraints on Pronoun Use

Even though the children in this study express relatively few subject pronouns, it is still possible that their usage is guided by the same schemas guiding adult usage. To test this hypothesis, each verb was coded for the six linguistic variables discussed above: person, reference, TMA, clause type, semantic class, and reflexive, described in detail here:

1. *Person/number* included five factors: 1sg (*yo*, 'I'), 2sg (*tú*), 3sg (*él/ella* 'he/she'), 1pl (*nosotros/nosotras*, 'we'), and 3pl (*ellos/ellas*, 'they').[11]
2. *Reference* included two factors: same and switch reference. Recall that these contexts are operationalized here in terms of the relationship between two consecutive grammatical subjects. Reference to the same referent across subjects is considered "same reference," while a change in reference is considered "switch reference."
3. *TMA* included eight factors: simple present indicative (*bailo*), preterit (*bailé*), imperfect (*bailaba*), future (*bailaré* or *voy a bailar*), conditional (*bailaría*), subjunctives (*baile, bailara*), perfect compounds (*he bailado, había bailado, habré bailado*), imperative (*baila*).
4. *Clause type* included three factors: main, subordinate, and coordinate clauses.
5. *Semantic class* included three factors: mental/estimative (*creer*), stative (*ser, estar*), and external activity verbs (*bailar, cantar, caminar*).
6. *Reflexive* included two factors: verb occurs with a reflexive pronoun (*me bañé*), verb does not occur with a reflexive pronoun (*creo*).

Two logistic regression analyses—one for the children and one for the adults—were performed using presence/absence of the subject pronoun as a dependent variable and the six variables listed above as independent predictor variables. Logistic regression is a type of multivariate analysis that examines the relative contribution of each predictor variable on the dependent variable. For discussion of the advantages of multivariate analysis, see Guy (1993, 237–238) and Otheguy and Zentella (2012, 130). The results of logistic regression analyses run in SPSS provide a WALD statistic (See Otheguy and Zentella 2012, 158–161), used here to construct variable hierarchies, which rank predictor variables in order of highest to lowest WALD value. The higher the value, the stronger the constraint. The column with the title *p* tells us whether or not each variable reaches statistical significance as a predictor of pronoun use, with two asterisks indicating significance at the <.01 cut-off value, and one asterisk indicating significance at the <.05 cut-off value, while *ns* means "non-significant."

The hierarchy presented on the left panel of table 9.2 shows that the ranking for the Mexican adults is person, reference, TMA, clause, semantic, and, finally, reflexive. This ranking is mostly consistent with Otheguy and Zentella's (2012, 182) ranking for recent arrivals to NYC hailing from Latin American mainland countries (Colombia, Ecuador, and Mexico).[12] The results for the children, presented on the right panel of table 9.2, show evidence of an emerging adult-like system. The two variables that are ranked the highest for the adults, person and reference, significantly impact the pronoun expression of the children and also appear in the same order in their constraint ranking. The third variable, TMA, does not reach significance for the children; nevertheless, as we will see below, the strongest factors within the TMA variable—the imperfect and the imperative—are significant predictors of pronoun use among the children.

Table 9.2 Predictors of SPP use for Mexican adults and children

Adults (N Vbs = 8270), R^2 =.16			Children (N Vbs = 2150), R^2 = .13		
Variables	**Wald**	**p**	**Variables**	**Wald**	**p**
1. Person	334.05	**	1. Person	63.22	**
2. Reference	152.68	**	2. Reference	31.80	**
3. TMA	149.90	**	3. TMA	10.31	ns
4. Clause	39.22	**	4. Clause	5.79	ns
5. Semantic	30.32	**	5. Reflexive	1.89	ns
6. Reflexive	27.41	**	6. Semantic	.80	ns

The impact of the factors within each variable is analyzed by examining the probability of pronoun use expressed as an *Exp(B)* value. Exp(B) values above 1.0 indicate that a factor promotes pronoun use, whereas values below 1.0 indicate that a factor promotes pronoun omission. The further away from 1.0, the stronger the factor. So, a factor with an Exp(B) value of 2.0 is a stronger promoter of pronoun use than a factor with a value of 1.5. Conversely, a factor with a value of .2 is a stronger promoter of omission than a factor with a value of .5. Exp(B) values are used to generate constraint hierarchies *within* each variable by ranking each factor in order of the strongest to weakest promoters of pronoun use. For example, the constraint hierarchy for person (table 9.3) shows that the person factor that most strongly promotes pronoun use among both adults and children is 1sg. This means that *yo* is more likely to be expressed than, for example, *tú* or *él/ella*. At the opposite pole is 1pl, the person factor that most strongly disfavors pronoun use. This means that *nosotros* is less likely to be expressed than *yo, tú, él/ella,* or *ellos/ellas*. We also report the range, which is useful for assigning different degrees of predictive strength to variables in different groups of speakers (Otheguy and Zentella 2012, 165; Tagliamonte 2012, 127). Ranges are calculated for each variable by subtracting the Exp(B) value of the strongest disfavoring factor from the value of the strongest favoring factor. In the current paper we only examine the constraint hierarchies for the top three variables, person, reference, and TMA. In tables 9.3 and 9.4, we present the constraint hierarchies for person and reference.

Table 9.3 Constraint hierarchy for person among Mexican adults and children

Adults				Children			
Factor	**N vbs**	**Exp(B)**	**p**	**Factor**	**N vbs**	**Exp(B)**	**p**
1sg	4009	2.39	**	1sg	401	2.89	**
3sg	1122	2.29	**	2sg	111	2.05	*
2sg	1226	.91	ns	3sg	1113	.89	ns
3pl	1224	.64	**	3pl	380	.45	**
1pl	689	.32	**	1pl	145	.42	*
Range		2.07		*Range*		2.47	

Table 9.4 Constraint hierarchy for reference among Mexican adults and children

Adults				Children			
Factor	**N vbs**	**Exp(B)**	**p**	**Factor**	**N vbs**	**Exp(B)**	**p**
Switch	4604	1.46	**	Switch	979	1.62	**
Same	3666	.69	**	Same	1171	.62	**
Range		*.77*		*Range*		*1.00*	

As demonstrated by the hierarchies in tables 9.3 and 9.4, not only are person and reference significant for both adults and children, the trends demonstrated within the variables are nearly identical. For both, 1sg pronoun *yo* is the most likely to be expressed. Also, the generalization that singular pronouns are more likely to be expressed as compared to plural pronoun holds for both adults and children. In other words, for both children and adults, plural pronouns *ellos/ellas* and *nosotros/nosotras* are likely to be omitted. With respect to reference, we see the same effect for adults and children: Switch reference promotes pronoun presence while same reference promotes pronoun absence. It is also worth noting that the children's ranges between the top and bottom factors in both person and reference are larger than the adults' ranges. This is further evidence suggesting that the children have approximated adult-like competence with respect to these two variables.

Although TMA is not significant for the children in terms of the WALD statistic associated with the variable as a whole (see table 9.2), table 9.5 illustrates that several factors within the variable do constrain the children's pronominal behavior, providing further evidence of an emerging adult-like pattern.

Table 9.5 Constraint hierarchy for TMA among Mexican adults and children

Adults				Children			
Factor	**N vbs**	**Exp(B)**	**p**	**Factor**	**N vbs**	**Exp(B)**	**p**
Imperfect	1257	2.60	**	Imperfect	343	1.94	*
Conditional	54	2.08	*	Conditional	5	1.38	ns
Subjunctive	343	1.75	**	Perfect	41	1.38	ns
Preterit	1786	1.34	*	Preterit	928	1.22	ns
Perfect	350	1.28	ns	Present	676	1.17	ns
Present	4072	1.09	ns	Future	37	1.02	ns
Future	233	.69	ns	Subjunctive	66	.69	ns
Imperative	175	.08	**	Imperative	54	.26	*
Range		*2.52*		*Range*		*1.68*	

Five TMA factors are significant among the adults: The imperfect, conditional, subjunctive, and the preterit all promote pronoun expression, while the imperative promotes pronoun omission. As in previous studies of adult Spanish, the TMA combination that is the strongest promoter of pronoun use here is the imperfect, while the one that is the strongest deterrent to pronoun use is the imperative. Only two TMA factors are significant among the children, but it is noteworthy that those two factors, the imperfect and the imperative, are identical in rank and direction to the adult data. In other words, the factor hierarchy within TMA is similar to variable hierarchy presented in table 9.2, where the strongest predictors of usage among adults, and crucially *not* the weaker ones, are those that appear to emerge first in the child data.

DISCUSSION

This study of subject pronoun expression in the speech of monolingual Spanish-speaking children, ages six to eight, provides three major findings. First, children in this age group produce far fewer subject pronouns than adults do. Second, girls advance more quickly than boys in the acquisition of adult-like pronoun rates. Third, the children's patterns of usage provide evidence of an emerging grammar, similar in structure to that of the adults. In this discussion section we address each of these three findings.

The children's comparatively low pronoun rate suggests that the crosslinguistic underproduction of subject pronouns found among very young children acquiring Catalan, Italian, Spanish, and Portuguese (Grinstead 2004, Valian 1991, Valian and Eisenberg 1996) persists into early school age. This finding, which is corroborated by the results for monolingual Mexican children studied by Montrul and Sánchez-Walker (this volume), has important implications for the study of child language, as it demonstrates that some parts of a child's grammar take a rather long time to develop. Furthermore, there is growing evidence that variability in the input has an effect on child language development: The more variable a structure is in the adult variety of a language, the longer it takes for children to master (Miller 2012; Miller and Schmidt 2010, 2012). In adult Spanish, subject pronouns are more often omitted than expressed. The implication of the relative scarcity of overt pronouns in adult speech is that positive evidence in the input is rather limited. This decreases the available data upon which children can formulate hypotheses regarding how and when to use pronouns. Our study suggests that, rather than inserting pronouns haphazardly, or liberally overusing pronouns initially, children are instead decidedly conservative in their pronominal behavior. They appear to postpone regular use of pronouns until they have acquired a richer understanding of how to use these forms appropriately. This behavior is consistent with a substantial body of evidence demonstrating that children are conservative language learners.

A second important finding in our study is that between ages six and eight girls outpace boys in the progression towards adult-like rates of pronoun use. As girls get older their pronoun rates increase. By age eight, the girls in our study used pronouns with a frequency similar to that found in adult Mexican Spanish. This finding complements the large body of literature reporting that girls proceed more quickly than boys in all aspects of language development (e.g., Eriksson et al. 2012; Locke, Ginsborg, and Peers 2002; To, Cheung, and McLeod 2013; among others). Furthermore, given that the girls achieve adult-like pronoun expression rates at age eight, our study lends support to the observation that this age represents a major milestone in the childhood acquisition of referring expressions (Shin and Cairns 2012, 31).

The third finding relates to our primary research question: Do children use subject pronouns in a systematically variable way? We conclude that the answer to this question is yes, on the basis of two findings. First, the two most powerful constraints on adult subject pronoun use, person/number and reference, are similarly operative in the children's speech. Second, while TMA does not, as a variable, make a significant contribution to the logistic regression model of the child data, significant results do emerge for specific factors *within* the variable, namely, the TMA factors of the *imperfect* and *imperative*. Together, these results clearly indicate the presence of structured variability, and strongly suggest that the developmental sequence of pronoun use follows directly from the patterns found in adult language: The strongest predictors among adults are the first to emerge among children.[13]

This study raises several challenging questions, the first of which relates to the issue of directionality: Does the adult pattern trigger the developmental sequence, or is the developmental sequence the very source of the adult pattern? And then, what sustains its transmission and use across generations? Are there inherent functional, psychosocial, or cognitive advantages to the hierarchy of constraints routinely reported for this "showcase variable"? Consensus on this issue remains elusive. What does seem to be clear is that the study provides evidence of children's acute sensitivity to probabilistic information in variable linguistic input in general and to patterns of morphosyntactic variation in particular. Indeed, it is rather unlikely to be mere coincidence that the first indications of structured variability among children are found in the effects of the strongest constraints on adult behavior. It is much more likely that this pattern emerges because the children are making direct use of adult behavior to tune the settings of the variable components of their own grammar. Future research might aim to make this case truly compelling, by substituting control data such as ours with a direct analysis of the input that children receive in their own individual speech communities.

ACKNOWLEDGMENTS

This research was supported by grants from the University of Montana awarded to the first author. We are also grateful to Ricardo Otheguy and Ana Celia Zentella, for allowing us to use data from their corpus; two anonymous reviewers, who provided excellent suggestions and feedback; Rafael Orozco and Ana Carvalho; and the editorial staff of Georgetown University Press.

NOTES

1. The corpus was developed at the Graduate Center of the City University of New York (CUNY) with support from the National Science Foundation (BCS 0004133), Professional Staff Congress of CUNY (62666-00-31), and a CUNY Collaborative Grant (09-91917).
2. Pronoun omission is more common than expression, with two exceptions: The polite form *usted* tends to have especially high rates of expression, ranging between 76 percent expressed in Madrid (Enríquez 1984, 191) and 88 percent in Buenos Aires (Barrenechea and Alonso 1977, 338). Likewise, impersonal *uno* can reach rates of 85 percent expressed (Cameron 1992, 233).
3. The impact of topic continuity on pronoun expression has also been investigated by examining co-reference with a preceding object, as well as the impact of intervening clauses (e.g., Abreu 2009, Balasch 2008, Bayley and Pease-Alvarez 1997, Hurtado 2005, Travis and Torres Cacoullos 2012).
4. Not all scholars agree that the TMA effect has to do with ambiguity. Some argue that in natural discourse true ambiguity is rare, and thus there is no need for pronouns to help disambiguate reference (Ávila-Shah 2000, 242; Travis 2007, 118). An alternative explanation has been offered by Silva-Corvalán 2001 (161–163), who posits that the imperfect promotes pronoun expression, not because of morphological ambiguity, but rather because of the backgrounding function associated with it (See also Bayley and Pease-Alvarez 1997, 363; Torres Cacoullos and Travis

2011, 253). Recently, Shin (2014) tested Silva-Corvalán's hypothesis, and finding no support for it, she concludes that the TMA effect is related to the avoidance of ambiguous reference.

5. Enríquez (1984, 351) found 19 cases of expressed *tú* out of 73 imperative contexts. Cantero Sandoval (1978, 264) notes that some imperative + pronoun constructions, such as *pon tú que*, are repeated so often that they become fixed expressions.
6. Abreu's results for her monolingual, but not bilingual, participants follow this hierarchy. Person is excluded from Hurtado (2005) and Torres Cacoullos and Travis (2010, 2011), as their data are restricted to specific grammatical persons. In Claes (2011) and Orozco and Guy (2008), reference is ranked lower than TMA, presumably because reference is operationalized differently than in other studies.
7. Almost all variationist child language research to date has investigated phonological (Cameron 2010; Chevrot, Beaud, and Varga 2000; Díaz-Campos 2005; Foulkes and Docherty 2006; Foulkes, Docherty, and Watt 1999; Roberts and Labov 1995; Romaine 1978) and morphophononological (Guy and Boyd 1990; Labov 1989; Roberts 1997; Smith, Durham and Fortune 2009) phenomena. See Nardy, Chevrot, and Barbu (2013) for an overview. What we have learned so far is that some (morpho) phonological patterns emerge early in child development; others emerge late. For example, Roberts (1997) found that many of the constraints on variable (-t/-d) deletion typically found among adult English speakers were evident in the speech of three- and four-year-old children. Nevertheless, -t/-d deletion patterns with "semi-weak" verbs, such as 'slept' and 'told', do not emerge until adolescence (Guy and Boyd 1990).
8. In the case of third-person referents there are, of course, a variety of NP types that could be used in subject position. In the children's data there were 989 expressed lexical NP subjects, which, following much of the literature on Spanish subject pronoun expression, were not included in the current study. Nevertheless, we agree with an anonymous reviewer that analyses of all types of third-person referents could shed light on how the use of referring expressions develops during childhood. Lexical NP subjects have been studied by Dumont (2006) in a study of adult New Mexican Spanish, as well as Geeslin and Gudmestad (e.g., 2010, 2011) in their research on second language acquisition.
9. The number at the end of each example refers to the identification number given to the participant.
10. The exclusion of a potential outlier among the male sample amplifies the main effect of this variable, increasing the difference in rates between the sexes from 3.2 percent (9.9 vs. 6.7) to 4 percent (9.9 vs. 5.9).
11. Cases of *usted*, *ustedes* (both 'you-formal') and *uno* ('one') were excluded from the current study due to the scarcity of these forms in the children's data.
12. Here the ranking of Semantic and Clause is reversed. In Otheguy and Zentella's (2012, 182) analyses of newcomers from Mainland Latin America, Semantic (which they call 'Lexical') is ranked higher than Clause.
13. Geeslin, Linford, and Fafulas's study (this volume) suggests that the same generalization applies to second language acquisition. The strongest predictors of pronoun expression among adult native speakers of Spanish are the first to emerge during both first and second language acquisition.

REFERENCES

Abreu, Laurel. 2009. "Spanish subject personal pronoun use by monolinguals, bilinguals, and second language learners." PhD diss., University of Florida.

———. 2012. "Subject pronoun expression and priming effects among bilingual speakers of Puerto Rican Spanish." In *Selected Proceedings of the 14th Hispanic Linguistics Symposium*, edited by Kimberly Geeslin and Manuel Díaz-Campos, 1–8. Somerville, MA: Cascadilla.

Austin, Jennifer, María Blume, David Parkinson, Zelmira Núñez del Prado, and Barbara Lust. 1998. "Interactions between pragmatic and syntactic knowledge in the first language acquisition of Spanish null and overt pronominals." In *Theoretical analyses on romance languages,* edited by José Lema and Esthela Treviño, 36–47. Amsterdam/Philadelphia: John Benjamins.

Ávila-Jiménez, Bárbara. 1995. "A sociolinguistic analysis of a change in progress: Pronominal overtness in Puerto Rican Spanish." *Cornell Working Papers in Linguistics* 13:25–47.

———. 1996. "Subject pronoun expression in Puerto Rican Spanish: A sociolinguistic, morphological, and discourse analysis." PhD diss., Cornell University.

Ávila-Shah, Bárbara. 2000. "Discourse connectedness in Caribbean Spanish." In *Research on Spanish in the US*, edited by Ana Roca, 238–251. Somerville: Cascadilla Press.

Balasch, Sonia. 2008. "La conectividad discursiva en el discurso interactivo." In *Selected Proceedings of the 10th Hispanic Linguistics Symposium*, edited by Joyce Bruhn de Garavito and Elena Valenzuela, 300–311. Somerville, MA: Cascadilla Proceedings Project.

Barrenechea, Ana María, and Alicia Alonso. 1977. "Los pronombres personales sujetos en el español hablado en Buenos Aires." In *Estudios sobre el español hablado en las principales ciudades de América*, edited by Juan M. Lope Blanch, 333–49. México: Universidad Nacional Autónoma de México.

Barriga Villanueva, Rebeca. 2002. *Estudios sobre el habla infantil en los años escolares ... un solecito calientote.* Mexico City: El Colegio de México.

Bayley, Robert, Norma L. Cárdenas, Belinda Treviño Schouten, and Carlos Martin Vélez Salas. 2012. "Spanish dialect contact in San Antonio, Texas: An exploratory study." In *Selected Proceedings of the 14th Hispanic Linguistics Symposium*, edited by Kimberly Geeslin and Manuel Díaz-Campos, 48–60. Somerville, MA: Cascadilla.

Bayley, Robert, and Lucinda Pease-Alvarez. 1996. "Null and expressed pronoun variation in Mexican-descent children's Spanish." In *Sociolinguistic variation: Data, theory, and analysis*, edited by Jennifer Arnold, Renee Blake and Brad Davidson, 85–99. Stanford: Center for the Study of Language and Information.

———. 1997. "Null pronoun variation in Mexican-descent children's narrative discourse." *Language variation and change* 9:349–371.

Bel, Aurora. 2003. "The syntax of subjects in the acquisition of Spanish and Catalan." *Probus* 15:1–23.

Bentivoglio, Paola. 1987. *Los sujetos pronominales de primera persona en el habla de Caracas*. Caracas: Universidad Central de Venezuela.

Boyd, Jeremy, and Adele E. Goldberg. 2012. "Young children fail to fully generalize a novel argument structure construction when exposed to the same input as older learners." *Journal of Child Language* 39(3):457 481

Bybee, Joan. 2001. *Phonology and language use.* Cambridge: CUP.

———. 2010. *Language, usage and cognition.* Cambridge: CUP.

Cameron, Richard. 1992. "Pronominal and null subject variation in Spanish: constraints, dialects, and functional compensation." PhD diss., University of Pennsylvania.

———. 1993. "Ambiguous agreement, functional compensation, and nonspecific tú in the Spanish of San Juan, Puerto Rico, and Madrid, Spain." *Language Variation and Change* 5:305–34.

———. 1995. "The scope and limits of switch-reference as a constraint on pronominal subject expression." *Hispanic Linguistics* 6/7:1–27.

———. 2010. "Growing up and apart. Gender divergences in a Chicagoland elementary school." *Language Variation and Change* 22(2):279–319.

Cantero Sandoval, Gustavo. 1978. "Observaciones sobre la expresión innecesaria de los pronombres personales sujeto en el español de México." *Anuario de Letras* 16:261–264.

Carvalho, Ana M., and Michael Child. 2011. "Subject pronoun expression in a variety of Spanish in contact with Portuguese." In *Selected Proceedings of the 5th Workshop on Spanish Sociolinguistics*, edited by Jim Michnowicz and Robin Dodsworth, 14–25. Somerville, MA: Cascadilla Press.

Chevrot, Jean-Pierre, Laurence Beaud, and Renata Varga. 2000. "Developmental data on a French sociolinguistic variable: Post-consonantal word-final /R/." *Language variation and change* 12:295–319.

Cifuentes, Hugo. 1980–1981. "Presencia y ausenceia del pronombre personal sujeto en el habla culta de Santiago de Chile." *Boletín de Filología de la Universidad de Chile* 31:743–752.

Claes, Jeroen. 2011. "¿Constituyen las Antillas y el Caribe continental una sola zona dialectal? Datos de la variable expresión del sujeto pronominal en San Juan de Puerto Rico y Barranquilla, Colombia." *Spanish in Context* 8(2):191–212.

Díaz-Campos, Manuel. 2005. "The emergence of adult-like command of sociolinguistic variables: A study of consonant weakening in Spanish-speaking children." In *Selected Proceedings of the 6th Conference on the Acquisition of Spanish and Portuguese as First and Second Languages*, edited by David Eddington, 56 65. Somerville, MA: Cascadilla Proceedings Project.

Dumont, Jenny. 2006. "Full NPs as subjects." In *Selected Proceedings of the 9th Hispanic Linguistics Symposium*, edited by Nuria Sagarra and Almeida Jacqueline Toribio, 296–296. Somerville, MA: Cascadilla Proceedings Project.

Enríquez, Emilia V. 1984. *El pronombre personal sujeto en la lengua española hablada en Madrid.* Madrid: Consejo Superior de Investigaciones Científicas.

Eriksson, Mårten, Peter Marschik, Tiia Tulviste, Margareta Almgren, Miguel Pérez Pereira, Sonja Wehberg, Ljubica Marjanovič-Umek, Frederique Gayraud, Melita Kovcevic, and Carlos Gallego. 2012. "Differences between girls and boys in emerging language skills: Evidence from 10 language communities." *British Journal of Developmental Psychology* 30:326–343.

Erker, Daniel. 2005. "Functional compensation for morphological ambiguity in New York City Spanish." MA thesis, University of New York.

Erker, Daniel, and Gregory Guy. 2012. "The role of lexical frequency in syntactic variability: Variable subject personal pronoun expression in Spanish." *Language* 88(3):526–557.

Flores-Ferrán, Nydia. 2002. *A sociolinguistic perspective on the use of subject personal pronouns in Spanish narratives of Puerto Ricans in New York City.* Munich: Lincom-Europa.

———. 2004. "Spanish subject personal pronoun use in New York City Puerto Ricans: Can we rest the case of English contact?" *Language Variation and Change* 16:49–73.

———. 2010. "*¡Tú no me hables!* Pronoun expression in conflict narratives." *International Journal of Sociology of Language* 203:61–82.

Foulkes, Paul, and Gerard Docherty. 2006. "The social life of phonetics and phonology." *Journal of Phonetics* 34:409–438.

Foulkes, Paul, Gerry Docherty, and Dominic Watt. 1999. "Tracking the emergence of structured variation– Realisations of (t) by Newcastle children." *Leeds Working Papers in Linguistics and Phonetics* 7:1–23.

Geeslin, Kimberly, and Aarnes Gudmestad. 2010. "Exploring the roles of redundancy and ambiguity in variable subject expression: A comparison of native and non-native speakers." In *Refereed Proceedings from the 12th Hispanic Linguistics Symposium*, edited by C. Borgonovo, M. Español-Echevarría, and P. Prevost, 270–283. Somerville, MA: Cascadilla Press.

———. 2011. "Using sociolinguistic analyses of discourse-level features to expand research on L2 variation: Native and non-native contrasts in forms of Spanish subject expression." In *Selected Proceedings of the 2009 Second Language Research Forum: Diverse Contributions to SLA*, edited by L. Plonsky and M. Schierloh, 16–30. Somerville, MA: Cascadilla Press.

Grinstead, John. 2004. "Subjects and interface delay in child Spanish and Catalan." *Language* 80(1):40–72.

Guy, Gregory. 1993. "The quantitative analysis of linguistic variation." In *American Dialect Research*, edited by Dennis R. Preston, 223–249. Amsterdam: John Benjamins.

———. 2011. "Variability." In *The Blackwell companion to phonology, Vol. 4*, edited by Marc Van Oostendorp, Colin J. Ewen, Elizabeth V. Hume, and Keren Rice, 2190–213. Malden, MA: Wiley-Blackwell.

Guy, Gregory, and Sally Boyd. 1990. "The development of a morphological class." *Language Variation and Change* 2:1–18.

Hochberg, Judith. 1986. "Functional compensation for /-s/ deletion in Puerto Rican Spanish." *Language* 62:609–621.

Holmquist, Jonathan. 2012. "Frequency rates and constraints on subject personal pronoun expression: Findings from the Puerto Rican highlands." *Language Variation and Change* 24:203–220.

Hurtado, Luz Marcela. 2005. "Syntactic-semantic conditioning of subject expression in Colombian Spanish." *Hispania* 88(2):335–348.

Kovac, Ceil, and Hugh Douglas Adamson. 1981. "Variation theory and first language acquisition." In *Variation omnibus*, edited by David Sankoff and H. Henrietta Cedergren, 403–410. Edmonton: Linguistic Research, Inc.

Labov, William. 1984. "Field methods of the project of linguistic change and variation." In *Language in use: Readings in sociolinguistics*, J. Baugh and J. Scherzer, 51–72. Englewood Cliffs: Prentice Hall.

———. 1989. "The child as linguistic historian." *Language Variation and Change* 1:85–97.

———. 1994. *Principles of linguistic change: Internal factors.* Mass: Blackwell.

Lieven, Elena. 2010. "Input and first language acquisition: Evaluating the role of frequency." *Lingua* 120:2546–2556.

Locke, Ann, Jane Ginsborg, and Ian Peers. 2002. "Development and disadvantage: Implications for the early years and beyond." *International Journal of Language and Communication Disorders* 37(1):3–15.

MacWhinney, Brian. 2004. "A multiple process solution to the logical problem of language acquisition." *Journal of Child Language* 31(4):883–914.

Miller, Karen. 2012. "Not all children agree: Acquisition of agreement when the input is variable." *Language Learning and Development* 8(3):255–277.

Miller, Karen, and Cristina Schmitt. 2010. "Effects of variable input in the acquisition of plural in two dialects of Spanish." *Lingua* 120(5):1178–1193.

———. 2012. "Variable input and the acquisition of plural morphology." *Language Acquisition: A Journal of Language Development* 19(3):223–261.

Nardy, Aurélie, Jean-Pierre Chevrot, and Stéphanie Barbu. 2013. "The acquisition of sociolinguistic variation: Looking back and thinking ahead." *Linguistics* 51(2):255–284.

Orozco, Rafael, and Gregory R. Guy. 2008. "El uso variable de los pronombres sujetos: ¿Qué pasa en la costa Caribe colombiana?" In *Selected Proceedings of the 4th Workshop on Spanish Sociolinguistics,* edited by Maurice Westmoreland and Juan Antonio Thomas, 70–80. Somerville, MA: Cascadilla Proceedings Project.

Ortiz López, Luis. 2011. "Spanish in contact with Haitian Creole." In *Handbook of Hispanic Sociolinguistics*, ed. Manuel Díaz-Campos, 418–445. Malden, MA: Blackwell.

Otheguy, Ricardo, and Ana Celia Zentella. 2012. *Spanish in New York: Language contact, dialectal leveling, and structural continuity.* Oxford: Oxford University Press.

Otheguy, Ricardo, Ana Celia Zentella, and David Livert. 2007. "Language and dialect contact in Spanish in New York: Towards the formation of a speech community." *Language* 83:770–802.

Paradis, Johanne, and Samuel Navarro. 2003. "Subject realization and crosslinguistic interference in the bilingual acquisition of Spanish and English: What is the role of the input?" *Journal of Child Language* 3(2):371–93.

Poplack, Shana, and Stephen Levey. 2010. "Contact induced grammatical change: A cautionary tale." In *Language and space: An international handbook of linguistic variation. Volume I,* edited by Peter Auer and Jürgen Erich Schmidt, 391–419. Berlin: Mouton De Gruyter.

Poplack, Shana, Lauren Zentz, and Nathalie Dion. 2012. "Phrase-final prepositions in Quebec French: An empirical study of contact, code-switching and resistance to convergence." *Bilingualism: Language and Cognition* 15(2):203–225.

Posio, Pekka. 2011. "Spanish subject pronoun usage and verb semantics revisited: First and second person singular subject pronouns and focusing of attention in spoken Peninsular Spanish." *Journal of Pragmatics* 43(3):777–798.

Prada Pérez, Ana de. 2009. "Variation in subject expression in Western Romance." In *Romance linguistics,* edited by Sonia Colina, Antxon Olarrea, and Ana M. Carvalho, 267–84. Amsterdam: John Benjamins.

Ranson, Diana L. 1991. "Person marking in the wake of /s/ deletion in Andalusian Spanish." *Language Variation and Change* 3:133–152.

Roberts, Julie. 1997. "Acquisition of variable rules: A study of (-t,d) deletion in preschool children." *Journal of Child Language* 24:351–372.

Roberts, Julie, and William Labov. 1995. "Learning to talk Philadelphian: Acquisition of short a by preschool children." *Language, Variation, and Change* 7:101–112.

Romaine, Suzanne. 1978. "Postvocalic /r/ in Scottish English: Sound change in progress?" In *Sociolinguistic patterns in British English*, edited by Peter Trudgill, 144–157. Baltimore MD: University Park Press.

Serratrice, Ludovica. 2005. "The role of discourse pragmatics in the acquisition of subjects in Italian." *Applied Psycholingusitics* 26:437–462.

Shin, Naomi Lapidus. 2006. "The development of null vs. overt subject pronoun expression in monolingual Spanish-speaking children: The influence of continuity of reference." PhD diss., City University of New York.

———. 2012. "Variable use of Spanish subject pronouns by monolingual children in Mexico." In *Selected Proceedings of the 14th Hispanic Linguistics Symposium, edited by* Kimberly Geeslin and Manuel Díaz-Campos, 130–141. Somerville, MA: Cascadilla Proceedings Project.

———. 2014. "Grammatical complexification in Spanish in New York: 3sg pronoun expression and verbal ambiguity." *Language Variation and Change* 26, 303–330.

Shin, Naomi Lapidus, and Helen Smith Cairns. 2012. "The development of NP selection in school-age children: reference and Spanish subject pronouns." *Language Acquisition: A Journal of Developmental Linguistics* 19(1):3–38.

Shin, Naomi Lapidus, and Cecilia Montes-Alcalá. 2014. "El uso contextual del pronombre sujeto como factor predictivo de la influencia del inglés en el español en Nueva York." *Sociolinguistic Studies* 8(1):85–110.

Shin, Naomi Lapidus, and Ricardo Otheguy. 2009. "Shifting sensitivity to continuity of reference: Subject pronoun use in Spanish in New York City." In *Español en Estados Unidos y en otros contextos de contacto: Sociolingüística, ideología y pedagogía*, edited by M. Lacorte and J. Leeman, 111–136. Madrid: Iberoamericana.

———. 2013. "Social class and gender impacting change in bilingual settings: Spanish subject pronoun use in New York." *Language in Society* 42(4):429–452.

Silva-Corvalán, Carmen. 1994. *Language contact and change: Spanish in Los Angeles.* Oxford: Oxford University Press.

———. 2001. *Sociolingüística y pragmática del español.* Washington DC: Georgetown University Press.

Silva-Corvalán, Carmen, and Noelia Sánchez-Walker. 2007. "Subjects in early dual language development: A case study of a Spanish–English bilingual child." In *Spanish in contact: Policy, social, and linguistic inquiries*, edited by Richard Cameron and Kim Potowski, 3–22. Amsterdam/Philadelphia: John Benjamins.

Smith, Jennifer, Mercedes Durham, and Liane Fortune. 2009. "Universal and dialect-specific pathways of acquisition: Caregivers, children, and t/d deletion." *Language Variation and Change* 21:69–95.

Tagliamonte, Sali. 2012. *Variationist sociolinguistics: Change, observation, and interpretation.* Malden, MA/West Sussex: Wiley-Blackwell.

To, Carol K. S., Pamela S.P. Cheung, and Sharynne McLeod. 2013. "A population study of children's acquisition of Hong Kong Cantonese consonants, vowels, and tones." *Journal of Speech, Language, and Hearing Research* 56:103–122.

Tomasello, Michael. 2003. *Constructing a language. A usage-based theory of language acquisition.* Cambridge, Mass: Harvard University Press.

Toribio, Almeida Jacqueline. 2000. "Setting parametric limits on dialectal variation in Spanish." *Lingua* 10:315–341.

Torres Cacoullos, Rena, and Catherine E. Travis. 2010. "Variable *yo* expression in New Mexico: English influence?" In *Spanish of the U.S. southwest: A language in transition*, Susana Rivera Mills and Daniel Villa Crésap, 189 210. Madrid: Iberoamer icana/Vervuert.

———. 2011. "Testing convergence via code-switching: priming and the structure of variable subject expression." *International Journal of Bilingualism* 15(3):241–267.

Travis, Catherine. 2007. "Genre effects on subject expression in Spanish: Priming in narrative and conversation." *Language Variation and Change* 19:101–135.

Travis, Catherine, and Rena Torres Cacoullos 2012. "What do pronouns do in discourse? Cognitive, mechanical, and constructional factors in variation." *Cognitive Linguistics* 23(4):711–748.

Valian, Virginia. 1991. "Syntactic subjects in the early speech of American and Italian children." *Cognition* 40:21–81.

Valian, Virginia, and Zena Eisenberg. 1996. "The development of syntactic subjects in Portuguese-speaking children." *Journal of Child Language* 23:103–128.

10

Variable Subject Expression in Second Language Spanish

Uncovering the Developmental Sequence and Predictive Linguistic Factors

Kimberly Geeslin, Bret Linford, and Stephen Fafulas

As the breadth of the current volume indicates, the (non)expression of verbal subjects in Spanish is of great interest. Such inquiry is not limited to the expression of subjects by native speakers, but also includes research on the expression of subjects by second language (L2) learners. Such investigations take place at the intersection of L2 acquisition research and research on sociolinguistic variation and thus contribute to both fields. One of the central goals of this cross-disciplinary research is to understand the path through which language develops among L2 speakers, using tools from sociolinguistics to describe the changes in rates of occurrence of a given form as well as the changing factors that predict such occurrence across levels of proficiency. This research also provides additional information about those factors to sociolinguists whose primary pursuit is to understand how language is used across geographic, social, and linguistic contexts. The current study contributes to L2 acquisition and sociolinguistic study by providing the first account of how the rates of subject pronoun expression (SPE) and the linguistic factors that predict it change as the L2 proficiency of learners of Spanish increases.

SUBJECT EXPRESSION IN SPANISH

Spanish allows the grammatical subject of a tensed verb to be expressed or unexpressed phonetically. Although there are several forms that may be used to express the subject overtly, most variationist research on subject expression in Spanish analyzes the variation between expressed (overt) and unexpressed (null) subject pronouns (e.g., Otheguy, Zentella, and Livert 2007). For the sake of comparability, we follow this tradition. Variationist research has shown that while pronoun rates vary across dialects, the same linguistic factors influence subject pronoun expression across varieties of Spanish (e.g., Cameron 1995). Our study is the first multi-level examination of L2 Spanish to focus precisely on those factors identified as central predictors of subject expression in sociolinguistic research. Some of the most influential factors include switch reference; tense, mood and aspect (TMA) of the verb; TMA continuity between verbs; and person and number of the referent.[1] This research has shown that subject pronouns tend to be expressed more often in contexts of switch reference than same reference (Bayley and Pease-Alvarez, 1997; Cameron, 1995; Otheguy and Zentella, 2012; Shin and Otheguy, 2009), with verbs that have TMA morphology that is ambiguous for person rather than with those that are person-specific (Bayley and Pease-Alvarez, 1997; Holmquist, 2012; Otheguy and Zentella, 2012; but see Bayley and Pease-Alvarez, 1997: 363; Silva-Corvalán, 2001, 161–163; and Torres Cacoullos and Travis, 2011, 253 for alternative explanations), and when the TMA differs from that of the previous verb (Bayley and Pease-Alvarez, 1997; Geeslin and Gudmestad, 2011). With regard to person and number, singular persons are associated with higher rates of overt subject pronouns than plural ones (Bayley and Pease-Alvarez 1997; Otheguy and Zentella 2012). Additionally, when considering the two most frequent forms in oral data, first person singular (1sg) forms are associated with higher rates of overt subject pronouns than third person singular (3sg) forms (Cameron 1992; Geeslin and Gudmestad 2008; Bayley and Pease-Alvarez 1997; Shin 2012).

SECOND LANGUAGE ACQUISITION OF VARIABLE STRUCTURES

Historically, L2 acquisition research has focused on the development of accuracy in the use of structures that are presumed to be invariant in the standard/educated variety. More recently, however, L2 inquiry has sought to incorporate native speaker variability into both the research design and the means by which learner data are analyzed. Such work has incorporated sociolinguistic techniques in order to describe how learner grammars change over time without relying on an assessment of accuracy. For example, Geeslin (2000) described changing rates of the use of *estar* and changes in the factors that predict such use across four levels of proficiency. This approach to research on L2 variation has since been applied to the subjunctive (Gudmestad 2012), the contrast between the present indicative and present progressive (Fafulas 2013), the use of direct object pronouns (Geeslin et al. 2010), the contrast between the preterit and present perfect (Geeslin et al. 2012), object marking (Killam 2011), future-time marking (Gudmestad and Geeslin 2013), and several other structures (see Geeslin 2011 for a review). What these studies all have in common is the value they place on recognizing that native languages are variable, and as such, the target for learners is not categorical use of every form but rather the ability to vary speech across linguistic as well as interactional contexts in native-like ways. In sum, the field of L2 variation now views development in terms of rates of use, predictors of use, and the direction of the effects of those predictors. The goal of the present chapter is to add a study of the development of SPE in L2 Spanish to the growing body of research on L2 variation.

SECOND LANGUAGE STUDIES OF SUBJECT EXPRESSION IN SPANISH

Subject expression in L2 Spanish has been investigated from a variety of theoretical frameworks. Within the generative framework, researchers have examined learners' development of the properties associated with the Null Subject Parameter (e.g., Al-Kasey and Pérez-Leroux 1998; Lozano 2002a) or the Overt Pronoun Constraint (e.g., Pérez Leroux and Glass 1999; Lozano 2002b; Rothman and Iverson 2007). Overall, this research demonstrated that learners acquire the relevant properties of the parameter or constraint outlined for subject expression. Nevertheless, this line of investigation has not explained the acquisition of subject forms in contexts where syntax alone does not constrain use. This limitation led researchers first to examine the interaction between syntactic and discourse-pragmatic properties in determining L2 Spanish subject expression (e.g., Lozano 2009; Montrul and Rodríguez Louro 2006; Rothman 2009), and later to conduct research that focused exclusively on subject expression in light of discourse-pragmatic variables. Approaches to L2 Spanish subject expression from a discourse-pragmatic perspective have investigated the pragmatic rules or constraints that guide subject expression in speech (e.g., Blackwell and Quesada 2012; Quesada and Blackwell 2009). These studies have shown that learners can acquire the pragmatic rules that constrain subject expression for native speakers, specifically those based on referent saliency, cognitive focus, contrastive focus, and pragmatic weight (Quesada and Blackwell 2009) as well as those based on cognitive status (Blackwell and Quesada 2012). One important contribution of this work is that it demonstrates how researchers might explore the discourse-pragmatic constraints on subject expression and describe acquisition of native-like use that cannot be determined by syntax alone.

The research reviewed thus far has explored the acquisition of L2 Spanish subject forms in contexts of *obligatory* use. That is, subject forms were examined in terms of accuracy as compared to the expected (categorical) patterns for native speakers. Nevertheless, sociolinguistic research has been dedicated to examining and explaining the linguistic and extra-linguistic factors that influence the *variable* use of Spanish subject forms (e.g., Bayley and Pease-Alvarez 1997; Cameron 1995; Otheguy and Zentella 2012); thus, it can be expected that these same factors may influence variable subject expression by L2 learners of Spanish. Research conducted on the acquisition of variable Spanish subject forms has largely been carried out in Geeslin and Gudmestad (2008, 2011) and Gudmestad and Geeslin (2010), and focuses on how highly advanced learners of Spanish express subjects as compared to native speakers.[2] These studies showed that use of subject forms differs between advanced learners and native speakers according to factors such as person and number and specificity of the referent. For example, Geeslin and Gudmestad (2008) showed that native speakers used more null subjects in 1sg and 3pl contexts while learners used more null subjects in all other contexts. Also, specificity of the referent demonstrated qualitative differences in the expression of null subjects between advanced learners and native speakers in that learners used fewer subject pronouns for non-specific referents than did native speakers. Gudmestad and Geeslin (2010) investigated the influence of three variables: TMA, potential verb form ambiguity, and switch reference. They found that switch reference explained the effects associated with TMA for both advanced learners and native speakers while potential form ambiguity did not, suggesting the need to examine discourse-related features of subject expression in more detail. By investigating the relationship between referent cohesiveness and perseveration of forms of subject expression by the same two groups, Geeslin and Gudmestad (2011) found that both advanced learners and native speakers demonstrated sensitivity to these discourse-level features in a similar manner. A key contribution of these studies is that they have allowed us to describe how highly advanced learners express

Spanish subjects and to identify those factors that can help account for similarities and differences across groups. What remains to be examined in greater detail is the development of subject expression over time as L2 learners move along the path of acquisition.

One project that begins to address this gap in the literature is Geeslin and Linford's (2012) cross-sectional study of subject expression in L2 Spanish by English-speaking learners. In addition to looking at the development of variable subject expression in Spanish across five levels of L2 proficiency, Geeslin and Linford employed a controlled task to examine constraints on subject forms. Previous studies (e.g., Geeslin and Gudmestad 2011) elicited data through sociolinguistic-style interviews from which tensed clauses were identified and analyzed according to a series of linguistic variables. One interesting result of the analysis of these interviews is that L2 learners actually produced more nulls than the native speakers, despite the fact that such forms rarely occur in their first language.[3] Geeslin and Gudmestad (2011) questioned whether the difference was indicative of greater ambiguity in the speech of learners or whether this was simply a reflection of linguistically less complex discourse created by learners. They suggested that a more controlled elicitation method would ensure that the discourse to which all participants responded was the same. Geeslin and Linford (2012) employed this type of elicitation task to examine the distribution of subject forms and how the discourse-level variables of referent cohesiveness and perseveration influenced subject form selection. They found that learners did not demonstrate native-like distribution of subject forms (i.e., nulls > overt personal pronouns > lexical NPs) until the fourth year, and also that it was not until the graduate level that rates of form selection were no longer statistically different from those demonstrated by native speakers. Sensitivity to the referent cohesiveness constraint was demonstrated by the second year, but as learners' proficiency increased, the relationship between decreasing use of overt subjects and less cohesive referents was not a linear one. Furthermore, within the discourse cohesiveness variable, only the distance to the previous mention of the referent was a significant predictor of subject form selection, while grammatical function of the previous form and TMA continuity did not significantly predict subject form selection for any group. Finally, with regard to perseveration, graduate-level learners demonstrated native-like trends for selection of a null form when the previous mention was also null. Thus, the work by Geeslin and Linford (2012) provided a first step in exploring the development of subject form expression across levels of proficiency and presented an appropriate methodology for such inquiry. A limitation of that project, however, is that the primary sentence-level factors known to be some of the greatest influences on subject expression were not examined. Thus, the current study seeks to expand on that work by providing a detailed account of how subject pronoun development proceeds over time with regard to pronoun rates and those variables known to predict subject form expression for native speakers.

THE CURRENT STUDY

As mentioned previously, the current study was designed to further our knowledge of the development of subject pronoun expression in L2 Spanish and to examine the developmental path that learners follow as they acquire this variable structure. In order to accomplish these goals, the current study is guided by the following research questions.

1. For each level of proficiency:
   (a) How frequently are overt subject pronouns selected on a written contextualized task?

(b) Which of the variables manipulated in the written contextualized task significantly predict subject pronoun selection?

2. How do the rates of selection and the factors that predict that selection:

   (a) Change across levels of proficiency?

   (b) Differ from those of native speakers on the same written task?

In the sections that follow, we describe the methodology employed to elicit and analyze data in order to answer these questions. Subsequently, we present our findings and discuss the implications for the fields of L2 acquisition and sociolinguistics.

PARTICIPANTS

The participants in the current study were 180 L2 learners of Spanish enrolled in six different levels of university Spanish courses which ranged from first-year to graduate level. All L2 participants were native English speakers from the United States. An additional 27 native speakers (NS) of Spanish from a variety of origins (Argentina, Colombia, Costa Rica, Mexico, Peru, Puerto Rico, Spain, and the United States) also participated in the study.[4] At the time of data collection, all of the NSs resided in the United States and were at least bilingual in English and Spanish. Moreover, all the NSs and graduate students were instructors of Spanish at the same university in which the undergraduate learners were enrolled. We only included the data gathered from the Spanish-dominant bilingual speakers residing in the United States for our NS group because it is reasonable to assume that these speakers are the best representation of the native target to which our classroom-instructed L2 learners are exposed. The characteristics of the participants are summarized in table 10.1, which includes the course level of each group, the number of participants per group, the groups' mean scores on a grammar test, and the percentage of participants with more than three weeks' experience in a Spanish-speaking country. Although the data collection times were somewhat staggered throughout the semester, these small differences are insignificant relative to the extent of the differences between groups in terms of overall proficiency level.

Table 10.1 Distribution of participants

Group	N	Mean percent on grammar test	Percent of participants with experience abroad
1st year[a]	30	36.3	0.0
3rd semester	30	46.0	0.0
5th semester[b]	30	46.8	6.7
3rd year	30	55.9	20.0
4th year	30	73.3	73.3
Graduate	30	92.5	100
NS	27	97.6	n/a

a. The students included in the 1st year group were enrolled in an introductory course designed for students with two or more years of high-school Spanish. The one-semester course covers material which would normally span two semesters.

b. This course is the first course beyond the basic language requirement. The third-year and fourth-year groups represent learners who are enrolled in junior- and senior-level Spanish major courses.

Each learner group contained 30 participants, while the NS group consisted of 27 participants. The results of the grammar test showed that the groups' mean scores increased with level of enrollment. An ANOVA showed that these differences were statistically significant [$F(6, 198) = 133.3$, $p < .001$]. However, post hoc Games-Howell tests demonstrated that there was no significant difference between the fifth-semester group and the third-semester group ($p = 1.00$) or the third-year group ($p = .127$). In addition, there was no significant difference between the graduate-level learners and the NSs ($p = .059$). Finally, beginning at the fifth semester, we see an increase in the percentage of students that have experience abroad as their course level increases.

Elicitation Tasks and Procedure

All participants completed three tasks in the following order: (1) a written contextualized task (WCT), (2) a short grammar test, and (3) a background questionnaire. The WCT consisted of a fictional dialogue in Spanish. Embedded in the dialogue were 16 items, each consisting of two response choices. These response choices were clauses that were identical except that the first option contained a null subject pronoun and the second option contained an overt subject pronoun. For each item, the four linguistic factors discussed previously (switch reference, TMA, person, and TMA continuity) were manipulated, and each category of these factors was evenly distributed across items so that each item contained a different combination of the categories of the four factors. Table 10.2 describes these factors, how they were operationalized, their categories, and the direction of the effect for each factor based on previous sociolinguistic research with native speakers of Spanish.

Several features of the dialogue were held constant for each item. Each item contained a verb in a main clause that was not a fixed expression, the previous mention of the referent in the item was always null, and the verbs preceding the items were either singular preterit or imperfect forms.[5] English translations in parentheses were added for 22 less common words or phrases in order to avoid miscomprehension. Example (1) is a sample item taken from the WCT. This particular item was coded as *switch reference*, *preterit*, *same TMA*, and *3sg*.

(1) Sample item taken from the WCT:

Pedro: *Bueno yo estaba seguro que él no sabía a dónde iba pero cuando le pregunté, ...*

☐ *... me dijo "¡Claro que sí! ¿No confías en mí o qué?"*

☐ *... él me dijo "¡Claro que sí! ¿No confías en mí o qué?"*

The second task the participants completed was a 25-item multiple-choice grammar test embedded in a fictional narrative in Spanish. Each item required participants to select the missing word that completed the phrase grammatically and also tested formal rules of grammar generally taught in the Spanish language classroom. As explained in the description of the participants, this test was used to corroborate groupings of our participants and has been found to be a statistically reliable measure (Linford, 2014).

The final task completed by the participants was a 53-item background questionnaire that elicited information regarding the social attributes of the participants (e.g., age, gender, native language), their experience with Spanish in various contexts, and their beliefs and attitudes toward Spanish. The results from this instrument were used to construct the preceding description of the participants. The roles of some of the individ-

Table 10.2 Descriptions of the factors manipulated in the WCT

Factor	Operationalization	Categories	Attested direction
Switch reference	Is the subject in the item the same as, or different from, the subject of the previous verb?	*(1) Switch reference*: the previous referent is different from the referent in the item. *(2) Same reference*: the previous referent is the same as the referent in the item.	More overt subject pronouns in switch reference contexts than in same reference contexts
TMA	What is the tense, mood, and aspect of the verb?	*(1) Imperfect indicative:* (e.g., *cantaba*) *(2) Preterit:* (e.g., *cantó*)	More overt subject pronouns with imperfect verb forms than with preterit forms
TMA continuity	Is the TMA of the verb the same as, or different from, the TMA of the previous verb in the discourse?	*(1) Same*: the TMA of the verb is the same as the previous verb *(2) Different*: the TMA of the verb is different from the previous verb	More overt subject pronouns when the TMA is different than when it is the same
Person[a]	What is the grammatical person of the referent?	(1) First person singular (2) Third person singular	More overt subject pronouns with 1sg than with 3sg

a. Including only these two persons allowed us to test the effects of TMA and morphological ambiguity. Additionally, the first person singular and third person singular were the most frequent forms produced in the oral interviews elicited in previous research (Geeslin & Gudmestad, 2008).

ual differences (e.g., motivation toward learning Spanish) fall outside the scope of the present analysis but are discussed in more detail in Linford (2014).

Data Coding and Analysis

The dependent variable in the current study was the selection of a null or overt subject pronoun. Each of the 16 items in the WCT was coded for switch reference, TMA, TMA continuity, and person of the verb form. In addition, the data were coded for grammar test scores and experience in Spanish-speaking countries. Both the linguistic and the extra-linguistic variables were examined for each proficiency level.

In order to address the research questions involving rates of subject pronoun selection, we identified the distribution of selection of null and overt subject pronouns by level of proficiency. We performed ANOVAs to determine if the differences in rates of selection of overt pronouns for each group were statistically significant. To examine the role of the independent variables, we performed separate binary logistic regressions using the Generalized Estimating Equations procedure for each group to determine which of the manipulated variables were statistically significant in the model (i.e., which variables significantly predicted subject pronoun selection for that group). Finally, the distribution of the rates of selection of null and overt subject pronouns within each category of the independent variables was determined in order to examine the direction of the significant effects for each group.

RESULTS

In this section, we first present the distribution of the selection of the null and overt subject pronouns for each group. This is followed by a description of the results of the logistic regressions for each participant group, showing the significant predictors of subject pronoun selection on the WCT.

Distribution of Forms

The data elicited using the WCT in the current study yielded a total of 3,303 tokens for analysis. The percentage of overt subject pronouns selected by each group of participants on the WCT ranged from 32.5 percent to 46.3 percent, and for nulls selection ranged from 53.7 percent to 67.5 percent. Table 10.3 summarizes these rates for each participant group.

Table 10.3 Distribution of null versus overt subject pronoun selection by level/group of participants

	Null pronouns		Overt subject forms		
Level/Group	#	%	#	%	**Total tokens** [a]
1st year	316	65.8	164	34.2	480 (100%)
3rd semester	292	61.1	186	38.9	478 (100%)
5th semester	266	55.5	213	44.5	479 (100%)
3rd year	257	53.7	222	46.3	479 (100%)
4th year	293	61.6	183	38.4	476 (100%)
Graduate	317	66.0	163	34.0	480 (100%)
NS	291	67.5	140	32.5	431 (100%)

a. A total of ten items were left blank by the participants.

The NS group demonstrated the lowest rate (32.5 percent) of selection of overt subject pronouns. Within the NS group, the participants from Costa Rica, the United States and Mexico exhibited the lowest rates of selection of overt pronouns (around 20 percent) and the speakers from Puerto Rico and Colombia demonstrated the highest rates of selection of overt pronouns (50 percent). The remaining participants from Spain, Bolivia, Argentina, and Peru selected overt forms between 30 and 44 percent of the time. In sum, the NSs behaved as anticipated based on the findings of previous sociolinguistic research, with the caveat that the speakers from Colombia were from coastal regions.[6] Importantly, our NS baseline is balanced across high-producing and low-producing backgrounds, and they represent the full range of typical rates of selection for the Spanish speaking world.

Looking at the L2 participant groups, the lowest average rate of overt subject pronoun selection was found among the graduate-level group, at 34 percent, followed by the first-year group with a 34.2 percent rate of overt subject form selection. The next lowest selection of overt pronouns was found among the fourth-year and third-semester groups, with averages of 38.4 percent and 38.9 percent, respectively. The highest overall rates of selection of overt pronouns were observed among the fifth-semester and third-year groups, with 44.5 percent and 46.3 percent overt pronouns, respectively.

Visually, the rates of selection of overt subject pronouns by each group of participants in the current study can be described as an inverted U-shaped curve, which is illustrated in figure 10.1. The figure also includes the NS group at the far right for the sake of comparison.

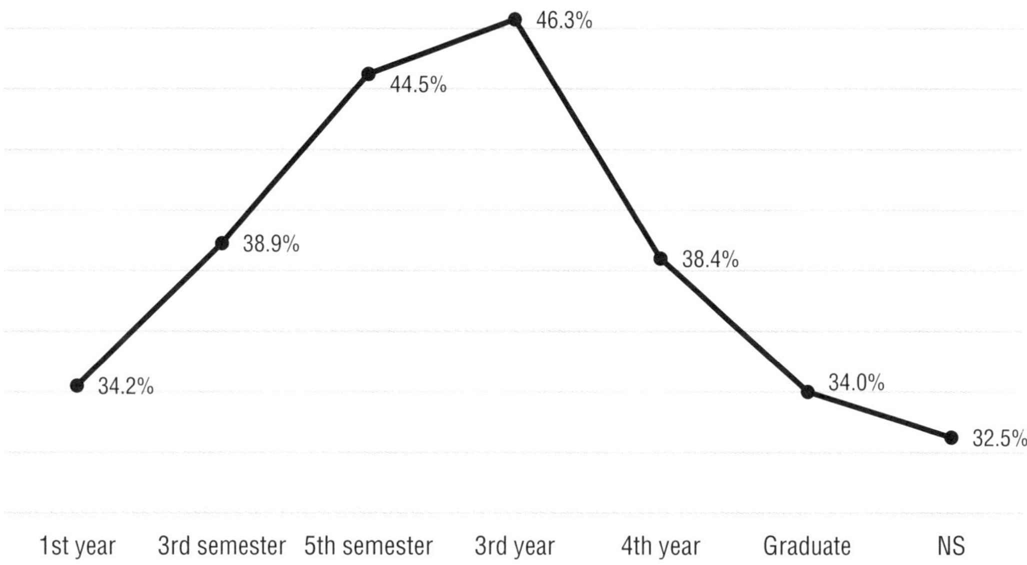

Figure 10.1 Rates of overt subject pronoun selection by group

As seen from left to right, on a continuum from least to most proficient in Spanish, the rate of selection of overt pronouns begins low with the first-year group, almost on par with NS selection rates. However, the rate of selection of overt subjects increases steadily until reaching its high point in third-year Spanish. Then, the rates of selection of overt pronouns steadily decrease through the fourth-year and graduate levels. The NS rates of overt pronoun selection are slightly lower than those of the graduate-level group. The results of an ANOVA reveal significant differences between the groups, $F(6, 200) = 2.717$, $p = .015$. However, post hoc Tukey tests show that only the third-year and NS groups were significantly different from each other ($p = .051$).[7]

Linguistic Predictors of Selection

As mentioned previously, we examined the role of switch reference, TMA, TMA continuity, and person. The results of each of the logistic regressions (one for each participant group) are summarized in table 10.4, where an "X" indicates that the factor was significant in the predictive model and asterisks indicate the degree of statistical strength. With the exception of the TMA factor for the third-semester group and person for the third and fourth year groups, when each of the factors included in the regression were significant predictors of subject pronoun selection, the direction of the effect was in line with the previously attested tendencies found in sociolinguistic research on native speakers (see table 10.2).

The selection of subject pronouns was significantly predicted by at least one factor for all groups except the fifth-semester group. For the first-year group, TMA continuity was the only significant predictor of subject pronoun selection and the effect of this variable was in the expected direction: More overt subject pronouns were selected

Table 10.4 Summary of regression analyses for each group with linguistic predictors of selection

Level/Group	Switch reference	Person	TMA	TMA continuity
1st yr.				X*
3rd sem.			X*	
5th sem.				
3rd yr.	X**	X**		
4th yr.	X***	X***	X*	
Graduate	X***		X***	
NS	X***		X***	

when the TMA was different between verbs than when the TMA was the same. For the third-semester group, only TMA was found to be a significant predictor of subject pronoun selection. In this case, however, the learners selected more overt subject pronouns with preterit forms than imperfect forms, which is the opposite of the previously attested trend for native speakers. At the fifth semester, none of the factors analyzed significantly predicted subject pronoun selection, but the switch reference variable did approach significance ($p = .066$). In contrast to the fifth-semester group, in the third-year group both switch reference and person significantly predicted subject pronoun selection but the effect of person was not consistent with the previously attested NS tendencies (these learners showed higher rates of selection of overt subject pronouns with 3sg than 1sg). Next, the fourth-year group showed a further increase in the strength of predictive power for switch reference and person (both in the same direction as the third-year group) and also added TMA to their model. At the graduate level, only switch reference and TMA were significant predictors of subject pronoun selection, aligning the model for this group with that of the NS group.

DISCUSSION

The objective of the current study is to observe the development of subject pronoun expression in L2 Spanish. We first discuss the overall rates of selection of subject pronouns by each group of NNSs (non-native speakers) and the NS group on the WCT. This section is followed by a discussion of the linguistic predictors of subject pronoun selection for each group. Finally, we describe the development of SPE across levels of proficiency based on our findings.

Distribution of Forms

As described previously, the WCT allowed us to elicit 3,303 tokens for analysis. The rates of selection of overt subject pronouns can be described as starting with relatively low rates of overt pronoun selection, increasing across levels until the third year, and then gradually decreasing again, ultimately reaching a rate of selection slightly lower than the first-year start rate. Despite this apparent trend, the statistical results showed no significant differences between learner groups. Finally, the rates of selection of overt pronouns for the NSs were slightly lower than the first-year and the graduate-level groups and constituted the lowest rates of selection of overt pronouns of any group. The finding that the first-year group showed similar rates of overt pronoun selection to the graduate-level learners and NSs appears to contradict previous research, which found higher rates of overt pronouns for lower-level learners (e.g., Pérez-Leroux and Glass 1999), but this may be a result of the specific task employed. In another study using a similar instrument (Geeslin and Linford 2012), a comparable trend to that of the current study was found: Learners began with lower rates, moved toward higher rates, and then decreased again with higher proficiency. As with grammatical structures which do not vary in native speech, there is evidence that this u-shaped behavior is characteristic of the process of acquiring subject pronoun use for first and second language learners alike. In an experimental study of Mexican children's preferences for overt and null subject pronouns, Shin and Cairns (2012, 16–19, 29) found that 6/7-year-olds were the most adult-like in their preference for null pronouns in same-reference contexts, while children between the ages of 8 and 13 tended to overselect overt pronouns in these contexts. Thus the general developmental trajectory for children and adults alike appears to move from a preference for null pronouns, then overt pronouns, and finally back to null pronouns.

Linguistic Predictors of Rates of Selection

Turning to the linguistic predictors of the rates of selection, we found that even at the two lowest levels of proficiency there were factors that significantly predicted subject pronoun selection, but these factors were either not significant at other levels or demonstrated effects that were not expected based on the tendencies reported in the sociolinguistic literature for native speakers. For the first-year learners, TMA continuity significantly predicted subject pronoun selection, but this is the only group for which this factor was significant. For the third-semester group, TMA was a significant predictor of the subject pronoun form selected, but in the opposite direction of the other groups. At the fifth-semester level, none of the factors significantly predicted subject pronoun selection but switch reference did approach significance. The significance of switch reference increased across levels of proficiency and was also significant for the NSs. TMA was not a significant predictor of subject pronoun selection in a manner consistent with previous findings reported for native speakers until the fourth year, but this factor was important for the two highest proficiency levels as well as for the NSs. As mentioned earlier, the effects of TMA are generally associated with the potential ambiguity of the verb form (e.g., Gudmestad and Geeslin 2010). In the current study, this effect was isolated to contrast the potential ambiguity of the 1sg and 3sg imperfect forms with the lack of ambiguity associated with those same forms in the preterit. It may be the case that because other features of the discourse also contribute to potential ambiguity, or that other verb forms make this effect more complex, we would see an earlier effect for TMA in less constrained elicitation measures. In the current study, however, the careful design of the instrument indicates that this effect is due only to the contrast between preterit and imperfect forms for 1sg and 3sg. The person of the verb form showed somewhat different results in that it was significant for the third-year and fourth-year groups but not in the same direction that has been found in previous NS research. This factor was not statistically significant for the graduate-level group or the NSs. Two effects are normally associated with the factor person. The first is that singular subjects tend to be associated with a higher expression rate of overt forms than plural subjects are. Because our elicitation instrument includes only singular forms, this effect is not pertinent for our analysis. The second effect is that 1sg forms are associated with more overt subject pronouns than 3sg forms. While the third- and fourth-year groups' selections of pronouns were significantly predicted by person, the native-like tendency found in previous sociolinguistic research of higher rates of overt subject pronouns with 1sg rather than 3sg was not demonstrated by the participants. In fact, there was no effect of person on pronoun selection for the graduate-level group or the NSs. In both cases, this finding is possibly a result of the design of our study, which intentionally controlled for a number of additional factors that are often associated with the effect of person, such as priming (e.g., Travis and Torres Cacoullos 2012).

Description of Development across Levels of Proficiency

Moving to the predictors of the rates of selection for the learner groups, there are several details about the path of development that can be ascertained. First, despite similar rates of selection of overt pronouns between the lowest and the highest proficiency groups, the predictive models reveal that while the higher groups selected pronouns in response to the same linguistic factors that condition NS patterns on this task (i.e., switch reference and TMA), lower-level learners did not. In the case of the first-year group, only TMA continuity significantly predicted the selection of subject pronouns. While this factor was not significant for any other group, for the first-year group, its effect was congruent with the native-like pattern found in previous sociolinguistic research: More overt subject pronouns were selected when there was a switch in TMA between verbs. As discussed below, although the direction of the effect is as expected, learners at this level are at a stage where morphosyntax is not fully developed. To us, this suggests that this factor likely operates differently for these lower-level learners than the influence one might anticipate this factor would have for native speakers. For example, it is possible that other sentence-level factors present in the context, coupled with the learners' lack of sensitivity to the factors guiding NS selection of subject pronouns on the same instrument, are also related to this finding. This becomes even clearer upon exploration of the results of the next highest learner group, third semester. By third semester, the selection of subject pronouns by the learners is significantly predicted by TMA of the verb used in the task item but in the opposite direction than that found for the NSs. These learners selected more overt subject pronouns with preterit forms than with imperfect forms. Geeslin et al. (2013) note that this may be due to increased processing load when object pronouns are present because, in the WCT, none of the imperfect forms in the questionnaire items were accompanied by object pronouns while five of the eight items that had preterit forms included an object pronoun. Thus, the first clear change to be noted as proficiency increases is that learners move away from patterns of selection that are conditioned by linguistic factors particular to their level(s) of development (i.e., TMA continuity for the first-year group), or patterns in a direction not typically associated with native-speaker trends (i.e., TMA for the third-semester group), or both of these (i.e., person for the third- and fourth-year groups). Additionally, switch reference becomes important starting at the third-year level, and then, at the fourth-year level, TMA also begins to constrain patterns of selection. Thus, those factors that predict selection are not acquired simultaneously. Instead, learners develop sensitivity to each factor individually over time. The appropriate combination of these predictive factors may take several years to acquire. There are two reasons that sensitivity to switch reference may be acquired before TMA. First, TMA is linked to morphosyntactic development, which has been shown to pose a challenge at earlier levels of proficiency in Spanish, particularly for native speakers of English (e.g., Comajoan 2013). The second reason is that switch reference is tied to cognitive principles of coreference, including topic, focus, informativeness, and pronominal anaphora (Quesada and Blackwell 2009), which are likely universals of human experience, cognition, and referencing of the world through language (Givón 1983). In other words, the learners in our study may be better equipped to "notice" linguistic cues through cognitive/discourse principles than they are through morphosyntactic means, at least at the earlier stages of acquisition. This may point to a general developmental trend, as it has been shown that, like second language learners, monolingual children become sensitive to switch reference before TMA (Shin and Erker, this volume). A final observation is that some factors that are not important for the NS group, such as TMA continuity and person, may enter into the predictive models at intermediate stages and be eradicated at higher levels of proficiency. In other words, learners do not simply develop sensitivity to the appropriate linguistic predictors, but rather must also learn to rely on only those factors that are shown to constrain native patterns in order to demonstrate both target-like rates and patterns of selection.

Using these observations as our guide, we propose an acquisitional sequence of null/overt subject pronouns by learners of Spanish in variable contexts, based on rates of selection as well as predictors of those rates. The proposed stages of development are outlined in table 10.5.[8]

Table 10.5 Developmental sequence for L2 Spanish null/overt subject pronouns by native speakers of English

Stage 1 Allowance of null pronouns
Overt and null pronouns are readily selected in contexts permitted by Spanish
Rate of selection of overt subjects is only slightly higher than for NSs of Spanish
When selection of subject pronouns is dependent on linguistic factors, these effects are either particular to the level of development or in the opposite direction of NSs
Stage 2 Emergence of linguistic predictors of selection for null/overt subjects
Increase in rate of selection of overt pronouns
Selection of null/overt pronouns is no longer constrained by any factor examined in the study
Stage 3 Extension of linguistic predictors and high point in inverted U-shaped curve
Selection of overt subjects continues to increase to its highest point
Switch reference becomes a predictor of subject pronoun selection
Person is incorporated into predictive model but not in line with the attested NS tendencies
Stage 4 Decreased rate of selection of overt pronouns and realignment of linguistic predictive factors
Rate of overt subject form selection begins to decrease again
TMA is significant predictor of form selection
Stage 5 Late stages of acquisition of null/overt subject forms
Overt subject form selection continues to fall, reaching native-like rates
Person factor is dropped from the predictive model
Learner model matches that of NSs; switch reference and TMA reach native-like constraint strength

Comparison to NS Participants

The final research question guiding the current project was whether the learners exhibited patterns of subject form selection similar to the NS group. When looking at the rates of selection, we see that both the highest and the lowest proficiency groups showed similarities to the NS group, and it is the intermediate levels that are furthest from the NS norm. Nevertheless, our analysis of the predictors of these rates clearly indicates that only the fourth-year and graduate-level participants arrive at these similar rates by responding to the same linguistic predictors as the native speakers. The fourth-year learners, however, demonstrate different levels of significance of certain factors as well as a greater difference in rates of selection than the graduate level. Thus, only the graduate-level group displays close similarities to the NS group with regard to rates and predictors of subject pronoun selection. We note that the finding that the highest proficiency learner level is indeed similar to the NS group on the measures used in the current study is of considerable interest and adds to the body of literature that explores native-like attainment by advanced learners (e.g., Birdsong, 2004).

One final observation regarding our results for NS and learner groups is that our research also shows similarities to research on subject expression by bilinguals in other contexts. For example, Otheguy, Zentella, and Livert's (2007) study of subject pronoun expression in New York City (NYC) Spanish supports the hypothesis that language contact is a predominant force pushing Spanish pronoun use in the direction of English (778). They conclude that "contact with English is causing an increase in the use of overt pronouns in Spanish in New York City …" (783). Based on their conclusion, one might expect that the use of overt subject pronouns would be highest among our lowest-level learners, as they represent a point on the bilingual continuum characterized by the greatest influence of English. However, our results show that the lowest level-group in our study, first-year Spanish, was closest to the highest learner level and NS groups in their rates of overt subject selection. Thus, the results for rates of selection of overt forms in the current study do not constitute a clear case for crosslinguistic influence. Another interesting question resulting from the previous discussion is whether or not factors such as length of residency, which result in the weakening of certain predictive factors, parallel the increase in those same factors as learners gain proficiency in Spanish. Previous research has shown the weakening of predictors such as switch reference and referent specificity on subject pronoun variation among bilingual Spanish–English speakers born and raised in the United States (e.g., Lapidus and Otheguy 2005; Shin and Otheguy 2009) but it remains to be seen the extent to which language attrition in bilingual communities in the United States mirrors language acquisition with regard to predictive factors. Previous research indicates that this is indeed the case for the copula contrast (Geeslin 2002), and we hypothesize that a similar relationship might exist for subject pronouns.

CONCLUSION

Following the work of L2 variationist sociolinguistics, our study set out to detail the developmental sequence for learner selection of null and overt subject forms in L2 Spanish. Our results provided some support for predictions, hypotheses, and conclusions derived from previous sociolinguistic studies of Spanish–English contact and subject pronoun expression (e.g., Otheguy, Zentella, and Livert 2007). However, the main contributions of the current study come in the identification of the linguistic predictors of selection and the developmental sequence for L2 subject pronoun form selection in Spanish. It was shown that, as learners begin to acquire native-like sensitivity to the linguistic predictors of selection of subject pronouns, their selection of overt pronouns increases in the opposite direction of the NS target. With greater proficiency in the target language, their selection of overt pronouns realigns with NS selection rates, exhibiting an inverted U-shaped pattern of development.

The results of the current study provide a number of avenues for future research on the L2 acquisition of subject expression in Spanish. Firstly, more participant groups and learners from earlier levels of proficiency will add to our understanding of the initial stages of acquisition of subject expression in Spanish. Secondly, the data of the current study should be compared to corpora of learners' oral data to uncover possible register-based or task-based differences. Thirdly, contexts of acquisition and individual differences between learners should be addressed in order to determine whether learners in other learning environments display similar patterns of development for subject form expression as the classroom learners observed in the current study. Finally, the analysis should be expanded to include other linguistic predictors of selection in order to offer a more thorough assessment of the developmental pattern of subject pronoun expression by L2 learners.

NOTES

1. Other factors such as linguistic priming (Abreu 2009; Cameron and Flores-Ferrán 2004; Travis 2007) and discourse pragmatics (e.g., Flores-Ferrán 2009) constrain subject forms but fall outside the scope of the current study.
2. See also Abreu (2009), which describes priming effects and the role of discourse cohesion in data elicited from heritage and intermediate-level second language speakers of Spanish.
3. There are cases of omitted subjects in English, and work on this topic suggests that similar factors may constrain this phenomenon (see Torres Cacoullos and Travis, this volume).
4. One native Spanish speaker from the United States was also included because her parents were born in Mexico and her patterns and rates of use were comparable to those of the other speakers, especially those from Mexico.
5. Given the known effects of priming (i.e., that null forms tend to be followed by null forms), this type of control may set the stage for priming of the null form. Nevertheless, the advantage of the written task is that all tokens are comparable across groups and this benefit outweighs the potential disadvantages for the purposes of the current study.
6. Means of overt subject pronoun selection by native speaker origin is as follows: Costa Rica (1 speaker) 19 percent; United States (1 speaker) 19 percent; Mexico (5 speakers) 22 percent; Spain (10 speakers) 30 percent; Bolivia (1 speaker) 32 percent; Argentina (2 speakers) 35 percent; Peru (1 speaker) 44 percent; Colombia (2 speakers) 50 percent; Puerto Rico (4 speakers) 50 percent.
7. Only two items elicited categorical responses from the native speakers and the graduate-level participants. All other items produced variable responses for all groups.
8. The generalizability of these findings must be confirmed through additional studies that include a broader range of tasks and participant backgrounds. Nevertheless, these stages describe development in terms of the changes seen across levels of proficiency for our participants.

REFERENCES

Abreu, Laurel. 2009. "Spanish Subject Personal Pronoun Use by Monolinguals, Bilinguals and Second Language Learners." PhD diss., University of Florida.

Al-Kasey, Tamara, and Ana Teresa Pérez-Leroux. 1998. "Second Language Acquisition of Spanish Null Subjects." In *The Generative Study of Second Language Acquisition,* edited by Suzanne Flynn, Gita Martohardjono, and Wayne O'Neil, 161–183. Hillsdale, NJ: Lawrence Erlbaum.

Bayley, Robert, and Lucinda Pease-Alvarez. 1997. "Null Pronoun Variation in Mexican-Descent Children's Narrative Discourse." *Language Variation and Change* 9:349–71.

Birdsong, David. 2004. "Second Language Acquisition and Ultimate Attainment." In *Handbook of Applied Linguistics,* edited by Alan Davies and Catherine Elder, 82–105. London: Blackwell.

Blackwell, Sarah E., and Margaret Lubbers Quesada. 2012. "Third-Person Subjects in Native Speakers' and L2 Learners' Narratives: Testing (and Revising) the Givenness Hierarchy for Spanish." In *Selected Proceedings of the 14th Hispanic Linguistics Symposium*, edited by Kimberly Geeslin and Manuel Díaz-Campos, 142–164. Somerville, MA: Cascadilla Proceedings Project.

Cameron, Richard. 1992. "Pronominal and Null Subject Variation in Spanish: Constraints, Dialects, and Functional Compensation." PhD diss., University of Pennsylvania at Philadelphia.

———. 1995. "The Scope and Limits of Switch Reference as a Constraint on Pronominal Subject Expression." *Hispanic Linguistics* 6–7:1–27.

Cameron, Richard, and Nydia Flores-Ferrán. 2004. "Perseveration of Subject Expression across Regional Dialects of Spanish." *Spanish in Context* 1(1):41–65.

Comajoan, Llorenç. 2013. "Tense and Aspect in Second Language Spanish." In *Handbook of Spanish Second Language Acquisition*, edited by Kimberly Geeslin, 235–253. New York: Wiley-Blackwell.

Fafulas, Stephen. 2013. "First and Second-Language Patterns of Variation: Acquisition and Use of Simple Present and Present Progressive Forms in Spanish and English." PhD diss., Indiana University.

Flores-Ferrán, Nydia. 2009. "Are You Referring to Me? The Variable Use of UNO and YO in Oral Discourse." *Journal of Pragmatics* 41:1810–1824.

Geeslin, Kimberly L. 2000. "A New Approach to the Study of the SLA of Copula Choice." In *Spanish Applied Linguistics at the Turn of the Millennium*, edited by Ron Leow and Cristina Sanz, 50–66. Medford, MA: Cascadilla Press.

———. 2002. "Semantic Transparency as a Predictor of Copula Choice in Second Language Acquisition." *Linguistics: An Interdisciplinary Journal of the Language Sciences* 40:439–468.

———. 2011. "Variation in L2 Spanish: The State of the Discipline." *Studies in Hispanic and Lusophone Linguistics* 4:461–517.

Geeslin, Kimberly L., Lorenzo J. García-Amaya, Maria Hasler-Barker, Nicholas C. Henriksen, and Jason Killam. 2010. "The SLA of Direct Object Pronouns in a

Study Abroad Immersion Environment Where Use Is Variable." In *Selected Proceedings of the 12th Hispanic Linguistics Symposium,* edited by Claudia Borgonovo, Manuel Español-Echevarría, and Philippe Prévost, 246–259. Somerville, MA: Cascadilla Proceedings Project.

———. 2012. "The L2 Acquisition of Variable Perfective Past Time Reference in Spanish in an Overseas Immersion Setting." In *Selected Proceedings of the 14th Hispanic Linguistics Symposium*, edited by Kimberly Geeslin and Manuel Díaz-Campos, 197–213. Somerville, MA: Cascadilla Proceedings Project.

Geeslin, Kimberly L., and Aarnes Gudmestad. 2008. "Variable Subject Expression in Second-Language Spanish: A Comparison of Native and Non-Native Speakers." In *Selected Proceedings of the 2007 Second Language Research Forum*, edited by Melissa Bowles, Rebecca Foote, Silvia Perpiñán, and Rakesh Bhatt, 69–85. Somerville, MA: Cascadilla Proceedings Project.

———. 2011. "Using Sociolinguistic Analyses of Discourse-Level Features to Expand Research on L2 Variation in Forms of Spanish Subject Expression." In *Selected Proceedings of the 2009 Second Language Research Forum*, edited by Luke Plonsky and Maren Schierloh, 16–30. Somerville, MA: Cascadilla Proceedings Project.

Geeslin, Kimberly L., and Bret Linford. 2012. "A Cross-Sectional Study of the Effects of Discourse Cohesiveness and Perseveration on Subject Expression." Paper presented at the 6th International Workshop on Spanish Sociolinguistics, Tucson, AZ, April.

Geeslin, Kimberly L., Bret Linford, Stephen Fafulas, Avizia Long, and Manuel Díaz-Campos. 2013. "The Group vs. the Individual: Subject Expression in L2 Spanish." In *Selected Proceedings of the 16th Hispanic Linguistics Symposium*, edited by Jessi Aaron, Jennifer Cabrelli Amaro, Gillian Lord, and Ana de Prada Pérez, 156–174. Somerville, MA: Cascadilla Proceedings.

Givón, Talmy, ed. 1983. *Topic Continuity in Discourse: A Quantitative Cross-Language Study.* Amsterdam: John Benjamins.

Gudmestad, Aarnes. 2012. "Acquiring a Variable Structure: An Interlanguage Analysis of Second-Language Mood Use in Spanish." *Language Learning* 62:373–402.

Gudmestad, Aarnes, and Kimberly L. Geeslin. 2010. "Exploring the Roles of Redundancy and Ambiguity in Variable Subject Expression: A Comparison of Native and Non-native Speakers." In *Selected Proceedings of the 12th Hispanic Linguistics Symposium,* edited by Claudia Borgonovo, Manuel Español-Echevarría, and Philippe Prévost, 270–283. Somerville, MA: Cascadilla Proceedings Project.

———. 2013. "Second-Language Development of Variable Future-Time Expression in Spanish." In *Selected Proceedings of the 6th Workshop on Spanish Sociolinguistics*, edited by Ana Carvalho and Sara Beaudrie, 63–75. Somerville, MA: Cascadilla Proceedings Project.

Holmquist, Jonathan. 2012. "Frequency Rates and Constraints on Subject Personal Pronoun Expression: Findings from the Puerto Rican Highlands." *Language Variation and Change* 24:203–220.

Killam, Jason. 2011. "An Interlanguage Analysis of Differential Object Marking in L2 Spanish." PhD diss., Indiana University.

Lapidus, Naomi, and Ricardo Otheguy. 2005. "Overt Nonspecific *ellos* in the Spanish of New York." *Spanish in Context* 2:157–176.

Linford, Bret. 2014. "Self-Reported Motivation and the L2 Acquisition of Subject Pronoun Variation in Spanish." In *Selected Proceedings of the 2012 Second Language Research Forum: Building Bridges between Disciplines*, edited by Ryan T. Miller, Katherine I. Martin, Chelsea M. Eddington, Ashlie Henery, Nausica Marcos Miguel, Alison Tseng, Alba Tuninetti, and Daniel Walter, 193–210. Somerville, MA: Cascadilla Proceedings Project.

Lozano, Cristóbal. 2002a. "Knowledge of Expletive and Pronominal Subjects by Learners of Spanish." *ITL Review of Applied Linguistics* 135:37–60.

———. 2002b. "The Interpretation of Overt and Null Pronouns in Non-native Spanish." *Durham Working Papers in Linguistics* 8:53–66.

———. 2009. "Selective Deficits at the Syntax-Pragmatics Interface: Evidence from the CEDEL2 Corpus." In *Representational Deficits in SLA: Studies in Honor of Roger Hawkins*, edited by Neal Snape, Yan-kit Ingrid Leung, and Michael Sharwood Smith, 127–166. Amsterdam: John Benjamins.

Montrul, Silvina, and Celeste Rodríguez Louro. 2006. "Beyond the Syntax of the Null Subject Parameter: A Look at the Discourse-Pragmatic Distribution of Null and Overt Subjects by L2 Learners of Spanish." In *The Acquisition of Syntax in Romance Languages*, edited by Vincent Torrens and Linda Escobar, 401–418. Amsterdam: John Benjamins.

Otheguy, Ricardo, and Ana Celia Zentella. 2012. *Spanish in New York: Language Contact, Dialectal Leveling, and Structural Continuity.* Oxford: Oxford University Press.

Otheguy, Ricardo, Ana Celia Zentella, and David Livert. 2007. "Language and Dialect Contact in Spanish in New York: Towards the Formation of a Speech Community." *Language* 83:770–802.

Pérez-Leroux, Ana Teresa, and William R. Glass. 1999. "Null Anaphora in Spanish Second Language Acquisition: Probabilistic versus Generative Approaches." *Second Language Research* 15:220–249.

Quesada, Margaret Lubbers, and Sarah E. Blackwell. 2009. "The L2 Acquisition of Null and Overt Spanish Subject Pronouns: A Pragmatic Approach." In *Selected Proceedings of the 11th Hispanic Linguistics Symposium*, edited by Joseph Collentine, Maryellen García, Barbara Lafford, and Francisco Marcos-Marín, 117–130. Somerville, MA: Cascadilla Proceedings Project.

Rothman, Jason. 2009. "Pragmatic Deficits with Syntactic Consequences? L2 Pronominal Subjects and the Syntax-Pragmatics Interface." *Journal of Pragmatics* 41:951–973.

Rothman, Jason and Michael Iverson. 2007. "On Parameter Clustering and Resetting the Null-Subject Parameter in L2 Spanish: Implications and Observations." *Hispania* 90:328–341.

Shin, Naomi Lapidus. 2012. "Variable Use of Spanish Subject Pronouns by Monolingual Children in Mexico." In *Selected Proceedings of the 14th Hispanic Linguistics Symposium*, edited by Kimberly Geeslin and Manuel Díaz-Campos, 130–141. Somerville, MA: Cascadilla Proceedings Project.

Shin, Naomi Lapidus, and Ricardo Otheguy. 2009. "Shifting Sensitivity to Continuity of Reference: Subject Pronoun Use in Spanish in New York City." In *Español en Estados Unidos y en otros contextos: Cuestiones sociolingüísticas, políticas y pedagógicas*, edited by Manel Lacorte and Jennifer Leeman, 111–136. Madrid: Iberoamericana.

Shin, Naomi Lapidus, and Helen Smith Cairns. 2012. "The Development of NP Selection in School-Age Children: Reference and Spanish Subject Pronouns." *Language Acquisition* 19(1):3–38.

Silva-Corvalán, Carmen. 2001. *Sociolingüística y pragmática del español*. Washington, DC: Georgetown University Press.

Torres Cacoullos, Rena and Catherine E. Travis. 2010. "Variable *yo* Expression in New Mexico: English Influence?" In *Spanish of the U.S. Southwest: A Language in Transition*, edited by Susana Rivera-Mills and Daniel Villa Crésap, 189–210. Madrid: Iberoamericana.

———. 2011. "Testing Convergence via Code-Switching: Priming and the Structure of Variable Subject Expresssion." *International Journal of Bilingualism* 15(3):241–267.

Travis, Catherine E. 2007. "Genre Effects on Subject Expression in Spanish: Priming in Narrative and Conversation." *Language Variation and Change* 19:101–135.

Travis, Catherine E., and Rena Torres Cacoullos. 2012. "What Do Subject Pronouns Do in Discourse? Cognitive, Mechanical and Constructional Factors in Variation." *Cognitive Linguistics* 23(4):711–748.

11

The Acquisition of Grammatical Subjects by Spanish–English Bilinguals

Carmen Silva-Corvalán

A crucial question posed by studies of bilingual first language acquisition (BFLA or 2L1) concerns the causes of crosslinguistic influence. Studies share the same insight that although the languages of a bilingual develop on the whole autonomously, bilinguals show signs of crosslinguistic influence or transfer. This influence may be manifested in the acceleration or delay in the acquisition of some constructions that do or do not have parallels in the contact language, in a higher frequency of a parallel construction compared to a monolingual variety, or in the production of non-target constructions not attested in monolingual acquisition. Researchers have examined a number of reasons for why influence may occur and have proposed that the syntax-pragmatics interface appears to be especially vulnerable to crosslinguistic interaction (e.g., Müller and Hulk 2001; Serratrice, Sorace, and Paoli 2004; Yip and Mathews 2005). Furthermore, some scholars predict that the influence is unidirectional, from the stronger to the weaker language (Silva-Corvalán 2014, Yip and Matthews 2007).

This chapter addresses the central issue of crosslinguistic influence through a study of subject pronoun expression (SPE) in the speech of two Spanish–English developing bilingual siblings who have acquired these two languages from birth and have attained different levels of proficiency in Spanish. Specifically, I ask (a) whether at the early age stage the siblings overproduce null subjects in English, and/or overproduce overt subjects in Spanish compared to their adult input, to their monolingual counterparts, and also compared to each other; and (b) whether subject realization changes within the siblings' first three years of life.

English and Spanish differ with respect to the realization of grammatical subjects. Subjects are (mostly) required in English; Spanish is a pro-drop language in which the expression of subjects is mainly constrained by discourse-pragmatic factors. This domain of the grammar of Spanish provides a nice test case, therefore, for the examination of a hypothesis on crosslinguistic influence at the syntax-pragmatics interface and of the possible differential effects of the influence in relation to language proficiency levels. The hypothesis predicts that only English (the siblings' stronger language) will influence Spanish (unidirectionality), and that the siblings with different levels of proficiency in the two languages will exhibit the same type of influence—in particular, (1) high frequency of expressed subjects; and (2) the use of subjects in discourse contexts that do not validate them. These predictions are examined in a longitudinal corpus of diary records and transcribed audio recordings obtained from the siblings between the ages of 1;6 and 3;0.

The analysis indicates that neither child differs from monolinguals in their acquisition of English subjects: They reach almost 100 percent expression by age 2;3. By contrast, both children evidence a gradually increasing percentage of overt pronominal subjects in Spanish as their exposure to English increases. The child with a somewhat lower amount of exposure to and production of Spanish (and consequently lower level of proficiency) shows much higher frequencies of use of pronominal subjects in Spanish than his older brother. Some subjects appear redundantly in his speech. This outcome indicates that the acquisition of grammatical subjects supports a model of autonomous development with interlinguistic influence affecting a syntax-pragmatic interface in the weaker language.

SUBJECTS IN ENGLISH AND SPANISH: THE ADULT SYSTEMS

The complete set of personal pronouns in (Latin American) Spanish and in English include: *yo* 'I', *tú* 'you-SG-familiar', *usted* 'you-SG-formal', *él* 'he', *ella* 'she', *nosotros* 'we-MASC', *nosotras* 'we-FEM', *ustedes* 'you-PL', *ellos* 'they-MASC', *ellas* 'they-FEM'.[1] In addition, English has the third singular pronoun *it*, which may be non-referential (*it's cold*) or may refer to inanimate objects (*it broke*, that is, a glass), and other non-human referents. Contemporary Spanish does not have a pronoun that functions like *it* in English.[2] Thus, reference to known inanimate objects is accomplished with a demonstrative (*Esto se quebró* 'This broke'), with verb inflection (*Se quebró*-3PSG '(it) broke') or by repeating the noun phrase (*El vaso se quebró* 'The glass broke').

Differently from Spanish, which requires that subject pronouns be referential, English is a non-null subject language (non-NS) that requires the subject to be expressed in tensed clauses even in non-referential contexts. Nonetheless, English allows unexpressed subjects in imperatives (commands, requests) and in some statements and questions in colloquial discourse (examples (1) and (2)).

(1) Wanna play?

'¿Quieres jugar?'

(2) (I) Gotta go now.

'Tengo que irme ahora.'

English also allows co-referential subjects of non-initial coordinate clauses to remain unexpressed, even if there is an intervening subordinate clause with a switch subject as in example (3), but it requires the expression of a co-referential subject in subordinate clauses, as in (4). Spanish, by contrast, does not favor an expressed subject in examples of the type of (4), as I indicate with a question mark in the translation.

(3) Mary ran to the phone when we won the game, and Ø called Sue to tell her about it.

(4) Mary always pays cash when she/*Ø goes shopping.

'María siempre paga al contado cuando Ø/ella(?) va de compras.'

In the English input they receive, children are exposed to subjectless sentences, but only imperatives have a significant presence. In my data, almost all adult statements with a verb in English occur with an overt subject (134 overt pronouns out of 136 statements, that is, 98.5 percent). Adult statements in Spanish, by contrast, provide frequent subjectless models to the child, as in the interaction between Nico (N) and the author (C) in (5). In the examples, I indicate a null subject position with a zero(Ø), and place the English subject in square brackets in the translation.

(5) *N: ¿Dónde está la Lupe?* (1;9:16)
C: Ø está en la casa de ella. Ø no está en la casa de granma.
'N: Where's Lupe?'
'C: [She]'s in her home. [She]'s not in granma's home.'

Structurally, the observation that Spanish has the option of expressing or not expressing a subject appears to be valid for most de-contextualized sentential contexts. Examined in the normal flow of speech, however, the complexity of the question of variable subject expression becomes clear. The phenomenon is not optional in every possible environment, as shown in (6), where a null subject is unacceptable in the conjoined sentence because it is the focus of a contrast with the subject of the preceding verb.

(6) *Pepe fue al cine y yo/* Ø me quedé en casa.*

'Pepe went to the movies and I/* Ø stayed at home.'

Speakers may also have the option of expressing a noun phrase (NP) subject, as illustrated in (7).

(7) *Me trajo chirimoyas de Chile. Las chirimoyas/ Ø estaban riquísimas.*

'[She] brought me chirimoyas from Chile. The chirimoyas/[they] were delicious.'

It appears appropriate to consider NPs in the analyses of subject realization, but previous studies have focused almost exclusively on pronominal subjects. For comparison reasons, then, here I focus on pronominal subjects only.

When the subject is co-referential with the referent of a constituent in the preceding sentence, or when it is in any way identifiable, three alternatives may be allowed: full NP, pronoun, or null subject (Paredes Silva 1993; Silva-Corvalán 1994, Ch. 5). The factors conditioning the expression of a subject have been considered in studies applying a variationist methodology, which have shown that the variable expression in main clauses is responsive to cognitive, semantic, and discourse factors (Travis and Torres Cacoullos 2012, among others). The presence of an overt subject is required under two conditions: a) when it is focal, either because it conveys new information, or is the focus of contrast, or is complemented by *solo*, *mismo* 'on one's own, by oneself' or a relative clause; and b) when it is needed to identify its referent.[3]

Overt subjects are favored probabilistically by a number of other factors; in particular, a) the establishment of an entity as the topic of more than one sentence; b) subject switch reference, as in (8); c) verbs of volition (e.g., want, wish, prefer), of saying or speaking (e.g., say, tell, affirm, declare, state, assert), and of mental processes (e.g., think, believe).[4] Pérez Brabandere (2010, 49) reports a range of 51 percent to 67 percent overt subjects with these three types of verb in two studies of adult monolinguals: Bentivoglio in Caracas, Venezuela; and Travis in Cali, Colombia.

(8) *a) Tu hermano quería saber b) si yo enseño en USC.*
a) 'Your brother wanted to know b) if I teach at USC.'

(9) *a) Pepe es mi vecino. b) Es un escritor muy conocido.*
a) 'Pepe is my neighbor. b) [He]'s a well-known writer.'

Example (8) illustrates a switch in the subject referent of two contiguous finite verbs: *your brother* in (a) switches to *I* in (b). Discontinuity of reference favors probabilistically the expression of the subject. By contrast, continuity of reference (also referred to as *co-referentiality*), as in (9 a–b), has consistently been shown to disfavor overt subjects in a number of Spanish dialects. On average, in various Spanish dialects over 40 percent of non-co-referential subjects are overt, while only about 25 percent of co-referential subjects are expressed (cf. Shin and Cairns 2012).

There are other linguistic factors that have been argued to affect subject expression, such as genre (e.g., narrative or conversational dialogue), structural priming, tense, person of the subject, and subject specificity, yet there is no general agreement about their effect. Indeed, the only indisputable facts are that subjects must be overt if they are focal and if they are needed to identify the referent. All other factors leave a sizable percentage of cases to a large extent unexplained. Consequently, researchers incorporate quantification to find out similarities and differences in subject expression rates across dialects. The assumption is that in a large corpus of data, the various factors that constrain subject expression become neutralized and, therefore, it is valid to calculate overall percentages of overt subjects to compare dialects and to reveal possible processes of change.

Importantly, Spanish varieties differ with respect to the rate of subject expression: Caribbean varieties have been shown to have the highest rate of overt subjects, while varieties in Spain evidence the lowest rates. In the siblings' case, the average percentage for the Santiago (Chile) variety, 38 percent (Cifuentes 1980–81), is of interest because this is the variety spoken by their family. Since the percentages are calculated over large numbers of tokens that neutralize possible discourse-pragmatic differences, the differences across dialects appear to indicate that subject pronoun expression is not validated only by discourse-pragmatic factors. Silva-Corvalán (2003) has suggested that the expression of a non-required subject is a sign of the speaker's intent to call the listener's attention toward the subject referent. This pragmatic function may be more or less weakened in the various Spanish dialects, thus leading to different rates of expression. A number of overt subject pronouns, then, may be expressed simply because they are an available alternative in the grammar, and Spanish dialects make use of this alternative at different rates. Furthermore, higher versus lower rates of expression do not appear to be motivated by contact with a non-null-subject language, at least not in Chile (cf. Otheguy and Zentella 2012).

SUBJECTS IN BILINGUAL ACQUISITION

The question of subject realization in languages that are being acquired simultaneously has been the focus of a number of studies carried out from syntactic and discourse-pragmatic perspectives; among others, Ezeizabarrena (2012) for Basque (in contact with Spanish); Juan-Garau and Pérez Vidal (2000) for Spanish–Catalan; Liceras, Fernández Fuertes, and Alba de la Fuente (2012), Liceras, Fernández Fuertes and Pérez-Tattam (2008), and Paradis and Navarro (2003) for Spanish–English. These studies include one to six children ranging in age from 1;7 to 4;11 and thus provide valuable comparable information to assess whether the siblings' behavior conforms to the developmental patterns uncovered. Some of these studies have found evidence of crosslinguistic interaction, others have not, but they all agree in pointing out that the acquisition of NS (null subject) and non-NS language pairs develops autonomously.

In their study of English–Spanish bilingual twins living in Spain, Liceras, Fernández Fuerte, and Pérez-Tattam (2008) note that English does not lead to overusing subject pronouns in the Spanish of the two bilingual speakers. In a more recent study, Liceras, Fernández Fuerte, and Alba de la Fuente (2012) compare the bilingual data with monolingual data from three children growing up in Spain in order to provide further evidence that English does not motivate the overuse of overt subjects in bilingual Spanish. They examine the bilingual twins' realization of subjects in their two languages in three age stages (2;4–2;6, 3;1–3;9, and 4;4–4;11) and conclude that the twins' balanced command of both English and Spanish may explain the absence of crosslinguistic influence. They also suggest that different configurations of language dominance—for example, lower Spanish proficiency—could lead to different results, (such as higher percentages of overt pronouns in Spanish).

The presence of pragmatically unexpected uses of subjects has been identified in data from Manuela (Paradis and Navarro 2003), an English–Spanish developing bilingual whose mother is a native speaker of southern British English and father a native speaker of Caribbean Spanish.[5] Paradis and Navarro compare this child with two monolingual children from Spain and also examine the input these three children are exposed to in order to find out not only if the bilingual's grammar differs from that of the monolinguals' but also what effect the parents' input might have on the children's realization of subjects. Manuela is shown to express subjects more frequently (35.3 percent) than the two monolingual children (18.5 percent) with whom she is compared, but the authors can reach only a very cautious conclusion concerning influence from English, mainly because the comparison is done between two very different varieties of Spanish: Caribbean and Castilian, already known to differ with respect to frequency of subject realization. Furthermore, the two monolinguals they examine differ from Juan, a monolingual studied by Liceras, Fernández Fuerte, and Alba de la Fuente (2012), who expresses subjects at a rate higher than Manuela's (41.7 percent expression between the ages of 1;7.2 and 2;10.21). If Paradis and Navarro had examined this monolingual child, their conclusions might have been different.

Deuchar and Quay (2000), who also study Manuela, do not commit themselves to a concept of dominant language or language proficiency, but they give information about the child's language environment, about aspects of her bilingual development to age 2;3, and about the amount of time that Manuela was exposed to each language between the ages of 1;0 and 2;0: She was exposed to English 48 percent of the time and Spanish 52 percent of the time. Based on this information, I conclude that the child was developing as a balanced bilingual. The same situation of balanced bilingualism, or perhaps slight Spanish dominance, may be assumed for the bilingual twins studied by Liceras, Fernández Fuerte, and Alba de la Fuente (2012), whose subject expression ranges from 16.0 percent to 27.1 percent. The siblings who are the focus of the present study, however, are English-dominant, as the following section will show.

DATA AND PARTICIPANTS

The siblings' language production is examined in a longitudinal corpus of diary records and transcribed audio recordings obtained in a variety of natural discourse situations. The children, Nico and Bren, have been exposed to unequal amounts of Spanish and English.

Detailed diary notes and audio recordings are included in this study between the ages of 1;6 and 3;0 for Nico, and for Bren between the ages of 1;10 and 3;1. They also include adult speech addressed to the children. Nico was the only child in the home during the age period examined for him; the second child, Bren, is 3 years younger. The children have grown up in an ethnically mixed home in Los Angeles: Their mother is an English speaking Euro–American, while the father is a bilingual Hispanic. The "one parent/one language rule" was applied fairly consistently until Nico was 3 years old, albeit in a bilingual environment insofar as the parents spoke to each other in English. Beyond this age, the father frequently broke the rule and spoke to the children in English; thus, the second child was not exposed to Spanish as much as his older brother. The two children received Spanish input mainly from the author, their paternal grandmother, and secondly from their father. The children spoke almost exclusively in Spanish with the author. They addressed their father in either Spanish or English. The siblings also interacted in Spanish with their uncles and, occasionally, with other Spanish-speaking people in Los Angeles. They were also exposed to children's movies, storybooks, and songs in Spanish. Nico started attending an English-only day-care center when he was 1;3 and Bren when he was 2 months old.

It is estimated that, on average, Nico was exposed to English and Spanish 67 percent and 33 percent of the time, respectively.[6] Bren was exposed to English and Spanish 74 percent and 26 percent of the time, respectively, throughout the period studied. By their third birthdays, English was the children's dominant language, but Spanish also appeared to be well-developed for their age. Nico evidences a higher level of proficiency in Spanish than his younger brother during the age period studied. This estimate is based on the fact that Nico uses more verb tenses in Spanish, he makes fewer person marking errors, his vocabulary includes a higher number of adjective and verb types, and he speaks with fewer repairs than his brother.[7]

Let us at this point consider the siblings' path of acquisition of subject pronouns.

THE SIBLINGS' ACQUISITION OF SUBJECTS FROM 1;6 TO 1;11.30

This section examines the realization of null and overt subjects in the siblings' data from the appearance of the first contexts for the production of a subject at age 1;6, to age 1;11.30, when the children have started to produce a sufficient number of sites for the occurrence of a subject to permit some comparisons and quantifications.

It is a well-established fact that the earliest appearing verbs in child language occur without a subject both in NS languages, as in Spanish (10), where it is a grammatical option, and in non-NS languages such as English, where the omitted subject in (11) is ungrammatical in the adult language. At the same age, the siblings produce utterances with expressed NP subjects in (12) and (13).

(10) C: *Es de la Bibi, el tic-tac es de la Bibi.* (1;10.10)
B: *Ø No alcanzo.*

'C: [It]'s Bibi's. The clock is Bibi's.
B: [I] can't reach [it].

(11) N: ~Ø push Kiko. [when seeing a picture of a girl who had pushed him] (1;6:23)[8]

(12) B: *Moto cayó.* (1;9.5)
'The motorcycle fell down.'

(13) N: Kakak broke. [kakak = the duck] (1;7.25)

Different explanations have been offered for the fact that subjects (and other constituents) are missing in the production of infants acquiring English or Spanish. I do not concern myself with the syntax versus processing deficit debate in monolingual child language acquisition, but rather with the issue of crosslinguistic interaction and its possible correlation with language proficiency.[9]

Examined in the earliest age period are a total of 236 utterances with a verb in English (180 from Nico and 56 from Bren), and 550 in Spanish (295 from Nico and 255 from Bren). The number difference in English is due to the data collection method. Bren's data come almost exclusively from audio recordings, and the tape recorder was not as readily available as the notebook I used for Nico. In addition, most of the recordings in this period include Bren in a Spanish-speaking context.

Of the 786 utterances, only declarative clauses containing a verb that had or could have had a subject were included in the analyses. Also included were utterances that were evaluated as lacking a copula or an auxiliary (*be*, *ser*, *estar*), as in *Kiko hiding*, which is missing the auxiliary *is*.

Not included in the analyses were rote imitations, utterances part of a song or rhyme, unintelligible utterances, impersonal constructions (e.g., with *haber* 'there to be'), interrogatives, and imperatives.[10] There are instances of a present tense form in Spanish used instead of an imperative form. If the situation was clearly one in which the imperative meaning is obtained in the context where the utterance was produced, the utterance was not considered a possible site for an overt subject and was excluded. Subjectless utterances in English that are clearly not imperative, such as (14), were included and considered to have an unexpressed subject.

(14) Mom: Bren, what are you doing?
B: Jump couch. ['[I'm] jumping on the couch'] (1;10.29)

In example (14) the child is evidently answering his mother's rhetorical question and not asking her to jump on the couch. In the cases when the Spanish or English context did not clarify the meaning, the utterances were discarded.

Utterances with a clause-internal language switch between the subject and the verb were included to calculate overall subject expression. For purposes of quantification, these utterances were considered to be either Spanish or English, depending on the language of the verb. Example (15) illustrates a subject in English and a verb in Spanish; it was coded as Spanish. No subject pronouns in Spanish with a verb in English occur at this age.[11]

(15) C: *¿Yo lo tapo?*
'Do I cover it?'
N: *I* tapo, ¿okay? [*I* in English; *tapo* in Spanish] (2;0.3)
'I cover [it], okay?

Table 11.1 displays the number and percentage of overt and null subject pronouns out of the total number of possible occurrences of a subject in the siblings' English and Spanish data for the earliest age period (1;6–1;11.30). Here and elsewhere in this chapter, pronominals include only personal pronouns in Spanish and English. Wh- and yes/no questions are not included in any of the quantifications, because subject realization in these types of utterance may be controlled by factors that have not been studied.

Table 11.1 Overt versus null subject pronoun use in Spanish and English to age 1;11.30

	Spanish				English			
	Nico		Bren		Nico		Bren	
	N	%	N	%	N	%	N	%
Overt	0/33	0	15/103	14.6	94/102	92.2	15/25	60.0
Null	33/33	100.0	88/103	85.4	8/102	7.8	10/25	40.0

The quantitative results show that from early on the siblings treated subjects differently in their two languages: The overall proportion of overt subjects in the English data is much higher than in the Spanish data. Nico's percentages of overt subjects in English are almost at ceiling in this early age period (average mean length of utterance by word [MLUw] is 2.3). Bren's English data are scant. Nonetheless, the 40 percent of null subject pronouns in his English data could suggest that he may be somewhat delayed in the acquisition of the obligatory rule of subject expression in this language. A comparison of his behavior with one of the groups in Valian's (1991, 45) study of 21 monolingual American children indicates the contrary, however. Bren's average MLUw in this age period is 1.53. The youngest group in Valian's study ranges in age from 1;10 to 2;2 (older than Bren), with an MLU by morpheme (MLUm) of 1.77, and their average use of subjects is 69 percent, only nine percentage points higher than Bren's even though they are older and have a higher MLU.[12] Bren's use of subjects in English is monolingual-like, therefore, showing no delay as a possible consequence of his bilingualism.

Studies of subject realization have focused almost exclusively on the production and absence of subject pronouns. This is justified on the basis that the unexpressed subject in adult Spanish is almost always a pronoun. In colloquial English, it is pronouns that may be licensed to be null. Thus, the results by month of age presented in table 11.2 include the overt number of pronouns over the total number of sites for the occurrence of a subject pronoun.

The first site for the occurrence of a pronoun in Spanish occurred at 1;7 and 1;9 in Nico's and Bren's data, respectively. In English, the first sites in Nico's data were identified at 1;8. Only one site was identified for Bren at 1;8, none at 1;9, and from 1;10 on the number of sites increased. Before these ages and beyond, many verb forms produced by the children in both languages functioned as requests and were therefore not considered to have a null subject (e.g., *go, get down*, *vamos* 'let's go', *abre* 'open'). A dash (-) in table 11.3 indicates the absence of a site for the expression of a subject pronoun.

In English, Nico started using pronouns at 1;8.2 in the utterance *I get it* (playing with a ball with an adult). Bren started using the first singular pronoun *I* at 1;10. This is the only pronoun he used during the early age period. Of the 15 cases of null subjects in Bren's English, only one is in the context of a second person singular; all other null subjects correspond to *I* with a missing auxiliary (e.g., *No like it*, *All done*). Shared

Table 11.2 Percentage of overt subject pronouns by language and age (1;7–1;11)

	Spanish				English			
	Nico		Bren		Nico		Bren	
Age	**N**	**%**	**N**	**%**	**N**	**%**	**N**	**%**
1;7	0/1	0	-	-	-	-	-	
1;8	0/6	0	-	-	13/15	86.7	0/1	0
1;9	0/8	0	0/6	0	8/11	72.7	-	
1;10	0/9	0	5/44	11.4	25/27	92.6	2/9	22.2
1;11	0/9	0	10/53	18.9	48/49	98.0	13/15	86.7

knowledge with the surrounding adults, as well as the physical and discourse context, compensate for excessive null subjects during the children's initial stage of subject omission.

In Spanish, Nico did not use pronominal subjects (but he did use overt nominal subjects). He started using overt subject pronouns in Spanish quite late; the first pronoun (*yo* 'I') is recorded at age 2;3. He referred to himself and others by name ('Kiko' for himself, with 3PSG verb inflection). Bren's first overt subject pronoun was also *yo* 'I'; it occurred much earlier, at age 1;11.0. A reasonable explanation for the asymmetry in the age of appearance of pronouns in the children's data is Bren's position as the second child. In Spanish contexts, he hears Nico, his older brother, using *yo* quite frequently (68.2 percent of *yo* from 4;0 on in Nico's data, when Bren is about one year old), while Nico was exposed only to an adult input with an approximate 54 percent of overt *yo*. The higher frequency of exposure to *yo*, coupled with the need to differentiate himself from his older brother, may have facilitated Bren's learning of this pronoun earlier than his older brother.

The next question that arises is whether the siblings violate pragmatic constraints for subject realization at this early stage. Are subjects expressed in contexts where monolingual speakers would not express them, or omitted where they should not be? I have encountered only one instance of pragmatic misuse in the English data: omission of a new-information subject in example (16). Most of the omitted pronouns in English match such adult uses as *All done?* (for *Are you all done?*), *All gone* (for *It's all gone*), *Whatcha doin*'? (with an indiscernible *you*). In Spanish, the context and shared knowledge among the children and the adults clarify the referent even when the children use the wrong person inflection, as in the interaction in (17), where continuity of reference would have made any type of subject redundant in the child's answer.

(16) N: ~Pushing, mommy. (1;8.25)
D: Who's pushing?
N: ~Pushing Christian.[13] [telling his mom about Christian pushing him at school]

(17) C: *¿Qué hiciste con la araña, Bren?*
'What did you do with the spider, Bren?
B: *¡Pató*-3PSG,PAST! (1;10.21)
(Literally: kicked-3PSG)
'I kicked it!'

At almost the same age, the children produced co-referential subjects in English, and new and contrastive subjects in Spanish, in accordance with the rules of these languages. Thus, they give evidence of early knowledge of some of the discourse-pragmatic principles of Spanish. Claims that children are unable to access their discourse-pragmatic competence (Grinstead 2004) do not find support in this study.

In sum, from age 1;6 to 1;11.30 the children's use of different proportions of subject pronouns supports the observation that there is no crosslinguistic interaction at this stage of bilingual development in this domain of the grammars of English and Spanish. The siblings follow a developmental path that does not differ from that of monolinguals in these languages. Sufficient exposure to two typologically different languages at this early age appears to have helped the siblings grasp the contrasting structures sooner (and perhaps more easily) than a monolingual child.[14]

The observation made about monolingual acquisition (Grinstead 2004) that overt pronominal subjects begin to be used at an earlier point in development by child speakers of non-NS languages compared to child speakers of NS languages is also valid for developing bilinguals in these two types of language. Children in fact tend to match the functions and distribution of subjects in the adult input from each language, including such principles of discourse-pragmatics as the requirement to express focal and new information subjects, and the tendency not to express a co-referential subject in Spanish. At this very early age children do not lack pragmatic knowledge concerning subject use.

SUBJECT PRONOUN EXPRESSION FROM 2;0 TO 2;11.30

This section examines subject realization in English and Spanish at a developmental stage when utterances are getting to be more complex, with different pronouns and many novel verbs, and determines if differing amounts of exposure to the weaker language make the children's production more or less vulnerable to deviations from a typical monolingual norm. To this end, I compute overt and null subject pronouns and compare the two siblings with each other, with monolinguals and bilinguals, and with the adults in their environment.

One observation about subject pronouns in English concerns gender and case. Nico and Bren did not make any subject gender errors (use of *she* instead of *he* and vice versa), but they started using third person pronouns well into their third year. Sensitivity to gender may have been helped by contact with Spanish, which marks gender on nouns, determiners, pronouns, and adjectives. But both children make a typical case error in English: They used *me* as subject, though infrequently. In addition, there is in Nico's data one example of *her* as subject at 2;1.25 (*Her's leaving*).

Table 11.3 displays the overall proportions of subject pronoun use from 2;0 to 2;11.30 for each child. A total of 2,348 affirmative and negative utterances where a subject could have been expressed were examined (1,279 from Nico and 1,069 from Bren). Of these, 661 are in English, and 1,687 in Spanish.

At first glance, the results in table 11.3 confirm the hypothesis that a lower amount of exposure to the weaker language and consequent lower proficiency in this language make Bren more vulnerable to influence from English in the domain of subject use. His rate of expression of pronominal subjects is 15 percentage points higher than that of his brother (51.2 percent compared to 36.1). By contrast, Nico's rate of overt pronouns is comparable to those of Manuela (a balanced English–Spanish bilingual) and Juan (a Spanish monolingual) (see section on Subjects in Bilingual Acquisition, above). Unlike Manuela, Nico is exposed more frequently to English than to Spanish, yet an approximate one-third exposure time to Spanish is sufficient for him to model the distribution of

Table 11.3 Overt versus null subject pronouns in Spanish and English; ages 2;0–2;11.30

	Spanish				English			
	Nico		Bren		Nico		Bren	
	N	%	N	%	N	%	N	%
Overt Pros	329/912	36.1	397/775	51.2	351/367	95.6	273/294	92.9
Null Pros	583/912	63.9	378/775	48.8	16/367	4.4	21/294	7.1

subjects typical of Chilean adults, shown to use 38 percent overt subject pronouns (Cifuentes 1980–81).

Interestingly, the rate of overt pronouns in the adult speech addressed to Nico and Bren is lower by 11 percentage points compared to speakers of the same dialect who live in the country of origin. I examined affirmative and negative utterances that could have had an expressed subject pronoun in the adults' data from various recordings that extended over Nico's ages 4;0 to 5;5, and Bren's ages 1;3 to 2;7. Adhering to variationist methodology, I selected a contiguous passage containing eighty to one hundred sites for the possible expression of a subject from each recording. The results show that adults express 27.0 percent (176/653) of the subjects in Spanish and 98.5 percent (134/136) in English.

The adults have a lower percentage of expression of pronominal subjects than the children. An examination of the data indicates that this asymmetry has interactional explanations. Adults frequently use the children's names when describing their actions since *tú* 'you' or *él* 'he' would not clearly distinguish between the children. Examples (18)–(19) illustrate.

(18) *Bren no necesita eso.* [addressing the child]

'Bren doesn't need that.'

(19) *Nico puede alcanzarla.* [the light] [addressing the child]

'Nico can reach it.'

One further crucial difference between the children's and the adults' discourse which has implications for the realization of subjects concerns the use of the verb *querer*, an issue that I discuss below.

The data in table 11.4 are grouped into four age stages, each stage comprising three months. Percentages for overt subjects only are reported. These were calculated by contrasting them to null subjects, as in previous tables; the denominator in each case is the sum of overt and null subjects. Thus 4/13 overt subjects implies 9/13 null subjects.

If we assume, along with Valian (1991, 48), that 84 to 94 percent expression is "evidence that children understand that subjects are obligatory," then we can conclude that both bilingual children acquired full control of the grammar of English regarding the overt subject requirement by 2;2. The children have the lowest percentage of overt subject pronouns at the first age stage, Nico 91.5 percent and Bren 85.5 percent, higher than that of an older child (84.1 percent at 2;3) in Valian's study. There is no doubt that BFLA has not affected this domain of the grammar of English. Indeed, some of the examples with null pronominals produced at the first age stage, and all those produced

Table 11.4 Percentage of overt subjects by language and age (2;0–2;11)

	Spanish				English			
	Nico		Bren		Nico		Bren	
	N	%	N	%	N	%	N	%
2;0–2;2	4/13	30.8	36/178	20.2	86/94	91.5	59/69	85.5
2;3–2;5	48/145	33.1	97/185	52.4	159/166	95.8	40/41	97.6
2;6–2;8	124/373	33.2	176/261	67.4	59/60	98.3	56/58	96.6
2;9–2;11	153/381	40.2	88/151	58.3	39/39	100	118/126	93.7

beyond this stage, as in (20) and (21), are acceptable in colloquial English. Some are also acceptable in formal varieties of English, as in the conjoined sentence in (21).

(20) B: Don't, don't know how to play the game. (2;10.16) [a spelling game]
(21) N: I hurt my finger and Ø screamed. (2;6.7)

In Spanish, Nico's overall proportions of overt pronominal subjects range from 30.8 percent to 40.2 percent and are thus comparable to those of the monolingual counterparts discussed in the section on Subjects in Bilingual Acquisition, above. But his use of pronominal subjects did increase throughout the year. With the exception of the first age stage, Bren also expresses subject pronouns much more frequently, from 52.4 percent to a high 67.4 percent. The steady increase observed throughout this one-year period suggests that Bren's Spanish is experiencing some degree of pressure from English as the patterns of this language become more entrenched. His behavior in this grammatical domain warrants an explanation, as does Nico's increase of almost ten percentage points of pronominal subjects.

The neutralization of influencing factors in a large corpus produces more valid results for interindividual comparisons of subject realization than smaller corpora collected in shorter periods of time. This is so because variability in subject expression owes much to the nature of the sample on which computations are based. If the sample contains more or fewer factors that favor expression, then the percentage of overt pronominal subjects increases or decreases. The effect of this situation is seen in the dissimilar percentages of overt subject pronouns in the speech of two Spanish monolinguals of approximately the same age, Emilio (27.9 percent) and Juan (41.7 percent), studied by Liceras, Fernández Fuerte, and Alba de la Fuente (2012), and to a certain extent also in the results obtained for Nico and Bren (table 11.4). I proceed to illustrate this observation with an examination of two factors that have been shown to correlate with subject realization, person of the subject and type of verb. The interaction of these two factors increases the probability that the subject will be overt.

It has been shown that first and second person singular subjects in Spanish are expressed more frequently than other persons (Enríquez 1984, Morales 1986). This is naturally so given that these two persons can only be referred to by means of a pronoun.

From 2;0 to 2;11 the distribution of subjects by person in the children's data patterns like that of the adults in their adult input (and in other dialects, Silva-Corvalán 2014, Ch. 4): First and second person singular subjects are expressed more frequently than other persons, and plural subjects are expressed much less frequently than singular subjects (see table 11.5). This indicates that the siblings understand the function of subject pronouns and can produce them appropriately.

Table 11.5 Percentage of overt subject pronouns by person of the subject: Nico and Bren (2;0–2;11), and their adult input

	Nico		Bren		Adult input	
	N	%	N	%	N	%
1st Yo	251/560	44.8	368/589	62.5	85/157	54.1
2nd Tú	48/134	35.8	17/26	65.4	45/173	26.0
3rd Él/Ella	21/143	14.7	12/95	12.6	31/198	15.7
1st Nosotros/as	2/31	6.5	0/15	0.0	6/51	11.8
3rd Ellos/as	6/46	13.0	0/50	0.0	8/73	11.0

There is, however, a difference between the siblings. While Nico's percentages are within the range of those of the adults, Bren's rate of expression of *yo* 'I' and *tú* 'you' is much higher than Nico's and the adults'. An examination of his data indicates that he steadily increases the rate of expression of *yo* from 25.2 percent at age 2;0–2;2, to 61.5 percent at 2;3–2;5, to 79.4 percent at 2;6–2;8, and to a high 83 percent at 2;9–2;11. By contrast, Nico's percentages decrease from 44.4 percent to 43.3 percent to 41.9 percent in the first three age stages, and increase to 48.4 percent at 2;9–2;11, a percentage that is still within the range of monolingual and bilingual adults. Bren's lower amount of exposure to Spanish has had an effect on the frequency of use of subject pronouns, then, such that some uses of *yo* and *tú* have no pragmatic motivation and appear to be redundant.

The semantics of the verb has also been shown to correlate with the likelihood of overt subject realization. Verbs of volition (e.g., *querer* 'want') and estimative or "mental activity" verbs (e.g., *creer* 'believe') favor an overt subject (Bentivoglio 1987, 48–53; Enríquez 1984, 152, 235–245). Estimative verbs are those that tend to present the speaker's point of view as implicitly distinct from that of others (e.g., *think*, *believe*, *assume*, *agree with*). This implicit idea of contrast may explain their positive correlation with overt subjects. As observed before, explicit contrast predicts the overt expression of the subject. A verb of volition like *querer* favors an overt subject as a form of emphasis, or as an attention pointer toward the speaker, especially in the case of a child who wants to draw the attention of the adult who may fulfill his wish.

An examination of the 653 sites for the occurrence of a pronominal subject in the adult input (table 11.6) indicates that a) an estimative verb, *creer* 'believe', and a verb of volition *querer* 'want', occur much more frequently with a realized subject than the average 27 percent of overt subjects over all types of verb, and b) that *querer* is less frequent in the adults' data than in the children's data (4.9 percent of all verb types in the adults' data).[15] There are 10 of 14 (71.4 percent) tokens of *creer* 'believe' with an overt first person singular subject in the adults' data. Of 32 tokens of *querer* 'want', 8 of 12 (66.6 percent) with a first person singular subject have a phonetically realized *yo* 'I', and 10 of 20 (50 percent) with second and third person subjects have an overt subject, thus supporting the favoring effect of these types of verb and also the idea that factor interaction is a strong predictor of subject realization (Allen 2007). Table 11.6 shows that while the siblings use *creer* 'believe' only rarely, *querer* 'want' is much more frequent than in the adults' data, especially to communicate personal wishes.

There is an obvious correlation between the children's overall frequency of overt subjects and their use of *querer* with the first person singular expressed subject. Nico's

Table 11.6 Percentage of overt subject pronouns with *querer* 'want' and *creer* 'believe' (Nico, Bren, and their adult input)

	***Querer* 'want'**				***Creer* 'believe'**				**% of total overt pros**	
	1st person		**2nd/3rd person**		**1st person**		**2nd/3rd person**			
	N	**%**	**N**	**%**	**N**	**%**	**N**	**%**	**N**	**%**
Adults	8/12	66.6	10/20	50	10/14	71.4	0	0	28/176	15.9
Nico										
2;0–2;2	0	0	0	0	0	0	0	0	0	0
2;3–2;5	6/27	22.2	0	0	0	0	0	0	6/48	12.5
2;6–2;8	10/36	27.8	2/3	66.7	0	0	0	0	12/124	9.7
2;9–2;11	14/21	66.7	2/2	100	1/1	100	0	0	17/153	11.1
Bren										
2;0–2;2	4/8	50	0	0	0	0	0	0	4/36	11.1
2;3–2;5	26/29	89.7	0/3	0	0	0	0/1	0	26/97	26.8
2;6–2;8	53/60	88.3	1/1	100	0	0	0	0	53/176	30.1
2;9–2;11	15/15	100	1/4	25.0	0	0	0	0	15/88	17

overt subjects increase from 33.2 percent to 40.2 percent at age 2;9–2;11, and it is also at this later age that he has a higher percentage of *querer* with an overt first person subject, 66.7 percent, a percentage that is almost exactly the same as that of the adults. Bren's rate of first person singular overt subjects with *querer* is unusually high, 89.7 percent at age 2;3–2;5 and 100 percent at 2;9–2;11. In addition, at the age when he has the highest percent of overt subjects, 67.4 percent at 2;6–2;8, 30.1 percent of these correspond to subjects of *querer.* Person of the subject and type of verb, then, account to a large extent for the high proportion of expressed subjects at this age. But Bren has taken the frequency of subject realization to an extent that signals the possible weakening of the discourse-pragmatic function of overt subject pronouns as attention pointers and produces redundant co-referential subjects, as those underlined in example (22).

(22) B: *Es, es Superman.* [he pretends to be Superman] (2;10.25)
C: *Hey, Superman aquí hay unos hombres muy malos y necesito que Superman me ayude.*
B: *Pero (a) yo no puedo, porque (b) yo no puedo ir a tu casa.*
C: *¿No puedes venir a mi casa? ¿Por qué, Superman?*
B: *Porque (c) yo estoy en mi casa y (d) yo no puedo abrir la puerta porque está em,* locked.

B: 'This is Superman. [he pretends to be Superman]
C: Hey, Superman, there are some bad men here and I need Superman to help me.
B: But (a) I can't, because (b) I can't go to your house.
C: You can't come to my house? Why, Superman?

B: Because (c) I'm in my house and (d) I can't open the door because it's uhm, locked.'

DISCUSSION AND CONCLUSION

This chapter has examined the developmental path followed by the siblings Nico and Bren in their acquisition of subjects in English and Spanish and has shown that the stronger language, English, does not evidence any negative effect from contact with Spanish. On the other hand, a lower degree of exposure to Spanish, the weaker language, results in deviations from the norm concerning the frequency of overt subjects. Nico's SPE percentages are comparable to those of monolingual adults and children, but Bren, the child who has had less exposure to Spanish, expresses subject pronouns much more frequently, suggesting that his Spanish is experiencing some degree of stress as English patterns become more entrenched.

Two factors are found to account to a large extent for the rise in the percentages of pronominal subjects: the higher number of first person singular sites for the occurrence of a subject, and the increased number of tokens of *querer*, a verb that favors overt subjects in the siblings' data, as well as in many varieties of Spanish. There are no violations of the rule requiring new information and contrastive subjects to be expressed, but pragmatically unjustified co-referential subject pronouns start to appear at 2;3 in Bren's data. Nico, however, the child with higher exposure to and proficiency in Spanish, rarely produces what I consider to be an unmotivated subject pronoun.[16]

I have noted that the only indisputable fact about Spanish subjects is that they must be overt if they are focal and if they are needed to identify the subject referent. All other factors favor an overt subject only probabilistically and leave a sizable percentage of cases to a large extent unexplained. It is also the case that native speakers do not always agree on the appropriateness of expressing a subject pronoun or leaving it null, a fact that most likely underlies some of the frequency differences within and across Spanish dialects. The input to the child is variable and inconsistent, thus making this domain of the grammar of Spanish highly vulnerable to being affected during the process of acquiring it alongside a stronger non-NS language. Expectedly, the child with less exposure to and use of Spanish, Bren, is more affected than Nico, who has received more Spanish input and has developed a higher level of proficiency in Spanish.

Some studies of subject realization in BFLA have not found evidence of crosslinguistic interaction between a non-NS and an NS language. They note, for instance, that while in the non-NS language (English), the production of overt subjects increases developmentally, in the NS languages (e.g., Spanish) overt subjects are maintained at quite a constant rate over time (Ezeizabarrena 2012). These authors report subject acquisition by developing balanced bilinguals. The simultaneous acquisition of a non-NS and an NS language in a fairly balanced situation, then, does not affect the acquisition of subjects in either language. Furthermore, Nico's not-so-balanced exposure to the non-dominant language for approximately 32 percent of his waking time to age 3;0 is sufficient for him to gain control of the semantic and discourse-pragmatic factors that favor or require the phonetic expression of a pronominal subject in Spanish.

The picture is different when the amount of exposure to and use of a language is reduced to less than a third, as in Bren's case. Bren's overuse of subjects starts at an early age and increases substantially as his English becomes stronger. As Liceras, Fernández Fuerte, and Alba de la Fuente (2012) suggest, different configurations of language proficiency lead to different results.

A possible mechanism accounting for the high rate of pronouns in Spanish is the child's copying of the overt subject requirement of his stronger language, English, that is, an external influence. Indeed, there is general consensus that in bilingual contexts both languages are activated regardless of the language currently in use.[17] Thus, the English [subject pronoun + verb] string could also be active in the child's mind, leading to its copy onto Spanish and the higher rate of pronouns attested. The high frequency of the English structure primes the realization of overt subjects in Spanish.[18] That is, the processing of the English syntactic form affects the subsequent processing of the Spanish form (Cameron and Flores-Ferrán 2004; Hartsuiker, Pickering, and Veltkamp 2004).

There is a direct correlation, then, between an increase in amount of exposure to and use of English, the dominant non-NS language, and an increase in the production of overt subject pronouns in the NS language. This quantitative increase is accompanied by violations of co-referentiality, the discourse-pragmatic factor that disfavors subject expression in the NS language. Clearly, a language is particularly vulnerable when a syntactic phenomenon is constrained by semantic and discourse pragmatics.

NOTES

1. This is a very simplified presentation of the forms of address, but sufficient for the purpose of this study. English does not differentiate between formal and familiar pronouns and marks gender only in the third person singular. The Latin American Spanish variety that the children are acquiring does not differentiate singular and plural second person pronouns, nor does it include *vos*. For a fuller treatment of personal pronouns in Spanish, see Fernández Soriano (1999).
2. Fernández Soriano (1999, 1,244) reports that a non-referential pronoun *ello* was used in earlier stages in the history of Spanish. She cites examples from three to five hundred years ago and adds that some Caribbean varieties have retained this non-referential pronoun.
3. See Amaral and Schwenter (2005), Silva-Corvalán (2003), and Travis and Torres Cacoullos (2012) for in-depth analyses of the "contrast constraint" on subject expression in Spanish.
4. A sentential topic is a referent about which new information is added in the proposition (Lambrecht 1994, 131).
5. Manuela was recorded approximately between the ages of 1;0 and 2;3.
6. These are average percentages based on language exposure in typical daily life and calculated based on an average of 12 waking hours (cf. Deuchar and Quay 2000). See Silva-Corvalán (2014) for further information.
7. See Silva-Corvalán (2014) for further details about the siblings' levels of proficiency.
8. The symbol '~' is used to indicate that an utterance is ungrammatical in the corresponding adult utterance. In the examples, B stands for Bren, N stands for Nico, C for the author, and D for the mother.
9. See Silva-Corvalán (2014) for a review of this debate.
10. Something the child repeats immediately after the adult has said it, as in:

    C: *Ándate, gato malo.* 'Go away, bad cat.'

    B: *Ándate, gato malo.* 'Go away, bad cat.' (1;10.29)
11. Mixed utterances with a lexical NP subject in one language and the predicate in the other do occur and continue to occur beyond age 2;0.

12. Although Valian's MLUm is based on a morpheme count, I assume it is more or less comparable with a word-based MLUw at an early age when morphology is still simple. Be that as it may, a word MLUw should result in a lower score than a morpheme MLUm.
13. Silva-Corvalán 2014 examines the position of subjects in Spanish and English.
14. Compare Meisel's (1990, 18) hypothesis that bilinguals tend to focus more on formal aspects of language and that this helps them acquire certain grammatical constructions faster and with fewer errors than many or most monolinguals.
15. Pérez Brabandere (2010) reports a range of 51 percent to 67 percent overt subjects with these types of verb.
16. Silva-Corvalán (2014, Ch. 4) shows that as exposure to English increases, so do overt pronominal subjects in the siblings' Spanish. Beyond age 4;0, Bren evidences the attrition or loss of the co-referentiality constraint.
17. The language switches in examples (15) and (22) are evidence of parallel activation.
18. I thank Richard Cameron for bringing the priming issue to my attention.

REFERENCES

Allen, Shanley E. M. 2007. "Interacting Pragmatic Influences on Children's Argument Realization." In *Crosslinguistic Perspectives on Argument Structure: Implications for Learnability*, eds. Melissa Bowerman and Penelope Brown, 191–210. New York: Lawrence Erlbaum.

Amaral, Patricia Matos, and Scott Schwenter. 2005. "Contrast and the (Non-) Occurrence of Subject Pronouns." In *Selected Proceedings of the 7th Hispanic Linguistics Symposium,* ed. David Eddington, 116–27. Somerville, MA: Cascadilla Proceedings Project.

Bentivoglio, Paola. 1987. *Los sujetos pronominales de primera persona en el habla de Caracas.* Caracas: Universidad Central de Venezuela.

Cameron, Richard, and Nydia Flores-Ferrán. 2004. "Perseveration of Subject Expression across Regional Dialects of Spanish." *Spanish in Context* 1(1):41–65.

Cifuentes, Hugo. 1980–81. "Presencia y ausencia del pronombre personal sujeto en el habla culta de Santiago de Chile. Homenaje a Ambrosio Rabanales." *Boletín de Filología de la Universidad de Chile* 31:743–52.

Deuchar, Margaret, and Suzanne Quay. 2000. *Bilingual Acquisition: Theoretical Implications of a Case Study.* Oxford: Oxford University Press.

Enríquez, Emilia V. 1984. *El pronombre personal sujeto en la lengua española hablada en Madrid.* Madrid: Instituto Miguel de Cervantes.

Ezeizabarrena, María José. 2012. "Overt Subjects in Early Basque and Other Null Subject Languages." *International Journal of Bilingualism.* Published electronically May 28, 2012. doi:10.1177/1367006912438997.

Fernández Soriano, Olga. 1999. "El pronombre personal. Formas y distribuciones. Pronombres átonos y tónicos." In *Gramática descriptiva de la lengua española,* eds. Ignacio Bosque and Violeta Demonte, 1:1209–73. Madrid: Espasa.

Grinstead, John. 2004. "Subjects and Interface Delay in Child Spanish and Catalan." *Language* 80:40–72.

Hartsuiker, Robert, Martin Pickering, and E. Veltkamp. 2004. "Is Syntax Separate or Shared between Languages? Cross-Linguistic Syntactic Priming in Spanish–English Bilinguals." *Psychological Science* 15:409–414.

Juan-Garau, María, and Carmen Pérez-Vidal. 2000. "Subject Realization in the Syntactic Development of a Bilingual Child." *Bilingualism: Language and Cognition* 3:173–91.

Lambrecht, Knud. 1994. "Information Structure and Sentence Form: Topic, Focus, and the Mental Representations of Discourse Referents." Cambridge: Cambridge University Press.

Liceras, Juana M., Raquel Fernández Fuertes, and Anahí Alba de la Fuente. 2012. "Overt Subjects and Copula Omission in the Spanish and the English Grammar of English–Spanish Bilinguals: On the Locus and Directionality of Interlinguistic Influence." *First Language* 32:88–115.

Liceras, Juana M., Raquel Fernández Fuerte, and Rocío Pérez-Tattam. 2008. "Null and Overt Subjects in the Developing Grammars (L1 English / L1 Spanish) of Two Bilingual Twins." In *A Portrait of the Young in the New Multilingual Spain,* eds. Carmen Pérez-Vidal, María Juan-Garau, and Aurora Bel, 111–34. Clevedon: Multilingual Matters.

Meisel, Jürgen. 1990. "Grammatical Development in the Simultaneous Acquisition of Two First Languages." In *Two First Languages: Early Grammatical Development in Bilingual Children,* edited by Jürgen Meisel, 5–22. Dordrecht: Foris.

Morales, Amparo. 1986. *Gramáticas en contacto: Análisis sintácticos sobre el español de Puerto Rico.* Madrid: Playor.

Müller, Natascha, and Aafke Hulk. 2001. "Crosslinguistic Influence in Bilingual Language Acquisition: Italian and French as Recipient Languages." *Bilingualism: Language and Cognition* 4:1–21.

Otheguy, Ricardo, and Ana Celia Zentella. 2012. *Spanish in New York: Language Contact, Dialectal Leveling, and Structural Continuity.* Oxford: Oxford University Press.

Paradis, Johanne, and Samuel Navarro. 2003. "Subject Realization and Crosslinguistic Interference in the Bilingual Acquisition of Spanish and English." *Journal of Child Language* 30:371–93.

Paredes Silva, Vera Lúcia. 1993. "Subject Omission and Functional Compensation: Evidence from written Brazilian Portuguese." *Language Variation and Change* 5:35–49.

Pérez Brabandere, Vanessa. 2010. "Los sujetos pronominales de primera persona en el español de Caracas 2004–2010." MA thesis, Universidad Central de Venezuela.

Serratrice, Ludovica, Antonella Sorace, and Sandra Paoli. 2004. "Crosslinguistic Influence at the Syntax-Pragmatics Interface: Subjects and Objects in English–Italian Bilingual and Monolingual Acquisition." *Bilingualism: Language and Cognition* 7:183–205.

Shin, Naomi Lapidus, and Helen Smith Cairns. 2012. "The Development of NP Selection in School-Age Children: Reference and Spanish Subject Pronouns." *Language Acquisition* 19:3–38.

Silva-Corvalán, Carmen. 1994. *Language Contact and Change: Spanish in Los Angeles.* Oxford: Clarendon.

———. 2003. "Otra mirada a la expresión del sujeto como variable sintáctica." In *Lengua, variación y contexto,* eds. Francisco Moreno Fernández, Francisco Gimeno, Juan Antonio Samper, Mariluz Gutiérrez, María Vaquero, and César Hernández, 849–60. Madrid: Arco/Libros.

———. 2014. *Bilingual Language Acquisition: Spanish and English in the First Six Years.* Cambridge: Cambridge University Press.

Travis, Catherine, and Rena Torres Cacoullos. 2012. "What Do Pronouns Do in Discourse? Cognitive, Mechanical, and Constructional Factors in Variation." *Cognitive Linguistics* 23:711–48.

Valian, Virginia. 1991. "Syntactic Subjects in the Early Speech of American and Italian Children." *Cognition* 40:21–81.

Yip, Virginia, and Stephen Matthews. 2005. "Dual Input and Learnability: Null Objects in Cantonese–English Bilingual Children." In *ISB4: Proceedings of the 4th International Symposium on Bilingualism,* eds. James Cohen, Kara T. McAlister, Kellie Rolstad, and Jeff MacSwan, 2421–31. Somerville, MA: Cascadilla Press.

———. 2007. *The Bilingual Child: Early Development and Language Contact.* Cambridge: Cambridge University Press.

12

Subject Expression in Bilingual School-age Children in the United States

Silvina Montrul and Noelia Sánchez-Walker

This chapter presents the results of a cross-sectional study investigating subject expression in Spanish–English bilingual children or child heritage speakers with specific focus on overt and null subjects, pronominal subjects, and the distribution of null and overt subjects by reference in discourse context. The term *heritage speaker* is widely used in the United States to refer to young adult early bilinguals who grow up exposed to a minority language, typically an immigrant language; in this study we use the term to refer to school-age children as well. The heritage language often develops under reduced input conditions due to pressure from English, the societal majority language. The use of null and overt subjects in the Spanish of Spanish–English bilingual children has been studied in very young children (Liceras et al. 2008, 2012, Paradis and Navarro 2003, Silva-Corvalán, this volume) and in adults (Montrul 2004, Silva-Corvalán 1994, Otheguy and Zentella 2012, among others). This study provides new data from children spanning the entire school-age period (ages 6–17), and contributes to documenting the development of subject expression in Spanish in contact with English during childhood and adolescence.[1]

Our study addresses a variable that has proved significant in many studies of the grammatical development of bilingual children and heritage speakers in general and which has not been controlled in studies of subject expression so far: type of early bilingualism (simultaneous vs. sequential), characterized by age of onset of bilingualism and length of extensive exposure to the majority language (English). This is an indirect way to estimate quantity of input in early childhood, when the structural basis of the native language develops in children. Several studies have found that heritage speakers who are simultaneous bilinguals show lower proficiency in the heritage language in middle and late childhood than sequential bilinguals who learned the majority language later, as a second language (see Montrul 2008), after a period of monolingualism or dominance in the heritage language. Classifying bilinguals in this way allows us to indirectly address the role of cumulative quantity of input in Spanish and English on the rate of null and overt subject expression in the Spanish of child heritage speakers.

Previous studies have shown that heritage speakers in the United States retain the strong syntactic agreement features that license null subjects in Spanish (Montrul 2004, 2006; Silva-Corvalán 1994). At the same time, their frequent overextension of overt subjects suggests developmental vulnerability, erosion, or incomplete acquisition of the pragmatic topic/focus features of Spanish overt subjects (Silva-Corvalán 2014), and a tendency towards structural convergence with English (Otheguy and Zentella 2012). An alternative explanation instead emphasizes the complexity of the syntax-pragmatics interface in null subject languages, where the pragmatic features of overt subjects play an important role (Sorace 2004). That is, bilinguals resort to the overt subject option not because they are influenced by English but because overt subjects are linguistically less complex or unmarked (Silva-Corvalán 1994; Sorace 2005). By turning our attention to children who vary in age of onset of bilingualism we consider these potential explanations together with the role of quantity of input.

Quantity of input refers to the actual amount of language available in the environment, namely, daily hours of exposure and use of the language and its cumulative frequency (every day, every other day, interrupted for a while, uninterrupted, etc.). Language development can only take place through sufficient exposure to input during the critical period in childhood (Mueller Gathercole and Hoff 2009). Monolingual children are exposed to their language more than ten hours a day, every day, for several years. Bilingual children's daily input to either language is much less than that, and if the language is a minority language and not instructed at school, the daily input can be less than five hours a day for school-age children. Furthermore, any changes in the linguistic environment of bilingual children affect the daily proportion of input in each language. Therefore, children's length of exposure to their heritage language varies and fluctuates significantly in terms of quantity, quality, and frequency of daily input. Simultaneous bilingual children are more vulnerable to language loss than sequential bilingual children who are minority-language dominant until they go to school. Simultaneous bilinguals have the longest exposure to the majority language and receive less input in the minority language (see Montrul 2008 for discussion).

Using an oral narrative task, our study investigates whether null and overt subject use attested in adult heritage speakers can be traced back to developmental patterns exhibited by school-age bilingual children (one group of sequential bilinguals and a group of simultaneous bilinguals). Montrul (2004) found that young adult heritage speakers tended to overuse overt subjects when maintaining reference across two consecutive grammatical subjects ('same reference') and to overuse null subjects when switching reference ('switch reference'). We show that child heritage speakers in the United States demonstrate knowledge of the syntactic constraints on null and overt subjects in Spanish, but a few individuals within each bilingual group exhibit instability or changes with respect to the pragmatic constraints on the distribution of null and overt subjects. The bilingual children in general produce more overt subjects than a group of age-matched monolingual children from Mexico, as well as higher rates of pragmatically illicit overt subjects in same reference contexts. Consistent with our predictions, we further show that the simultaneous bilinguals exhibit the highest rates of overt subjects in pragmatically illicit contexts. Our results contribute to providing data on a critically important stage of language development in bilingual children by documenting the evolution of subject expression in Spanish in contact with English. Before presenting the details of our study, we provide a selective review of related studies.

SUBJECT EXPRESSION IN MONOLINGUAL AND BILINGUAL VARIETIES OF SPANISH

As a null subject language Spanish licenses both null and overt subjects. Null subjects (Ø) are possible because Spanish has rich verbal inflection, allowing person and number information about the subject to be recoverable, as in (1) and (2).

(1) *Ella/mi amiga/María/Ø llegó de Madrid.*
(She/my friend/Maria arrived-3rd-sg from Madrid)
'She/my friend/Maria arrived from Madrid.'

(2) *Ellos/Ø llamaron a la puerta.*
(They called-3rd-pl to the door)
'They knocked on the door.'

Overt subjects can be pronominal (e.g., *ella, ellos;* 'she, they') or lexical (*mi amiga, María;* 'my friend, Maria'). Syntactic analyses of Spanish and English establish that these two languages vary in the values of the Null Subject Parameter (Rizzi 1982), as related to the strength of nominal features of the functional categories agreement and tense. Spanish has strong nominal (person and number) and verbal (tense) features in agreement that license the empty category *pro*, a null subject. By contrast, English has weak nominal and verbal features of agreement, and subjects are realized overtly, as pronouns or lexical noun phrases (NPs). English does not typically allow null subjects, except for imperative sentences (*Open the door*) or diary registers (*Came home tired. Cooked dinner. Went to bed*) (Haegeman and Ihsane 2002). (Torres Cacoullos and Travis, this volume, provide information about subject expression in English.)

In cases of personal subjects, as in (1) and (2), the possibility of expressing them overtly or non-overtly depends on the context. More specifically, the distribution of null and overt subjects is regulated by discourse-pragmatic factors such as topic, focus, contrast, and same versus switch reference. Overt subjects are strictly required when new information is introduced and a contrast is established in discourse, as in examples (3) and (4). The answer to question (3) requires a focused NP, and it must be expressed by an overt subject. In (4), the overt subject *él* is a topic if unstressed, but it can also be a contrastive focus if it is stressed. The pronoun in this case can co-refer with the subject of the previous clause because it emphasizes the subject.

(3) *¿Quién vino?Él/Mario/*Ø vino. focus*
'Who came?He/Mario/*Ø came.'

(4) *El periodista*$_i$ *dijo que él*$_i$*/ÉL*$_i$ *no había escrito ese reporte.topic*
(The journalist said that he (himself) not had written that report.)
'The journalist said that he had not written that report.'

The use of null and overt subjects is also relevant to establish reference in discourse. For example, when there is no switch in reference between a series of sentences, null subjects are appropriate to establish topic continuity and overt subjects are pragmatically infelicitous, as in (5). By contrast, overt subjects are appropriate when there is topic shift and a different referent is introduced, as in (6). Null subjects are infelicitous in these switch reference contexts (examples from Silva-Corvalán 1994, 148).

(5) *Pepe no vino hoy a trabajar. *Pepe/?él/Ø estará enfermo.same reference*
(Pepe no came today to work. *Pepe/?él/Ø will be sick.
'Pepe did not come to work today. He must be sick.'

(6) *Hoy no fui a trabajar. Pepe/él/*Ø pensó que estaba enferma.switch reference*
(Today [I] no went to work. Pepe/él/*Ø thought that I was sick.)
'Today I did not go to work. Pepe/he/*Ø thought I was sick.'

Summarizing, Spanish overt and null subjects in discourse are regulated by topic, focus, and topic-shift features (as proposed by Sorace 2000 for Spanish and Italian). In contrast, while the distribution of overt and null subjects in English may also be regulated by discourse-pragmatic factors, null subjects are rare in English (Torres Cacoullos and Travis, this volume).

Studies of subject expression in monolingual and bilingual varieties converge on the finding that speakers from the Caribbean (Cuba, Puerto Rico, and the Dominican Republic) produce a higher rate of overt subjects, and especially pronominal subjects, than speakers of other Latin American varieties (Bentivoglio 1987; Cameron and Flores-Ferrán 2004; Morales 1997) and of Peninsular Spanish (Enríquez 1984). These findings are also confirmed by Otheguy and Zentella's (2012) study of Spanish spoken in New York. Their sample included 19 recently arrived immigrants (newcomers) from the Caribbean and 20 from mainland Latin American countries. The Caribbean speakers' rate of overt subject pronoun production was 36 percent, while the mainlander's was 24 percent, a difference that was statistically significant. Shin and Cairns (2012), who summarize the use of overt pronouns in same reference and switch reference contexts from different corpus studies, also confirmed that speakers of Madrid Spanish use about 11 percent overt pronouns in same reference contexts, whereas speakers of Caribbean varieties use more than 30 percent. For some researchers, the higher rate of overt subjects in Caribbean varieties is indication that the Caribbean varieties are changing the setting of the null subject parameter (Ticio 2002; Toribio 2000), much like Brazilian Portuguese, which has been undergoing similar changes in the last century (Duarte 1993, 2000).

Studies reporting the acquisition of subjects in monolingual Peruvian (Austin et al. 1997) and Peninsular varieties of Spanish (Grinstead 2004) show that children do not produce any overt subjects during the earliest stages (before age 2;0). However, Ticio (2002) found that two monolingual Puerto Rican children already produced overt subjects at the age of 1;7 (about 18 percent of their subjects were overt). Villa-García, Snyder, and Riqueros-Morante (2010) further confirmed that the acquisition of null and overt subjects by children acquiring a Caribbean variety is different from that of children acquiring mainland and Peninsular varieties. Their findings support the proposal that Caribbean and mainland varieties have different grammars of null subjects. Taken together, these studies suggest that Spanish-speaking children develop knowledge of the morphosyntactic conditions that license null and overt subjects in Spanish very early, by age 2;0. The differential rate of overt subjects in the Puerto Rican children and in the children from other varieties also suggests that Spanish-speaking children converge on the adult grammars of their linguistic environment early on.

However, the pragmatic distribution of subjects, and the production of third person singular subject pronouns in same reference and switch reference contexts in particular, come much later. This is not surprising given that discourse-pragmatics and the referential dependencies of pronouns are not typically mastered in monolingual children until about age 9 (Goodluck 1991). Ortiz López (2009) analyzed overt and null subject pronouns in the spontaneous oral production of Dominican children ages 4 to 12 years old. In general, the children produced fewer overt pronouns than the monolingual adult comparison group, especially in contexts of switch reference, which tend to trigger higher overt pronoun rates. In two studies of Mexican monolingual children, ages 6 to 8, Shin (2012) and Shin and Erker (this volume) found that the children produced particularly low rates of personal pronouns (6.3 percent and 9 percent, respectively). These figures are markedly lower than studies of Mexican adults, which report rates around 20 percent (Lastra and Martín Butragueño, this volume; Michnowicz, this volume; Otheguy and Zentella 2012; Silva-Corvalán 1994). In an experimental study with Mexican children ages 5;9–15;8, Shin and Cairns (2012) elicited preferences for null and overt third person subject pronouns in same reference and switch reference contexts. They found that by age 8 or 9, children correctly chose overt pronouns significantly more than null pronouns in switch reference contexts, but not as often as adults did. The only children who reached adult-like rates of above 80 percent were the oldest ones, ages 14 or 15. Since null subjects in switch reference contexts were pragmatically infelicitous in this study, the authors interpret their results as an indication that children tolerate ambiguity. Shin and Erker (this volume) confirm this tolerance for ambiguity: The monolingual Mexican children in their study produced 361 null subjects with unrecoverable referents. Thus, all these studies show that children produce fewer pronouns than adults, especially third person pronouns (Bel 2003; Serratrice 2005; Shin 2012), and the pragmatic distribution of null and overt pronouns does not seem to be fully acquired until ages 14 to 15, when the linguistic behavior of the children matches that of the adults.

If children in a monolingual environment take more than nine years (according to Shin and Cairns 2012) to converge on the adult pragmatic distribution of null and overt subjects, such a phenomenon is likely to remain underdeveloped and highly vulnerable to structural influence from the majority language in bilingual contexts where children receive suboptimal amount and frequency of input in Spanish and restricted opportunities to use the language. For example, Paradis and Navarro (2003) analyzed the rate of null and overt subject production in Manuela (ages 1;9–2;6), a Cuban Spanish–British English bilingual child (CHILDES database, Deuchar corpus). Manuela produced significantly more overt subjects as compared to her parents, as well as two monolingual children. Furthermore, 32 percent of Manuela's overt subjects were pragmatically illicit. In this volume, Silva-Corvalán addresses the potential role of crosslinguistic influence in a longitudinal study of two simultaneous bilingual siblings. The children were raised in the United States and were recorded between the ages of 1;6 and 5;11. The children followed the monolingual route in their acquisition of overt subjects in English, converging on the monolingual grammar by age 2;3. While the children also demonstrated knowledge that Spanish has both null and overt subjects, the rate of overt subject expression increased with age, especially in the child who exhibited lower proficiency in Spanish. Silva-Corvalán (2014) shows that by age 5;11 the siblings had not yet reached complete mastery of the referentiality factors that regulate the use of null and overt subjects in discourse. These findings strongly suggest that the child with less input and use of Spanish did not fully acquire the pragmatic features regulating the distribution of subjects at an age-appropriate level in Spanish, his weaker language. Although the siblings were both simultaneous bilinguals, one was less proficient in Spanish than the other. Silva-Corvalán found a direct correlation between an increase in amount of exposure to and use of English, the dominant language, and an increase in the production of overt subject pronouns in Spanish.

Similar findings apply to bilingual adults, suggesting that the instability found in adulthood could potentially be related to late or incomplete acquisition of this phenomenon earlier in childhood resulting from insufficient input. Studies of subject expression in Spanish–English adult bilinguals suggest that bilingual speakers do produce significantly more overt subjects than monolinguals (Otheguy and Zentella 2012; Shin and Otheguy 2013). Bilinguals do not lose the morphosyntactic ability to license null subjects in Spanish, but what seems to be affected are the pragmatic features governing the distribution of null and overt subjects, which corresponds to the findings for child bilinguals. Similar findings have been reported for other null subject languages, including Russian (Polinsky 2006), Italian (Sorace 2000, 2011) and Greek (Tsimpli et al. 2003). Silva-Corvalán's (1994) study of Los Angeles Spanish showed that the children of first-generation immigrants evidenced an increased frequency of pronominal subjects compared to speakers who were more dominant in Spanish, and similar results are reported by Montrul (2004, 2006). Montrul (2004) used a narrative task to elicit subjects, objects, and past verb tenses in speakers of Mexican heritage with intermediate and advanced proficiency in Spanish. The heritage speakers with lower proficiency in Spanish produced significantly more overt subjects than the heritage speakers with advanced proficiency and the recent arrivals, respectively. When pragmatic context was examined, 8.5 percent of the lower proficiency speakers' subjects in same reference contexts were overt, and 15.5 percent of their subjects in switch reference contexts were null. The heritage speakers with advanced proficiency in Spanish produced half those rates and the native speakers tested as control produced almost no incorrect forms. What that study did not examine was the overall use of personal pronouns, since both lexical and pronominal subjects were collapsed for the analysis.

THE STUDY

Using the same methodology employed in Montrul (2004) with adults, the purpose of our study is to examine bilingual children between the ages of 6 and 17, to see whether the bilingual patterns reported by age 5 (Silva-Corvalán 2014, this volume), and in young adults (Silva-Corvalán 1994, Montrul 2004), can also be traced back to this important age group, when input in Spanish is more severely reduced due to schooling in English. Looking at school-age children adds to our current understanding of the development of subject expression in Spanish in contact with English from birth until adulthood.

Research Questions and Hypotheses

Silva-Corvalán (this volume) showed that lower proficiency in Spanish and amount of input in the language play a role in the degree of development of both the morphosyntactic and pragmatic features of Spanish subject expression in simultaneous bilingual children between the ages of 1 and 4. The question we pursue in this study is whether the apparent instability of pragmatic features of overt subjects in Spanish evidenced in these pre-school-age simultaneous bilingual children is also attested in school-age and adolescent heritage speakers. Silva-Corvalán showed that the child with less exposure to Spanish and lower proficiency in the language produced a higher overt pronoun rate. We ask whether quantity of input also affects older bilingual children. Because our study is cross-sectional rather than longitudinal, we can only investigate the potential role of quantity and quality of input indirectly, by including in our study participant groups who differ in age, length of residence in the United States (LoRUS), and age of onset of bilingualism and concomitant exposure to English as the majority language.

Our study focuses on the overall rate of null and overt subjects in Spanish oral production, and the pragmatic distribution of null and overt subjects, including an analysis of pronominal subjects, in same reference and switch reference contexts only (following Shin 2012). We address the following research questions and hypotheses:

1. Does the null/overt subject distribution in bilingual children differ from that of monolingual children? Do bilingual children overuse null subjects in switch reference contexts like monolingual children? Or do they overuse overt subjects in same reference contexts like adult bilinguals?
2. Do age of onset of bilingualism and length of exposure to English affect the rate of overt subjects and their pragmatic distribution in child heritage speakers?

If school-age bilingual children produce higher rates of overt subjects than those documented in the monolingual literature, then weakening of pragmatic features associated with Spanish overt subjects due to influence of English may be assumed in the children. If they produce high rates of null subjects in switch reference contexts like monolingual children younger than 12 (Shin and Cairns 2012), this will also suggest that they have not fully developed pronoun reference in Spanish.

In her study of age effects in bilingualism, Montrul (2008, 98) advanced the hypothesis that first language attrition is subject to age effects: Adult immigrants with a mature native grammar would be less vulnerable to attrition of their native language than child immigrants. Among pre-pubescent children, simultaneous bilinguals (exposed to the two languages very early) would exhibit more extensive attrition than sequential bilinguals (those who acquire one language before the other). Several studies of young adults have shown that heritage speakers who are simultaneous bilinguals tend to have weaker command of the heritage language than sequential bilinguals (Montrul 2002; Kim, Montrul and Yoon 2009), but this has not been directly investigated with respect to subject expression. We predict that if cumulative quantity of early input matters, simultaneous bilinguals exposed to Spanish and English before age 4 will show higher rates of overt subjects in same reference contexts than sequential bilinguals who had five years of exposure to Spanish at home and subsequently learned English at school.

Participants

We recruited 35 Spanish–English bilingual children ages 6 to 17 growing up in Chicago (n = 20) and in New York City (n = 19). Twenty-two were of Mexican origin; the rest were from Puerto Rico, Colombia, Ecuador, Honduras and El Salvador. Judged by parental reports, 15 children were simultaneous bilinguals exposed to English and Spanish since birth, and 20 were sequential bilinguals for whom exposure to English began after age five. Because most of the children came from Mexico, we also tested a group of 20 monolingual children in Guanajuato, Mexico, ages 6;0–17;0 (M = 11 years). The simultaneous bilinguals were younger (M = 10.8 years) than the sequential bilinguals (M = 12.2 years), but a one-way ANOVA indicated that the three groups did not significantly differ in age ($F(2,54) = 1.20$, $p = .308$). The parents of all the children completed a short background questionnaire eliciting information about their language and about the children's linguistic abilities and patterns of language use in Spanish and English. In addition, the bilingual children were administered the standardized *Peabody*

Picture Vocabulary Test–Revised (PPVT–IV; Dunn and Dunn 2007) and the *Test de Vocabulario en Imágenes Peabody* (TVIP; Dunn et al. 1986). The Spanish version has fewer items than the English version and was standardized with Puerto Rican and Mexican populations. Each item has four simple black-and-white illustrations arranged in a multiple-choice format. The interviewer pronounced the word, and the child pointed to the matching illustration. Items increased in difficulty, and testing was discontinued when the respondent reached the ceiling. The children in Mexico also took the TVIP in Spanish.

The two bilingual groups differed in parental assessments of English ($t(33) = 2.34$, $p = .03$) but not in PPVT standardized scores ($t(33) = .68$, $p = .50$). Yet, they were significantly different in parental assessment of Spanish ($t(33) = 3.45$, $p = .002$). The simultaneous bilinguals were also significantly less proficient in Spanish than in English as per parental estimates ($t(15) = 4.8$, $p < .0001$), whereas the sequential bilinguals did not differ on these measures in Spanish and English ($p > .1$). A one-way ANOVA on the standardized scores of the Spanish vocabulary task, the TVIP, showed significant differences between the monolingual children and the two bilingual groups ($F(2,52) = 25.51$, $p < .0001$), but the two bilingual groups did not differ from each other (Tukey, $p = .91$). Table 12.1 summarizes basic descriptive information about the children in the study.

Table 12.1 Information about the child participants (standard deviations appear in parentheses)

Child Groups	N	Age (in years)	Parental-rating English (max = 5)	Parental-rating Spanish (max = 5)	English PPVT (standard scores)	Spanish TVIP (standard scores)
Simultaneous bilinguals	15	10.4 (3.4)	5 (0)	3.8 (.8)	98.9 (11.1)	83.1 (21.6)
Sequential bilinguals	20	12.4 (3.7)	4.7 (.5)	4.5 (.5)	97.0 (8.5)	86.9 (20.9)
Mexican monolinguals	20	11 (4.1)	--	--	--	122.1 (14.3)

Task

The main task was the Story Retelling Task used in Montrul (2004) and in Montrul and Sánchez-Walker (2013). All participants were provided with 14 colored pictures of the children's tale *Little Red Riding Hood* and were asked to look at the pictures and narrate the story in Spanish and in the past, with as much detail as possible. The research assistant who administered the task could see the pictures. All the oral narratives were audio recorded, transcribed, and coded for analysis. Sorace (2004) questioned the suitability of this methodology to investigate the pragmatic distribution of subjects for two reasons: 1) the number of tokens produced by each subject differs, and 2) because the story is universally known and there is no information gap between the participant and the researcher, perhaps it makes the participant produce more null subjects in shared knowledge context than expected. We are aware of this criticism and acknowledge that using a narrative of this sort limits our ability to control for context and draw clearer conclusions about the children's knowledge of null and overt subjects. At the same time, this task is valuable for comparing the children to adults that we have previously studied using the same task, as well as for identifying emerging trends in the data that can be the focus of a future experimental task. Finally, we share Sorace's concern that this narrative and the way it was administered may have prompted some participants to use null subjects in switch reference contexts because the null subjects were licensed by the shared context of the narrative. We considered this possibility in the analysis of our data.

RESULTS

Since the narrative is in the third person, it mostly elicits third person subjects. The few first and second person pronouns produced were not included in the analysis. Counts and percentages of verbs with subjects were calculated for each participant. We also calculated counts and percentages of types of subjects, including lexical NPs and null and overt subject pronouns. In cases of null and overt subjects, these were also coded for pragmatically licit and illicit or redundant uses. That is, we calculated correct and incorrect uses of lexical subjects, pronominal subjects and null subjects in same reference and switch reference contexts. For example, overt subjects were considered redundant when they referred to the same referent mentioned in the previous sentence (a context where a null pronoun would be felicitous), and they were considered correct if they were used when there was a change of referent in the discourse, or to establish emphasis. See (7) and (8) for examples of each, respectively.

(7) *. . . el muchacho tienen unas estijeras. El muchacho le está poniendo bolas de piedras en su barriga.* (participant 304)

'*. . . the young man have scissors. The young man is putting balls of stone in his belly.*'

(8) El lobo malo atacó al Capurecita Roja. El señor llega. (participant 10)

'The bad wolf attacked Little Red Riding Hood. The man arrives.'

Similarly, null subjects were considered illicit when there was a change of referent in the story line, and the participant used a null subject, making the context ambiguous or unclear.

(9) *Ahí el leñador oyó los gritos de Caperucita Roja y Ø se la comió.* (participant 5)

'There the woodcutter heard the screams of Little Red Riding Hood and Ø ate her.'

However, as mentioned earlier, there were some null pronouns that appeared to be licensed by the researcher's and participant's shared knowledge and joint attention to the story, as in (10). These task-related null subjects in switch reference contexts occurred in both monolinguals and bilinguals. They were very few (less than 2 percent of all the data) and were excluded from the analysis.

(10) *Después vino un cazador y vio el lobo. Ø Encontraron a su abuela.*

(Then came a hunter and saw the wolf. Ø found-3rd-pl her grandmother)

'Then a hunter came and saw the Wolf. They found her grandmother.'

(Participant 311) [In the picture the hunter comes in with a dog, thus the third person plural in the second sentence can refer to the dog and the hunter.]

Only finite verbs were included, except for weather verbs. All sentences with negation (*no*, *nadie*, *ninguno*, etc. 'No, nobody, none, etc.') were excluded from the analysis, as were questions and existential and pleonastic constructions. Ambiguous cases such as (11) were also excluded.

(11) *Un hombre mató la wolf porque comió qué.* Ø Lo mataron María.
A man killed the wolf because he ate what. They killed him María.
(participant 308)

In (11), the subject of 'Lo mataron' is third person plural, but it can also be argued that the participant inflected *matar* incorrectly when trying to say that the wolf killed Maria. In other words, perhaps 'the wolf' is the intended subject. It is also possible that *lo mataron* was produced as an impersonal construction, not blaming the man (which leaves an unexplainable 'Maria' in the sentence). Because we could not state with certainty whether there was a clear referent or not, this type of sentence was excluded from the analysis.

Percentages of production in each category were submitted to statistical analysis. Two Spanish speakers counted and categorized the data, and there was over 90 percent agreement between them on the 40 percent of the data that was submitted to inter-rater reliability. Table 12.2 presents the distribution of overt and null subjects by age of onset of bilingualism and type of bilingual group.

Table 12.2 Percentage of null and overt subjects by child group

Child Groups	N	Total verbs	Overt subjects	Null subjects
Mexican monolinguals	20	569	57.6%	42.4%
Simultaneous bilinguals	15	339	67.5%	32.5%
Sequential bilinguals	20	583	63.6%	36.4%

A two-by-three ANOVA showed that the children produced more overt subjects than null subjects ($F(2, 52) = 44.43$, $p < .0001$), but there were no subject by group interactions. Even though the children in Mexico produced the highest rate of null subjects (42.4 percent) their rate was not significantly greater than the rate produced by the sequential bilinguals (36.4 percent) and the simultaneous bilinguals (32.5 percent), as also confirmed by a one-way ANOVA ($F(2,54) = 2.13$, $p = .12$). Thus, overall, the bilingual and monolingual children know that Spanish allows both null and overt subjects and their production of overt subjects is 60 percent or above.

Table 12.3 focuses on types of overt subjects, namely, lexical (*la abuelita, caperucita, el lobo, el cazador*) and pronominal (*él, ella, ellas, ellos*). The vast majority of subjects produced by the children were lexical, and not all participants produced pronouns. Only 8 of 20 Mexican children (40 percent of the sample) produced pronouns, as compared to 13 sequential bilinguals (65 percent) and 8 simultaneous bilinguals (53.3 percent). The rate of pronoun use was higher in the bilingual than in the monolingual children, according to a one-way ANOVA and Tukey post hoc tests ($F(2,34) = 3.36$, $p = .042$). Although the simultaneous bilinguals produced more pronouns than the sequential bilinguals, the 8.3 percent difference did not reach statistical significance.

Finally, table 12.4 displays the distribution of lexical, pronominal, and null subjects by context. Recall that among adults overt subjects (lexical and pronominal) are

Table 12.3 Types of overt subjects by type of bilingual group

Child Groups	N	Total verbs	Lexical subjects	Pronominal subjects
Mexican monolinguals	20	328	94.7%	5.3%
Simultaneous bilinguals	15	229	81.5%	18.5%
Sequential bilinguals	20	371	89.8%	10.2%

Table 12.4 Pragmatic distribution of subjects by context (# = pragmatically infelicitous)

		Switch Reference Context			Same Reference Context		
Child Groups	N	lexical	pron.	#null	#lexical	#pron.	null
Mexican monolinguals	20	95.9%	93.7%	5.9%	4.1%	6.3%	94.1%
Simultaneous bilinguals	15	86.7%	75.3%	10.9%	13.2%	24.7%	96.3%
Sequential bilinguals	20	89.9.7%	80.9%	12.7%	10.1%	19.1%	96.9%

more frequent in switch reference contexts whereas null subjects are preferred in same reference contexts. We calculated the percentages of the three types of subjects in the two contexts, and the distribution reflects the expected pattern in the three groups. For example, of all lexical subjects produced by the monolinguals, 95.9 percent were used in switch reference contexts and only 4.1 percent in same reference contexts.

An ANOVA comparing the three subject types in switch reference contexts revealed a main effect for type of subject ($F(2, 31) = 64.4$, $p < .0001$), since null subjects were in general not preferred in this context, and a main effect by group ($F(2,31) = 3.81$, $p = .033$). The Mexican children produced lower rates of null subjects in switch reference contexts (less than 10 percent) than the simultaneous and sequential bilingual children (more than 10 percent). The bilingual children also produced significantly higher rates of overt pronouns in same reference contexts than the monolingual children ($F(2,33) = 3.66$, $p = .037$). However, there were no significant differences between bilingual groups ($p > .05$).

To summarize, the results of our study show that monolingual and bilingual children produce comparable rates of overt subjects. Even so, the bilingual children produced higher rates of subject pronouns than monolingual children from Mexico. In general, monolingual and bilingual children know the distribution of null and overt subjects in Spanish. At the same time, the monolingual and the bilingual children produced few null subjects in switch reference contexts. However, the bilingual children produced more overt subjects, and especially overt pronominal subjects, in same reference contexts than the monolingual children. The tendency was also for the simultaneous bilinguals to produce more infelicitous uses of pronouns than the sequential bilinguals, although this difference between the simultaneous and sequential bilinguals was not significant.

DISCUSSION AND CONCLUSION

The goal of our study was to provide new data on the development of subject expression in Spanish–English bilingual children and adolescents, an age group that has not been the focus of any previous studies. This group is crucial to inform the route of language development between pre-literate bilingual children and young adult heritage speakers with respect to the role of input in minority language development, when most schooling takes place in the majority language. We examined the rate of overt subjects, pronominal subjects, and the distribution of null and overt subjects in a child narrative context administered to school-age Spanish–English bilingual children in the United States (ages 6–17, mean 11) and age-matched monolingual children from Mexico. The bilingual children varied in age of onset of bilingualism and age of exposure to English, the majority language. Controlling for age of onset of bilingualism in children allows us to indirectly test the effect of cumulative input in the development of Spanish as a heritage language. The simultaneous bilingual children in our study received lower parental ratings in Spanish (mean 3.8 over 5) than the sequential bilingual children (mean 4.7 over 5), and the difference was significant. But the two groups did not differ on their standard TVIP scores, a measure of receptive vocabulary in Spanish.

We found that the expression of subjects in Spanish may be subject to developmental effects in monolingual children from Mexico when compared to younger and older adults from the same region. When types of subjects were examined in discourse, the monolingual children were different from the adults in Montrul (2004) in their higher rate of null pronouns in switch reference contexts, as found by Shin and Cairns (2012). Recall that Shin and Cairns found in their experimental study that monolingual Mexican children did not select overt subject pronouns in switch reference contexts at adult levels until age 14 or 15. The mean age of the children we tested was 11, although our sample included children who were older than 12. When we looked at individual children, we found that some of the children who produced errors were older than 12. Nine children made errors with null subjects, such as in (12), where the null subject of 'had given' is the grandmother, and (13), where the null subject of 'ate her' should refer to the wolf. Of these nine children, five of them were younger than 12 and the other four were older than 12.

(12) *Había una vez una niña que se llamaba Caperucita Roja. Y era como su cumpleaños y estaba bailando la niña porque Ø le había regalado una capa roja y Ø estaba bailando.*

'Once upon a time there was a little girl named Little Red Riding Hood. And it was like her birthday and was dancing the girl because Ø had given her a red hood and was dancing.'

(13) *Ahí el leñador oyó los gritos de Caperucita y Ø se la comió.*

'There the woodcutter heard the screams of Little Red Riding Hood and Ø ate her.'

Seven monolingual children used redundant lexical subjects; one of them also used a redundant pronominal subject. Four of these children made errors with both null and overt subjects and their ages were 8, 9, 16, and 17. In general, children of all ages made errors.

The bilingual children produced more overt subjects than the monolingual children, although this difference between the bilingual and monolingual children did not reach statistical significance. The mean rate of overt subjects was about 65 percent for the bilingual children, but four simultaneous bilingual children and four sequential bilingual children produced rates above 70 percent, 80 percent, and 90 percent. The bilingual children produced pragmatically illicit null subjects like the monolingual children, but also much higher rates of redundant overt subjects as has been attested in younger bilingual children and adults (Montrul 2004; Paradis and Navarro 2003; Silva-Corvalán 1994, this volume). No bilingual child produced 100 percent redundant overt subjects in same reference contexts: Rates ranged between 10 percent and 30 percent for lexical subjects and 10 percent and 50 percent for pronominal subjects. As in the monolingual data, children of all ages produced null subjects in switch reference contexts and overt subjects in same reference contexts.

Our second research question asked whether age of onset of bilingualism and length of exposure to English affect the expression of subjects in child heritage speakers when compared to native speakers of the same age in Mexico. We hypothesized that if child bilinguals produce higher rates of overt subjects and of pragmatically infelicitous subjects than age-matched monolinguals, it can be assumed that the bilinguals may not have had a chance to develop the pragmatic features of Spanish subjects fully. We found that, as predicted, the simultaneous bilingual children displayed the highest rates of redundant lexical and pronominal subjects. Thus, our hypothesis stating that simultaneous bilinguals would produce more overt subjects and more pragmatic errors than sequential bilinguals was confirmed. As for infelicitous uses of null pronouns in switch reference contexts, our hypothesis stated that if the bilingual children produce null subjects in switch reference contexts like monolingual children younger than 12 (Shin and Cairns 2012), this will also suggest that they have not fully developed pronoun reference in Spanish. This hypothesis was also supported because the bilingual groups were comparable to the monolingual children from Mexico in this respect. Thus, what we observe in our data with overt subjects is the typical pattern of overextension observed in bilingual grammars in general whereas with respect to null subjects we see the developmental pattern attested in monolingual children. At the same time, we should be cautious interpreting these results because the range of ages covered in the groups in our study was wider than that covered in the groups studied previously by Shin and Cairns (2012). Ideally, in future studies we should separate children in at least two or three age groups to capture these developmental changes as they occur.

Finally, we note that there is another potential explanation for the results of the simultaneous bilingual children, which has to do with where the children were living. Twenty of the children were recruited in Chicago: Nineteen were of Mexican heritage and one was from Colombia. Fifteen of these children were sequential bilinguals, and five were simultaneous bilinguals. The other nineteen children who participated in the study were tested in New York City, and ten of them were simultaneous bilinguals. Only two of the children tested in New York were of Mexican heritage. The rest were from Honduras, Ecuador, Colombia, and El Salvador. According to Otheguy and Zentella's (2012) study of the Spanish in New York, Spanish speakers of non-Caribbean varieties residing in New York produce higher rates of overt pronominal subjects than newcomers from the same regions due to contact with speakers of Caribbean Spanish (Puerto Rico, Cuba, Dominican Republic). In addition to contact with English, a non-null subject language, what is going on with subject expression in the Spanish of New York is dialect leveling: All varieties of Spanish are converging on a higher use of overt subjects (Otheguy and Zentella 2012). We suspect that given the distribution of our children by region, the results of the simultaneous bilingual children may also have to do with dialect contact and dialect leveling in New York City, in addition to age of acquisition, proficiency, and contact with English.

We reanalyzed the results of the children by region: Mexico, Chicago, and New York City, and we found no differences between the children by age. When the children from Chicago were compared to the children from New York on parental ratings of Spanish, parental ratings of English, PPVT scores, and TVIP scores, there were no differences between the groups either. However, there were significant differences in production of overt subjects and pronominal subjects between the three groups, mostly due to the children from New York who were very different from the children from Chicago and the children from Mexico. Recall that the monolingual children from Mexico produced 5.8 percent null subjects in switch reference contexts. The Chicago bilinguals produced 20.1 percent but the children from New York hardly made these errors (1.7 percent). At the same time, the children from New York produced 72 percent of overt subjects, whereas the children from Chicago produced 61 percent and were not different from the monolingual children from Mexico who produced 59 percent. The Mexican children produced 5.2 percent of overt pronominal subjects, the Mexican children from Chicago 8.1 percent, and the bilingual children from New York 29 percent. The highest rate was with redundant pronominal subjects in same reference contexts. Here, the Mexican monolinguals and the Chicago children were not different from each other, producing 6.2 percent and 8.9 percent rates, respectively. However, 30 percent of the New York City children's same reference subjects were overt. In other words, the New York bilinguals produce a much higher rate of redundant subjects compared to the Chicago bilinguals or the Mexican monolinguals. Taken together, the results for analyses of same and switch reference contexts suggest that the Chicago children who are 95 percent from Mexican heritage and are 75 percent sequential bilinguals have problems establishing reference with null subjects in a discourse narrative, whereas the children from New York City do not have this problem but produce instead redundant overt pronominal subjects in same reference contexts. In future work, we should recruit simultaneous and sequential bilingual children in both cities, to see if these apparent differences hold by variety of Spanish as well.

In conclusion, this study has shown that subject expression remains a vulnerable area in child bilingual grammars during the school-age period. The patterns we find are also the same ones found in monolingual development, except that the magnitude of the effects is higher in Spanish speakers who live in a situation of language contact with English, as in the United States. Our results also show that it is not possible to pinpoint a single cause or factor underlying these changes, but it seems that many factors contribute to the degree of indeterminacy of the pragmatic distribution of null and overt subjects in Spanish. These include strong pressure from English, structural complexity of overt subjects in Spanish, integration of syntactic and pragmatic features, contact with other dialects, and age of onset of bilingualism, among others. Whether this is a representational or a processing problem as Sorace (2004) suggests, would need to be pursued with a more suitable experimental methodology along the lines of Shin and Cairns (2012), with more children per age group.

ACKNOWLEDGMENTS

This material is based in part upon work supported by the National Science Foundation under Grant Number BCS-0917593, ARRA. Any opinions, findings, and conclusions or recommendations expressed in this material are those of the author(s) and do not necessarily reflect the views of the National Science Foundation. We are grateful to all the participants in the study, as well as to Kirsten Hope and Laura Romani, who helped with data collection and transcriptions. Hélade Santos also helped with inter-rater reliability.

NOTE

1. Due to scope limitations, we could not present the data we collected with adult heritage speakers, first-generation immigrants and adult native speakers from Mexico. When we compared statistically the monolingual adults and the children from Mexico, the children produced more overt subjects than the adult native speakers.

REFERENCES

Austin, Jennifer, María Blume, David Parkinson, Zelmira Núñez del Prado, and Barbara Lust. 1997. "The Status of Pro-Drop in the Initial State: Results from New Analyses of Spanish." In *Contemporary Perspectives on the Acquisition of Spanish,* edited by Ana Teresa Pérez-Leroux and William R. Glass, 37–54. Vol. 1, *Developing Grammars.* Somerville, MA: Cascadilla Press.

Bel, Aurora. 2003. "The Syntax of Subjects in the Acquisition of Spanish and Catalan." *Probus* 15:1–26.

Bentivoglio, Paola. 1987. *Los sujetos pronominales de primera persona en el habla de Caracas.* Caracas: Universidad Central de Venezuela.

Cameron, Richard, and Nydia Flores-Ferrán. 2004. "Perseveration of Subject Expression across Regional Dialects of Spanish." *Spanish in Context* 1(1):41–65.

Duarte, Maria Eugênia L. 1993. "Do pronome nulo ao pronome pleno: a tragetória do sujeito no português do Brasil." In *Português Brasileiro: Uma viagem diacrônica,* edited by Ian G. Roberts and Mary Aizawa Kato. Campinas: Unicamp.

———. 2000. "The Loss of the 'Avoid Pronoun Principle' in Brazilian Portuguese." In *Brazilian Portuguese and the Null Subject Parameter,* edited by Mary Aizawa Kato and Esmeralda Vailati Negrão, 17–35. Frankfurt: Verveuert.

Dunn, Lloyd M., and Douglas M. Dunn. 2007. *The Peabody Picture Vocabulary Test, Fourth Edition.* Pearson Assessments.

Dunn, Lloyd, Eligio Padilla, Delia Lugo, and Leota Dunn. 1986. "Test de Vocabulario en Imagenes Peabody: TVIP: Adaptacion Hispanoamericana [Peabody Picture Vocabulary Test: PPVT: Hispanic-American Adaptation]." Circle Pines, MN: American Guidance Service.

Enríquez, Emilia V. 1984. *El pronombre personal sujeto en la lengua española hablada en Madrid.* Madrid: Instituto Miguel de Cervantes.

Goodluck, Helen. 1991. *Language Acquisition.* Oxford: Blackwell.

Grinstead, John. 2004. "Subjects and Interface Delay in Child Spanish and Catalan." *Language* 80:40–72.

Haegeman, Liliane, and Tabea Ihsane. 2002. "Adult Null Subjects in the Non-Pro-Drop Languages: Two Diary Dialects." *Language Acquisition* 9:329–346.

Kim, Ji-Hye, Silvina Montrul, and James Yoon. 2009. "Binding Interpretation of Anaphors in Korean Heritage Speakers." *Language Acquisition* 16(1):3–35.

Liceras, Juana M., Raquel Fernández Fuertes, and Anahí Alba de la Fuente. 2012. "Overt Subjects and Copula Omission in the Spanish and the English Grammar of English–Spanish Bilinguals: On the Locus and Directionality of Interlinguistic Influence." *First Language* 32:88–115.

Liceras, Juana M., Raquel Fernández Fuertes, and Rocío Pérez-Tattam. 2008. "Null and Overt Subjects in the Developing Grammars (L1 English / L1 Spanish) of Two Bilingual Twins." In *A Portrait of the Young in the New Multilingual Spain,* edited by Carmen Pérez-Vidal, María Juan-Garau, and Aurora Bel, 111–134. Clevedon, UK: Multilingual Matters.

Montrul, Silvina. 2002. "Incomplete Acquisition and Attrition of Spanish Tense/Aspect Distinctions in Adult Bilinguals." *Bilingualism: Language and Cognition* 5(1):39–68.

———. 2004. "Subject and Object Expression in Spanish Heritage Speakers: A Case of Morpho-Syntactic Convergence." *Bilingualism: Language and Cognition* 7:125–142.

———. 2006. "Bilingualism, Incomplete Acquisition, and Language Change." In *L2 Acquisition and Creole Genesis: Dialogues*, edited by Claire Lefebvre, Lydia White, and Christine Jourdan, 379–400. Amsterdam: John Benjamins.

———. 2008. *Incomplete Acquisition in Bilingualism: Re-examining the Age Factor.* Amsterdam: John Benjamins.

Montrul, Silvina, and Noelia Sánchez-Walker. 2013. "Differential Object Marking in Child and Adult Spanish Heritage Speakers." *Language Acquisition* 20:1–24.

Morales, Amparo. 1997. "La hipótesis funcional y la aparición de sujeto no nominal: el español de Puerto Rico." *Hispania* 80:153–165.

Mueller Gathercole, Virginia, and Erika Hoff. 2009. "Input and the Acquisition of Language: Three Questions." In *The Blackwell Handbook of Language Development*, edited by Erika Hoff and Marilyn Shatz, 107–127. Malden, MA: Wiley-Blackwell.

Ortiz López, Luis A. 2009. "Pronombres de sujeto en el español (L2 vs L1) del Caribe." In *El español en Estados Unidos y otros contextos de contacto*, edited by Jennifer Lehman and Manuel Lacorte. Madrid: Iberoamericana.

Otheguy, Ricardo, and Ana Celia Zentella. 2012. *Spanish in New York: Language Contact, Dialectal Leveling, and Structural Continuity.* Oxford: Oxford University Press.

Paradis, Johanne, and Samuel Navarro. 2003. "Subject Realization and Crosslinguistic Interference in the Bilingual Acquisition of Spanish and English: What Is the Role of the Input?" *Journal of Child Language* 30:1–23.

Polinsky, Maria. 2006. "Incomplete Acquisition: American Russian." *Journal of Slavic Linguistics* 14:191–262.

Rizzi, Luigi. 1982. *Issues in Italian Syntax.* Dordrecht: Foris.

Serratrice, Ludovica. 2005. "The Role of Discourse Pragmatics in the Acquisition of Subjects in Italian." *Applied Psycholinguistics* 26:437–462.

Shin, Naomi Lapidus. 2012. "Variable Use of Spanish Subject Pronouns by Monolingual Children in Mexico." In *Selected Proceedings of the 14th Hispanic Linguistics Symposium*, edited by Kimberly Geeslin and Manuel Díaz-Campos, 130–141. Somerville, MA: Cascadilla Proceedings Project.

Shin, Naomi Lapidus, and Helen Smith Cairns. 2012. "The Development of NP Selection in School-Age Children: Reference and Spanish Subject Pronouns." *Language Acquisition* 19:3–38.

Shin, Naomi Lapidus, and Ricardo Otheguy. 2013. "Social Class and Gender Impacting Change in Bilingual Settings: Spanish Subject Pronoun Use in New York." *Language in Society* 42:429– 452.

Silva-Corvalán, Carmen. 1994. *Language Contact and Change: Spanish in Los Angeles.* New York: Oxford University Press.

———. 2014. *Bilingual Language Acquisition: Spanish and English in the First Six Years.* Cambridge: Cambridge University Press.

Sorace, Antonella. 2000. "Differential Effects of Attrition in the L1 Syntax of Near-Native L2 Speakers." In *Proceedings of the 24th Boston University Conference on Language Development,* 719–725. Somerville, MA: Cascadilla Press.

———. 2004. "Native Language Attrition and Developmental Instability at the Syntax-Discourse Interface: Data, Interpretations, and Methods." *Bilingualism: Language and Cognition* 7:143–145.

———. 2005. "Syntactic Optionality at Interfaces." In *Syntax and Variation: Reconciling the Biological and the Social*, edited by Leonie M. E. A. Cornips and Karen P. Corrigan, 46–111. Amsterdam: John Benjamins.

———. 2011. "Cognitive Advantages in Bilingualism: Is There a 'Bilingual Paradox'?" In *Multilingualism: Language, Power and Knowledge*, edited by Paolo Valore, 335–358. Pisa: Edistudio.

Ticio, Emma. 2002. "Dialectal Variation in the Acquisition of the Null Subject Parameter." In *Proceedings of GALA 2001,* edited by João Costa and Maria João Freitas, 271–278. Lisboa: Associacão Portuguesa de Linguística.

Toribio, A. Jacqueline. 2000. "Setting Parametric Limits on Dialectal Variation in Spanish." *Lingua* 10:315–341.

Tsimpli, Ianthi, Antonella Sorace, Caroline Heycock, Francesca Filiaci, and Maria Bouba. 2003. "Subjects in L1 Attrition: Evidence from Greek and Italian Near-Native Speakers of English." In *Proceedings of the 27th Annual Boston University Conference on Language Development,* 787–797. Somerville, MA: Cascadilla Press.

Villa-García, Julio, William Snyder, and José Riqueros-Morante. 2010. "On the Analysis of Lexical Subjects in Caribbean and Mainland Spanish: Evidence from L1 Acquisition." In *Proceedings of the 34th Boston University Conference on Language Development,* 433–444. Somerville, MA: Cascadilla Press.

Contributors

Ana M. Carvalho is an Associate Professor at the University of Arizona, where she also directs the Portuguese Language Program. Her research interests include the sociolinguistics of border communities, language variation and change, and language contact. She has published extensively about the contact between Spanish and Portuguese on the Uruguayan-Brazilian border, and has begun to explore sociolinguistic issues on the contact between Spanish and English on the US-Mexican border.

Rafael Orozco is an Associate Professor of Spanish Linguistics at Louisiana State University. His teaching and research interests include Spanish sociolinguistics, Colombian Spanish, Caribbean Spanish, and Spanish in New York City. His research mainly explores variation in *Costeño*, the variety of Spanish spoken in the Caribbean region of Colombia.

Naomi Lapidus Shin is an Assistant Professor at the University of New Mexico. Her research focuses on Spanish in contact with English in the United States, childhood acquisition of Spanish, and how functionality influences the trajectory of language change and development. Shin's work has appeared in journals such as *Language Variation and Change, Language in Society, Language Acquisition, Spanish in Context, Studies in Hispanic and Lusophone Linguistics,* and *Sociolinguistic Studies.*

Gabriela G. Alfaraz is an Associate Professor of Spanish Linguistics at Michigan State University. Her research interests include variationist sociolinguistics, language contact, bilingualism, language attitudes, Caribbean Spanish, and Spanish in the United States. Her research has focused mainly on attitudes and sociolinguistic variation in Cuban Spanish.

Ryan M. Bessett is a Ph.D. student in Hispanic Linguistics at the University of Arizona. His major research interests center around language variation and change, Spanish in contact, and Spanish phonology. He is especially interested in differentiating contact-induced change from language-internal variation through the variationist methodology. To this end, he has written on comparisons between Sonoran Spanish in Arizona, USA, and Sonora, Mexico.

Daniel Erker is an Assistant Professor of Spanish and Linguistics at Boston University. His research areas include sociolinguistics and language variation. He is particularly interested in the sociophonetic mechanisms and outcomes of language contact.

Stephen Fafulas is an Assistant Professor at East Carolina University, and director of the ECU SoCIOLing Lab. His area of specialization is sociolinguistics, with an emphasis on morphosyntactic variation in native, learner, and bilingual grammars. Currently, he is working on a number of projects that analyze Spanish in contact with endangered languages of the Peruvian Amazon, including Bora and Yagua. His work has appeared in journals such as *Spanish in Context* and *Boletín de Filología*.

Kimberly Geeslin is a Professor at Indiana University. Her research focuses on second language Spanish and the intersection of second language acquisition and sociolinguistics. She is the author of *Sociolinguistics and Second Language Acquisition* (Routledge 2014) and editor of the *Handbook for Spanish Second Language Acquisition* (Wiley-Blackwell 2013). Her research also appears in *Studies in Second Language Acquisition, Language Learning, Hispania, Spanish in Context, Bilingualism: Language and Cognition, Linguistics*, and *Studies in Hispanic and Lusophone Linguistics*.

Yolanda Lastra is a researcher at the *Instituto de Investigaciones Antropológicas* of the *Universidad Nacional Autónoma de México* and the coordinator of the *Archivo de Lenguas Indígenas de Mexico* at *El Colegio de México*. Her publications include books on Náhuatl and Otomí as well as articles on those languages and Chichimeco. She is the autor of *Sociolingüística para Hispanoamericanos, una Introducción*.

Bret Linford is a Ph.D. candidate in Hispanic Linguistics at Indiana University. His main research interest is the second language acquisition of variable structures in Spanish. He is currently working on projects that examine the importance of individual differences, context of learning, and lexical frequency on the second-language acquisition of variable structures.

Pedro Martín Butragueño is a professor at El Colegio de México where he co-coordinates the Laboratorio de Estudios Fónicos. He is co-director of the "Sociolinguistic Corpus of Mexico City" and the "Sociolinguistic History of Mexico" projects. His main area of interest is the study of change and variation in Spanish. He currently co-directs the "Oral Corpus of Mexican Spanish" (a dialectogical and sociolinguistic study of twelve Mexican cities).

Jim Michnowicz is Associate Professor of Spanish at North Carolina State University. His research focuses on language and dialect contact, with a particular interest in the Spanish of Yucatan, Mexico. His work has also explored questions of linguistic expressions of identity, and he is beginning a project to examine the newly formed contact situation between Spanish and English in North Carolina.

Silvina Montrul is Professor of Spanish and Linguistics at the University of Illinois at Urbana-Champaign. She is co-editor of *Second Language Research* and author of *The Acquisition of Spanish* (Benjamins, 2004), *Incomplete Acquisition in Bilingualism,* (Benjamins, 2008), *El bilingüismo en el mundo hispanohablante* (Wiley-Blackwell 2013), and *The Acquisition of Heritage Languages* (forthcoming, Cambridge University Press).

Ricardo Otheguy is professor of linguistics at the Graduate Center of CUNY. His theoretical work is in the areas of functional semiotic grammar and language and dialect contact. His applied work has centered on bilingual education and Spanish textbook materials. He is co-author of *Spanish in New York: Language Contact, Dialectal Leveling, and Structural Continuity* (Oxford University Press). His papers have appeared in major journals such as *Language*, *Language in Society*, *Lingua*, *Modern Language Journal*, *TESOL Quarterly*, and *Harvard Educational Review*. His work has been supported by the Rockefeller Brothers Fund, the Fulbright Program, and the National Science Foundation.

Pekka Posio studied Romance languages and General Linguistics at the University of Helsinki, Finland. His research interests include the variable expression of pronominal subjects in Spanish and Portuguese, the uses of human impersonal constructions, and other strategies of referring to human participants in spoken discourse. He is currently a postdoctoral researcher at the University of Cologne working on a project focusing on human impersonal constructions in Spanish and Portuguese within a usage-based perspective.

Ana de Prada Pérez is an assistant professor of Hispanic Linguistics in the Department of Spanish and Portuguese Studies at the University of Florida. She obtained her Ph.D. from The Pennsylvania State University in 2009. Her research focuses on language contact outcomes of Spanish-English and Spanish-Catalan bilingualism. At UF she has taught a variety of graduate and undergraduate linguistics courses including: Introduction to Hispanic Linguistics, Foundations of Hispanic Linguistics, and Spanish syntax, bilingualism, language acquisition, and code switching.

Noelia Sánchez-Walker is pursuing her Ph.D. in Spanish linguistics and Second Language Acquisition and Teacher Education at the University of Illinois, Urbana-Champaign under the direction of Professor Silvina A. Montrul. Her research interests include acquisition and development of Spanish as a second language and as a heritage language in adults and school-age children.

Carmen Silva-Corvalán is Professor of Spanish Linguistics at the University of Southern California. Her publications include *Language Variation and Change: Spanish in Los Angeles* (Oxford U. Press, 1994), *Sociolingüística y Pragmática del Español* (Georgetown U. Press, 2001), *Bilingual Language Acquisition: Spanish and English in the First Six Years* (Cambridge U. Press, 2014), and articles in journals such as *Language*, *Spanish in Context*, and *Bilingualism: Language and Cognition*.

Rena Torres Cacoullos is Professor of Spanish and Linguistics at the Pennsylvania State University, and editor of Language Variation and Change. Her work combines variationist and usage-based perspectives in the quantitative analysis of Spanish, English, and Greek varieties. She is co-principal investigator of the New Mexico Spanish-English Bilingual project.

Catherine Travis is Professor of Modern European Languages and Head of the School of Literature, Languages and Linguistics at the Australian National University. Her research focuses on the way in which grammar emerges through discourse, which she investigates through the study of variation in spontaneous speech, in monolingual and bilingual contexts. She is co-principal investigator of the New Mexico Spanish-English Bilingual project, and is a Chief Investigator on the ARC Centre of Excellence for the Dynamics of Language.

Index

D

E

F

G

H

I

L

M

N

O

P

Q

R

S

T

U

V

W

Y

Z